A Carpetbagger in Reverse

A Carpetbagger in Reverse

Arthur W. Mitchell, America's First Black Democratic Congressman

JOHN MORRIS KNAPP

THE UNIVERSITY OF ALABAMA PRESS
Tuscaloosa

The University of Alabama Press
Tuscaloosa, Alabama 35487-0380
uapress.ua.edu

Typeface: Minion Pro

Cover image: Congressman Arthur W. Mitchell; Chicago History Museum, ICHi-183707, Norma Lloyd for Bruno Studios, photographer
Cover design: Sandy Turner Jr.

Cataloging-in-Publication data is available from the Library of Congress.
ISBN: 978-0-8173-2215-1 (cloth)
ISBN: 978-0-8173-6175-4 (paper)
E-ISBN: 978-0-8173-9535-3

For Nathanael Greene of Wesleyan University and all the students inspired by his passion for history.

Contents

Illustrations

Figures

Table

Prologue

"Everybody Knows the Character of the Negro"

IN 1913, WILLIAM Gilbert, the young son of the local postmaster, stands on a corner in Geiger, a small town in Sumter County, Alabama, near the border with Mississippi. In the heart of cotton-growing country, the community was so isolated that five years before, most of its residents had never seen a railroad. It was home to a small minority of white landowners who maintained control over a large number of Black sharecroppers through intimidation, violence, and an occasional lynching. Geiger's representative to Alabama's 1901 constitutional convention had recommended this method to his colleagues because, he said, "everybody knows the character of the Negro and knows that there is no punishment in the world that can take the place of the lash with him. He must be controlled that way." Not surprisingly, Black Geigerites doffed their hats to whites, addressed them as "sir" and "ma'am," and stepped off the sidewalk to allow their betters to pass.

A horse and carriage approach, the best team in town. In it Gilbert sees an impeccably dressed man, his wife, and their young son. They go past, waving to him, and disappear into the piney countryside. An everyday occurrence in rural Alabama, Gilbert thinks, with one astonishing difference: the man, his wife, and their son are Black.[1]

Acknowledgments

My thanks go to so many for their help in the preparation of this book. In Chicago, I am deeply indebted to the staff at the Research Center of the Chicago History Museum and particularly to Leslie Martin and Michael Featherstone for helping me navigate the enormity of the Mitchell and Barnett archives. Thanks also go to the staffs at the Joseph Regenstein Library of the University of Chicago for assisting at every level. The staffs at Carter J. Woodson Regional Library of the Chicago Public Library and the Newberry Library helped with the search for short-lived, small newspapers.

I am also indebted to Lucious Edwards, archivist emeritus at Virginia State University for his explanation of the existence of a second Mitchell archive and for a visit to Mitchell's home in Petersburg, Virginia. The staff of the Franklin D. Roosevelt Presidential Library and Museum in Hyde Park, New York, were also extremely helpful as were those at the Hoole Special Collection at the University of Alabama, the Alabama Department of Archives and History in Montgomery, and the Julia Tutwiler Library of the University of West Alabama.

Thomas Aeillo of Valdosta State University helped with my inquiry into Davis Lee, and Ms. Bettye Browne of the Columbus-Lowndes (MS) library supplied valued information about Sylvester Harris. Charles Branham of the University of Chicago Laboratory Schools and Senator Carol Moseley Braun shared many insights into the labyrinth that is, and was, Chicago politics. Special appreciation is also expressed to the staffs of Tulane's Amistad Research Center and the Dallas Historical Society for the searches of the papers of William J. Edwards and Hatton Sumners for relevant materials.

On many occasions I tried the patience of my wife, Carla Young, my son, Philip, and Peter Mattison, all of whom played a vital role in the preparation of the manuscript. Christopher Hellwig, Carol Connell, and Penelope Cray were particularly helpful in its final preparation, as was Dr. Robert Crootof, who supplied expert advice on photography. At various stages, the work benefitted from suggestions offered by Professors Nathanael Greene and Ronald Schatz of Wesleyan University; Lawrence Squeri, emeritus professor of history, East Stroudsburg University of Pennsylvania; Joanne and Charles Hadlock, John Stephens, and Mrs. Frances Clawson.

Special thanks go to Claire Lewis Evans, who saw potential in an unsolicited text by an unknown author and brought the work safely to the harbor at the University of Alabama Press, where Arthur Mitchell would have wanted his unwritten autobiography to have been published.

None of these friends and colleagues are responsible for any errors of fact or interpretation contained herein. They remain exclusively the responsibility of the author.

A Carpetbagger in Reverse

Introduction

A Forgotten Man and His Unwanted Papers

MANY OF THOSE reading this book will know little about Arthur Wergs Mitchell, the man driving the carriage. He has virtually disappeared from the national historical narrative, much like Communist officials out of favor in Stalin's Soviet Union would vanish from photographs of those standing atop Lenin's tomb during parades. But in his day, he was a major political figure whose influence and accomplishments deserve attention if we are to understand the evolution of the Civil Rights Movement.

Born in 1883, Mitchell established and ran rural schools in western Alabama until 1919, when he moved to Washington, DC, and then to Chicago in 1928. In 1934, he won an election there that made him the first Black Democrat to sit in the House of Representatives. His eight years as a congressman were highlighted by bills he introduced to protect Black rights in the workplace through the creation of an Industrial Commission and anti-lynching legislation. He also made a major contribution to Franklin Roosevelt's sweeping 1936 victory, attempted to integrate the service academies, supported the nomination of Hugo Black to the Supreme Court, proposed reforms to civil service, advocated for a "Back to the Farm" program to return destitute Black southerners who had migrated to the North back to the South, and championed equal treatment for Black members of the armed forces. Beyond these efforts, he considered his greatest contribution to the fight for racial equality to have been his four-year effort with Richard Westbrooks to eliminate the Jim Crow transportation system in the South through a court case, *Mitchell v. United States*. When the Supreme Court found unanimously in their favor, it was both a landmark decision and an early instance of Black attorneys arguing successfully before the highest court in the land.

While in Congress, his name recognition among Black college students ranked third among Black public figures, trailing only Joe Louis and Jesse Owens. In the aftermath of Franklin Roosevelt's overwhelming victory in 1936, a reporter for *Opportunity*, the magazine of the National Urban League, asserted that Mitchell was "the foremost Negro politician in the country." Four years later, his Supreme Court victory made him something of a folk hero to Black residents of Columbia, South Carolina. When the decision was announced, a newspaper editor there informed Roy Wilkins of the National Association for the Advancement of Colored People (NAACP) that "you would have thought that Joe Louis had just won the heavyweight championship of the world."

Despite this, history has largely ignored Arthur Mitchell, a void noted by Melvin G. Holli, who observed that "it is surprising how little scholarly attention Arthur Mitchell has gotten."[1] The only biography of Mitchell, by Dennis S. Nordin, appeared in 1997. In it, the author makes his opinion of his subject explicit in the final sentence of the first paragraph of the preface. Mitchell, Nordin writes, "was neither admirable nor respectable." Rather, he was a "scoundrel . . . who does not deserve a biography for what he did for Blacks; he deserves it because his career demonstrates how far an African American in the age of Franklin Roosevelt could go by making himself the tool of a power structure that also did not 'care a thing' about the people he had been elected to represent." The text that follows expands on this interpretation. A random sample of two pages finds these words used to describe Mitchell: "twisted," "irksome," "backhanded," "exaggerating," 'preposterous," "greed[y]," "unscrupulous," "unsavory," and "unpopular."[2]

This three-hundred-page critique ignores Mitchell's many skills: his remarkable talents as a politician, his rhetorical abilities, his tenaciousness, and his willingness to expose himself to personal assault in what he saw as the long struggle to establish Black equality through adherence to the societal norms set by white society. He did not, as Nordin asserts, view "most African Americans with contempt."[3] Rather, he saw his mission as calling his race to a higher standard; his unrelenting call was for others to look at him and what he had accomplished. "Stop excusing the unfairness of your circumstances for your status. I succeeded and you can too" was his message. All it took was grit, determination, courage, and a willingness to work hard. His job as the sole Black member of Congress was to create opportunities for individuals; it was up to them to advance themselves through self-help.

Contrary to Nordin's assertion that "to most of his contemporaries, he was neither admirable nor respectable," Mitchell had many admirers, largely concentrated among southern Black elites to whose betterment he was passionately devoted. But he did not "put down his bucket" among them. Rather, he moved to Chicago seeking to be an agent for political change in the South by halting the exodus of Black talent from the region. There, he sought and won election to Congress from the only area in the country that would elect a Black candidate, the city's First Congressional District with its high concentration of Black voters.

When first elected in 1934, he seemed to one Black southerner "a beacon light in the sky from which no star was expected." When he retired eight years later, Julius J. Adams, managing editor of the *New York Amsterdam News*, New York's leading Black newspaper, praised him as "the one Negro in America closer to the situation confronting his own people, [who] commands the respectful attention of the thinking and far-sighted people of both races." George Washington Carver, the famed agronomist under whom Mitchell studied at Tuskegee, agreed: "Your brilliant career as a Congressman . . . has interested everyone who gets far enough away from themselves to think of real service." Kelly Miller, a leading Black intellectual and a close friend, thought his years in the House of Representatives constituted "a new chapter in the history of the Negro race." R. R. Wright, president of Wilberforce University, saw him as "the greatest Negro political leader of the century and most practical legal mind today." Westbrooks remembered him as "without doubt one of the most able and earnest men I have ever known. Every bill you have introduced has been for the benefit of the common people and particularly the Negro. . . . What more could be asked of any man serving the people? You are the people's man."[4]

Critics, usually representatives of Black northern establishment politics, held equally strong and opposing views. Claude Barnett, founder of the Associated Negro Press, denounced him as a tool of southern racists, a man "making a strenuous effort to win the presidency of the Banjo picker's club." He was a "four flusher," "an egotist of the first water," "crude, ruthless, and arrogant." The NAACP's Roy Wilkins dismissed him as a "little, narrow election accident strutting around in shoes too big for him" and "the greatest mistake of Negro political history." Just after Mitchell's first election, Nathan S. Taylor hung a label on him that he carried the rest of his public life: "His fawning after white leaders has become so notorious . . . that he is already known as 'Uncle Tom Mitchell' among his people." During the 1936 election, the *Chicago Defender* published a letter from J. A. Williamson of Driver, Arkansas, who described him as "an educated fool, a characterless dog, who has done all he could to hurt the Negro." Another from J. J. Stenky of Augusta, Georgia, portrayed Mitchell as "the Negro Benedict Arnold." At the moment of Mitchell's retirement, Edgar G. Brown, a prime mover in the National Negro Congress, wrote that he "leaves none to mourn him. He goes to his own retirement unsung and unheralded by members of his own race and colleagues with whom he served."[5]

Mitchell himself seemed resigned to such assaults, having "been viciously attacked a thousand times because of my stand on many public matters" despite having "simply spoken the facts as I saw them." "My motto," he told his brother, "has always been to make sure that I am right and then go ahead." "I have my own way of making enemies," he conceded. "I have had fifty years of practice at the art." But he also believed that someday history would recognize his accomplishments. "I know," he wrote to a dentist in Barbertown, Ohio, in 1941, "that people who read the history of this period will see the effectiveness of my work. I know it will be understood at some time and this knowledge is the basis of my satisfaction."[6]

To aid future historians, Mitchell originally proposed to write an autobiography that would "attract universal interest." He intended to base it on his private papers, a collection that had grown by the time he retired to seventy-three large boxes stacked in the basement of his Virginia home. When he showed the collection to visitors, it drew praise as "priceless papers and documents" and "a gold mine for biographers." Shown a portion of the material, a contemporary thought it a "fine show of mental honesty" as it displayed materials both praising and critical of the collector.[7]

Despite a twenty-five-year retirement, Mitchell never went beyond creating two rough outlines for his autobiography. But his papers survive, their disposition underlining their importance to American history. Before his death, and unbeknownst to his wife, Mitchell signed a deed gifting them to the Chicago Historical Society, now the Chicago History Museum, where Archie Motley was the archivist. After his death, Clara, his third wife, contacted Virginia State College (now University) asking if the school was interested in acquiring the archive. Dr. Edgar Toppin, a distinguished professor at Virginia State and a leader of the 1976 drive to elevate Black History Week into Black History Month, met with her to evaluate the holding. As this meeting was taking place, Motley arrived at the Mitchell house with the Chicago deed. After a discussion, and to avoid dispute, a verbal agreement was reached in which VSU received copies of most of the materials. There they were later arranged by Lucious Edwards Jr., university archivist. The VSU deposit is supplemented by the original records of Mitchell's real estate company and a few personal letters.

Meanwhile, the originals went to Chicago, where they were catalogued but have lain largely unused for fifty years. A 2002 obituary of Motley reveals that when he was asked why he had been so successful in gathering collections such as Mitchell's, he answered, "Nobody else was interested." As a result of this process, two copies of the Mitchell papers exist, one in Chicago and the other in Petersburg, Virginia.[8]

The existence of two sets of Mitchell papers underscore their importance to all interested in the Black struggle for racial equality during the 1930s. Forming the basis for this study, they are indeed a "gold mine" for students of American history. Largely covering his years in Congress, from 1935 to 1943, they offer a unique, detailed perspective of the national landscape as seen through the eyes of an individual who served for eight years as the only Black member of the House of Representatives.

If there is an overarching perception that emerges from the collection, it is the sense that Mitchell was a fighter, convinced that he was correct and that those who disagreed with him were either knaves or fools. But this certainty of rectitude was based on a passionately held belief in his cause: creating the condition that would halt the exodus of Black Americans from the South, their natural home, by creating a more equal society in which they could succeed.

The Mitchell who emerges from fifty thousand pages of documents was a remarkably intelligent individual, perhaps one of the most astute members ever to serve in Congress. Although born into a semi-literate world, by the time he arrived in Washington he could quote freely from obscure biblical verses, Greek stoic philosophers, and Thomas Carlyle. His mind was detail-oriented and his ability to remember large sets of data remarkable. Beginning with his role as a census-taker in 1910, he displayed a fascination with numbers. By 1936, he could recite from memory the congressional districts with more than one thousand potential Black voters as well as the name of the local barber whose influence in the local community could bring them to the polls.

Mitchell proved himself to be a surprisingly private individual for such a public figure. His papers reveal little about his family life. We do know that he was married three times, no wife playing a significant role in his career. In 1905, at the age of twenty-two, he wed Eula May King, a graduate of Tuskegee, who bore him his only child, Arthur Jr., nicknamed Wergs. She died from pellagra in 1910 at the age of thirty, an obituary describing her life "as an example to her race [and as being] universally respected by both white and colored people." A year later, he remarried Annie Cornelius Harris of Watertown, Connecticut. Theirs was a happy union, she addressing her letters to him as "My dearest precious." Often in poor health, his "pal and partner" during his congressional years died in 1947 at the age of fifty-seven. In 1948, he took a third wife, Clara Mann, whom he had originally met during a trip to New Bern, North Carolina, in 1935. Often, they did not get along. Clara told Dennis Nordin that she once fired a shotgun at his car in retaliation for his ongoing affair with "the white lady from across the road." In a 1952 letter, Mitchell referenced his and Clara's incompatibility and his thoughts about a divorce.[9]

Unlike his wives, who rarely appear in the Mitchell papers, Wergs hovers as a tragic figure. A graduate of the University of Michigan who did advanced work at the University of Chicago, he suffered from depression and was given to violence. He was first institutionalized in 1937 after he locked himself in a room at a YMCA believing that he was being followed by a mysterious stranger. Never close to his father, Wergs blamed parental neglect for many of his problems. His father, who spent considerable time and effort on his son's treatment, saw Wergs's "breakdown" as due to the "dissipation, gambling, and drinking" of the friends with whom he associated. To get better, his son needed to be "taken away from the influence of Chicago." Despite occasional furloughs, Wergs spent most of his adult life confined at the Elgin State Hospital in Illinois, dying in 1965.[10]

An intensely private individual, Mitchell appeared only at social events that were of a "political significance" and compelled his attendance. He maintained that this reticence extended to often refusing "a standing invitation" to the White House "because of the attendant fanfare." It certainly influenced his refusal to attend the numerous formal dinners, "smokers," and receptions where alcohol and tobacco flowed freely. Something of a prude, he disapproved of both and of the role they played in Black politics. "Whenever business interferes with pleasure," he asserted, Black people "usually [proceed] to cut business out." To be effective representatives of the race, "the Negro has got to meet less at the banquet table and more in council chambers." "I never cared much for social affairs," he admitted, "when there is so much work to be done." "I was not elected to eat," he told E. M. Hennessey of the *Boston Globe*, "I was elected to work."[11]

Mitchell's personal finances were free from scandal. By his election, Mitchell was wealthy, not attracted to the lures that often haunt politicians. The origins of his prosperity in Alabama are mysterious, but he supplemented them with very successful investments in the Washington real estate market of the 1920s that guaranteed him financial freedom throughout his life. When Mitchell moved to Chicago in 1928, he came "with money" but lived in a modest way, a pattern he continued in office.[12]

Despite this affluence, he could be remarkably uncharitable and miserly in daily life. Almost every personal appeal for money brought an immediate rejection. Campaign workers in 1936 had to detail the number and cost of the pencils they purchased if they wanted to be reimbursed. Comic relief in the Mitchell papers is offered by the years-long exchange between him and Harry Englestein, from whom he rented office space in Chicago. In numerous exchanges Englestein demanded what he saw as back-due rent while Mitchell proffered various excuses for not paying.[13]

Conversely, he spent freely from his personal funds on issues that he considered important to his career and legacy. Unable to raise money for either the primary or general election in 1934, he financed both from his own purse. Underfunded by the Democratic National Committee (DNC) in 1936, he supplemented what money he received with his own. Famously, he refused all offers of financial support for legal expenses associated with *Mitchell v. United States*, seeing that as his gift to Black Americans. Similarly, he intended his retirement home in Virginia, referred to by enemies as a "plantation," to meet a larger need than his personal desire for comfort. Built exclusively by Black engineers and construction workers, he proposed to leave it to a foundation dedicated to the effort to continue the work toward racial harmony that he felt he had espoused.[14]

Mitchell appears to have been a regular attendee at church services. During his early years in Alabama, he profiles as devoutly religious, frequently singing and preaching at local churches. Elements of these beliefs remain in his speeches as a congressman, which contain references that only a student of the Bible could have known. However, as his criticism of the leadership provided by Black churches waxed, his Christian zeal waned. By 1939, he described himself as "spiritual but non-partisan" in his religious beliefs. He attended church regularly, but where he worshipped depended on where he was.

Hard work did not deter him from pursuing hobbies that he believed contributed to the "efficacy of those who have heavy and grave responsibilities." Among these diversions, he listed playing pool, working jigsaw puzzles, gardening, farming, and fishing. Driving alone was also a recreational activity for him, particularly when facing difficult decisions. When dealing with these, he told a reporter, he "simply gets behind the wheel and steps on the gas, and thinks his way out."[15]

His papers suggest a linkage between gardening, farming, fishing, and driving alone. All were solitary activities that sheltered Mitchell from incessant racism he confronted on a daily basis. Farming is particularly suggestive. As a child, he took pride in having the straightest rows in his mother's garden, as a young educator in his school's crop yields, and as a retiree in the quality of roses his gardens produced. His relationship with the soil was one reason for his deep attachment to the South. "The earth," he frequently said, "doesn't discriminate." If he could not achieve equality in the human world, he could in the natural world, where the playing field was level. The same could be said for fishing.[16]

Driving alone not only relaxed him but relates to another important character trait: personal courage. Just as he did not care what others thought of him or the enemies he made, he was fearless in exposing himself to risk. He drove alone over thousands of miles in the South at a time when such behavior by a Black motorist was considered extremely dangerous. That same bravery enabled him to be prepared to withstand a lynch mob, standing at the door of his school, rifle in hand.[17]

Mitchell's attention to correspondence with those he thought worthy of his attention was also a pleasure, some of these exchanges continuing for years. Given his other duties, many evenings spent with Annie must have been given over to answering his voluminous mail. As "there is nothing like the sense of immediate contact with personality one gets from reading someone's letters," the traits he displayed in his letters contribute to understanding Mitchell.[18]

He responded to most letters within two or three days, a promptness that drew praise from Raymond Pace Alexander, a prominent civil rights lawyer. So did the candor and specificity of his answers, proof that Mitchell had read the letter and thought about his reply. C. S. Boothby, the president of the Jahn & Ollier Engraving Company in Chicago, serves as an example. He and Mitchell disagreed for years on many issues, but Boothby appreciated the "frankness of [Mitchell's] letter and the time [he] took to write it." Most of the time, Boothby complained, he received an "ambiguous reply . . . which generally comes from the Representative telling his secretary to 'send that bird no. 67.'" But Mitchell was different. He read and carefully answered questions.[19]

But there was a darker side to this talented correspondent. Mitchell suffered fools lightly, a politically incorrect rebuke awaiting those who did not advance arguments he considered worthy of his attention. These unfortunates received torrents of abuse in letters that ended with outbursts such as "Go straight to 'h' where you and all your kind belong" or "Why the 'h' should I have to explain myself to a numbskull like you."[20]

Few were spared. Mitchell told Booker T. Washington Jr., the son of his supposed beloved mentor, that his "life is the best example of a misspent life I have ever known." When Stafford B. Ash, a nephew, asked him for a donation in order to attend Tuskegee, not only was he refused but Ash was also lectured on self-help: "I did not ask anyone to do for me under the most serious handicap—far more serious than you have ever known and I think any boy who is worthwhile can find a way for himself in this country of unusual privilege and opportunities. In fact, I think you should be ashamed to want somebody else to carry what you yourself should carry if you were thoughtful and earnest in your endeavor."[21]

Many of these tongue-lashings went unanswered, but a few brave correspondents responded, some with telling effect. When John H. Broadhead was told to "stop fore-flushing and know what is going on in the country," he was unintimidated. "Your letter," he wrote back, "showed a lack of self-control and tact. Were you to include . . . the consideration of the feelings of Negroes whom you represent among other fine qualities you possess, you would achieve even greater success."[22]

Among these "fine qualities" were Mitchell's eye for detail and disciplined research. The care with which he prepared his legislative proposals and the tortuous process that eventually brought him success before the Supreme Court testify to this. But such disciplined research was not limited to issues of national import. Mitchell also devoted inordinate time and energy to righting perceived wrongs done to individuals (frequently himself) or members of his race. Here the example of Harrison Dunnigan, a District of Columbia truck driver, is instructive.

When Mitchell found Dunnigan not only blocking his driveway but also burning refuse in it, he informed the driver that both were violations of the law. Dunnigan responded "with vile oaths" (Mitchell's euphemism for the "n" word) and declared, in Mitchell's words, that "he did not care anything about [Mitchell] or the law" and that Mitchell could call the police if he did not like it. When he did, Dunnigan "used a great many more vile oaths and drove away." Mitchell complained, contending that "a man of this type should not be driving a truck in the District of Columbia. The man belongs in prison or some reformatory." But he did not write to some unknown official; he wrote to William A. Van Duzen, the director of traffic and vehicles for the District of Columbia, including in his letter the time of the incident, his address, and the license number of the truck, specifics that he hoped would force Van Duzen to "have attention called to this matter."

Van Duzen did act, reporting to Mitchell that he had spoken with Dunnigan, who admitted to blocking the alley but denied cursing Mitchell and said he had nothing to do with the fire. If Mitchell wanted to follow up, Van Duzen advised, he could go to Police Court or the Board of Revocations. Mitchell thanked Van Duzen for the information, telling him that his only reason for writing had been the "extreme length" to which Dunnigan had gone to show "his utter disregard" for the police, Mitchell himself, and the "rights of citizens." "Men of his type, if allowed to go unchallenged will produce trouble for innocent citizens," Mitchell warned.

He had decided to write Dunnigan a letter inviting him "to talk it over." He told Van Duzen, "If he shows the right spirit, I shall be willing to drop the whole matter with the hope that he was reformed in his conduct." Mitchell wrote to Dunnigan, "If you come to see me, I propose to drop [my complaint]." If Dunnigan didn't, the congressman added, he was going to swear out a warrant for the suspension of Dunnigan's driving license. After that final meeting, an undated note to Van Duzen relates that Dunnigan had come to see him and had apologized. "He has learned his lesson," Mitchell concluded.[23]

While it is difficult to imagine members of Congress today devoting their time and energy to such incidents, similar scenarios played out for others Mitchell judged to be prejudiced against him as an individual: taxi drivers who refused to service or overcharged him, an elevator operator with whom it was "unfair, unsafe and dangerous for Colored people to come in contact," a stationer who substituted a picture of the Lincoln Memorial for the Supreme Court on his Christmas cards, a neighbor who had Mitchell's car towed, a clerk who wouldn't cash his check, a courier who threw a telegram at his secretary, and a red cap who refused to handle his bags.[24] Winning small battles against racial prejudice was part of his calling.

He also sprang to defend the individuals he saw as defamed in the media.

Hearing radio station WRC in Washington refer to a woman injured in a car accident as a "negress" merited the following: "This term, like the despicable term 'Nigger,' is objectionable to all well-thinking colored people."[25]

Letters from young people drew his special attention, some stirring him to dramatic action. When James Clinton wrote to Mitchell from a Virginia prison where he was awaiting execution for "stealing peanuts," Mitchell answered that he would drive to Richmond and "hope to be of service in your fight to save your life."[26]

When the Black victim of prejudice was also a prominent member of society, he was even more aggressive. Two years before she was denied permission to perform at Constitution Hall, the famed contralto Marian Anderson came to his attention because of a discourteous reference to her in the *Washington News*. "I was dumbfounded," Mitchell wrote to the paper, "to read the insulting headline in which you speak of that great artist, Miss Marian Anderson, as 'Dusky Marian Anderson.' I think you owe it to the Colored people of Washington to explain why you thus insult us."[27]

In 1939, when the Daughters of the American Revolution (DAR) denied Anderson permission to perform at Constitution Hall, Mitchell claimed to have been the first to protest this slight. If he was not the first, he was among the most strident, writing to the president-general of the DAR that this refusal was "of the same mind as the Nazis in their treatment of Jews in Germany. I wouldn't be surprised, if Hitler knew of this, the D.A.R. would get a metal from him."

When the Corcoran Gallery of Art refused to display Paul Meltsner's portrait of Anderson despite a critic's judgment that it was "an enormously sensitive work, full of quiet dignity and grace," Mitchell saw the action as "a slap in the face" to all Black Americans. "None of these things do more than to spur me on toward the greatest possible achievement. The Negro must fight; his friends must be uncompromising. This is the only way I know to break down the terrible discrimination which is recognized as part of American democracy."[28]

This defense of Anderson was only one example of the role Mitchell was asked to play and to which he devoted considerable effort: acting as a cultural consultant on Black contributions to the arts. Once, when he was introduced to a Morgan State audience with a classical fanfare, he prefaced his speech by complaining about the absence of a Black spiritual: "I think I should say something about the regretful way in which you turned to our music. . . . No people would have ever reached their highest point in intelligence or of possibilities if they were ashamed of their own productivity. . . . Those who believe that we ought to forget our songs and stop singing spirituals—those Negroes are hardly worth considering."[29]

Figure 1. Carter G. Woodson, Mitchell's friend and creator of Negro History Week, precursor to Black History Month. Mitchell shared Woodson's advocacy for the preservation of Black culture and was an enthusiastic speaker at events promoting the cause. Scurlock Studios.

As a self-styled guardian of Black culture, Mitchell became an active participant in his friend Carter Woodson's Negro History Week, the purpose of which was "not to focus on how Blacks had been victimized but instead on how Blacks had influenced United States and world history." He became a popular speaker at events, reporting to Woodson in 1940 that he had been invited to a dozen states to make more than fifty speeches "in celebration of what you started." "Could you," he asked, "send me something I could use to explain your work?" Woodson responded with a five-page, single-spaced letter outlining Black achievements "in order that the race may not become a negligible factor in the thought of the world." The document, which detailed Black accomplishments from their African origins to the present day, was designed to "force scientists to revise their estimate as to the Negro who has long been regarded as an inferior." To the contrary, the race should be regarded as "equal to others belonging to the family of mankind." Mitchell read Woodson's letter into the *Congressional Record*.[30]

To imbed this message for future generations, Mitchell became an early advocate for the teaching of courses dedicated to Black American history and achievements in colleges and universities. It was a goal he emphasized in a 1935 speech where he called upon institutes of higher learning to offer classes designed "to foster and formulate better race relations." He renewed the call when he wrote to the University of Michigan in 1938, offering his "unqualified endorsement" to a student resolution in support of a Black history course, "perhaps leading to a department of Negro history." "The Negro," Mitchell wrote, "suffers more from a lack of his History than any other group. I believe you could do nothing better, in the way of helping the movement of racial good will, [than to offer this course]."[31]

Black authors seeking to make a future contribution to the culture enjoyed his special attention. Irene West, later celebrated as the "real mother" of the Montgomery boycott, submitted her poem "De-Mockery vs. Democracy" to him for review. He read it "with great interest" and said he would "refer to the splendid thoughts contained in the poetic lines which you sent." After she sent him more unpublished pieces, Mitchell said he was "overwhelmed by [her] work": "It is unique in that no white woman has . . . ventured to write of this problem in such strong terms and express it in poetry." Chandler Owen, a close friend of A. Philip Randolph, sent Mitchell a draft of his essay "What Will Happen to the Negro if Hitler Wins?" Mitchell found it a "splendid job." Forced to decide between Nazi persecution and British-American discrimination, the choice of the latter was obvious and could only be opposed by an "error-laden Negro Mind." Owen went on to publish a pamphlet, *The Negro and the War*, that the Office of War Information distributed to 2.5 million Black Americans.[32]

But Mitchell was also in demand as a consultant to white authors seeking guidance when writing about Black southerners. Marie Owen was both the sister of William Bankhead, the Speaker of the House and director of the Alabama Department of Archives and History from 1920 to 1955. She sought his help in her attempt to publish a novel, *Children of the Night*, that she saw as presenting Black Americans as "normal human beings aspiring to fill their places in the world." She had run into problems because, she wrote, "Eastern publishers want to show how badly the Negro is treated in the South or presented as the criminal class." After reading more than half of her *Children*, Mitchell told her he was "deeply impressed" and offered to help her find a publisher. A week later, Owen complained about the lack of progress on this front: "If the book had a lynching or two, I might have got a publisher." Mitchell was still encouraging: "The theme is wonderful. It is quite unique in that it is the only case I know of a southern white woman writing, emphasizing so strongly the higher side of Negro life. I am sure if the book was published and read it would mean much for the cause of the Negro." In another instance, Grace Varney, a white woman moved by the experience of having her Black chauffeur refused admission to a restaurant, was trying to rid herself of prejudice. She had written a novel about race relations during the Great War and wanted

Mitchell's opinion of the idioms she had employed in creating Black speech. He answered that he was "much impressed by the dialect." Her work would "go a long way in softening and removing many of the racial prejudices to which we are now subjected."[33]

As a speaker, Mitchell had his critics. W. E. B. Du Bois prayed that "from the speeches of Congressman Mitchell, Good Lord deliver us," and Roy Wilkins dismissed him as a "neighborhood curbstone ranter." But many contemporaries considered Mitchell a spellbinding orator. Maury Maverick, a colleague from Texas, thought him "one of the ablest and most effective speakers in our nation's capital." So did vast numbers in his audiences. Among the hundreds of testimonials to his ability to inspire, his papers contain this from two sisters: "As young people of the Negro group, it is our sincere endeavor to be one more star like you to help light the way for our race. . . . You have given us courage when we thought we were venturing into endless darkness . . . to carry on and expect more from life by putting more into it."[34]

What inspired the sisters was that these speeches often invited Black audiences to be self-critical and face the shortcomings of their own communities. Mitchell began one by telling the story of the lifeguard who saved a drowning man by striking him across the face. Likewise, what he was about to say "may seem cruel and brutal," but he was there to tell them what they needed to hear, not what they wanted to hear. This included critiques of Black social habits, the sensationalism in Black newspapers, and what he saw as the propensity of the race to see themselves as "victims" of white society. Once, when asked how he responded to the news that 69 percent of Black residents of St. Paul, Minnesota, were on welfare, Mitchell answered that it showed "there must be too many good-for-nothing Negroes in St. Paul." After this comment, the *St. Paul Recorder* remarked on his combative style: "It takes courage to tell the Negro his faults. It's an unpopular and unpleasant task." "Wherever Mitchell goes," the paper continued, "he leaves in his wake heated discussions which last for weeks. It is good for the communities he visits." Calling him "the most positive voice of the Negro today," the *Dayton Forum* agreed. "The most overwhelming point in his favor is his brutal frankness," the paper opined. "Congressman Mitchell is the major prophet of the Negro race today. We had better hear him."[35]

To this speaking ability Mitchell added a rare facility to think strategically and act in a detail oriented fashion when facing the future. Responding to a question about his famous prediction in 1928 that he would go to Congress someday, he mused after his election six years later, "I don't know what it is, but in a number of . . . situations I have predicted almost to the letter how events were going to come out. I guess it's just luck, but a lot of my predictions have worked out." But, he added, "I don't just sit still after I make my predictions."[36]

His move to Chicago in 1928 proved the point. He took the step because it offered him an opportunity to win a seat in the House of Representatives from the only congressional district in the country that could elect a Black candidate. Once there, he followed a disciplined six-year strategy to achieve his goal. Wily, old Michael J. "Hinky Dink" Kenna, a wizened survivor of Chicago's political wars, saw him for what he was. "I'm not for Mitchell," he announced after their first meeting, "because he's a carpetbagger." To be more accurate, Kenna should have called Mitchell a reverse carpetbagger, a man who moved north to accomplish something that was impossible in the South.[37] When he managed the "get out the vote drive" to elect Democratic congressmen in 1936, he did so not only because he believed in the New Deal but also to advance his own legislative agenda. After he took his famous ride on the Rock Island, Mitchell pursued a calculated, four-year strategy that led to victory before the Supreme Court but only after reversals he hoped and planned for by pursuing his initial suit before the Interstate Commerce Commission and not lower courts.

He was also a skilled political chameleon, able to adapt to any event with the agility, a man, as Julius J. Adams put it, "who understood publicity as well as any man I have ever met." In doing this he had no compunction about misleading or dissembling. Was the day he met Booker T. Washington the "red letter day" of his life, an epiphany, the day the scales fell from his eyes? Did he really believe that Franklin Roosevelt was "greatest humanitarian this nation or any other nation has [ever] seen . . . second only to the Christ?" Probably not, but it was good political theater designed to advance his causes by casting him in a nonthreatening light. He, like Washington, was "incessantly travers[ing] the border between accommodation and resistance, seeking a middle ground where resistance conflated with accommodation." Ben O'Brien, a reporter for California newspapers, grasped the point of this fluidity. Mitchell, he wrote, had to be "beloved rather than despised if he were to be effective." He was "relentlessly squeezed between opposing forces," southern power in Congress and Black demands for change. By navigating between the two, he served "the best interests of his people and accomplished far more than he otherwise could." His technique, Mitchell boasted to Malcolm Smith of the *Courier*, was to recognize "that there are many ways of putting out a fire aside from calling out the fire department." Those who were truly interested in accomplishing a goal worked quietly and behind the scenes rather than "grand-standing for publicity."[38]

Despite these talents, Mitchell was a flawed change agent, with his feet firmly planted in the clay of what contemporaries termed "a difficult personality." He was, as Robert Vann, editor of the *Pittsburgh Courier*, told him, often "his own worst enemy." He had a tendency to lecture others and could be quarrelsome, self-centered, vindictive, and convinced of his own rectitude. P. L. Prattis, the city editor of the *Pittsburgh Courier*, thought that there was never a moment when Mitchell "was not convinced that he was absolutely right. There is a common term for such an attitude . . . bullheadedness."[39]

Fits of uncontrolled anger dot Mitchell's physical actions as well as his writing. Examples include his 1935 confrontation with a reporter who he reputedly "charged like a wild beast . . . smashing his camera." "I'm no coward," he proclaimed afterward. "People may call me a 'hat in hand' Negro, but I'm afraid of no man, white or black." On another occasion, after Mitchell hung his phone up on reporter William Jones, who was mid-sentence, Jones devoted considerable ink to an analysis of the congressman's behavior. "That," Jones wrote, "newspapermen told me, is the habit of Mr. Mitchell."[40]

One of the things that provoked him was being forced to live in Chicago. Not only had its licentiousness ruined his son, the city was, he complained, a place "where the sun refuses to shine and where the weather is cold and everybody is buttoned up in the heaviest clothes imaginable." When first elected to Congress in 1934, his victory parade did not go down Michigan Avenue. It was a tour of the South, centered on Alabama. At its conclusion, he confessed to a friend that it had been a "real vacation," that "my only regret was my inability to remain in the South longer."[41]

As a congressman, Mitchell spent little time in Chicago, neither seeking public acclaim nor backslapping with local politicians. Charles R. Branham observes that, during those years, Mitchell "built no organization and did not advance the career of even one major leader within the [Democratic] party." In turn, many of his constituents felt alienated from their absentee representative. "He doesn't belong in Chicago," one Democratic party worker complained. "He has no part in Chicago life, either civic or social." Mitchell acknowledged the accuracy of this assertion, admitting to a friend, "I do not know what's going on in the political world of Chicago except as I get a hint now and then such as you give and such as I see in the newspapers."[42]

What he did like and used to his advantage was the similarity between "elections" in the Alabama of his youth and those in the Chicago of the 1930s. Results in both depended on who counted the votes. That being the case, the Windy City's political structure promoted an unspoken but real marriage of convenience between him and the city's bosses. He committed to following the guidance of Mayor Edward J. Kelly and chairman of the Cook County Democratic Party Patrick Nash on issues critical to Chicago. The most important of these was the free flow of patronage, the "mother's milk" of politics, to the Kelly-Nash "machine." In return, they guaranteed his election and reelection until the time when a suitable Democrat with stronger ties to the Chicago emerged to replace him. This arrangement freed Mitchell from the typical responsibility of answering to his constituents on election day. "I really have no contest here," he bragged. "My future is perfectly safe."[43]

With Kelly and Nash turning a blind eye toward issues that did not affect them, Mitchell used his eight years in Washington to promote a vision of his "beloved Southland" reborn as a welcoming home for a Black population that lived on an equal legal footing with white residents.

The key to understanding Mitchell's congressional career lies in dividing it into two distinct phases. During the first, from his election to April 1937, Mitchell saw his goals as attainable through the legislative process. To accomplish this, he adopted the costume and style of a successful white politician. He dressed impeccably, spoke proper English, and exuded success. He bragged, "I never saw a white man who wouldn't yield if you studied him long enough to find out how to approach him." Often, this meant behaving like him.[44]

The technique had some success. Mitchell proved a skillful politician, particularly as his rhetoric soothed fears among southerners about a frontal assault on the status quo. In quick order, he became the chief administration advocate to Black Americans for the New Deal, then a proponent for the thesis that the Democratic Party, not the Republican, was the natural home for Black citizens, and then the leading strategist for bringing Middle Western Black voters to the polls in 1936. These were steps by which he hoped to promote two pieces of landmark legislation necessary for the creation of his reborn South: one bill to create an Industrial Commission to safeguard Black interests in the workplace and another to make lynching a federal crime. A year after his arrival in Congress, he boasted to John J. LeFlore, the secretary of the Mobile branch of the NAACP, that he had enjoyed considerable success using this mollifying method, an achievement "which would not have been accomplished had I gone about it with the beating of drums and the flying of kites."[45]

At the same time, he was merciless in his attacks on the Black bastions of power that, he felt, had accomplished so little since the end of Reconstruction despite their constant braying about the sins of the South. Robert S. Abbott, the publisher of the *Chicago Defender*, the nation's largest Black newspaper, was "just plain ignorant" and his paper "a reactionary, hidebound journal." Robert Vann was "an unstable individual . . . whose natural gait is running away," and Carl Murphy of the *Afro-American* was "as big a liar as can be found in the country." To Mitchell, NAACP stood for the "National Association for the Advancement of Certain People," and was a "cheap racket, the primary purpose of which is to furnish money for [its leaders] so they can have fat salaries and newspaper notoriety." Walter White, the organization's executive secretary after 1931, was "the smallest and most silly man that I have ever seen holding what might be regarded as a responsible position."[46]

These victims of Mitchell's ire exacted their revenge. Despite moving personal appeals to his colleagues, neither of his bills ever became law. The Industrial Commission legislation died in committee; his anti-lynching bill got no further than the House floor, where the vote to even debate the bill was defeated. The critical moment for Mitchell came in the wake of his inability to secure that debate, a defeat that taught Mitchell that he had little future as a legislator.

Rather than retire from the field of battle, he then changed strategies. After April 1937, a rebranded Mitchell shifted what had been a national focus to one that concentrated on judicial, regional, state, and local forces as agents for change in his reconstructed South.

It was no coincidence that only two weeks after the defeat of his anti-lynching legislation, Mitchell instituted a legal process aimed at striking what he saw a death blow to the so-called Jim Crow railroad system in the South. If he could not accomplish his goals through the legislative process, perhaps he could through the judicial.

His legal campaign and eventual victory on this issue did much to alter the public's perception of him, enemies becoming friends and vice versa. The Black press's portrayal of him as an Uncle Tom evolved toward celebration of a heroic fighter for civil rights. In contrast, after his lawsuit was announced, Senator Pat Harrison of Mississippi, someone Mitchell had previously cultivated, denounced him as an arch foe who had begun a process that might lead the federal government "perhaps under the cover of bayonets . . . [compelling] every state to permit Negroes to vote in the white primaries of the South."[47]

A very different Mitchell now preached that necessary change could come only from below, not above, and that the South, not Congress, had to solve its own racial problems. He had long believed that Black leaders living in the North, be they members of the Republican Party, the NAACP, the Black press, or religious leaders, had accomplished little since the end of Reconstruction. Advice delivered from the safety of Washington, New York, or Chicago was counterproductive. Now he added to that list of adversaries most southerners who held political office. No matter their personal beliefs, they were unwilling to pay the political price for threatening the status quo.

Therefore, a new, younger generation of Black and white southern leaders was needed. Ralph Ellison, when writing his *Invisible Man*, captured Mitchell's revised vision in the words of Mary Rambo, a Black woman living in New York who befriended the author's protagonist: "It's you young folks what's going to make changes. . . . You got to lead and you got to fight and move us all up a little higher. And I'll tell you something else, it's the ones from the South that's got to do it, them what knows the fire and how it burns. Up here, too many forgits. They find a place for themselves and forgits the ones on the bottom."[48]

Mitchell toured eleven southern states in 1937 and North Carolina in 1939, seeking allies from both races for his vision of the future. During these travels he insisted on only speaking before racially mixed audiences with white attendees seated onstage with him. His new cadre of leaders should consist of Black students, teachers, and ministers who were college educated but who had remained in the South. To these he joined white allies who did not hold political office. He believed that there were many of these. It was convenient to paint all white southerners with a broad "racist" brush; the discredited Wise Men of the North had been doing that for decades. Admittedly, there were some unrepentant bigots, but they were a relic of the past, the "narrowest, meanest, prejudiced and most intolerant men I have ever met," the "most conceited and biggest hypocrites in our nation. In fact, I do not believe the agitators of this kind of doctrine believe it themselves."[49] A broad swath of white southern public opinion knew that change was needed and inevitable. Typical of this group was Hugo Black, whose nomination to the Supreme Court Mitchell passionately defended despite Black's voting record in the Senate and previous membership in the Ku Klux Klan. Black, he thought, was the type of southerner who, freed from the chains of being answerable to voters, would evolve into a champion for Mitchell's cause.

During these tours, Mitchell became convinced that his physical presence in the South was "one hundred percent more important" than his serving in Washington. You once told me, he reminded a friend, that I should "get out of Congress as early as possible and give my time and ability in helping in the move to make the education of the Negro in the South a practical reality. I am deeply inclined to a program of this kind." School must be "an integral part of community life" and he aimed to "make a contribution toward achieving that goal." After careful consideration, he moved to Virginia in 1939 in preparation for his retirement from Congress.[50]

There he rededicated himself to the education of the new generation of southern leaders as the key to a different approach in the fight for civil rights. "Our progress," he told a conference of Black Alabama primary schoolteachers, "depends more on education than upon all other factors combined."[51] From his new home, he launched a campaign to improve the quality of primary education through the distribution of federal pamphlets to teachers. The time and effort previously devoted to cultivating congressional colleagues now went to addressing Black college audiences. It was students' duty, Mitchell thought, to stay in the South. He wanted them to be proud of who they were, reject victimhood as an excuse for their troubles, and strive to accomplish as he had.

Above all, these new leaders should involve themselves at the local level. Alter a neighborhood's culture, the new Mitchell taught, and you eventually affect national attitudes in ways that would be impossible had you waited for change to come from Washington where power was held by those committed to the status quo. Once he had thought that sending Democrats to Congress was the key to passing anti-lynching legislation. Now he believed that "if you elect a sheriff, you have no need for an anti-lynch law. . . . Instead, we should try to educate the White man to our problems through sane, sound, quiet reasoning."[52]

With this younger, proud leadership in place, Mitchell believed that Black southerners could be persuaded to remain in the South. As important, many who had fled to the North could be convinced to return. Those who had enjoyed success by insinuating themselves into white society would not come back. But what of the sharecropper's family whose land of "milk and honey" had turned out to be a wasteland? There were no jobs for them in the large urban centers of the North where those lacking industrial skills had been "swallowed up and in most cases destroyed by the contaminating influence of city life." This corroding impotence had led to institutionalized poverty, which was no better than slavery. Why could not the federal government use the same monies that went into relief underwriting Black homesteading in the South, just as they had supported white immigrants from Europe in the Middle West after the Civil War? Such grants would give farmers the opportunity to "go forward and develop that which is at your fingertips, the soil."[53]

This radical shift in tactics between the two phases of Mitchell's congressional career confused both friend and foe who recognized that years would pass before an objective assessment of Arthur Mitchell could be undertaken. "It will be some time," an anonymous columnist of the *Amsterdam News* wrote in 1942, "before his own race will have a proper conception of his incomparable contribution to public service and racial betterment." W. J. Edwards thought that, with the passage of time, Mitchell would "go down in history as one of the great men of our time." So did Emory B. Smith, a Black attorney in Washington with whom Mitchell had studied. His student had "nobly taken on the burden of your entire race. I hope that historians will properly appreciate your contributions to American life." Even P. L. Prattis, a frequent critic, thought that Mitchell deserved a chance to appear before the bar of history: "I am sure that he carries within his breast the hope that some day he will be understood, that many of the commendable things he has undertaken . . . will be exposed . . . and that he . . . will be reevaluated in terms of his honest, constructive efforts. [But] I doubt that he will ever be understood. . . . I suspect that he will be forgotten before anyone will listen with an open mind to an interpretive analysis of his record."[54]

Arthur Schlesinger Jr. could well have been thinking of Mitchell when he warned that historians have "no license to roam through the past, handing down moral verdicts on individuals. . . . This reductionism denies historical figures the validity of their own judgments and thereby denies them their human dignity. . . . When participants explain in urgent words why they lived, fought, and bled, is it not hubris for historians to dismiss their testimony?" Schlesinger also reminds us that revisionism is "an essential process by which history, through the disclosure of new sources, the posing of new problems, and the investigation of new possibilities, enlarges its perspective and enriches its insights."[55]

Drawn in great part from the Arthur Mitchell papers, the following narrative offers us a chance to revise our thinking about the path forward toward racial justice in the United States. It does not advocate for Mitchell's opinions or methods; it only presents them and calls attention to their currency today. An objective study of Arthur Mitchell does ask us to confront the nature of enduring change. To be lasting is it massive and fought on high ground of principle or incremental and fought in the trenches of unedifying detail?

Arthur Mitchell will delight some while infuriating others. The point is not whether he was right or wrong but that his was and is an important, almost forgotten, voice in this national discussion. It is in that spirit that we should heed Prattis's advice "to listen with an open mind to an interpretive analysis of his record."

That listening is difficult given Mitchell's controversial character but important given his accomplishments. As Jill Lepore warns in *These Truths*, "Between reverence and worship, on the one side, and irreverence and contempt on the other lies an uneasy path." This book seeks to tread that path, neither celebrating nor condemning Mitchell but explaining him in the context of the age in which he lived while bearing in mind the mistake made by attempts to conflate today's values with yesterday's realities. To place Arthur Mitchell in his historical context, we need to evaluate him by what he achieved in his day compared to what he could have accomplished.[56]

1
"The Place of My Birth, Which Is Very Dear to Me"

Arthur Mitchell began many addresses to college audiences with the observation, "I don't think of many things more interesting than my [own] life." Perhaps, but with a few exceptions, all that we know about his first twenty-five years was based on stories he or Clara Mitchell, his third wife, told. According to them, three of Mitchell's biological grandparents had been slaves; the fourth was a white man. His father, Taylor, was born near Cusseta, Georgia. Ammar, his mother and the dominant personality in the family, had a white father. Family lore held that she had been a disobedient slave who tried to escape and once was punished for trying to learn the alphabet. Neither of his parents could read or write. Taylor was unschooled; Ammar had three weeks of formal education.

The first of six children, Arthur was born on a farm near Stroud in "the very backwoods of Alabama," in 1883. The village was twelve miles from any railroad, "amid cotton patches, corn fields, and briar patches." Shortly after his birth, the family moved to the land of R. W. Allen in Lafayette and then to that of M. M. Carlisle in Chapel Hill. There, depending upon the season, Taylor raised cotton or felled timber. He was prosperous enough to avoid being forced into sharecropping and might have owned land at one point, either in Chambers or Randolph County. Mitchell claimed that his childhood there connected him with one of the most famous Alabamians of the first half of the twentieth century. He and Joe Louis "were born and reared in the same settlement" and their fathers were "the best of pals and lived a few blocks from each other." Although his mother valued education, Arthur received little formal education as a child. If he received religious training, it was not from the "Negro preachers" who called upon his parents. When ministers stopped at the Mitchell home for chicken dinners, "they devoured the best pieces, leaving only neck bones, backs, and wings for everyone else."[1]

The family fell apart between 1896 and 1901 after Taylor and two of his sisters died of dysentery. In an effort to make ends meet, a teenaged Mitchell hired himself out for thirty cents a day picking cotton, digging ditches, shucking corn, and gathering fodder while sustaining himself on sweet potatoes, corn bread, molasses, and butter milk. Despite his efforts, unpaid doctors' bills and other debts led to financial hardship so extreme that he and his mother gleaned the field they once had owned at night to feed the remaining family.

This destitution led Arthur to leave home. In a recounting that bears striking similarities to Booker T. Washington's tale of finding his way from the salt mines of Walden, West Virginia, to the Hampton Institute in Virginia, Mitchell walked the sixty-five miles from his home to the Tuskegee Institute in search of an education. He carried all of his worldly possessions with him: "a dress suit-case, an extra pair of trousers, one suit of underwear, and a few shirts." Along the way, he ate oranges that had fallen to the side of the road.[2]

It was a dangerous journey for the young Mitchell to undertake in Alabama at the dawn of the twentieth century, a state where "Black men and women were hunted like sport," a pursuit that could result in a public lynching. Between 1901 and 1918, 102 such killings occurred, 82 percent of which involved a Black victim. No participants in these "executions" were ever held to account by a jury, a body from which Black Americans were excluded.[3]

At almost the same date as Mitchell's walk, a convention in Montgomery adopted the 1901 Constitution, a document that effectively denied almost all Black Alabamians the right to vote because "as a race, [the Negro] is incapable of self-government and the intelligent exercise of the power of voting."[4]

Compounding these injustices, poor Black residents of the state, such as Mitchell's family, would become virtual prisoners in the county of their birth, thanks to a 1903 vagrancy law, legislation "so vague that any Black not under the protection of a white could be arrested," jailed, and then leased to large industrial corporations under appalling conditions.[5]

Under these circumstances, the majority of the Black poor were prisoners on the land they farmed, locked in place by a sharecropping system that Blackmon called an "economic serfdom far worse . . . than personal slavery had ever been." But even the few having the resources to travel—Black professionals—declined the opportunity. Ray Stannard Baker, a muckraking journalist who toured in South in 1904 and 1907, was surprised to learn this. Despite all of the persecution and danger they faced, when Baker asked Black southerners "What is your chief cause of complaint?" "the first answer nearly always referred to Jim Crow cars or Jim Crow railroad stations" and the public humiliation they faced as a result of the *Plessy v. Ferguson* Supreme Court decision in 1896 that created the "separate but equal" standard for public transportation.[6]

Lacking the means to subject himself to this embarrassment, a foot-weary Mitchell appeared at Tuskegee sometime in 1901 with fifteen cents in his pocket. He was so poor, he liked to say, that he couldn't afford a two-cent stamp to write and tell his mother that he had arrived safely. Once there, he was denied admission by the registrar, as Washington had been at Hampton, because he lacked the entry fee of two dollars. Undaunted, Mitchell went into town and washed dishes for two weeks, reappearing with the required deposit. There he met Booker T. Washington, who refused to accept the payment, instructing the bursar to "Charge it to me, this boy is going places." Mitchell always maintained that this original meeting with Booker T. Washington was the "*Red Letter* day of my life." After his election in 1934, he returned to Tuskegee, where he told the students, "The older I grow and the richer my experience, the more do I appreciate that everything I have done or may do that is worthwhile will come from the contacts I had with Dr. Washington and others here at Tuskegee."

He spent his first days at Tuskegee washing out his only set of underwear every evening. At night, he prayed that someday he would be given the opportunity to "do all in my power to help poor, worthy, struggling boys and girls" such as himself.

Washington soon appointed Arthur to be his office boy. In that role, he met visiting dignitaries such as Andrew Carnegie, John D. Rockefeller, and William Howard Taft. But his position also entailed danger. In October 1901, "it was my duty to stand guard all night long with a rifle in my hand to protect the property of that institution and protect the life of that great man" from death threats following the "Wizard of Tuskegee's" reception at the White House by President Theodore Roosevelt.[7]

When in Congress, Mitchell always emphasized his time at Tuskegee, a period he fondly remembered. With friends, he reminisced about the "good old days," including joint participation in the Willing Workers Debating Club. The deepest personal relationship Mitchell formed at Tuskegee was with George Washington Carver, the famed agronomist, who ignited in him a lifetime interest in agriculture, taught him advanced farming techniques, and impressed upon him the importance of a diversified agriculture that moved away from an exclusive reliance on cotton for prosperity. "I knew [Carver] very intimately when I was a student at Tuskegee," Mitchell remembered, disdainfully dismissing students who didn't want to sit in the school's dining room with "this man with a brain with which he has accomplished great things . . . because he was a farmer and worked with his hands as well as his brain."

Mitchell and Carver remained close for decades. During his 1934 visit, he introduced his teacher as "the greatest scientist in the world." After Mitchell delivered the Founder's Day speech at Tuskegee in 1939, Carver wrote to him that his address made his former teacher feel "very chesty and you can't blame me for it. We all have a right to feel proud of you. With so much love." Mitchell responded with unusual effusiveness: "I shall keep this letter as long as I live. I want to assure you that I cherish it because it comes from the heart of a great soul and a great patriot. Cordially, sincerely, and gratefully yours." Following Carver's death, Mitchell was an active supporter of the movement to turn his teacher's birthplace into a national monument.[8]

Despite his sworn fealty to Washington, Mitchell's relations with the "Wizard of Tuskegee" proved more checkered over time. As a student he embraced Washington's concept of industrial education that would lead to acquisition of a trade as the way forward for Tuskegee students, a means of escaping the perpetual poverty imposed by sharecropping. With the tools necessary to function in society, the race could produce and provide for itself as a first step out of poverty.[9]

But, Washington preached, proper training had to be joined to grit and determination if an individual was to enjoy success. It was a lesson Mitchell internalized, frequently telling the story of the Wizard's humiliating his own stepbrother, who was Tuskegee's football coach. After a dismal season of losses, J. B. Washington gave a chapel talk explaining the defeats. "The Wizard" listened to the talk and responded, "Mr. Washington, you have brought us a beautiful story of excuses and failures but we sent you out to bring us success. The world will forget the excuses that you have brought us, but it will never forget the story on the scoreboard."[10]

The power Washington and his program exerted across the nation also awed Mitchell. During his student days at Tuskegee, "The Wizard" came to be seen as "race spokesman by the nation's political leadership." He blessed almost all Black political office holders and controlled the distribution of northern philanthropic money. "No Negro schools received contributions from Carnegie, Rockefeller and lesser donors without Washington's approval." Should any opposition to this arrangement arise, discipline was imposed by the "Tuskegee machine," a "ruthless instrument of Washington's power" that acted "unmercifully against the perceived enemy."[11]

After a stay of less than two years at Tuskegee, Mitchell left for unknown reasons and enrolled at the Snow Hill Institute, located in rural Wilcox County. William J. Edwards, himself a Tuskegee graduate, had founded the school ten years before, staffing it with graduates of Washington's enterprise. It was a "shining example of the influence of Tuskegee graduates" in the Black Belt, "an atoll [of educational excellence] in a vast sea of ignorance."[12]

For Mitchell, Snow Hill had the advantage of offering a curriculum that advanced "the Tuskegee program beyond its narrowing and limiting bounds" by placing greater emphasis on the humanities than Washington's school did. This gave the future congressman the chance to study literature, grammar, rhetoric, history, and geography.[13]

Several of Edwards's precepts had a profound influence on Mitchell's political development. While Washington was vague on direct political involvement, Edwards called for engagement. The reality of self-government in the South, he taught, meant "equal justice to [only] one race." It was impossible to build a civilization on such a "modified democracy." True democracy meant the "right to vote and make decisions about all social, political, and economic matters that affected [Negro] lives." Students who wanted to escape to the large cities of the North were doing only the "work that any ordinary man can do. Here in the South a great work is before us and the majority of our people are here." Rather than flee, Edwards taught his pupils that staying in the South was a "labor of love" and that those committed to the betterment of the race should "go out into the rural sections and teach."[14]

Figure 2. William J. Edwards, founder of the Snow Hill Normal and Industrial Institute from which Mitchell graduated in 1903. Mitchell always insisted that he was a "Tuskegee man" and Booker T. Washington's acolyte. But Edwards, with his insistence that Black citizens attempt to vote, may have had a greater influence.

Mitchell portrayed himself in Washington as a "Tuskegee man" without even mentioning his physical presence at Snow Hill. As a congressman, Mitchell downplayed Edwards's role in his development, sensing that presenting himself as a Washington acolyte was to his political advantage. Only late in his career did he acknowledge even his physical presence at Snow Hill. It was a ploy that offended Edwards, who had written in 1918, "when I think of Mitchell's work . . . I feel that my sacrifice has not been in vain." Privately, Mitchell seemed to admit the truth of Edwards's role in his development. In a 1912 letter to Snow Hill's principal, he confessed that "Tuskegee perhaps has had too large a share of the honor of my work, that is if I have done anything worthy of honor." Tuskegee's own publication celebrating its first fifty years also seems to support Edwards's position. Mitchell is listed only as "a former student."[15]

This, he boasted throughout his career, was because he had escaped crushing poverty and destitution by an act of will, and he asserted that other Black Americans should emulate his example if they wanted to be successful. "Your destiny is in your own hands," he told students, and "nobody in the world is going to do your work for you. I want to see boys willing to set out and fight the battle of life themselves. They make real men. . . . I don't want to see a boy . . . depending upon parents to carry him on their shoulders." But Edwards helped prepare him for the battle, perhaps more than Booker T. Washington. The first surviving letter written by Mitchell was to Edwards shortly after his graduation. It bears testimony to that debt: "When I get in a tight [spot] I feel I am your son and you must help me. I must succeed. . . . You need not worry. If I live, I am going to reach the mark."[16]

By the time of his graduation from Snow Hill in 1903, Mitchell was as well-educated as any Black American of the day could be. Thus armed, he moved to Greensboro, twenty-five miles northwest of Selma. There, he taught and then served as principal of the Tullibody Academy, "one of the better Negro schools" that offered courses in Latin, Greek, geometry, English, grammar, and natural philosophy. A student at Tullibody later remembered Mitchell as "an earnest young man addressing a group of eager faced boys and girls . . . trying to teach them the right principles of living, trying to plant a spark of ambition in their souls—pleasant memories these."[17]

In Greensboro, "where his excellent conduct was held in esteem by all," Mitchell also set out to found his own school, the West Alabama Normal and Industrial Institute. Following the Tuskegee model, its course of study placed heavy emphasis on "trades . . . and particularly agriculture." "I make an earnest plea that all persons, both white and colored, join us in the building up of an agricultural school at this place," Mitchell wrote. "Our interests are so interwoven than one cannot be helped without effecting [*sic*] the other." The motto he gave the school was appropriate given the state of education for rural Black Alabamians of 1905: "Bend to the oar tho' the tide be against us."[18]

It certainly was. Trapped on the land, the children of rural Black southerners faced grim prospects. "Educate the Negro and you spoil a field hand" ran the popular expression. This belief was made more explicit by one Forrest Pope in a letter to the *Atlanta Georgian*. The thought that "education would solve the Negro problem" was false, he wrote. There was not "an honest, fearless, thinking man in the South but who knows that to be a bare-faced lie. Send an educated Negro out in the South with ever so good intentions on the part of his benefactor and himself, send him to take my work away from me and I will kill him."[19]

In fact, Alabama seemed to pride itself on restricting educational funding to all. Its white primary and secondary institutions were a "veritable hodgepodge of schools" with no uniform standards. Public schools in the Black Belt were "uncomfortable, unfurnished, and wholly unsuited to use." "If a man in a rural community owned a car," Albert Moore wrote about Alabama in 1914, "he had more invested in it than the whole community had invested in its school and he probably spent more on the upkeep of the automobile than the community spent maintaining its school, including the teacher's salary."[20]

Bad as they were, white schools compared favorably to Black ones. In 1892, Alabama had repealed a law that state funds had to be distributed equally to all schools on a per pupil basis. Under new legislation, the total number of students enrolled in a town or county would determine the funding a municipality received. It was left to local officials to divide those dollars "as they deem just and equitable." In 1908, the total value of all equipment in Alabama schools was recorded as $262,218. The Black schools' share of this total was $21,285. Even this pittance was under attack. "Stop the appropriations for Negro education," an opponent argued, "and the school hours in which it is taught will decay. [Then the] Negro will take the place the Creator intended that he should take in the economy of the world—a dutiful, faithful, and law-abiding servant."[21]

Not only did Alabama underfund its Black schools, but the state's elected officials joined other southern politicians in scorning northern financial assistance to them. Most white Alabamians agreed with James K. Vardaman, the governor of Mississippi, who warned that "Northern philanthropy" in support of Black education was a mortal threat. The only effect of such schooling was "to spoil a good field hand and make an insolent cook." What "the North was sending South was not money" but rather the liberating idea that education could raise up a segment of the population to become full-fledged citizens who voted, an imminent danger to the existing social structure. "I am opposed to the niggers voting," Vardaman declared. "It matters not what his advertised moral and mental qualifications may be. I am just as much opposed to Booker Washington, with all his Anglo-Saxon reinforcement, voting as I am to voting by the cocoanut-headed, chocolate-colored typical little coon, Andy Dotson, who blacks my shoes every morning. Neither one is fit to perform the supreme functions of citizenship."[22]

This attitude left Black schools in Alabama in an "abysmally poor" condition, although their exact status was hard to assess because "many were short-lived, most were small, and almost none preserved their records or even the story of their development." Fires destroyed school buildings on a regular basis. Classrooms had almost no equipment. Teachers were "generally incompetent, some barely literate." In the Black Belt, the Black school year, beginning after cotton had been picked and ending when it was time to plant the next crop, averaged five months, class size averaged sixty-nine students, and teacher salaries 80 cents a day as opposed to $14.55 for instructors in white schools. Statewide, 65 percent of white children attended school as opposed to 37 percent of Black children. Five percent of white residents were illiterate, compared to nearly one-third of the Black population.[23]

If they could read, Black Alabamians had access to only twenty-five of the state's 383 public libraries. Among the titles they could peruse were *The Negro: A Beast* and *The Negro: Menace to Civilization.* If they preferred a gentler approach, they could read Joel Chandler Harris's Uncle Remus stories peopled by happy Black characters, "nostalgic for the days of enslavement because their elites lacked the ability to lead and whom whites had a duty to control and shepherd through life."[24]

In 1908, just as white violence reached a crescendo against Black southerners, making it "seem like the whole South was insane," Mitchell left Greensboro to reestablish his institute at Panola in Sumter County. It was a bold move, perhaps motivated by a Tuskegee report that there were "very few black schools offering specific education in agriculture" but that "the rural people are receptive, want to learn, and will learn if leaders . . . can inspire their confidence and create a healthy sentiment for the best there is in American agriculture."[25]

Lying on the Alabama-Mississippi border, Sumter County had been the ancestral home of the Choctaws before the tribe had been forced west by Andrew Jackson's removal policies during the 1830s. Migrating slave owners replaced the Native Americans, establishing large cotton plantations designed to take advantage of the area's rich soil. By 1860, Sumter County counted five thousand white residents and eighteen thousand enslaved people. Largely untouched by Civil War battles, Sumter developed a reputation as a lawless region during Reconstruction. By 1908, it was one of the poorest counties in Alabama, one where disadvantaged white residents "could harass and assault blacks with little fear of legal consequences" and one of the "most prone to lynching African-Americans." Sumter and those counties immediately surrounding it in Alabama and Mississippi recorded 121 lynchings of Black residents between 1877 and 1950. It was, the future congressman wrote, "unsafe for an educated Negro to spend even one night in this section of West Alabama."[26]

Explaining his choice of Panola, an isolated clearing of 175 people, as the location for his school, twenty-five-year-old Arthur Mitchell wrote that he "purposely avoided the more prosperous section and settled on Panola" because he had discovered during a visit in early 1908 that of the area's twenty-eight thousand residents, twenty-four thousand were Black people "living largely as they did during the days of slavery . . . driven to work by white overseers." 10,934 Black children between the ages of seven and twenty-one lived in the vicinity and had no access to education of any sort. Seeing this next generation as "further behind and more neglected than in any other section of the whole South," this was his opportunity "to be of the greatest possible usefulness to both our maker and our fellow man." Guided by this thought, he "talked with some of the large planters about the condition of my people and was granted permission to open a little school and teach the children that could be spared from the cotton fields."[27]

One of these "large planters" was John A. Rogers, a state senator and 1880 graduate with highest honors of the University of Alabama. Not only an able student, he was also captain of the first Crimson Tide football team. He was, the *Sumter County Sun* reported in 1912, "a man of deep learning and gifted beyond the lot of many to make himself felt and understood: a master of language and oratory."[28]

When he met Mitchell, Rogers was the owner of the Fair Oaks estate, one of the largest land holdings in Sumter County. He was also a supporter of industrial education because "my ancestors were responsible for Negroes being in America" and "it was the duty of the strong to help the weak, to put these Negroes in the way of earning an honest living which must come through a thorough training of their hands, their minds, and their hearts." According to a local newspaper, his work crew living at Fair Oaks saw Rogers as a "great and good man" who had "always deported himself as a friend to needy and worthy people."[29]

Having deeded a section of Fair Oaks to the Alabama, Tennessee, and Northern (AT&N) Railroad, an enterprise that proposed to build a line connecting the coalfields west of Birmingham to Mobile and the Gulf of Mexico, this "great and good man" also had a financial interest in promoting the development of Sumter County. As he hoped to attract Black workers to settle on the land bordering the railroad, a Black school offering instruction in industrial education would be an important enticement. Mitchell impressed Rogers as a potential leader of such an enterprise. "Better than his energy and ability," the senator wrote in 1910, the head of the West Alabama Institute displayed "a spirit of morality and good citizenship that has had its effect on his people. I believe him to be worthy of aid and encouragement and that his example will be one of great benefit to the Negroes in this section."

Therefore, he gave the penniless Mitchell eighty acres of land on which to build a school, provided the task was accomplished within three years. In addition to the eighty-acre gift, Rogers made Mitchell a partner in the Afro-American Building, Loan and Real Estate Company of Sumter County, an undertaking to promote the sale of Fair Oaks plots to Black workers.[30]

Mitchell was deferential to his benefactor, writing that "we are not slow to admit that the man is our superior and we are dependent on him to a large degree. We cannot hope to do anything here without the cooperation of the white people." The aim of his West Alabama Institute was "to train Negroes in such ways as will render their lives more serviceable to their own people and the country . . . to have them, as far as possible, settle down in the country, work among the less fortunate, and reflect in the lives of the masses the training they themselves have received here." During Reconstruction, Mitchell wrote, the Black southerner had been "unlettered and untrained, and did not thoroughly understand how to handle himself in his new freedom." Leaders from other sections of the country took advantage of this ignorance to promote the view of education as a method of "becoming prominent in politics or evading work." The result was that many never learned to farm in a diversified manner that would move them away from reliance on cotton. As mechanization spread, this dependence on a single crop resulted in idleness during market turndowns, "one of the greatest causes of so much crime being committed. Our aim is to teach the Negro to love all honorable work, however humble, and to seek to be employed at all times." "If something is not done to change the result of the farm in a few years," he warned, "not only the Negroes who operate these farms but the white people who from year to year are putting out their money to support these farms will be paupered."[31]

Literally building his own school, Mitchell claimed that he "went into the woods with an axe and with his own hands felled the trees out of which rough lumber was cut for the first school building." It opened on October 28, 1908, "without one cent of money, with one teacher [Mitchell] and with three pupils." At first, it met out of doors, then in a Methodist church. To attract students, Mitchell taught during the day while speaking at nearby churches and local dances in the evening. A glimpse of the inspirational message he delivered may lie in clippings he left behind. Among these were "Life's Mirror," a poem by Madeline S. Bridges:

> There are loyal hearts, there are spirits
> There are souls that are pure and true
> Then give to the world the best you have
> And the best shall come back to you.
> For life is a mirror of king and slave. Tis just what you are or do
> Then give to the world the best you have And the best shall come back to you.

There is also a copy of "Hark, the Voice of Jesus Calling" by Daniel March, a Congregational minister:

> If you cannot cross the ocean and the heathen land explore
> You can find the hethen [*sic*] near you
> You can find them at your door
> If you cannot speak like angels
> If you cannot preach like Paul
> You can tell the love of Jesus
> You can say he died for all.

To this Mitchell added a note: the life of Jesus "was one of pure, genuine, practical religion." A school's job was to "engage the young men and the young women in the true sense of religion and teach that life means something."[32]

On August 26, 1909, an AT&N train stopped at Panola, the first time many older Alabamians had seen an "iron horse." Rogers addressed a festive crowd of fifteen hundred in a celebration that included a barbeque, a baseball game, and a dance. The opening of the railroad then permitted Mitchell to run a series of fairs during 1910 that took as their model the agricultural techniques taught by Carver "designed to emancipate the black farmers of the South from agricultural ignorance." Advertised in the local newspaper, the events were a combination of hoedown and serious education. One offered an excursion by train to "fair grounds one mile below Panola" with "cheap fares and all can go. The best of order assured on train and at the park." Once there, spectators could watch a baseball game featuring "the best teams in the county" while enjoying a barbeque and fish fry, complete with ice cream, soda, and watermelon. Good music was to be provided all day. Another fair featured "races and amusements for the young, foot, apple, potato and sack races, greased pole and sleek pole and other sports. Big piano concert at night." While the children were being entertained, adults could attend "lessons to learn better farming techniques." Classes included instruction on "how to break land for cotton and corn," "how to grow corn on sand land," and "the need for improved seed and the use of fertilizers."[33]

Spurred on by the Rogers's grant, the coming of the railroad, and contributions from both white and Black residents, the institute prospered. Sixteen months after its founding, four teachers instructed 150 students. Its one large building, Rogers Hall, was a three-story structure containing twenty-five classrooms. There was also a chapel, a blacksmith and wood shop, and some livestock. Mitchell put the school's value at $10,000. Fanoy Little, an acquaintance from these early days, remembered Mitchell as a "good teacher," determined to emulate Booker T. Washington. He was "very friendly," although he didn't particularly believe in church and didn't think much of Black preachers. Students of all ages went to class, in addition to working on the farm. But, Little remembered, his friend was hard to get along with, particularly when angry. Also troublesome to Little was the fact that Mitchell often didn't seem to be honest. "He wouldn't," Little remembered, "deal straight for five minutes."[34]

The success of West Alabama came to the attention of officials at Tuskegee. Robert C. Bedford, secretary of the Board of Trustees, was impressed after a visit: "You have shown a spirit of work that is equaled by few," he wrote to Mitchell. "I could plainly see that your example had taken hold of the people and was already bearing fruit in a determination on their part to do better than they had ever done before. I have rarely seen a nobler example of self-denial and devotion than that shown by your wife and yourself. Please use our friends—north and south. It gives me the greatest pleasure always to speak well of your work." This was followed two months later by praise from Washington himself in his *Annual Report* : "I cannot illustrate the far-reaching values of the work our graduates are doing in building up the schools in the rural districts of the South than refer to the West Alabama Institute which example indicates in a large degree the spirit of self help."[35]

Delight at this recommendation was cut short by the death of Mitchell's first wife, Eula Mae, in August 1910 from pellagra. Mitchell described to Edwards a heartrending scene where "his devoted wife," went to bed, lost her mind, and had to be "taken to the Hospital for the Insane," all in the space of six weeks.

More determined than ever to make his school a success, Mitchell told Edwards that "he had rolled up his sleeves and gone about the work with renewed energy and declared that with the Lord to help me I shall know no failure." This commitment led to his first fundraising expedition in the North, outreach he had seen modeled at both Tuskegee and Snow Hill.

His appeal, he told to a Springfield, Massachusetts, audience, was not for a school in the northern sense of the word. His aim was to create self-supporting students "by giving boys instruction in agriculture and the simpler trades and by teaching girls domestic science." At first, he admitted, this approach had been unpopular with those he sought to serve, but now the "eagerness of the students . . . is at times almost pathetic, many working through the day [in the cotton fields] to attend school at night."[36]

As he explained to gatherings in Massachusetts, Connecticut, and New York, he needed a small printing press that could be used to teach students a trade while lowering the cost of publications. In addition, the school required "another good pair of mules," $300 to complete a kitchen and dining room, $500 to finish a "cottage for teachers" with the construction work being done by students, and a machine to manufacture bricks. Donations of new and secondhand clothes and shoes for students "who have gone bare-footed all winter" would also help, as would books for the library as "scores of families are without easy reach of a school." He also appealed for scholarship monies. Because of financial constraints, the school had been able to accommodate only one-fifth of the students who had applied. Four young women had walked thirty miles to Panola only to be denied admission. "If we were able," he asserted, "we could enroll one thousand students within a month's time. There is not a section in the entire Southland where a few dollars invested in Negro education would reach a greater number and do more real good."[37]

In a letter to Edwards from Watertown, Connecticut, Mitchell reported, "We are doing a fine job on our trip . . . making many friends for our work." He usually addressed three audiences every Sunday, efforts that earned him praise as "a speaker of exceptional ability." But the next Sunday, he would speak four times: to two white churches in the morning, then to the YMCA and "to a colored church late in the evening." He wanted Edwards to appreciate that he was not only speaking in Black churches but also to clubs whose members represented the white power elites of the North. One gathering in Palmer, Massachusetts, was made up of "lawyers, Drs., newspaper men, and the best men of Palmer and is presided over by a man that has for six years been a member of the legislature. I think we shall made [*sic*] a move upward now."[38]

During 1911, enrollment grew to between 250 and 300 students. With Mitchell "having gained the confidence of many representative white men in this section," the future looked bright until a "very disastrous fire" occurred on October 29 when a stovepipe flue ignited, reducing Rogers Hall to ashes, a loss Mitchell estimated at $5,000. As the fire raged, Little remembered Mitchell sitting on the ground next to the school's piano, the one piece of equipment that had been rescued, crying.[39]

The fire inspired Mitchell to "demonstrate more than ordinary ability and energy to rebuild his school." With $195 "largely or wholly given by the colored people," he headed north with an appeal for two thousand "friends" to give five dollars apiece to help him with reconstruction. The solicitation listed Booker T. Washington as a "special reference" and focused on the progress the institute had made in promoting racial harmony in Sumter County. Until the establishment of the school, the appeal reported, an educated Black person had been "regarded as a menace to the welfare of the community." Now white people supported the school, attending its graduations and farmer institutes. "We are sure," Mitchell claimed, "that we have an opportunity for usefulness second to no other school of its kind in the South."[40]

On this trip, Mitchell spent much of his time in New York City and Connecticut, where the *Waterbury Republican* reminded its readers that "wherever he went [last summer] he made a very good impression and he is well recalled by many of the residents here as a very bright, interesting young man," who impressed listeners with "the earnestness of his purpose." Among those he visited was Horace Taft, brother of the president and headmaster of a prestigious boarding school that bore his name. In New York, he appeared at a mass meeting held at St. Mark's Methodist Episcopal Church on West Fifty-Third Street. There, speakers included Fred Moore, the editor of the *New York Age*, a "devout accomodationist" who was Washington's "journalistic spokesman," and A. Clayton Powell Sr., pastor at the Abyssinian Baptist Church.[41]

To Mitchell's surprise, the Washington endorsement that had seemed so powerful during his first visit appeared to be more a hindrance than a help during his second tour. This was because, in March 1911, "the Wizard" had been seen in New York's Tenderloin district, a "raucous strip of Manhattan's West Side famed for its licit and illicit entertainment venues." There, Washington had allegedly been caught staring through a peephole at a white woman undressing.[42]

Writing from New York, Mitchell warned Washington that the "New York affair" was being used against him by some Black ministers "sick of Tuskegee and Booker Washington's leadership." In particular, he reported that Taft "generally circulated through the North that you are a hard drinker and that at times you would come to the Manhattan hotel and get broiling drunk." Having delivered this assessment, Mitchell tried to soften the blow. "I love Tuskegee," he vowed, "and there is no man living that I esteem so highly as I do you. If my life means anything at all in the way of helping our people, I owe that impetus of feeling and inspiration to you."[43]

Washington, Mitchell was about to learn, was what Louis R. Harlan described as "a circumspect man, full of covert goals and secret devices that would not bear the light of day. His secret actions against his black opponents . . . showed little forbearance and drew less from the teachings of Jesus than those of Machiavelli." Rather than respond with gratitude to a young disciple telling truth to power, the Wizard sent a member of the "Tuskegee machine" to Sumter County to investigate the West Alabama Institute. This subordinate concluded that Mitchell had not been giving children a satisfactory education and should be shunned.[44]

The report, Mitchell told Edwards, was "false from start to finish; there had never been an investigation. Good white people are indignatt" and would "see to it that he retracts his statements. . . . While I do not wish to do the man any harm, I and my friends, who are many, are going to bring the truth to the people regarding the matter." Two days later, he wrote that a Tuskegee representative had agreed that the report "was rotten and assured me that it would be corrected in some satisfactory way immediately." "The only thing that has kept this matter out of the courts is the desire on my part not to injure [Washington] further than I am forced to do in order to take care of myself. I am in the dark," he disingenuously added, "as to the real motive. The whole thing seems shrouded in mystery."[45]

According to Clara Mitchell, what he did to protect himself from Washington was to "induce" a Tuskegee telegraph operator to steal copies of messages from "the Wizard" that ordered "quantities of whiskey" and arranged "visits to white mistresses." When Washington protested to the telegraph company about this theft, their inspector investigated, concluding that "these telegrams were gotten out of the office in an unscrupulous way through this man Mitchell and we think he deserves punishment." Mitchell denied involvement: "As I remember it there did come to us through the mails several months ago a badily mutilated package of what appeared to be old copies of telegrams. But as it was absolutely worthless as far as we could see, no effort was made to preserve it. . . . We have not the slightest idea who sent them or why they should have been sent to us."[46]

By the time he returned to Alabama, Mitchell had raised $25,000 and announced that his school would be rebuilt—but not at Panola. Rather, its new location lay eight miles to the south on the AT&N at Geiger on land owned by John Pinson. Like Rogers, he was a real estate developer who shared the former's vision for the economic development of the west Alabama corridor but on a grander scale. Also like Rogers, Pinson owned a large plantation, a portion of which he had also donated to the AT&N. He saw the opening of the railroad creating the possibility to turn the small town of Geiger into a trading center and supply point for eight hundred square miles of the richest farmlands in western Alabama and eastern Mississippi. A 1910 promotional pamphlet touted the "very fertile soil," "the finest land in the world for growing alfalfa," excellent corn yields, and the rewards of raising cattle and hogs in the area. "All the advantages to be found in the world's best farming centers are here," it boasted, "and in the center of it all is the new town of Geiger. We only want more white people and good people to develop it." For potential recruits, films shown as far away as New York depicted Geiger as "an alternative to the frustrations and uncertainties of industrial jobs in the cities." In his endorsement of the project, Rogers added that "the Negro, heretofore in the way of white immigration, is now drifting to the lumber camps and mineral centers of the south, leaving the farmlands to the white man who is now growing on twenty acres of land what was formerly grown on a hundred. . . . Bring many such white families among us. . . . They are needed."[47]

Pinson had Geiger plated and built a bank "as imposing as any in the Black Belt, a business district and a church." William Gilbert, son of the then postmaster, described the downtown as having a newspaper press, two drugstores, a brick factory, a cotton gin, a cotton-seed oil mill, grocery stores, a rail line, and even a Coca-Cola bottling plant. Gilbert also remembered the lottery Pinson organized to sell fifteen thousand acres of land to white farmers. For fifty dollars, a participant could purchase a lot and the opportunity to win farmland of between ten and forty acres. The raffle's grand prize was a house sitting on 160 acres.[48]

Black farmers were important to Pinson's plan. He needed them as an agricultural labor force but also believed that "since the colored people had had such a great part in making him prosperous, in simple justice he might well do something for [them]." His vision included "a large colored settlement of intelligent and progressive Negroes in Sumter County" modeled on Mound Bayou in Mississippi, a small city that had been founded in 1887 by a former enslaved person, Isaiah Montgomery.[49]

To build such a settlement in Alabama, Pinson proposed to sell one thousand acres of land to Black buyers at five dollars an acre. He also intended to construct a $15,000 school to be run by Mitchell on four hundred acres allotted to him for "agricultural instruction." The cornerstone on the school was to read: "This building donated to the Negro race by Pinson and Geiger, Geiger, Ala., who were friends of the Negroes as slaves and friends to them as freedmen."

The *Geiger Times*, a newspaper owned by Pinson, celebrated the prospect with the headline: "Colored Institute to Be Rebuilt. Mitchell Returns from East with $25,000." "Arthur Mitchell," it declared, "is destined to establish right here in Sumter County one of the largest institutions of its kind in the world. There are thousands of Negroes in this section who will be benefitted by the institution if it don't do any more than teach them to hold a plow in the ground properly. It will bring out skilled labor . . . and encourage the tenant to be less dependent on the land owner for all his requirements. Give us better farmers . . . and with our wealth of the world's greatest soils we have solved the problem." W. U. Lavender, head overseer for the Pinson and Geiger Land Corporation, supported this proposal in an open letter to Mitchell: "I was a skeptic, but I can give my hearty endorsement of the work you are doing for the young men and women of the black belt. The moral and religious training you give them has already had good results." Mitchell expressed gratitude to Pinson, Lavender, and white supporters of his new school. "We do not help our cause," he wrote, "by yielding to gusts of passion and words spoken in haste. . . . One wins more from the kindness of a friend than he is able to extort from an enemy."[50]

Pinson's newspaper glowed in anticipation of the groundbreaking, scheduled for July 19, 1912. The rebuilt West Alabama Normal and Industrial Institute represented "the greatest effort in the entire South" to advance the "proper training" of Black southerners. The life purpose of its principal was "to give his people the greatest aid toward making them industrial, self-sustaining workers," thus his motto: "Work with your hands as well as your head." The school was an effort that "white friends have lauded." A railroad excursion for the opening ceremonies had been arranged at a reduced rate to "an ideal spot for a big holiday picnic and thousands will be on hand to lend glad cheer to the institute."[51]

Figure 3. Mitchell during his Alabama years, the photograph probably taken at Geiger, circa 1912. Throughout his public career, Mitchell was an impeccable dresser, believing that what he wore made him a less threatening advocate for change. Chicago History Museum, ICHi-026226.

The keynote speaker for the occasion was a northern minister, William T. Holmes, the pastor of the First Congregational Church in Watertown, Connecticut, where Mitchell had spoken. In a report north, Holmes detailed the barbeque, baseball game, and religious ceremony that accompanied the opening, but it was Mitchell who caught his attention. "The Institute's most valuable asset," Holmes wrote, "is the personality of its founder and principal. . . . I talked with white men of all sorts and conditions and found that Mr. Mitchell commanded unanimously their confidence, their enthusiasm—really their pride." From these conversations, Holmes gleaned that white people agreed with Mitchell that Black education "must embrace the twin aims of moral character building and efficiency in labor." Institute parents also concurred: "Among Negroes . . . I found such confidence and affection to be well nigh universal. I found them emphatic in declaring the benefit the [Panola] school had been to them and their children." "I count it," he concluded, "that his situation and he are instances of the happy conjunction of the Opportunity and the Man."[52]

Thomas P. Ivy, a Harvard graduate and banker in Atlanta, was also in attendance and agreed with Holmes. He knew "of no cause more inviting and urgent" than the new school. There were fifty thousand Negro children "who need exactly the kind of training that Principal Mitchell aims to give." What augured so well for the West Alabama Institute's future were the new relations between the races that Mitchell was promoting. Before his arrival, white employers had regarded Black workers as "incapable of improvement" and therefore available "to be used" at the lowest wage rate possible. In response, Black residents, who saw "all law and land" in white hands, "gave as little in return for what he got as he could." With Mitchell's presence, both sides recognized the "prevalent racial and economic error" of this thinking. Now, a white employer wanted "the highest grade labor he can get" while a Black worker wanted "to earn the highest wage."[53]

He might have brought a new economic model to western Alabama, but the Nordin interviews, including one with John Pinson's son, portray Mitchell in Geiger as more than willing to display an unexplained, newfound prosperity. Both Gilbert and Pinson Jr. recalled seeing him drive through Geiger in an elegant carriage, pulled by a fine horse with equipment that "only the rarest of Black Americans owned." This, they felt, caused resentment in both the white and Black communities in Geiger. But Mitchell's flaunting of status was by design. Edwards had taught him that "you cannot do much to forsake the one room log cabin so long as you live in one. . . . You must teach by example as well as precept." If you acted downtrodden, Mitchell came to believe, you would be treated as downtrodden. Successful Black leaders should use symbols of that achievement—their clothes, vehicles, and homes—to demonstrate their penetration of white society. Mitchell and his carriage bespoke someone who "always wanted to better himself" and had succeeded where few others had. This attitude made him seem special. "He had something that a lot of people didn't have," the young Pinson recalled.[54]

Another trait that made Mitchell distinctive was his ability to form personal friendships with Geiger's leading white residents. Both Gilbert's and Pinson's sons remembered their fathers relating to Mitchell on a warm, intimate level. Gilbert's father thought Mitchell to be "pleasant" and "very well accepted." He remembered his father telling him about the occasion when the elder Pinson paid the medical bills that Mitchell's family had accumulated during a typhoid epidemic, expenses that would have ruined the principal had he not intervened.

Although no records of the Geiger school remain, the same interviews offer an overview of the institution. The physical plant was more "modern" than Panola. Unable to recruit capable instructors from the area, Mitchell hired teachers from the North. In addition, an impressive number of northern sponsors visited the school. Students ranged in age from seven to fourteen or fifteen and did not pay tuition. Relations between the school and Geiger were peaceful, and white townspeople generally supported the institute. Its fairs were well attended by both the white and Black communities, as were elaborate two- and three-day graduations.[55]

Notes in Mitchell's own hand for what might have been a graduation address in 1913 speak to his mindset in Geiger. "Life is a great spirit and a busy heart," he wrote. "We live in deeds not years, in thoughts not breaths. He most lives who thinks. He who most feels the noblest acts the best. Let those who know tell those who do not know. Retreat only for strategic reasons. We need courageous leaders . . . question of migration to the north . . . story of the gold seeker in the far west. If I fail my people in any crisis where my efforts and leadership are needed may my right hand forget its cunning and my tongue cleave to the roof of my mouth."[56]

Despite these cordial relations, there was apparently at least one crisis at Geiger, the details of which Mitchell revealed in a 1939 exchange of letters with Carl Murphy, publisher of the *Afro-American*. Was it true, the newspaperman asked, that a mob threatened the school and you told the teachers that "you proposed to stay and fight it out and that all who thought otherwise might leave?" Absolutely, the congressman wrote back. Only "the present Mrs. Mitchell" stayed. "We waited in the woods with rifle and pistol all night. A mob came within three miles of our home where it stopped and tried to recruit a local white man. He informed them that I was the owner of a Winchester rifle and that I knew how to shoot and would shoot. This stopped the mob. There was no charge of any kind against me other than that I was educating Negroes."[57]

Letters to Edwards trace the rise and fall of the institute between 1912 and 1915. In June 1912, Mitchell "never felt better over the outlook of our work." By February 1913, he had been so successful that Oswald Garrison Villard, editor of the *New York Post,* a cofounder of the NAACP and a liberal reformer, agreed to serve on the school's Board of Trustees. Eight months later, the West Alabama Institute had produced six bales of cotton on four acres, one acre of corn had yielded one hundred bushels, and the school had won a fifty-dollar gold prize in a local competition. "We have succeeded beyond our expectations," he told Edwards. In recognition of this, he had been asked to organize the industrial fair for western Alabama and eastern Mississippi. Then disaster in the form of an infestation of the boll weevil struck. This led to "the hardest year of our history. We have cut our number of teachers to four and it still seems as if we are going to be taxed to the limit to keep out of debt." The final blow fell when another blaze destroyed the school in January 1915.[58]

This second fire at a Mitchell school reignited speculation about his newfound wealth, prosperity he vaguely attributed to a land and timber arrangement with Pinson. Mitchell never offered a clear explanation for his newfound affluence. There was speculation about less innocent sources. Some locals conjectured that Mitchell had set fire to the schools at Panola and Geiger to collect insurance money. Pinson's son discounted this. "There was no earthly way of putting out a fire" in either Panola or Geiger, he observed, so what company would write insurance? Even the "better homes" in the area were not covered.[59]

Mitchell's third educational venture in Alabama involved the Armstrong Agricultural and Industrial School in Butler, fifty miles south of Geiger in neighboring Choctaw County and another stop on the AT&N. On February 24, 1915, the *Choctaw Advocate* announced the selection "of one of the best known educators of the Negro race" as principal. He was dedicated to "building a second Tuskegee," an enterprise to which local Black residents had already contributed $500 and "three grants of land." Four months later, the paper reported on "the most important educational meeting ever held among the Negroes of this section," one addressed by Arthur Mitchell, "a great leader and organizer. His success here has been simply phenomenal." The school sat on three hundred acres given by white donors and ten given by Black supporters. Its principal structure was a "handsome brick building" that contributed to its being "in high favor with the people of the county. The white people as well as the Negroes are enthusiastic in their support of Mitchell."[60]

As with the schools at Panola and Geiger, no records exist for Armstrong. Nordin did conduct interviews in 1979 with three students: Golden Chaney, Zola May, and Rachel Collins-Levy. They shared generally favorable memories of their experiences: mathematics lessons, learning to weave straw mats and baskets, sewing and cooking lessons, baseball games, but also at least one paddling by the principal for a disciplinary infraction. William R. Turner, an Armstrong trustee and father of four students, remembered Mitchell fondly. When the former principal ran for Congress for the first time, Turner wrote praising the candidate's intelligence, courage, and honesty during his years in Butler: "The colored people here will never forget how you fought for their rights in this section and the great sacrifices you and your wife made for their advancement."[61]

Mitchell enhanced his reputation as a gifted speaker at Butler. His "Fifty-Three Years of Negro Freedom in America," a talk given at the courthouse in Butler to a multiracial audience on Emancipation Day in January 1916, drew praise as being delivered "by a second Booker T. Washington." His agricultural fairs also added to his repute. One in March 1916 combined a memorial service for Washington, who had died the previous November, with a talk on "how to get ahead of the boll weevil, a topic that should interest all Negro farmers." In addition, he opened Armstrong facilities to the Black community as a place where they could hold public meetings. This drew an accolade for the "untiring and successful efforts [of] the Wizard of the moment, Prof. Arthur W. Mitchell . . . a humane Principal in heart and hand in welcoming colored people [of] the world."[62]

Despite these successes, Mitchell again irritated the local citizenry with displays of his affluence. When Wergs's sorrel pony went missing, his father placed an ad in the *Advocate* announcing a reward of twenty-five dollars that would "be paid for any reliable information that will lead to the location of either the horse or the thief." After the entry of the United States into World War I, Mitchell had the resources to purchase a $1,000 Liberty Bond. Most upsetting to locals was Mitchell's purchase of a car, an action he later justified because the "separate but equal" Jim Crow rules on railroads had created unsafe and unsanitary travel conditions for his wife. These regulations forced him to "buy an automobile, when I was not able to [afford] do so for the purpose of keeping [Annie] out of that condition that every decent and respectable colored woman is subjected to when she attempts to ride on the trains any distance." But Mitchell also saw his "machine," much like his fancy horse and buggy in Geiger, as a "highly valuable and visible symbol of conspicuous consumption," a sign of his success. Not only was he the first Black resident of Choctaw County to own a car, but his was a Packard, the preeminent luxury vehicle of the day. Among white locals, this provoked the "suspicion and hostility of African Americans who drove expensive cars." According to Clara Mitchell, the car "caused her husband so many problems that he began to fear serious trouble."[63]

Also worrying to him were increasingly less successful efforts to raise funds in the North. Mitchell blamed these disappointing results on the effects of the Great Migration, the movement of hundreds of thousands of rural Black southerners to northern cities beginning in 1916. After trips north from Butler, Mitchell observed two types of transplants, distinguishing between "doers" and "loafers" in a September 1916 letter to the *Birmingham Ledger*. He was fulsome in his praise of the former, using the example of three thousand Black college students who had harvested the tobacco crop in the Connecticut valley and were returning home. These "doers" had "made good. There was not a single case of friction reported." But he was contemptuous of "loafers," those who had been misled by labor agents to move north with false promises of jobs. They were "the element that is so frequently seen hanging around barber shops and pool rooms. . . . They are worthless here in the South and are more worthless in the North." He warned that the patience of the North for these idlers would be "exceedingly short. The sudden exodus of the Negro into the northern territory where conditions are so different is a very dangerous adventure for him." Not only was the migration dangerous for the "loafer," he explained to a Mississippi newspaper, but it also made southern reformers less effective. "The big [northern] papers," he complained, "where the Negro has been tried out and where he has failed have printed very bitter news . . . in a manner to injure the Negro in general." "It does this section [the South] no good for the worthless Negro to emigrate northward. It only gives the work we are doing a black eye. We should keep this people here and train them to be self-supporting and useful."[64]

When the United States entered the Great War the following year, Mitchell stressed his view of his race as patriots. A remark by an Alabama congressman that German spies were going to stir up a Black revolt in the South drew his ire. "No good thinking Negro," he declared, "would listen to such a plan. I have my finger on the pulse of the Negroes of this section and I know that to a man they can be trusted implicitly. Give us the sword, show us the enemy, and give us the orders and we assure you that we will charge. . . . There are no Benedict Arnolds among the Negroes."

He also criticized Black Americans who, when solicited for donations to the Red Cross, wanted to know if the money would go to members of their race. His advice was to contribute and not ask. "I have the greatest confidence in those who have charge of the work and know that the money will be used to help the most needy, whether white or colored. The colored people of this county have done very little as compared to what we should and must." His hope was that "there will not be found among our ranks a single slacker." As for "loafers" who sought shelter and food at Black homes, "none of us should take care of any tramp while the country is at war. . . . Report the matter to the authorities at once."[65]

Figure 4. John McDuffie, the Alabama congressman (1919–1935) who facilitated Mitchell's entrance into the Democratic Party and served as his mentor during Mitchell's early days in Congress.

It was also at Armstrong that Mitchell developed a close relationship with John McDuffie, the solicitor general for Alabama's First Judicial Circuit since 1909, who Mitchell met at a trial involving disputed property. A graduate of Auburn and the University of Alabama Law School, McDuffie was a rising political star, about to be elected in 1918 to Congress, where he would serve until 1935 when President Roosevelt elevated him to the federal bench.[66]

Compared to other southern political figures, McDuffie was an anomaly in ways that Mitchell found attractive. Both had been born in 1883, one to privilege and the other to poverty. Yet McDuffie would write in his memoirs about the "feudalism" that characterized his life on the family plantation as a young man, appreciating the support he received from the sharecroppers after being thrust into a leadership role following the murder of his father during a local feud. Moderate, perhaps even liberal by the southern standards of the day, on the race question, he saw Black Americans displaying "every standard of honesty, integrity, and sympathy. . . . They had all the qualities of ladies and gentlemen, as indeed they were." In particular, he developed a close relationship with his overseer, Jim Kelly, who had come to him through a "criminal court contract." Mutual confidence developed between them. "In temperament," McDuffie wrote, "we were very much alike."

As time went on, MacDuffie and Mitchell came to respect each other, sharing a concern that society deal fairly with Black Americans and an understanding of the importance of education in improving their conditions. McDuffie believed that bad Black behavior was almost always the result of white actions. "All too often," he wrote, "it has been the mean White man who has made the mean Negro."[67]

Over time, Mitchell would come to describe McDuffie as "my very best friend" and a mentor on dealing with white people. "I had," Mitchell recalled in retirement, "the occasion to try [McDuffie] out in many race matters before he became a member of Congress. . . . He has a high regard for the law and justice for all people . . . [and] can be depended upon to do the right thing as he knows it or as it is shown him."[68]

Mitchell closed the Armstrong Agricultural and Industrial Institute shortly after McDuffie won election to Congress, following his friend to Washington. It is noteworthy that Mitchell left Alabama not on a train as did most participants in the Great Migration. Clara Mitchell told Nordin that he exited driving his Packard with a suitcase in its trunk that contained $10,000 in cash. If true, the statement is remarkable testimony not only to his prosperity but also to his personal courage. In 1919, it was foolhardy indeed for a Black man to drive the eight hundred miles from western Alabama to Washington in a luxury car with a wife, young son, and $10,000 in cash. At that time, Black people "who traveled in the South, even for leisure, were always in harm's way," particularly when the journey involved "certain remote . . . pockets" of the region. Unfortunately, he left no record of the trip, but it is difficult to imagine where the Mitchells ate, slept, refueled, or relieved themselves given the few services available to Black southerners at the time. It is even more difficult to see him adhering to the informal "Rules of the Road" that applied to his group: always yield the right of way at intersections to white drivers and never pass them, particularly women, as you "might stir up dust that would get on white folks."[69]

After his departure, Armstrong trustees, suspicious of the circumstances under which Mitchell departed, filed suit seeking to invalidate Mitchell "land deals" that might explain the contents of the Packard's trunk. The litigation claimed that "a prominent, well educated, shrewd, intelligent, and influential member of the Negro race" had taken advantage of "most all ignorant, common every day, country darkies, living as farmers in the rural section of the state." The case lingered in the legal system until May 9, 1921, when a judge dismissed it as being based on circumstantial evidence.[70]

Despite these legal proceedings, Butler residents still spoke favorably about Mitchell's Armstrong venture years later. Local historian Ann Harwell Gay came to this conclusion in 1993: "For at least four years, Choctaw County was enriched by a black man with tremendous energy and persuasiveness who was, to local blacks, a fine example of dedication to education. He not only taught them how to fight the boll weevil, he showed them how to aspire to ever higher things in life."[71]

The Alabama years were over, but which parts of the story Mitchell told about them were history and which parts fiction? The Mitchell papers are less than revelatory about the first thirty-five years of his life, a period covered by less than 1 percent of the massive archive and for which corroborating documents are scarce. As Lepore reminds us, "most of what historians study survives because it was purposely kept. This inheritance is called the historical record, and it is maddeningly uneven, asymmetrical and unfair." And in this case it was Arthur Mitchell who did the keeping.[72]

As a generalization, his origin story seems to fit Waldo Martin's description of Washington's *Up from Slavery* as a "mixture of self invention and self-promotion," with emphasis on the latter. The truth about his Alabama years is undiscoverable, but it seems fair to conclude that the Arthur Mitchell we meet is the product of what could most charitably be described as profile enhancement. For example, even a cursory reading of his story of walking sixty-five miles to Tuskegee suggests an almost verbatim borrowing from Washington's account of his journey from West Virginia to the Hampton Institute.

Further, his portrayal of himself as a "Tuskegee man" came under sharp criticism once skeptics investigated Mitchell's background and discovered how short his stay there had been. The question of where Mitchell went to school remains an open question, as it was during his public career.

His claim to be a devotee of Booker T. Washington who wanted to "do everything in my power to make real the things for which he stood and the wonderful lessons I learned from him" compels the question of whether these "wonderful lessons" included blacklisting by one party and falsification of records by the other. In reality, his experience at Snow Hill, to which he only reluctantly admitted, with its emphasis on the humanities and direct involvement in the political process, seems to have played a larger role in his development than did his time at Tuskegee.

The same is true of his rendering of his years as an educator. Until late in his career, Mitchell conflated his experiences at Panola, Geiger, and Butler, describing the period from 1908 to 1918 as a time when he served, "without pay," as the president of the Armstrong Agricultural College. That was not the name of the institution, he did not serve there from 1908 to 1918, and it doubtful that he went unremunerated for his efforts.

But equally unconvincing is the charge that Mitchell's schools were examples of peonage, where token education was exchanged for compulsory labor, Mitchell "fleecing and fleeing" them when his schemes were discovered. The Mitchell papers contain several testimonials from students, parents, and philanthropists that his efforts to raise educational standards were real and appreciated.[73]

Likewise, the speculation that Mitchell burned schools down to collect insurance money flies in the face of Gilbert's observation that companies would not underwrite even the best residences in Sumter County because of their isolation and the fact that rural Black schools frequently burned. Snow Hill experienced serious fires in both November 1911 and January 1912.[74]

Finally, an incident during the 1936 election campaign leaves Mitchell's portrayal of himself as a selfless Alabama educator open to question. That August, Davis Lee, a firebrand reporter for the Scott Newspaper Syndicate, wrote to Mitchell, who was then directing the mid-western portion of President Roosevelt's reelection campaign among Black voters. Davis wanted a job and warned the congressman that he had been to Butler, where he had been told "interesting stories" about the Armstrong school. He had since been offered $100 a week to write pieces for Republican media outlets. "In your own language," he threatened, "if you don't give me some consideration, I am going to raise hell."[75]

Mitchell tried to put him off, insisting that his duties did not include the hiring of staff. Reacting to this excuse, Lee suggested that he was prepared to go to Alabama to "take pictures of the high school once managed by you. I am also going to run a series of articles on your early life in Alabama. A Negro of your type is not fit to be in Congress as a representative of our people or any other people and I will go plum to hell to bring about your defeat."[76]

On September 22, Mitchell, who prided himself on never yielding to extortion, offered Davis a position in Kansas: "Nothing will please me better than to have your full cooperation. . . . Please let me have a line from you direct stating in what capacity you wish to work." In October, he hired Lee for fifty dollars a week as an organizer of Roosevelt clubs, adding "if there is anything else I can throw your way, I will be glad to do it." After the election, Mitchell sent him a bonus that the latter acknowledged with "thanks for the unexpected check."[77]

Whatever the facts of his Alabama years were, Mitchell always placed a high value on his experiences in there. When Annie Lomax, a student of his at Tullibody, wrote to congratulate him on his 1934 election, he answered with emotion. The most meaningful letters he received came from those who knew of the challenges he faced as a young man. His present position had not been achieved "without the hardest kind of struggle, the greatest possible sacrifice, and the exercise of enduring patience." That battle cemented his belief that all individuals facing obstacles in life had within themselves the ability to be successful. "All my life," he wrote in 1936, "I have refused to believe that I couldn't go forward. I have insisted that I must go forward. In this [belief], I have found myself. . . . I believe that if anybody else can do the job, I too can do it." What he refused to believe was that there was an unbreakable caste system in the South, "that the Negro must haul down his social expectations and resign himself to relative immobility." He might have begun life in poverty but had succeeded by dint of his own efforts, not by leaving the South but by studying and understanding it.[78]

In notes to himself, Mitchell wrote that if his race wanted to "make our lives rich in usefulness" it had to be willing to pay the price. "A great life can no more be made without trials than a gold coin can be made without fire." Leadership would go to "men who have met opposition, grown strong in struggle, who have grappled with defeat . . . but have risen again, more eager for fight, more sure of victory." The fight against the "monstrous" evils in society "*cannot* be waged successfully by weaklings." His race had "too many talkers who tell us what ought to be done—and wait for somebody else to do it."[79]

Mitchell's Alabama experiences proved to him that he was a fighter, a "doer," an individual possessing great personal courage. Not only did he open schools for Black students, but he opened them in one of the most isolated and dangerous sections of the South, on the Alabama-Mississippi border. Fifty years later, the Freedom Riders of 1961 spoke of the fear they experienced when they approached the area. In 1964, three civil rights workers were murdered in Philadelphia, Mississippi, a town only thirty miles from one of Mitchell's schools.

Having survived—and even prospered—in that environment, Mitchell believed that the Great Migration would be a long-term disaster for Black Americans. The Great War might create temporary employment advantages above the Mason-Dixon line, but the prospects for long-term Black economic prosperity in the North were bleak. The end of the war would see Black workers lose their jobs in northern cities to returning veterans because of the prevailing bigoted concept that "the ordinary colored man can't do as much work nor do it as well as the ordinary white man." It was far better to remain in the South, where Black workers had the field of manual labor largely to themselves, "unsharpened by fierce competition from foreigners."[80]

Mitchell agreed with the *New York Age* that if the South wanted to stop the "dangerous adventure" of moving north, it should accord all Black Americans better treatment: higher wages, improved schools, more police protection, equal access to transportation and the elimination of lynching. "In a word, it means the treatment of the Negro as a fellow human being and an American citizen."[81]

To this, Mitchell added a specific context for Alabama, "the place of my birth, which is very dear to me." He had experienced the folly of an economy based on cotton alone. The answer was diversified farming. But "it is a great pity that in this county [Sumter] with thousands and thousands of acres of beautiful rich soil . . . there are so few who really understand how to farm." Rather than flee to the North, Black southerners would be better positioned if they remained in the rural South, their "historic home and hence the place where they would best progress," and were afforded the opportunity to advance from sharecropping to the status of independent farmers.[82]

Such reforms would require a home-grown Black elite that did not flee to the North in a vain attempt to experience success in the equally racist society there. Rather, real advocates for reform would remain in the South, calling for equal treatment of all Black citizens by demonstrating that they could succeed by the standards of white southern society.

In turn, this retention of talent required strategic dealings with the predominant white population in order to make success attainable. Here Mitchell's Alabama years had taught him to be a pragmatist. He was under no illusions about the motives of northern philanthropists who trekked to Tuskegee and who he himself had solicited on trips north. Ministers might be inspired impulses for justice, but there were also those industrialists who wanted to develop the resources of the South for their benefit through the exploitation of a cheap labor force.

Sympathetic white southerners, those who did not challenge the status quo but sensed instinctively that change was necessary, held the real key to improved conditions for Black southerners. The novelist Richard Wright might dismiss this group with the observation that "all southern white men fancied themselves as friends of niggers," but the Mitchell leaving Alabama in 1919 saw himself as proof of Charles Blow's recent assertion that "sometimes the greatest allies in the advancement of southern Blacks were southern whites who had been the children of the enslavers."[83]

Mitchell's three great benefactors in Alabama—John Rogers, John Pinson, and John McDuffie—were precisely this, children of enslavers. Although at least Rogers and Pinson stood to benefit financially from Mitchell's success, all three agreed with Washington's precept that "one man cannot hold another man down in the ditch without remaining in the ditch with him." This was a sentiment voiced by John Greenleaf Whittier in his poem "At Port Royal," a work Mitchell quoted frequently:

> The law of changeless justice
> Binds the oppressor with the oppressed
> And, as close as sin and suffering are joined,
> They march to fate abreast.

Rogers, Pinson, and McDuffie shared at least a rudimentary sense of not wanting to be the "oppressor" of the "oppressed." One saw this in Roger's explanation for why he first gave Mitchell land, in the cornerstone that Pinson envisaged for his Geiger school, and in McDuffie's autobiographical musings. If such allies could be found in rural Alabama, what did that imply for advancement if expanded to a larger arena?

That was a question for the future. In 1919, the Mitchells had reached "that station in life where we [should] do something for ourselves." That meant following McDuffie to Washington to make money and contacts.

2

"That Station in Life Where We Should Do Something for Ourselves"

A. Philip Randolph, the powerful leader of the Brotherhood of Sleeping Car Porters, once characterized the Washington to which the Mitchells moved in 1919 as "not only the capital of the nation [but also] the capital of Dixie. There crackerocracy is in the saddle." At its center sat Woodrow Wilson, a president who told "darkey stories" to his cabinet and whose administration was "the most Southern dominated, anti-Negro, national administration since the 1850s."[1]

Yet Washington differed from Chicago, Detroit, and New York in an important respect. The Black community the Mitchells joined was dominated by an elite "not submerged by a wave of ignorant farm hands from the rural South" during the Great Migration. This elect group consisted of longtime residents of the city possessing the ability to "pass" as white, individuals whose skin color enabled them to "move about in a white world with some freedom."[2]

Despite this difference, 1919 was a moment of peril for all Black Washingtonians. Mitchell's prediction that Black southerners moving north during the Great Migration had proved prophetic. East Saint Louis, Illinois, had experienced a race riot in 1919, as did Chicago two years later. Just as the Mitchells arrived, the same fate befell the nation's capital. Reports in the *Washington Post* of the rape of a white woman by Black "hoodlums" helped provoke a riot led by returning white veterans, many still in uniform. The result was "a night of terror unparalleled in Washington's history." Four days of mayhem followed, leaving fifteen dead. Lawlessness ended only when President Wilson mobilized the National Guard.[3]

In this fraught atmosphere, Arthur Mitchell made his first congressional appearance when he testified before the House of Representatives's Committee on Interstate and Foreign Commerce in September 1919. The nation's railroads had been nationalized in 1917 to facilitate the war effort, and the hearing centered on under what conditions they would return to private ownership.

Martin Madden, the Chicago representative for the district where many participants in the Great Migration had settled, proposed an amendment to the legislation stipulating that all Black travelers be given "equal and identical rights, accommodations, and privileges" as part of the return to private ownership.

Most likely invited to testify by McDuffie, Mitchell used this as an opportunity to rail against the public humiliation for Black riders created by the separation of races by southern railroads into white and so-called Jim Crow cars.[4] In his remarks, Mitchell attacked the concept of these cars, whose purpose was "rank discrimination against the colored people." Describing himself as well traveled in the South, he told House members that "nothing has done more to create a spirit of unrest and dissatisfaction in the heart of every self-respecting Negro . . . except perhaps lynching." Nowhere in the South, he asserted, was a serious effort being made to enforce the "equal" provision of *Plessy v. Ferguson*. To the contrary, Black travelers with first-class tickets were relegated to old, inferior baggage cars where they shared space with the conductor, the news dealer, "white laborers, drunken, low bred white men," and even prisoners. Black men and women had to share the only toilet in "filthy and unsanitary conditions."

Black professionals, church bishops, doctors, and lawyers could not purchase Pullman accommodations and were denied access to dining cars despite their ability to pay for the services. Wives of Black officers, on their way to say goodbye to their husbands before they "sailed to offer their lives for their country," were treated in the same way. Their husbands, returning from Europe wearing French and American decorations, were humiliated, not celebrated, by being forced into Jim Crow cars.

To make his point, Mitchell read into the record a comment from the *St. Luke Herald* of Richmond, Virginia, that "the Jim Crow car is worse than lynching; lynching occasionally kills one man; the Jim Crow car perpetually tortures 10,000." Black servicemen, the newspaper told its readers, who had to travel through the Deep South to embarkation points in the North, frequently sat up three days and nights "without a change of clothes or a bit of warm food." This, the *Herald* added, "was certainly good training for trench warfare." His race, Mitchell concluded in an argument he would advance to greater effect twenty years later in an even more prestigious venue, "should have every accommodation for the same money that is granted other races. He does not ask this as a matter of charity, but demands this as a right."[5]

His testimony before Congress aside, politics played only a minor role in Mitchell's early years in Washington. Remembering the lessons he had learned in Alabama about the profitability of owning land and a house, he accumulated capital through real estate investments. In 1921, Mitchell formed the Mutual

Housing Company, a corporation that purchased three apartment buildings in the Black district of the capital: the Oregonian, Luray, and Sherman Avenue. By 1924, the company was valued at $150,000 and paid a 10 percent dividend on common stock, 8 percent on preferred. Through this investment, Mitchell assured himself of a secure stream of income for the rest of his life. Even during the Depression, he told an investor, the Mutual Housing Company "has done better than any similar organization in the City of Washington." Profits from it enabled him to buy a home at 1320 River Street, NW, "where well-to-do Negroes" resided.[6]

Although he never attended law school, it was also at this time that Mitchell was admitted to the bar. A correspondence course with Chicago's Blackstone School of Law and study in the offices of several Black attorneys secured his entrance to the District of Columbia's legal profession in 1927, a status that was later honored by the State of Illinois on a reciprocal basis.[7]

In 1926, he was elected president of a national Black fraternity, Phi Beta Sigma, a post he held until 1935. It was a term in office that the *Atlanta Daily World* judged to demonstrate Mitchell's "remarkable ability as a leader and organizer." But it did not end well. By 1934, Mitchell's association with Phi Beta Sigma had frayed. "Bickerings and resentments were cropping up," the *Crescent*, the fraternity's magazine, reported. Denouncing his brothers as "ingrates," Mitchell broke off all contact with the organization after his election to Congress. "The Fraternity showed me the blackest and basest kind of ingratitude after I had spent thousands of dollars of my own money to put it on its feet," he groused in 1936. "I took the medicine they dished out to me without complaining, but I am through with the Fraternity for all time." This rupture did not prevent the *Crescent* from offering a favorable retrospective of his presidency: "He was a man of vigorous personality. He was scrappy. He was almost garrulous. He had a way of getting things done. He knew people and made excellent contacts. He brought great dignity and respect to the Fraternity. . . . No one unseated him because no one could. In fact, the boys loved him. The 'little Napoleon'—except he wasn't little in any sense of the term—dominated the Fraternity for nine years."[8]

As his circle of social contacts in Washington expanded, Mitchell formed relationships with prominent Black residents, several of whom became his friends and influenced his thinking as he matured from a narrowly focused Alabama educator into a serious thinker about broader issues affecting his race. Among them were Robert Russa Moton, Alain Locke, Carter G. Woodson, and Kelly Miller.

Through fraternity connections, Mitchell grew close to Moton, Booker T. Washington's successor as principal of the Tuskegee Institute, where Moton served from 1915 to 1935. While in Congress, Mitchell facilitated Moton's access to Roosevelt on several occasions. After Moton retired to Virginia, the two became fishing companions. When Moton died in 1941, Mitchell wrote to F. D. Patterson, then the principal at Tuskegee, that "Dr. Moton was my friend, as he was a friend to mankind. During the years I have been in Congress he was one of my closest advisors. I leaned heavily on his arm."[9]

He also met and formed a friendship with Alain Locke, a Harvard graduate who had gone on to become the first Black Rhodes Scholar. In Washington, Locke was in the midst of a distinguished if contentious career at Howard University. It saw him author *The New Negro* in 1925 and be considered by many to be "one of the most influential African American cultural critics of his era." Being a prosperous "virtual passer," Mitchell impressed Locke as a model for the modern Black politician.[10]

In both 1934 and 1936, Locke proved an enthusiastic supporter of this "politician of the new order, capable of effective and courageous participation in the counsels of the Democratic party." Later, he wrote Mitchell a letter endorsing the movement of Black voters from the Republican Party to Democratic Party. It was better, he thought, to accept "bread from a strange table" than "husks and taffy from a familiar hand." After the Democratic sweep in 1936, Locke congratulated Mitchell on the "good judgment by which you made President Roosevelt the main issue." Two years later, he reiterated his support through a letter to the *Defender*. In return, Mitchell helped distribute the publications of Locke's *Associates in Negro Folk Education* to Black schools.[11]

Like Locke, Carter G. Woodson was a member of the Howard faculty, serving as the Dean of the College of Arts and Sciences. In addition to their collaboration in promoting an awareness of Black history and culture, Woodson and Mitchell shared a belief that what little education Negro children were receiving was incomplete. In *The Mis-Education of the Negro,* Woodson cautioned that "our schools are daily teaching Negroes what they can never apply in life." These lessons included how to hand-stitch dresses and shoes, both trades made redundant by mechanical devices. Mitchell agreed, once writing to his friend that Negro education must be more up to date, "otherwise . . . we are going to suffer tremendously for the lack of training to do the things required of people living in this age." Both saw improvement in primary and secondary education of Black children as far more important than any single political act in advancing the prospects for the race. This could not happen so long as "the large majority of persons supposedly teaching Negroes never carry to the school room any thought as to improving their [the students'] condition. . . . Most of them are satisfied with receiving their pay and spending it for the toys and gewgaws of life."[12]

What also appealed to Mitchell was Woodson's belief that new types of Black political leaders were needed, public officials who were more interested in what they could do for others than in what could be done for them. The new leaders would be judged successful if they developed the younger generation into worthy citizens and leaders of their communities. They could even be Democrats. Among Woodson's teachings was the idea that "history does not show any race, and especially a minority group, has ever solved an important problem by relying altogether on what others may do for it, certainly not by parking its political strength on one side of the fence because of empty promises."[13]

At the beginning of his congressional career, Mitchell thanked Woodson for "the supreme effort and sacrifice which you have made in the interests of truth and Negro history." As his time in Congress drew to a close, he sent his friend a set of his speeches and a signed photograph that Woodson acknowledged with emotion: "I will safeguard these among my treasures that in years to come I may have as a reminder when I may not be able to gaze so frequently upon my friend."[14]

But Mitchell's closest companion from his early Washington days might well have been Kelly Miller, longtime professor of sociology at Howard. Regarded by H. L. Mencken as "the greatest black intellectual of his time," Miller authored a newspaper column that reached one hundred thousand readers every week during the 1930s. Among the many things upon which the two agreed was Miller's idea that "the farm offers a better chance to the Negro than the city. Already . . . the city contains more Negroes than can fit themselves to urban life." "When I was puzzling upon problems," Mitchell told the *Afro-American* after Miller's death, "I sent a cab to Dean Miller and he came to my office for many conferences." "It was upon his shoulders," Mitchell told the House in his eulogy, "that I leaned more heavily upon than upon the shoulders of any other leader in the country."[15]

More opaque is Mitchell's putative relationship with Franklin Roosevelt during these Washington years. At the time of his election, Mitchell made much of being "on speaking terms" with the president, a claim that he repeated in a 1936 letter to Agnes Levitt asserting, "I know Mr. Roosevelt very well. I have known him almost a quarter of a century." "There isn't a person in Washington," Mitchell declared on another occasion, "including the Speaker and the Vice President, that the President has listened to with more patience, tolerance, and consideration than he has listened to me." But evidence of an early friendship is nonexistent. Roosevelt, serving as Assistant Secretary of the Navy, lived in Washington when Mitchell arrived in 1919, but there is no correspondence between them during the 1920s in either the Mitchell papers or the Roosevelt Library.[16]

Mitchell, whose only overtly political act as an Alabamian had been to join the "Taft Republican Club" in 1910, was close to Perry Howard, the Black

Republican National Committeeman from Mississippi. They played pool together and Mitchell prepared for the bar examination in the Mississippian's law office. In 1928, it was at Howard's recommendation that the Republican National Committee sent Mitchell to Chicago to assist in efforts to ensure that the Black vote there went to Herbert Hoover. His charge was to pay special attention to the First Congressional District, a sprawling area south of the Chicago River made up of two very different groups of voters: poor white residents, who predominated in the First and Eleventh Wards, and the large Black population that had moved north during the Great Migration, concentrated in the Second. For his efforts, Mitchell was to be reimbursed at the rate of seventy-five dollars a week.[17]

Figure 5. Michael J. "Hinky Dink" Kenna, whose support helped elect Mitchell to Congress in 1934. Better government organizations thought him "totally unfit" to hold elective office; Mitchell described him as a "fine old Irish gentleman."

The business area south of the Chicago River, commonly known as "The Loop," made up much of the First Ward. It boasted of being "the richest square mile in America" because of the many banks and business establishments located there. But the captains of industry supervising these enterprises lived and voted in the suburbs. The majority of First Ward residents were poor first- and second-generation immigrants, living to the west and the south of the business district and under the political control of an aging but still powerful Michael J. "Hinky Dink" Kenna. Better government groups regularly described him as "utterly unfit" to hold office and "a dangerous man to have on the [City] Council." Balloting overseen by him was notoriously dishonest, characterized by one judge as "a plague spot so far as election fraud is concerned."[18]

Southwest of the First Ward lay the Eleventh, containing the Irish enclaves of Bridgeport and Canaryville, including the home of future mayor Richard J. Daley, and a large number of eastern European immigrants, many of whom worked in the nearby stockyards. Black men and women ventured into the Eleventh, "a major center of riot activity in 1919," at their own peril. One of Bridgeport's white associations voiced the prevailing views of the ward when it proclaimed that "there is nothing in the makeup of a Negro, physically or mentally, which should induce anyone to welcome him as a neighbor."[19]

Such views were anathema in the Second Ward, south of the First and east of the Eleventh, the most heavily populated ward in the congressional district. Thanks to the Great Migration, it had evolved into a Black electoral stronghold as well as being a cultural center for Chicago's version of the Harlem Renaissance. From 1910 to 1930, Chicago's Black population rose from 44,103 to 223,903, with the Second Ward's percentage soaring from 12.8 percent to 86 percent.[20]

In 1928, the Second Ward was solidly Republican. Not only had Black voters supported the "Party of Lincoln" for sixty years, but "Big Bill" Thompson, the Republican mayor often linked to Al Capone by the newspapers, held office, actively soliciting Black support. One analyst suggested that Thompson "exercised as strong an emotional and organizational hold on Chicago's Negroes as probably any politician has ever exercised on a like group in the history of American politics."[21]

But Thompson's mayoralty was marked by endemic violence. In the six months before Mitchell's arrival, sixty-two politically motivated bombings with political implications had occurred, almost all blamed on Big Bill's allies. Targets included the homes of a US senator and a State Attorney General. In one notorious incident, Octavius Granady, a reform candidate for City Council, had had his car forced off a city street on the day of the 1928 primary and had been gunned down by occupants of a car bearing Thompson banner.[22]

To add to the mayhem, three weeks later, Madden, the powerful Republican who had represented the district since 1904, dropped dead in his Washington office. To select a replacement, Republican committeemen gathered to recommend a replacement to Mayor Thompson. Characterized by Martin Kilson as "gamblers, successful hustlers, flophouse keepers, and occupants of other antisocial roles," those present at the selection process said much about the state Republican politics in 1928 Chicago.[23]

They chose Oscar De Priest, a former Alderman seen by reformers as tied to the underworld. Like Mitchell, De Priest had been born in Alabama, he at

Florence in 1871. Making his way to Chicago in 1889, he eventually entered politics, winning election as the first Black city councilor in 1915. His performance there had led the Municipal Voters League to assert that "no alderman in Chicago's history piled up a more notorious record in so short a time." Toward the end of his two-year term, he stood trial for corruption but was acquitted thanks in part to Clarence Darrow's vigorous defense. Out of office after 1917, he, like Mitchell, spent the 1920s amassing personal wealth through real estate speculation. In 1928, a contemporary theorized that De Priest had forced Mayor Thompson to select him for "certain services involving 'black and tan resorts,' vice rings, protection collection and other matters in which the two are said to have been associated."[24]

Mitchell's analytic mind took all of this in during his visit to Chicago from August 4 to September 8, 1928. He saw that the First Congressional District, its concentrated Black population not restricted by the blatant voter suppression devices employed in the South, offered a Black candidate the opportunity for election to the House of Representatives, the unique national political office to which a member of his race could aspire in 1928.[25] But, given the racial composition of the First and Eleventh Wards, the district as a whole was not overwhelmingly Black. In fact, a Black candidate with appeal to white voters and an ability to cut into the Republican stranglehold on the Second could be viable.

He also recognized that Chicago in 1928 was much like his native Alabama. There, he had seen Democratic election officials brag that "we don't have to steal elections," because the vote "as finally tabulated was not left to the whim of the voters." In Alabama, "the party controlled every aspect and avenue of nomination and election to public office. Nominations were awarded by the leadership to safe and loyal candidates by party caucuses. Democrats registered the voters, kept the voting lists, conducted the elections and, after counting the votes, announced the winners."[26]

Chicago was similar, the major difference being that Republicans were in control of the process, not Democrats. But the techniques for election manipulation were just as real, if subtler. In Chicago, votes were openly sold and registration lists notoriously fictive. Accepted practices included chain voting (the reuse of the same ballot), "colonization" (the importation of voters from outlying districts), and the use of floaters/repeaters (the same voter moving from polling place to polling place). If these techniques did not produce the desired result, "precinct captains and others went into a back room and evidently agreed on the number of votes to be given to the candidates, [and then] gave the numbers to the judges and clerks who recorded them."[27]

To this understanding of the mechanics of Chicago elections, Mitchell added his perception of where power lay. The city was a grouping of small political fiefdoms, wards that retained considerable autonomy so long as they followed the lead of the mayor. The key player in each of these units was not the aldermen, who sat on the City Council, but rather the committeemen who controlled the ward's patronage. They supervised the selection of which candidate should run for what office. They also counted the votes.[28] Therefore, Mitchell concluded, there were only six votes that counted in determining who would represent the First Congressional District in Congress: those of the mayor, the chairman of the political party in power, and the committeemen representing from the First, Second, Fourth, and Eleventh Wards.

Figure 6. Oscar De Priest, to many, the "iconic" Black representative for Chicago's First Congressional District. Mitchell considered him "a political hustler," totally unfit for the office he held. Chicago History Museum, ICHi-018076.

During his time in Chicago, Mitchell also developed a disdain for De Priest, whose victory in the upcoming election was a virtual certainty given the general prosperity of the times and the Black voter's loyalty to the Republican Party. To him, the about-to-be congressman represented the worst stereotype of a Black politician: corrupt, ill-educated, inarticulate, and supported by old party warhorses who were "self-satisfied, feeding off the patronage of white political machines and insensitive to the broader concerns of the race." When he compared "his own education and speaking ability" to De Priest's, it was clear that the Mayor Thompson's candidate was not "the kind of man who ought to represent Negroes in Congress."[29]

Interested in eventually replacing De Priest but questioning his chance for personal advancement as a Republican in Chicago, Mitchell returned to Alabama, where he faced a new threat: the takeover of that state's Republican Party by the "lily white" supporters of presidential candidate Herbert Hoover. There he was driven out of the Republican convention hotel and "saw whites march in and dare the colored delegates to come in." Nothing, he warned Hoover after the election, retarded Black progress more than "the incompetent and fraudulent leadership characteristic of Southern Republicanism." Rather than support this "extreme lilywhiteism, substantial colored men and women should be given a share of responsibility for reforming the Republican party."[30]

As Mitchell told the story, he then approached Jouett Shouse, a former Kansas congressman and future chairman of the Democratic National Committee, "because I could see that the Democratic Party was marching to power because of the stupendous blunders the Republican Party was making." What, Mitchell wanted to know, would the Democratic attitude toward the Negro be in 1932? Shouse's answer was that "the Democratic Party does not owe the Negro a damned thing. The Republican Party owes the Negro a hell of a lot and will not pay him. Republicans have the Negro in their vest pocket. Nobody tries to catch the fish that he has in the basket or in the pail. When we go fishing, we go after the fish in the pond." That, Mitchell claimed, "opened my eyes and I immediately began to work for the Democratic Party." He also wrote to Albon Holsey, an old Tuskegee friend and now secretary to Moton, that "I'm leaving Washington for Chicago. Don't worry. I'll be back in 1936 and when I do come back, I'll be representing the First Congressional District of Illinois."[31]

3

"He's a Carpetbagger"

MOVING TO CHICAGO in 1929, Mitchell registered as a Democrat and opened a South Side law office on Forty-Seventh Street to establish a name for himself in the local community by winning the friendship of the congregations of "store front" churches.[1] Shortly after his arrival, the Great Depression struck, devastating Black neighborhoods even more than white. "If conditions were terrible for Chicago's whites," Rita Gordon has written, "they were deplorable for Negroes." A Fisk University sociologist was even harsher. Unemployment, overcrowded housing, the erosion of savings, and the disruption of family life had led to "a loss of the spirit to carry on a determined struggle" for survival. In one small area of the Second Ward, 116 out of 125 homes were unheated. Living in a "hotel" might be a better option. Rooms rented for five cents a day. That entitled the guest to sleep standing up; a bed cost 25 cents more. A meal, if you could get it, was "State Street chicken," code for neck bones.[2]

As the Depression deepened, Chicago experienced a political earthquake. Spurred on by the effects of the economic downturn but also tired of the corruption and violence associated with Thompson's City Hall, "voters" had retired "Big Bill" in 1931, electing Democrat Anton Cermak in 1931 to replace him. That result meant that Democrats now controlled the city's levers of power.[3]

To Mitchell, a new-to-the-party Democrat, the combination of Cermak's election and economic depression opened a window of opportunity. On the neighborhood front, he heightened his profile by forming a "Free Advice Group" to protect Black citizens from credit bureaus, insurance agents, and "unscrupulous collectors who were preying on the South Side." In a letter to "Dear Rev. Powell," he volunteered to appear at the Powell's church and explain the program. He signed his note "yours for the rights of our people."[4]

In 1932, he accepted a role similar to the one he had played in 1928, but this time for the Democrats. Republicans had sent De Priest, sure of his own reelection in Chicago, to California in an attempt to keep that state's electoral votes in Hoover's column.

Mitchell took his assignment seriously, studying the radio addresses of James Farley, Chairman of the Democratic National Committee, Department of Commerce studies, Woodson's writings, and Hoover campaign literature, apparently to good effect. Robert Vann's *Pittsburgh Courier* reported that Mitchell "made a spectacular entry into Los Angeles," producing "a number of effective speeches." There were also naysayers. A critic told Claude Barnett that Mitchell "turned out to be a good deal of a cheap shyster. He made three speeches and pulled his freight back to Chicago."[5]

Results seemed to support the *Courier*'s assessment. Democrats did particularly well in the urban centers where Mitchell appeared. He boasted that his addresses to audiences in San Diego, Los Angeles, San Francisco, and Oakland had resulted in a 60–40 percent Roosevelt victory in those cities. While in California, he also revised the prediction he had made to Holsey in 1928. Given the conditions created by the Depression, he told several skeptical hosts that he was going to challenge and beat De Priest in 1934, not 1936.[6]

Shortly after the election, events took an unexpected turn in Chicago with the death of Cermak from wounds suffered in Miami in an assassination attempt on the life of President-Elect Roosevelt. To fill the vacancy, Patrick Nash, the chairman of the Cook County Democratic Committee, and the City Council of Chicago selected the unknown chief engineer of the Chicago Sanitary Commission, Edward J. Kelly, to serve as mayor until an election in 1935 under the provisions of a special piece of legislation passed by the Illinois State Legislature. This proved to be the beginning of the Kelly-Nash machine destined to dominate Chicago politics for fifteen years.[7]

With the levers of national and local political power in Democratic hands, Mitchell and Vann tried to organize a meeting of Democratic elected officials "to make out a working program for the Negro in the new administration." Vice President John Nance Garner and Senator Pat Harrison of Mississippi, the chairman of the powerful Finance Committee, were invited to attend but declined. McDuffie delivered the news of these refusals in a "Dear Arthur" letter that nevertheless ended with the hope that all Democrats would share "keen and friendly relations between our races in the South."[8]

Although rebuffed on the national level, Mitchell moved quickly to align himself with Kelly and Nash as potential benefactors for Black Chicagoans. He wrote to States' Attorney Frank Loesch that he admired how the prosecutor was "fighting day and night for good government and law enforcement" but that "our section [the South Side] of the city is entirely neglected. . . . Those who are in control seem to delight in putting political power in the hands of the most corrupt." Loesch proved receptive to the initiative, answering that the "great Industrialists showed no interest in needs, particularly housing, when bringing colored from the south. The responsible people of your race," he continued, "are doing more to curb the criminality and preach respect for the law than is the case with some foreign-born races who furnish the large contingent of white criminals."[9]

To Mitchell, criminality was not the only reason for Black misery. He explained to Kelly Miller that government monies were going to charities "simply to keep people alive." If the same funds were loaned to individuals to purchase livestock and seed and to facilitate the purchase of farms in the South, "it would only be a short time before the people would begin to make substantial contributions toward their own support, thus greatly strengthening their characters and their ability to become self-supporting." The dole, he confided to McDuffie, wasn't working. Black Americans were "the object of charity in our large cities and have absolutely no opportunity to make an honest living" in the North. They should be encouraged to return to the South.[10]

The suffering of the Black residents of Chicago and the fact that Democrats now controlled city government convinced Mitchell that his moment had come. De Priest was extremely vulnerable, being only a "political hustler" who was paid a great deal money to go around the country giving "inflammatory speeches instead of tending to the interests and needs of his constituents." In Mitchell's analysis, De Priest's loyal support for the Republican agenda of the Hoover administration made matters worse for the incumbent. It proved that he did not understand basic economics. Rather, De Priest appeared to be in agreement with Alden B. Baxter, who wrote in the *Chicago Commerce* that "we need Depressions—They mold men and Nations."[11]

Seeing his chance to gain the Democratic nomination in 1934, Mitchell first approached McDuffie, who wrote to James Farley, technically the postmaster general but in reality Roosevelt's "political fixer," to "unqualifiedly endorse" Mitchell as a potential candidate to oppose De Priest. "I do not know any colored man in the country," the Alabama congressman asserted, "who is a more active and loyal Democrat and I know he rendered valuable service in the last campaign." Farley, faced with the dilemma of not wanting to alienate southern Democrats by supporting a Black candidate but very much wanting to defeat De Priest, did not respond. McDuffie was nothing if not persistent. When Farley failed to answer to his first letter, he resent it on September 13. Again there was no answer.[12]

Mitchell approached Kelly personally, promoting himself as a potential ally. He assured the mayor that "nothing has happened within the Democratic Party that has been half so heartening and encouraging to honest and good-thinking Chicago negroes" as the mayor's being chosen to succeed Cermak. Gone were the days of vice-lords and racketeers leading the party. When Kelly faced his first election in 1935, Mitchell promised, Black voters would support him.[13]

Joseph Tittinger, the white Democratic committeeman for the Second Ward since 1930, needed less persuading. Mitchell wrote to him on January 12, 1934, detailing his "firm belief" that De Priest could be beaten. The Democratic aspirant argued that his speeches in California had been very effective in counteracting the congressman's rhetoric. Moreover, he was experienced in Washington, a college man, and the president of a national Black fraternity with seven thousand members. He would, he also pledged, be a loyal cog in the machine. "We can only succeed," he promised Tittinger, "as we work through and with our leaders."[14]

Tittinger, his position as dispenser of patronage increasingly threatened by loud Black demands that one of their race should occupy his post, saw Mitchell as heaven-sent. By supporting him, the committeeman would acquire an articulate, well-educated Black American to challenge De Priest, quelling some of the opposition to his leadership. Moreover, given the temper of the times, a Black Democratic candidate running in the First Congressional District might just win. This would create opportunities for additional patronage from Washington. Although he may not have ever met him, Tittinger declared that Mitchell was "his probable choice" to run for Congress on January 30, 1934.[15]

Unfortunately, Kenna, still a political power to be reckoned with, did not share Tittinger's enthusiasm for Mitchell. For years, there had been rumors of a marriage of convenience between the first ward boss and De Priest, one that insured an uninterrupted flow of patronage between a Republican-controlled Washington and Chicago. The speculation seemed substantiated by Kenna's repeated slating of the nondescript candidate, Harry Baker, as De Priest's opponent in general elections. Baker, a white store owner who had lived in the district for forty years while serving as a deputy sheriff and bailiff for Cook County, was, sniffed the Chicago *Tribune*, only "a job holder under the patronage of former Ald. Michael Kenna."[16]

Kenna would not abandon his stalking horse for an unknown quantity. "I'm not for Mitchell," he announced after meeting him for the first time, "because he's a carpetbagger. I would rather have De Priest, the devil we know, than Mitchell, the devil we don't know." To no one's surprise, Kenna prevailed in the argument. The oft-defeated Harry Baker would be the nominee.[17]

Faced by this reversal, Mitchell took a chance. He defied Kenna and ran anyway in the primary against Baker. In "Specific things Racial for which I shall Stand and Work," Mitchell outlined his platform. The most dangerous aspect of the Depression, Mitchell said, was "enforced idleness": "I shall be in favor of any program which tends to furnish work for people even though such a program incurs governmental expense, thus increasing taxation." He pledged to dedicate himself to wiping out racial discrimination, which "breeds hatred, prejudice, and injustice," and providing South Siders with a higher standard of living. He promised to author legislation in Congress to replace the use of photographs on civil service applications with fingerprints, to make sure that Black Americans enjoyed a "just proportion" of New Deal jobs, and to attempt "incessantly" to have Congress adopt an anti-lynching bill. He would also attempt to "re-enfranchise the Colored People of the South," who were being denied the ballot, and to see that American citizens, not aliens, were first to get job opportunities.[18]

A postcard circulated during the primary portrayed the candidate making these promises as a "prominent and successful lawyer" who had studied under Booker T. Washington, done graduate work at Columbia and Harvard, and was prominent in civic and fraternal affairs. McDuffie added to the fanfare, writing to Kelly that he had "known Arthur for many years" as a "man of the finest integrity as well as excellent ability." He was thoroughly dependable and "his service here [Washington] would be much more valuable than that of Oscar DePriest." Perhaps influenced by this, the mayor appeared at a Mitchell rally on March 19 and seemed to endorse him. According to the *Pittsburgh Courier*, Kelly asked his audience "to give my good friend Arthur Mitchell your vote for he is 100 percent for Chicago and should be elected." Three days later, Mitchell thanked Kelly for the "fine words you spoke for my candidacy."[19]

Financing himself, Mitchell ran a strong race. However, to nobody's surprise, Baker "won" on election day. When the votes were "counted" on April 10, Mitchell carried the Black Second and Fourth Wards by overwhelming margins. Baker prevailed by even stronger margins in the white wards, Kenna's First and Bridgeport's Eleventh. However, the narrowness of Baker's victory was surprising: 7,326 to 6,812. So was the fact that Kelly and Nash had permitted the race to be reported as so close.[20]

When critics referred to Mitchell as "lucky" or "an accident," they had a point. Three sequential, untimely deaths came together to make him a congressman in 1935. Madden's 1928 death in his own office had transferred the First Congressional District seat in Congress from a white to a Black member. Cermak's murder in 1932 replaced a mayor unsympathetic with the Black plight with one anxious to promote better conditions. And now, fate intervened for a third time. Harry Baker died of heart failure on May 8. This left the decision on who should oppose De Priest to the recommendation made by the six "electors": Kelly, Nash, and the four committeemen whose wards made up the First Congressional District: Kenna (1st Ward), Tittinger (2nd), Joseph Geary (4th), and Hugh Connelly (11th).

McDuffie offered his friend support ten days after Baker's death, writing, "I wish to be of every assistance I can to you" and adding that the Congressional

Campaign Committee shared this desire. It was Tittinger, however, who took the lead in advocating for Mitchell. The primary had given the Second Ward committeeman additional ammunition. His protégé had shown himself to be an able campaigner and a good speaker. He had run particularly well in Tittinger's bailiwick, beating Baker 5,205 to 294. He did not seem to have any interest in challenging the Kelly-Nash machine and that made him safe. So did the fact that he was virtually unknown. He was who he said he was, untouched by the internecine warfare that characterized Chicago politics. All of this meant that he might win.

In addition, party workers weighed in. One wrote to Joseph Geary that very few Black candidates were on the ballot, a fact that placed Democrats "at a terrible disadvantage. . . . For goodness sakes, do what you can to get Mitchell on the ticket. This will mean thousands of votes for Democrats all over the city." Precinct captains also applied pressure, assuring Kelly that Mitchell "can and will be elected if placed on the ballot." They went even further in their plea to Nash, predicting that with Mitchell replacing Baker, the Democrats would have "more than an even chance to carry the Second Ward."[21]

With apparent reluctance but lacking a viable alternative and impressed by Mitchell's showing in the April primary, Kenna gave way. It took most of the summer to persuade him, but on August 8, the Democratic Central Committee announced that Arthur W. Mitchell would be its candidate to oppose Oscar De Priest in the November general election. It would be a historic event: for the first time in American history, two Black candidates of opposing political parties would face each other in a general election to decide a seat in the United States House of Representatives.[22]

But, despite the devastations wrought by the Depression and the popularity of Roosevelt, November 1934 did not seem to be the ideal moment to oppose De Priest, who had transformed himself into something of a Black national hero during his three terms in Congress. His early days in Washington had been difficult, but the former house painter who had lived on the edge of respectability for decades had evolved into a "shrewd, resourceful, and utterly fearless" spokesman for his race over time. The *Washington Tribune* pictured Mitchell's opponent as "a national idol, inspiring . . . and to some extent uniting the race."[23]

Defying Democratic trends, De Priest had been reelected in 1930 and 1932. Moreover, in 1934, he added to his stature when an aide had been denied access to the House cafeteria. De Priest successfully petitioned against this action despite Democratic opposition, forcing the full House to appoint a committee to investigate the exclusion. At its heart, Black Americans saw the cafeteria dispute as a test of whether the "New Deal" extended to them or not. "It is either to be carried out impartially to every citizen alike or it is a hypocritical pretense," the *Defender* argued. "Oscar DePriest is making a fight for the 12,000,000 Colored people in the United States."[24]

What was beyond dispute to friend and foe alike was that Oscar De Priest in the summer of 1934 was "the best known, the most publicized, and the most striking personality in the Negro political world." As such, he seemed "virtually invulnerable."[25]

4
"What a Difference a Week Makes"

MITCHELL'S PROSPECTS FOR unseating De Priest were made easier by Roosevelt's popularity in Chicago. "Let Jesus lead you and Roosevelt feed you" was a popular slogan on the shores of Lake Michigan. "Everywhere and every place," the *Pittsburgh Courier* reported, "it's Roosevelt, Roosevelt, Roosevelt and vote the straight Democratic ticket."[1]

In addition, the president seemed to be personally fond of Mitchell. Edgar G. Brown, a publicity director for the Federal Emergency Relief Agency and the brother-in-law of Irwin McDuffie, the president's valet, reported from Hyde Park that Roosevelt was "wearing a 'Mitchell for Congress' button" and that De Priest's opponent was "considered a real new dealer here, in step with the President." In early October, the *Courier* reported that "the word has come down from the White House itself to 'get DePriest.'"[2]

However, these indirect signals of support did not translate into public endorsements. In addition to worrying about the corruption of the Kelly-Nash machine, Roosevelt felt that he could not afford to alienate the southern power brokers who dominated Congress by supporting a Black candidate. As the president had explained to Walter White during a May 1934 interview, he "did not choose the tools with which I must work. Had I been permitted to choose them I would have selected quite different ones. But I've got to get legislation passed to save America." In 1934, those tools included white southerners who held the offices of vice president, president pro temp of the Senate, Speaker of the House of Representatives, and chairs of many of the most important committees of both houses.[3]

Farley, the chairman of the Democratic National Committee, shared this reticence. "Never at the forefront of efforts to bring African Americans into the Democratic party," he wanted De Priest defeated but saw no guarantee that Mitchell would be well received by Democratic leaders. He and the DNC finessed the situation by endorsing Mitchell in private but not offering him financial support. "I am sure," Farley wrote to him on September 18, that "the people of your district, if they knew the stand-pat reactionary record of

Congressman DePriest, would endeavor to replace [him] and gain representation in the Halls of Congress. [They] are entitled to honest, fearless, and intelligent representation which we in Washington know only too well you are not getting at the present time." Two weeks later, he offered "every possible assistance" to Mitchell, but that did not include money or even Mitchell's being named as a formal candidate in a circular letter to Illinois's Democratic leadership. When Mitchell complained about this omission, Richard Roper, the executive secretary of the DNC, explained that "we didn't refer to you by name because in big cities we could not be sure as to district boundaries. Time was too limited to get the necessary information to make this possible."[4]

McDuffie tried unsuccessfully to loosen Democratic purse strings. On September 2, he assured Farley that he and Mitchell had enjoyed "long years of friendship" and that his fellow Alabamian "has always been a loyal Democrat" and now needed money desperately. Mitchell himself appealed to Emil Hurja, Farley's pollster, claiming that there were a dozen states north of the Mason-Dixon line that would hold the balance of power in 1936. His election in 1934 "would mean volumes for the Democratic Party in '36 and to the party in local elections."[5]

Mitchell was equally unsuccessful in his attempts to solicit financial support from friends in Washington and Chicago. Among local politicians only Adolph Sabath, another Chicago congressman, and Jacob Arvey, a powerful cog in the Kelly-Nash machine, contributed. No sitting Democratic congressman, senator, or member of the Roosevelt administration was prepared to give money to a Black Democrat running for Congress. Representatives from Alabama, California, Kentucky, Oklahoma, Tennessee, and Texas all turned his request for funding down, most using the expense of their own campaigns as an excuse. Even McDuffie, who was running unopposed, begged off. Since he was running virtually unopposed in his Alabama district, he offered the explanation that he was so cash strapped that he had had to borrow money for his daughter's college tuition. He did, however, send another plaintive letter to Farley urging the DNC to send money to "one of the highest type of our prominent colored citizens in the country."[6]

Given these refusals, Mitchell dipped into his personal resources to "educate colored voters on the issues and expose the hypocrisy of our present Congressman." Despite these outlays, Mitchell portrayed himself as underfunded. In particular, he regretted not being able to take Chandler Owen up on his suggestion to use the modern device of the radio to broadcast his message during the closing weeks "when lies will be spread thick." Modern campaigning methods "would have done much in reaching white Republicans."[7]

Believing that the misery of so many of his constituents could only be alleviated by federal programs, Mitchell committed his campaign to wholehearted support for Roosevelt and the New Deal legislation, a promise he was to honor throughout his time in Congress. In the late summer of 1934, this pledge took both courage and foresight as the first year and a half of Roosevelt's administration had engendered substantial opposition from Black Americans. They seemed to matter very little in the Democrats' political calculus during the early days of the New Deal as "it was clearly more important to the administration to keep southern political support than it was to court blacks."[8]

Many of them referred to the National Recovery Act as "Negro Rights Abused" or "Negroes Ruined Again," seeing the bill as "a hopeless shambles so far as Negroes are concerned." Likewise, hiring policies in the Civilian Conservation Corp (CCC) provoked outrage. But most odious to many was the Bankhead Cotton Bill of 1934 that licensed producers of cotton while imposing penalties on those who exceeded enumerated quotas. The *Defender* claimed that this piece of legislation would cut employment in cotton fields by 30 percent and reduce wages by one-half, "leading toward permanent pauperization of the Negro, and permanent pauperization is the same as slavery."[9]

While admitting these New Deal shortcomings, Mitchell urged Black voters to concentrate on the larger perspective. He was "100 percent for Roosevelt." Despite early stumbles, the president's agenda was on the right track. In the long run, conditions would improve for all. Roosevelt's agenda, he asserted, was "the only workable program by which this country and government can be saved." At the same time, he argued to white voters, who made up an important voting bloc in the First Congressional District, the area being one of the richest in the country, "it should be represented by someone who is versed in the affairs of business, in economic and social affairs."[10]

In truth, the De Priest-Mitchell contest was over before it even began because Chairman Nash, Mayor Kelly, and Committeeman Michael J. Kenna had decided it was. On September 19, Nash "predicted" in the *Public Service Leader*, the trade journal of the Cook County Democrats, that Mitchell would win "handily," De Priest forces being "disorganized." "The colored voters," Nash contended, "the first to feel the effects of the Hoover Depression, are determined to give the Roosevelt administration [and Mitchell] an endorsement of its job-creating projects."[11]

Kelly and Nash also had a vested interest in Mitchell's success. The mayor had been appointed by a fifty-member City Council, not elected by the public. He was scheduled to face the voters for the first time shortly after the 1934 election and a Mitchell victory would burnish his image as a winner. It would also signal the support of the Black community for a mayor who wanted to be known as a "second Thompson." From his point in view, Mitchell's slogan, "Forward with Roosevelt and Recovery," might just as well be "Forward with

Roosevelt, Mitchell, Kelly, and Recovery." No wonder that the mayor hoped to "tie this ticket to the Roosevelt kite and soar to victory."[12]

An incident in mid-October cemented the personal relationship between Kelly and Mitchell, who nurtured a lifelong commitment to improving Black education. Faced with overcrowding at Morgan Park High School on the South Side, the Chicago Board of Education had reassigned Black ninth graders to a satellite school. A Black state representative, the NAACP, the Urban League, and the parents of the affected students appealed to Kelly, who overruled the board and ordered the students readmitted. Two hundred white parents then stormed Kelly's office, a woman shouting "we moved out to Morgan Park to get away from these Niggers and now we have to contend with them again. We ought not stand for it." Kelly refused to yield and the students returned to Morgan Park.[13]

Mitchell praised the mayor's actions as "not only manly and right, but requir[ing] the highest type of courage. There is nothing in the career of Big Bill Thompson, or any other Republican, which is so heartening to the Negro. In this matter you have made thousands of friends among Negroes not only for yourself but for the Democratic Party." Kelly's response was equally warm. He expressed "a feeling of deep gratitude" to "Congressman Mitchell" for his note and assured him that "I will remember your message after November 6."[14]

Kenna remained the player who needed to be moved from a position of passive acceptance to active support. Kelly and Nash could have forced him to comply, but Mitchell understood that the veteran of so many Chicago political wars deserved to be persuaded, not coerced. So he went to see "Hinky Dink," who he described as "a fine old Irish gentleman nearly eighty," during the first week in October to ask for his endorsement. Kenna refused at first, saying that Black voters would never support a Democrat. He cited an example where he had paid a Black Republican ward leader $200 in cash to "find" votes for his candidate in a previous election and received nothing in return. Mitchell argued that times had changed, that De Priest was a Republican, the party which was out of power and liable to be weakened further in the upcoming election. He, on the other hand, was a Democrat and, if elected, would have access to increased patronage. As an outsider with no Chicago roots, Mitchell added he had no personal interest in who benefited from the distribution of pork. That was up to the machine.

Convinced that De Priest had outlived his usefulness, "the Hink" agreed to support the devil he now knew. On October 8, Mitchell wrote to a supporter that he had had a very satisfactory conference with "Alderman McKenna. He gave me his word that his organization is one hundred percent with me," that the First Ward "is going straight for the Democratic ticket."[15]

This political earthquake was reported in the *Courier*, which estimated the prized endorsement would gain Mitchell about twelve thousand votes. "What a difference a week makes," Vann's paper observed. "Seven days ago it appeared that DePriest might well hang on." Now, the *Courier* concluded, "with such tremendous odds against him, [DePriest's] victory [would] constitute the greatest political feat within the history of local politics."[16]

Virtually ignored by the *Defender*, Barnett's Associated Negro Press (ANP), and the *Tribune*, Mitchell received some coverage from Hearst's *Herald and Examiner* that found him to be "brilliantly educated with a background of teaching at the famous Tuskegee Institute and high scholastic attainments at Harvard and Columbia." In the Black community, Mitchell relied on the Chicago *World* to publicize his activities. Edited by Jacob Tipper and given out at local stores that advertised in it, the *World* had a circulation of about six thousand. After the Kenna endorsement, Tipper "advised his staff to use every effort to put [Mitchell] over." In the *World*'s eyes, their candidate was "one of the best known lawyers in the country . . . one of the wheel horses of the local and National Democratic Party." He had "never been indicted for graft, for being in league with commercialized vice . . . never removed from office . . . never charged his people high rent when there was no necessity for doing so." He was "educated . . . cultured . . . and refined."[17]

Not only was he extremely well qualified, Mitchell wrote to campaign workers, but "the Republicans have no money, no offices, and no argument except the old worn out statement that 'negroes should be Republican because they are black.'" To counter this, Mitchell advised supporters to "talk about the great promise being held out to the Negroes by the Democratic Party."[18]

As for his opponent, Mitchell compiled a litany of complaints that he returned to time and time again at his rallies. They included the charge that De Priest did not live in the First Congressional District; was unwilling to represent the interests of the entire district, a third of whom were white; had behaved in a "reprehensible" manner in Congress, having stirred up "race prejudice" and made "bitter enemies" of potential supporters; had shown little interest in his duties in Washington; was a "political hustler," paid from $50 to $200 for speeches delivered all over the country; had destroyed Republican harmony in the Second Ward by his actions in the 1934 primary; was explicit in his opposition to Roosevelt, as he had supported only seven of twenty-six New Deal pieces of legislation, with an attitude that "threatens all relief measures"; and was "out of favor with the party in power" and therefore could no longer deliver patronage to his constituents.[19]

These attacks enabled Mitchell to gain some support in traditionally Republican circles that formed themselves into a "Mitchell for Congress Club." He invited its chairman, Caswell Crewes, to "talk turkey" with him. After digesting the bird, Crewes wrote a public letter to the *Defender* praising Mitchell for his "intelligence, poise, courage, honesty and clean record." He added that the New Deal was "the greatest social, political, and economic program ever offered for the American people."[20]

Although Mitchell would later claim that his election was "the cleanest" in the history of Chicago politics, his letters also showed an understanding of how votes were secured in the city. Not only was he interested in "talking turkey" with Crewes, but another message to Reverend J. M. Foster was even more explicit. Thanking him for his support, Mitchell promised a "contribution" to anyone voting as Foster recommended. It was a donation he would "see to personally," if those entitled to it appeared at his headquarters.[21]

Hoping to take advantage of what he saw as his superior forensic skills and ability to demonstrate that De Priest was out of touch with the times, Mitchell challenged his opponent to debates, confrontations he told Locke his adversary would decline. In three taunting letters, he listed questions he intended to ask De Priest if they met. These included: 1) what extraordinary expenditures of the federal government would he eliminate?; 2) would he close relief stations and stop feeding the hungry?; 3) would he stop all public works?; 4) would he restore old banking methods?; 5) would he return to the policies of the Hoover administration?; and 6) "Have you any program by which you plan to hasten recovery and, if so, what is it?"[22]

De Priest temporized, saying he would consider a debate only if Mitchell published his correspondence with "Congressman Duffie who I understand is your principal sponsor." The *World* thought this answer an excuse "resorted to by one who fears that he may be shown up by an opponent." Mitchell also ridiculed it, reading its opening sentences to a crowd in a scene sketched by the *Chicago Daily News* : "Dear Mr. Mitchell: 'I understand that you are a candidate for Congress and I believe in my district.' That brought a howl of delight from the crowd. 'Mr. DePriest,' Mitchell mockingly lamented, 'has just discovered that I am running. I feel sorry for him.'" Three days before the election, Mitchell wrote a fourth letter to De Priest. "Your record is such," he charged, "that you should be retired to private life. You are finishing up your last year in Congress. . . . You are wholly unfit to represent the First Congressional District and the people will not be fooled into voting for you again."[23]

When not badgering De Priest, Mitchell sprang a master political stroke later judged by a friend to be "a clever piece of strategy" and by the *Atlanta Constitution* as having a major impact on the election result. He brought Sylvester Harris, an illiterate Black farmer from Columbus, Mississippi, to Chicago to campaign for him.[24]

Figure 7. Mitchell with Sylvester Harris in Chicago (1934). Harris's story of his Mississippi farm being saved from foreclosure by President Roosevelt's intervention contributed to Mitchell's 1934 victory and was an element in the Democratic appeal to Black voters in 1936. Chicago History Museum, ICHi-183204; Associated Press, photographer.

Harris's story had first surfaced in the Black press early in 1934. Having his name on a loan for a farm that was about to be foreclosed, he feared that his nine children would be left homeless and "would have called Satan if the connection could have been made" to save his land. In desperation, he drove his last cow into town, sold it, and with that money repeatedly called Franklin Roosevelt at the White House, asking for his help. When he finally spoke to the president, Roosevelt offered assistance and the farm was saved.[25]

During the closing days of the campaign, Harris came to Chicago under the guise of attending the World's Fair. According to a local Mississippi newspaper, it was Tittinger who promised to pay all of his expenses. With his crops in and nothing particular to do, Harris thought a "vacation" would be wonderful for him. So he got a haircut, shined his shoes, put on his Sunday suit, and ventured north. Before leaving, Harris volunteered that "he was ready to speak a good word on behalf of the Democratic party if any of the ward organizations there wanted him to."[26]

Harris in Chicago proved to be great political theater. He rekindled nostalgia for the South and farming in transplanted Black Chicagoans while demonstrating that conditions in the old Confederacy were improving under President Roosevelt. Wherever he went, Harris told and retold his story, followed by Mitchell, who stressed the "Roosevelt and Recovery" theme, pointing to Harris as proof of its validity. The farmer from Mississippi was so passionate that he proved an instant success at rallies, the ANP declaring that "folks flocked to hear him and a lot of them, moved by his homey philosophy, were to some extent guided by him." What they heard, the *Birmingham News* wrote, was a "poor negro farmer in overalls and unable to speak a correct sentence." When asked if somebody had written his speeches for him, Harris answered, "It wouldn't have done any good cause I can't read. I just got up and told [the audience] to quit talking about Abraham Lincoln. Why, I told them, Mr. Lincoln had been dead most 70 years and to think about who was President now.'"[27]

Mitchell's campaign rushed out a brochure titled "President Roosevelt Saved His Farm" showing its candidate and Harris shaking hands. In case anyone missed the point, Vann hammered it home after the election. When a man like Harris "got what was coming to him, I think the Negroes of the South must look to that sort of man [Roosevelt]," he wrote in the *Courier*. "It was a new day in politics when this government went to the rescue of this poor Mississippi Negro farmer."[28]

Mitchell benefitted from this "master move to be remembered when scribes recount in history the story of 1934." He emerged as the local embodiment of a Democratic administration that cared for the dispossessed of Chicago. Not only did the Democratic candidate understand the plight of Black Chicagoans, but he had a potential solution for it. Might they not be better off returning to the South? Harris made the same point when back in Mississippi. Asked what he thought of Chicago, he answered, "too much noise and too many folks."[29]

Two days before the election, the *Tribune* editorialized for De Priest and against the "socialism and radicalism" of the New Deal and Mitchell, who supported ideas created by a "professional brain trust," which "gave life to the national bureaucracy that has piled up billions of debt."[30]

The two most important Black media outlets in Chicago also supported De Priest in the closing days. The *Defender,* which had ignored Mitchell's candidacy up to that point, broke its silence with an October 20 editorial. Pointing to Mitchell's southern roots, it charged that "no man trained and educated in the cruel environments of the South lynch law can shake the effects of that influence from his thoughts." If Mitchell won, it would mean that the Black Chicagoan had "surrendered [his] manhood . . . to a political allurement that has for years lynched your men and prostituted your women." A week later, Douglass Bainbridge repeated the argument in the same paper. De Priest had been a champion of Black rights. His election would mean the continuation of northern "ideals and programs" in Washington. It was inconceivable that a "political creature of Southern influence . . . trained and educated in the cruel environments of Southern lynch laws, concubinage, and murder," could be elected. Choosing Mitchell, he warned, would sentence "Southern brothers and sisters to perpetual peonage."[31]

Barnett, who enjoyed "close ties to the Republican party," and his ANP also supported De Priest. To him, the incumbent's "fawning" opponent was "Uncle Tom Mitchell," whose election would be the result of the influence of "policy kings, bootleggers and other racketeers." On the other hand, De Priest had "developed into a most effective public figure with courage and fortitude."[32]

Despite this opposition, Mitchell remained confident. He insisted that he would win by fifteen thousand votes, carry the First Ward by nine thousand votes, receive a majority in the Fourth and the Eleventh, and get an "even break" in the Second, "the principal battleground." The Republicans were approaching "complete collapse." For them, it was "every man for himself." And the GOP had no one to blame but themselves for their predicament. De Priest had also voted against "practically every [New Deal] measure which would bring relief to the People of Chicago." When one added to this the fact that De Priest didn't live in the First Congressional District, had distributed no patronage since the election of Roosevelt, and displayed an attitude that "has made no friends for himself at home, nor for his race at large," victory was assured.[33]

During the final days of the race, the *Courier* backtracked on its October prediction of a Mitchell victory. It now pictured the "elephant and donkey locked in mortal combat," forecasting that De Priest would win by a narrow margin. The *New York Times* agreed that the incumbent seemed to be the "likely" winner. But Barnett feared that the opposite was possible. Mitchell might win, he wired subscribing newspapers the day before the election, and "editors will want to have at hand a picture of Oscar De Priest's political career as this will probably mean [its] end." A political obituary followed, highlighting De Priest's roots among the common people, his election successes, and the value of his time in Washington. His defeat, the tribute concluded, had been due to facing a "colored opponent" and strife within the Republican Party. Don't use this story, Barnett cautioned, if De Priest is reelected.[34]

On election day, one observer reported that "repeaters, non-existent persons, and floaters" swelled the total of votes cast. Republicans charged that citywide the Kelly-Nash machine cast perhaps as many as 250,000 counterfeit "Roosevelt and Recovery" ballots, some "well after the polls closed." Another eyewitness saw November 6 as "a resurrection day," unprecedented in Chicago with the "wholesale voting of the dead and the phantoms." Agreeing that perhaps 250,000 fraudulent ballots had been cast, it was "doubtful if there were honest returns from ten percent of the Chicago precincts."[35]

In the First Congressional District, confusion reigned until twenty hours after the polls closed. Barnett left perhaps the most detailed description of the counting process. The white wards (First and Eleventh) reported first, giving Mitchell a substantial lead. Early Wednesday morning, the Black wards (Second and Fourth) came in. They cut De Priest's deficit to twenty-six votes with three precincts unreported. By late morning, De Priest was ahead by sixty-one votes with two precincts outstanding. The count remained at that point for five hours, with speculation mounting as to the identity of the missing precincts. The afternoon newspapers of November 7 reported that De Priest had won. Then the election judges announced a Mitchell victory by slightly more than three thousand votes. You could not convince De Priest's friends that "something didn't happen on the inside," Barnett wrote. "The impartial observer, aware of Democratic control of the election machinery and everything else in the city and county, is forced to admit that almost anything is possible."[36]

At 5:40 p.m. on November 7, De Priest conceded defeat in a telegram congratulating Mitchell as the "first Negro Democratic Congressman." The victor answered on November 10 that he would "endeavor to carry forward the splendid work of looking after and protecting the interest of our group in which you have been so nobly engaged." The *Courier* 's summary headline of the election read: "Late Poll Shows DePriest Defeat by Mitchell. Most Startling Upset of Election."[37]

Official returns revealed that, despite his predictions, Mitchell did not come close to winning in the Second Ward. It remained staunchly Republican, if by a reduced margin. What carried him to victory in a much closer election than he had anticipated were his reported margins among voters in the two predominantly white wards. Before the election, Mitchell predicted that he would carry Kenna's First by nine thousand votes. He carried it by 9,077. Connelly's Eleventh Ward was also a bastion of support. Most of these were ballots cast by middle- and lower-class white voters, the irony of Mitchell's election. The first Black Democrat ever elected to Congress had been carried to victory by the same white precincts that had been the epicenter of the 1919 riots.[38]

Not only had Mitchell won in the First, but he also seemed to have coattails that extended into neighboring Indiana. During the campaign, he appeared in Gary in support of local Democratic candidates. Ray Madden, who was then the Gary Democratic Central Committee Chairman and would go on to a thirty-four-year career in Congress, told him after the election that "it is the consensus of opinion that your speech and visit was greatly instrumental" in ending twenty-nine years of Republican control.[39]

To the *Courier,* Mitchell's triumph was "an election upset that stunned and surprised almost everybody . . . but Mitchell." It represented "the political emancipation of the Negro with all the benefits that may accrue therefrom." Black voters would no longer be a "wheel horse" of the Republican Party as "colored voters are wedded to no one party. Perhaps the realization of that fact may have a profound effect on the political future of Negroes down South."[40]

Conversely, Mitchell's victory shocked the Black Republican establishment where his candidacy "had not been taken seriously and his election [was] viewed with amazement and alarm." Barnett found De Priest's defeat "disconcerting" to "those who felt that he had arrived at a place of usefulness beyond even what we had expected when he went [to Washington]." "We didn't realize," Judge Richard Harwood told Charles Branham in a 1979 interview, that "the Black man was going Democratic until Mitchell defeated De Priest. And then the bottom fell out."[41]

Mitchell had no doubt that Republican failure to understand the times had been decisive. He, on the other hand, had seen that change was necessary and that the early New Deal, however flawed, offered the best future for Black Chicagoans. "I pledge myself," he had declared early in the campaign, "to work to the end that the New Deal will mean as much, if not more, to our people than to any other group." The New Deal, he reaffirmed to Roosevelt, had been "his platform," and his election represented "a desire fully expressed for the new leadership." He was "100 percent in agreement with the President's program. I was elected partly on the achievement of your administration and partly on the promise that I would stand back of it."[42]

The pledge was a personal one, from Mitchell to Roosevelt. Farley, who had done little to help, was not thanked, nor were the Democratic functionaries who had ignored his campaign. The postmaster waited until November 14 to send word through an intermediary that he was "particularly glad that

Mr. Mitchell won. It was a marvelous victory and proved he has a lot of loyal friends, and we were very glad to see his opponent defeated because he was so against the President's program." When Farley did write to Mitchell it was only to advise him to "refrain from making any commitments or in any way tieing up with a special interest."[43]

McDuffie, who congratulated his friend on his "fine victory" the day after the election, was forgiven for his failure to offer financial support. "You will never know," Mitchell wrote, "the encouragement I have gotten from you and the part you have played in me reaching this point. I shall endeavor to keep in the closest possible touch with you and to profit through your advice and counsel in my new environment."[44]

In Chicago, "it was widely believed" that Kelly's support had been the key to victory. Mitchell seemed to agree, telling the mayor, "I want to thank you again for the unparalleled interest which you have shown in me personally and in my political career." Geary and Connelly also received letters of thanks. Tittinger and his precinct captains received special commendations for "roll[ing] up their sleeves and working like real soldiers." They received this promise: "I owe each and every one a debt of lasting gratitude and [will] always endeavor to help the organization." Mitchell, however, reserved special praise for Kenna: "I have never seen any organization function so perfectly with leaders so loved and trusted who were in complete control of their forces." "I want you to feel," he concluded, "that at any time you wish me to serve you, I stand not only ready and willing but most anxious."[45]

As to the press, the congressman-elect thanked Tipper for the "splendid service you rendered the Democratic Party and me in the last campaign." But when Mitchell did grant a post-election interview, it was not to Tipper or to any Chicago newspapers. Rather the honor went to Frank Marshall Davis, a prominent Black reporter then working for the Gary (IN) *American*. Reprinted in the *Daily News* and the *Defender*, Mitchell boasted to Davis that his "campaign will go into history as one of the cleanest ever waged in Chicago. We will let the record of the opposition speak for itself." No one, however, should misunderstand the election's larger meaning: it was an endorsement for Roosevelt and the New Deal but, Mitchell declared, "equally significant is the fact that it marks a turning point in a campaign of bitterness waged by some northern Negro leaders against southern white people. It is the repudiation of the attempt to bulldoze your neighbor. It is my belief that a man ought to make and retain all the friends he can. I shall continue to cultivate such friendly relations for the best interests of blacks and whites."[46]

In triumph, Mitchell snubbed Abbott and Barnett. The *Defender* tried to make amends, A. N. Fields writing on November 10 that "the new Congressman enters upon his responsibilities properly equipped, having been a college professor himself. . . . This, fortified with common sense and a deep spiritual desire to help his race, places him in an excellent position." When Mitchell ignored his requests for a quote and after he had read the Davis interview, Abbott reverted to form: "It smacks of ingratitude for a visiting gentleman who has made his residence in the North but a brief five years and to have been honored on such short acquaintance with a seat in Congress to assume to chastise his host."

Mitchell did not return Barnett's telephone calls. In frustration, the publisher of the Associated Negro Press pleaded with him to release a statement. It could contain "anything [Mitchell] wished," so long as the ANP had something to publish. He did not receive an answer.[47]

5

"A Political Abortion . . . Imprisoned in the Winds of Hate and Slander"

Of great symbolic importance, Mitchell's victory tour was not an excursion through the First Congressional District. Rather, citing a need to visit his ailing mother and the wish to thank his "many old white friends from all over the South" who had congratulated him on his election, he got into his car and drove south.[1]

Before leaving, he issued a promise to "address myself first to the interests of the people of the First Congressional District," who wanted "intelligent, courageous, honest, and capable representation," something they "have not had during the past six years. I think the people are tired of bombast, ballyhoo and noise." His agenda included:

- Any program which tends to furnish work for the people, even if it involved more taxes;
- The elimination of racial discrimination;
- The commitment to a higher standard of living, increased wages, and better housing conditions for Black Americans;
- The return of suffrage rights to southern voters;
- The elimination of photos in civil service applications;
- The promise that Black applicants would receive a "just proportion" of New Deal jobs;
- The promise to work "incessantly" on anti-lynching legislation; and
- The application of an "Americans first" policy to filling job openings.

He was "100 percent in agreement" with the president's program, but its execution had not been handled as it should have been: "These errors can and will be corrected."[2]

His first stop was in Louisville. There, the *Defender* informed its readers, he was received like a "conquering hero. Everywhere he went he was greeted with large crowds and cheers." At the end of his visit, Louisville's chief of police provided him with a ceremonial escort to the city limits. Remarkably, the *Louisville Courier,* the city's leading white newspaper, reported on his visit, the first time that newspaper had ever given front-page coverage to a Black politician.[3]

From there, it was on to Birmingham, where he told a crowd that the first Republican lie he had heard was when he had listened to the "40 acres and a mule" promise at an 1896 rally he attended with his father. He also reprised his version of his Tuskegee experiences and the exploits of Sylvester Harris in Chicago, and he reviewed the goals he had set for himself in Washington. "To show you how ridiculous are the thoughts of some," he added, "I was asked before leaving Chicago if I wasn't afraid to come to Birmingham as a congressman."[4]

When he arrived in Montgomery, Mitchell found that Grover C. Hall, the editor of the *Montgomery Advertiser* and a leading southern progressive, had prepared a special welcome for him. The winner of a Pulitzer Prize in 1928 for his editorials opposing the Ku Klux Klan, Hall praised Mitchell for his moral courage, "the first requisite of a useful public servant," in choosing to run for political office as a Democrat and not a Republican. "The latter lives in the past, the former looks to the rising sun of the future and is not unaware of the living present. If Mitchell will be faithful to his original impulse to be an American Congressman instead of a Negro agitator in Congress, he will reflect credit upon himself and his race." Mitchell could, Hall concluded, rival Booker T. Washington as "the wisest spirit ever born of African blood."[5]

Several other southern newspapers agreed with Hall. The *Florence* (AL) *Tribune* thought that his election made him the most distinguished Negro Democrat of the nation and heir to much of "the influence that Booker Washington exercised over the South." The *Nashville Banner* agreed: "What a blessing he will be in Washington where he can be relied on to bring to the problem of race relations a mellow understanding." Less complimentary, the *Jackson* [MS] *Daily News* viewed him merely as "a white folks Negro who will do anything they tell him to do."[6]

The climax of Mitchell's tour occurred with his return to Tuskegee. Dropping by "just to say howdy," he marveled at the new facilities that had been built since he was a student while acknowledging the value of the lessons he had learned from Washington. "I am in full sympathy with the teachings of Booker T. Washington," he told students. "I believe that anything the Negro gets, he will get by working for it. That is how I have got everything that I have." Responding to a question about his prediction that he would go to Congress, he mused, "I don't know what it is, but in a number of other situations I have predicted almost to the letter how events were going to come out. I guess it's just luck, but a lot of my predictions have worked out." But, he added, "I don't just sit still after I make my predictions."

In a clear reference to De Priest, he observed, "I am convinced that being a congressman should take all the best a man has to give with little time or energy left for bombast." As for those who criticized him for having white southern friends, he reiterated, "I have no apologies for these friends and only wish I had more of them."[7]

After his day with students, Mitchell spent the evening at the home of William Carter, Tuskegee's treasurer, where he proved to be a "very charming guest who talked from 9:30 p.m. to 2 a.m." Had he known that his enemies had launched a campaign designed to prevent him from ever taking a seat in Congress, Mitchell might not have been so charming.[8]

The effort began with a letter from Ligon A. Wilson, Edwards's successor as principal at Snow Hill. He wrote to Barnett that the new congressman's claim to be a Tuskegee graduate was a lie. Mitchell "received his training at Snow Hill and is an alumnus of the same, graduating in the Class of 1903." Snow Hill "aided him up the hill and influenced his educational activities in the state until 1918." While "it will be unfortunate to dig up old skeletons," it was time to pay Edwards the homage he deserved. In addition to challenging his academic pedigree, Wilson charged that Mitchell had once been arrested, convicted of a felony, and might have spent time in jail. If true, he was a convicted criminal and could not serve in Congress. Wilson hoped "you will put this matter before Mr. Mitchell either by placing this letter before him or by doing so in your own way. We must save him from sure embarrassment."[9]

In response to the challenge about Mitchell's academic credentials, an unknown official at the ANP admitted that that the agency knew very little about Mitchell's early years but was investigating them. So few people had taken his candidacy seriously that no one had bothered to check on the accuracy of his claims about his background. "Our files about Mr. Mitchell are chaotic at present," a Barnett associate told Wilson. "There are claims he attended Talladega, Tuskegee, Howard, Columbia, and Harvard. Howard and Harvard have no record of him. He spent six weeks at Columbia. [The record] contains no reference to Snow Hill. . . . In spite of the lack of scholastic background, Mr. Mitchell has pushed himself forward to recognition as one of the able thinkers of the race. With scarcely more, if as much scholastic background as Mr. De Priest, he has made himself felt as a scholar."[10]

Barnett found the assertion of criminal activity creditable, writing to Carter, "Dr. Moton and Dr. Mordecai Johnson (President of Howard University) agreed that nothing which could happen in public life to Negroes would be more disastrous at this time than to have aired in the White press circumstances behind Mr. Mitchell if they are true." Above all, the accusation should be kept from De Priest "because he would seek to take political advantage and would broadcast it." Rather, Barnett suggested, a committee of "outstanding people" such as Moton, Johnson, and Walter White should be formed. It would investigate the charges and, if it concluded that they were credible, "call Mr. Mitchell in and ask him to resign. If he did not care to do so without fuss, the committee itself could denounce him and ask for him not to be seated." "The accuracy of the conviction and the method of release," Barnett concluded, "should be verified at once."[11]

To investigate the accusations, Carter, Wilson, and Edwards traveled to Chambers County. They found that the "felony" involved the theft of pocketknives from a general store and was "more or less a prank." Moreover, Carter reported to Barnett, the new congressman "is well known in the community and well thought of." He had received "an invitation from very influential citizens, white and colored, to return to speak before a very large audience." Across the bottom of this letter, Barnett wrote, "let's forget the whole thing."[12]

Unaware of any of this, Mitchell ended his tour of the South with stops at Selma, Uniontown, Havana, and Tuscaloosa, Alabama, and at Hot Springs, Arkansas. A letter of thanks to Richard Harris, a friend he had seen at Tuskegee, hinted at his upcoming agenda in Washington. "Please send me clippings [from southern newspapers]," he wrote. "I am particularly interested in any expressions made relative to lynching and to the Negro franchise in the south."[13]

He was back in Chicago by December 1, in time to celebrate the Democrats' November triumph at a victory banquet before still disbelieving critics. The *Defender* 's Dewey Jones heard him declare that the editor of the *Birmingham Age-Herald* "is one of my best friends." "How in heaven's name can this be possible?" Jones wondered. How could you have a friend in the land of the Scottsboro boys,[14] Tom Heflin, Jim Crow, primaries where Black citizens were not allowed to vote, peonage, and white mobs? Jones was equally amazed at the deference paid to Tittinger, who was treated "like a conquering hero." How does a "plain, boyish-looking white man dominate a district that is 95 percent black?"[15]

After the celebration, Mitchell turned his attention to the many requests for him to speak that had accumulated since his election. This necessitated formulating a policy on where and under what conditions he would appear. He constructed a questionnaire to sort requests. It asked for the name and number of active members of the organization sponsoring the event, the location, date, and time of the speech, the seating capacity of the site, the estimated size of the audience, who else was scheduled to speak and for how long, other events Mitchell was expected to attend, whether or not an ad mission fee was to be charged, how was the meeting to be paid for, who was responsible for meeting Mitchell's expenses, and a list of references for the organization.[16]

Proposing to charge admission almost always guaranteed that Mitchell would not speak. De Priest had been notorious for this, but he would not countenance it. He also had to be guaranteed a large audience since he "could not afford to take up his time" with small gatherings. Mitchell also demanded to travel in first class on trains and stay at first-class hotels. This stipulation, he explained to H. H. Merritt, was not based on his need for creature comforts. Rather, it was an important political statement. Given his status, he should be treated as a model for all members of his race. "I cannot see," he explained, "how we will ever break down racial discrimination" if the only Black congressman "cannot stay in a good hotel."[17]

Mitchell honored two speaking engagements in late 1934. One was in Kansas City, where he shared the dais with newly elected Senator Harry S. Truman. There, he asserted that Roosevelt was a greater friend of his race than Abraham Lincoln had been and that his (Mitchell's) victory signaled that Black Americans had begun to desert the Republican Party. Repeating promises about civil service reform, anti-lynching legislation, and an effort to refranchise the voters, he reiterated that he was "in favor of any program that does away with idleness, the most dangerous element in our country today."[18]

The message was similar in Detroit, where he spoke after meeting with Congressman John Dingell Sr. to agree upon strategy for an anti-lynching bill. On this point, Mitchell emphasized his desire to knit together a biracial alliance to accomplish the task. "The blunt-edged needle used by Congressman De Priest," the *Afro-American* wrote in reporting about this meeting, will "be cast aside for one sharp with diplomacy."[19]

He returned to Washington days before the swearing in of the Seventy-Fourth Congress and set about making "friends for myself and for the race." He did not come there, he told E. M. Hennessey of the *Boston Globe,* thinking of himself as an inferior, with a chip on his shoulder. He did not intend to spend his time on issues of where he could eat or get his hair cut. Nor would he be another "calamity howler." His job was to help Roosevelt "feed the hungry and clothe the naked and provide work for all the idle of every race and creed."[20]

Before the opening of Congress, Kelly and Nash made sure that Mitchell was well positioned to be an effective dispenser of patronage. Originally, Democratic congressional leaders had slotted him for a seat on the Committee for the District of Columbia, an assignment that made perfect sense to them. Mitchell had lived there for ten years and was familiar with the needs of Washington's Black residents. But it didn't fit with Mitchell's plans. He complained that he "would be swamped with friends asking for jobs which I have no power to give. I want to be free to attend to the demands of my Chicago constituents." It also didn't make sense to Kelly and Nash. Patronage considerations demanded his assignment to the dispenser of most political pork in the 1930s, the Committee on Post Offices and Post Roads. An appeal to Adolph J. Sabath, the dean of the Illinois delegation in Congress, had facilitated this change in placement.[21]

With this coveted assignment in hand, Mitchell developed a system for the dispersal of patronage that he used for the next eight years. It enjoyed the dual advantages of freeing him from the time-consuming task of distributing patronage himself, a job he did not want, and placing that responsibility in the hands of those who did want it, Chicago's ward committeemen.

When he received letters seeking post office employment, Mitchell first checked to see if the applicants lived in his district. Frequently, they did not. These he referred to a fellow congressman through a form letter. If writers were his responsibility, Mitchell warned them that it did no good to apply to him directly for employment. As he told W. D. Britton at the very beginning of his first term, "it is a rule for all persons seeking work through the Democratic organization to make application direct to the Ward Committeeman. Congressmen have no jobs which they control. All the patronage in the Organization is controlled by the patronage committee together with the ward committeemen." He expanded on this explanation with explicit advice to Garnie Tennon: "Simply voting Democratic is not enough for a job. Form the closest possible alliance with Democratic leaders of your ward. . . . You cannot hope to get work through them until you have done some work for them. . . . They and they alone have charge of whatever patronage there is."[22]

If recommended by a ward committeeman, Mitchell forwarded the applicant's name to Ernest J. Kreutgen, postmaster in Chicago, keeping a "Jobs Secured" file for favorable outcomes. They were often low-paying, even temporary positions. Nevertheless, Mitchell's efficiency in supplying them satisfied Kelly and Nash and guaranteed his reelection to his congressional seat.[23]

However, it was not the Chicago machine but the giants of the Black press who made life difficult for Mitchell from the day he took office. Having first ignored him during the campaign because they thought he was bound to lose and then failed to block his assumption of office based on a rumor about his childhood, they now ridiculed his every action.

Mitchell's behavior gave them fodder for this campaign. When he failed to greet well-wishers after his swearing in, Barnett described this as "ineptitude in handling people." The *Defender* delighted in reporting on his outrage when a supporter addressed him as "Arthur." When he appeared at a Black social club waving the stub of his paycheck around and then had it stolen by a taxi driver, both the *Afro-American* and *Defender* gleefully reported the incident. When he supposedly attacked its photographer for taking an unauthorized picture of his wife, the *Afro-American* begged him to stop vandalizing its equipment, editorializing that he should be ashamed of himself, that "as our only congressman, everything you say, everywhere you go, everything you do becomes news. That is the penalty you must pay for sitting in Congress."[24]

But what really brought the Black establishment down on him were not small incidents but the first major speech he made after assuming office. At the Bethel AME church in Harlem at the end of January 1935, he announced his break with political orthodoxy. He intended to be "brutally frank" in his public dealing, exposing the "camouflage and ballyhoo" of those who "lead us further into darkness." Both the *New York Herald Tribune* and the *New York Amsterdam News*, the city's largest Black newspaper, reported that the audience sat in stunned silence at this and that "he spoke with such vehemence that at one point he paused and remarked 'I suppose you won't want me to come back here.'"

He began by attacking a previous speaker who had suggested that New York City should be redistricted so that Harlem could have a Black representative. If a white man who raised the color question was a "demagogue of the worst kind," he asked, what was the Black politician who did the same thing? Take him as an example. His margin of victory had been supplied by white voters. He expected to accomplish a number of things to help his "people," but he "refused to forget the white people who gave me the majority . . . I received." Stop whining, he urged his listeners, and use your ballots to choose representatives sympathetic to all citizens.

Further, he did not intend to be the "national buffer for the Negro in Washington. Do not 'snow me under' with petitions," Mitchell pleaded. He intended to serve his Chicago constituents, not take on responsibility for an entire race. Black Americans living outside his district should take their concerns to their own representatives, thereby increasing Black visibility in Congress. His responsibility was to cooperate with 434 white representatives in order to end lynching, Black disenfranchisement, and the use of photographs for civil service applications. As to Black dissatisfaction with the first two years of the New Deal, Roosevelt was a great president "who doesn't even know color": "The source is pure. The pollution that came in the stream is from below." Finally, Mitchell warned against "certain newspapers who resort to cheap sensationalism without proper investigation. I stub my advancing feet against their bigotry and move on without noticing them."[25]

The Bethel address found many admirers. The day after his speech, Samuel Westerfield, president of the Young Peoples' Lyceum of the church, wrote to Mitchell that "the community is still ringing from your powerful address. Practically all opinions are that it was the most potent and scholarly [speech] ever heard in this community." Michael Jones, executive secretary of Howard

University's alumni association, agreed on its impact. "My views are considerably changed. You are about 95% right. Like all pioneers, you showed you were prepared to pay the penalty of leadership." Eloise Keller concurred: "It means so much and is so fine when we can boast of a Negro leader who has the guts to tell Negroes just what they need to be told."[26]

But the speech offended many others, including Elijah Morris, who wrote to the *Defender* that the First Congressional District had "sold its birthright" for a "mess of porridge." Voters would have two years to repent "after which little Arthur will be relegated to the wood pile where he belongs." Abbot's journal agreed, describing Mitchell as "a political abortion . . . imprisoned in the winds of hate and slander."[27]

The Bethel speech also outraged the NAACP, which had remained silent until then on the 1934 election. Now Walter White attacked in an article titled "Smart Talk from Mr. Mitchell." The congressman, White complained, had insulted the Black press by his attitude and affronted the Black residents of Washington by his refusal to accept his original committee assignment. His comment that he was not in Congress to represent all Black Americans was offensive. Apparently, the denial of "constitutional citizenship rights" did not matter to him so long as the violation did not occur in his district. Even congressmen from states with fewer than one thousand Black residents paid attention to these rights, because they realized that denial of them was "part of the whole government with which every level-headed public servant should be concerned." But what should you expect, White asked, from a congressman the *Jackson* [MS] *Daily News* labeled "a white folks Negro who will do anything they tell him to do?" "Whether he does anything for us or not, he will be judged by his actions," White wrote. Therefore, "we set down the fervent hope that, if he cannot be discrete, he at least will remain silent."[28]

White's critique marked the opening salvo in what Mia Bay has accurately termed the "acrimonious relationship" between White and Mitchell, a feud that carried on for years with profound implications for the Civil Rights Movement. During it, White often proved as controversial and confrontational as his adversary. While many supported him, others thought the executive secretary had an administrative style that "generated friction within the organization" because "he was tough, arrogant, ambitious, . . . prone to vanity and egotism, and he often behaved in an autocratic manner." W. E. B. Du Bois was sharper in his criticism, describing White based on his experience as the editor of the *Crisis* as "one of the most selfish men I ever knew. He was absolutely self centered and egotistical to the point that he was almost unconscious of it. . . . I can work with stupidity. I can work with open and frank dishonesty. But the combination of that with charm, double-dealing and insincerity is something I can't waste time on."[29]

With a press war looming that would determine the coverage he received, Mitchell divided the Black fourth estate into two groups. There was, he believed, a northern branch, dominated by sensation-seeking scandal-mongers, bent on portraying race relations in the South in the worst possible light and free with advice on subjects about which they were ignorant. Into this group he placed the *Chicago Defender, Pittsburgh Courier, [Baltimore] Afro-American,* Barnett's Associated Negro Press, and the NAACP's magazine, the *Crisis.*[30]

On the other hand, he tended to regard Black southern newspapers that dealt with the realities of the day and were necessarily less militant as "friendly." Joseph E. Mitchell's *St. Louis Argus* belonged in this category. But it was P. B. Young's *Norfolk* (VA) *Journal and Guide,* the African American paper with the largest circulation in the South, that drew his special praise as "the best Negro newspaper in the United States. . . . You never smear a lot of filth and yellow stuff on the front page." In fact, "you do not carry the type of filth that characterizes a great many weekly newspapers."[31]

In this potential battle, the ANP saw Mitchell as a formidable opponent. "There is nothing he likes better," the service reported, "save two fights [rather than] one in defense of what he believed to be right." If the Black press wanted conflict, they would have it. Mitchell enjoyed a good feud, thinking he "could hurt [hostile Black newspapers] more than they could hurt him."[32]

While eager for combat on substantial issues, Mitchell saw most critiques of his early behavior as a tempest in a teapot. He reassured C. Francis Stradford, "I am able to take care of myself under all circumstances. As long as there is real progress why give a moment to thinking about criticism? I have done more constructive work the few weeks I have been here than most Congressmen do the first year." Woodson agreed, congratulating his friend for showing during his first two months in office "courage, common sense and statesmanlike vision. If you continue on this way, we shall have further reason for rejoicing that you have been thus honored by the people of Illinois."[33]

To Mitchell, his "constructive work" centered on two pieces of landmark legislation he authored during his first month in office. One proposed the creation of a "Negro Industrial Commission" to safeguard Black rights in the workplace and the other to make lynching a federal crime.

Of the two bills, the one creating the commission generated more immediate attention. House Bill 5733 called for the creation of a five-person board, three of whom had to be Black. Four members were to be appointed for six-year terms and earn an annual salary of $5,000. The chairman's compensation was set at $7,500.

The fourth article of the bill outlined the major responsibilities of the commission. It would:

- Study the economic condition of Black Americans and the labor problems in which they were "fundamentally interested"
- Stimulate and encourage "thrift and industry among Negroes"
- Promote the general welfare of Black Americans in industrial pursuits and "encourage [their] general uplift"
- Work out plans looking toward the solution of different problems confronting Black Americans
- Consider all questions referred to it by any department of the US government, governor, or any state's attorney general to recommend what may be necessary for the stability of labor in the different states
- Discourage "subversive doctrine and propaganda" and
- Work toward the formation of a policy for "mutual understanding and confidence between the races."

The Mitchell press release announcing its introduction stated that the proposal would be referred to the Committee on the Judiciary, chaired by Hatton W. Sumners of Texas, "one of the greatest constitutional lawyers in the United States" who "to a large extent influences the action of his committee on proposed legislation." Sumners was, the release added, "loud in his praises of the Mitchell bill."[34]

The effort to pass anti-lynching legislation, Mitchell's second effort, had taken on particular urgency because of an event in Florida just before the 1934 election. Claude Neal, a young Black man, had been accused of murdering a white woman. When a lynch mob formed at the local jail, he was moved to Alabama for his own safety. Members of the mob followed him there, seized him, and brought him back to Florida where he was publicly lynched before a large crowd that had been brought together by a radio announcement advertising the event.[35]

In this explosive atmosphere, Walter White had written to Mitchell just after his election asking him to support a NAACP-sponsored bill, jointly authored by Senators Edward Costigan of Colorado and Robert Wagner of New York, that would make lynching a federal crime. The legislation defined a "mob" as "a group of three or more persons lacking a legal basis who set about to harm another or to deprive him or her of life." Any state or local official who failed to protect potential victims of a mob could be fined up to $5,000 and sentenced to prison for five years. If thirty days passed after a lynching and no action had been taken by state or local authorities, "a federal district court and its law enforcement agency" could enter the case. If it was found that a lynching had occurred, the county in which it had taken place was to be fined $10,000. If the victim had been seized in one county and murdered in another, both counties were to be fined.[36]

When Mitchell responded with a "cool, non-committal attitude" to the request for his support, White was "considerably taken aback." The chagrin increased when Congressman Thomas Ford of California, a supporter of Costigan-Wagner, confirmed to White that the only Black member of the House of Representatives "does not approve our bill and intends to introduce his own."[37]

Mitchell doubted White's sincerity in sponsoring anti-lynching legislation. He had reason to be skeptical. Buffeted by both the Depression and its handling of the Scottsboro case, contributions to the NAACP had dropped by 50 percent, leaving it in a dire financial condition. Its board hoped that an anti-lynching campaign, a specialty of White, would turn attention away from Scottsboro and prove "a better issue for fund-raising than pushing an economic agenda."[38]

Further, as a political realist, Mitchell also doubted that Costigan-Wagner would ever become law. If it passed the House, it would be filibustered in the Senate. If that filibuster was broken, President Roosevelt would not sign the bill for fear of alienating southern senators whose votes he needed to advance New Deal legislation. As early as December 1933, Mark Ethridge had written in the *Washington Post* that the NAACP "does not expect—and really does not care for the bill to go through, but is rather using it for the moral effect." Leonidas C. Dyer, a retired Republican congressman from Missouri who had seen a similar bill he introduced filibustered in 1922, 1923, and 1924, shared the skepticism. "You are too smart and you have had too much experience with this subject," he cautioned White, "to believe that the present Democratic congress will enact any legislation of this kind." Black supporters of Costigan-Wagner "were wasting their time and postage in even writing to members of Congress."[39]

Mitchell saw mob violence "one of the most vicious and unnecessary crimes in our country." But he did not think that a law "would prevent lynching any more than a law against murder prevents murder, [but] I do believe there should be laws against every crime." He also hoped to "have the support of the best people of the South in my efforts to uplift my race" in offering a modest piece of anti-lynching legislation that might navigate its way into law. Something in the federal codes that made mob violence a crime was better than nothing. Once enshrined in law, minimal legislation could later be strengthened. With this in mind, he had set about writing a bill that passed constitutional muster, could win approval in the House, and had a chance, however remote, of gaining Senate approval.[40]

Mitchell approached this task cautiously. Louis Lautier, a reporter who later became the first Black journalist admitted to the National Press Club, told White that the Illinois representative had consulted with Benjamin Gaskins, "whom I regard as the ablest colored lawyer at the bar of the District of Columbia" and who had advised Mitchell that he (Gaskins) thought Costigan-Wagner was vague and doubted that it was constitutional.[41]

Although there were differences in penalties and definition from Costigan-Wagner, the bill that Gaskins and Mitchell authored was unique in creating a specific definition for the prima facie evidence that a crime had been committed during a lynching. Once an officer took a suspect into custody, it stated, it became his duty to safely deliver that individual before a magistrate or judge. If the suspect was injured, killed, or taken from the arresting officer, the state had denied the prisoner the equal protection of the law, which is a federal crime. According to a Mitchell press release, the draft had been "submitted to a half-dozen of the leading law schools of the country for criticism and suggestions." It "differs radically from every measure ever before introduced in Congress" and was being "hailed as a masterpiece of federal legislation."[42]

6

"The Shame of American Democracy"

WHEN MITCHELL SET about securing endorsements for his Industrial Commission from "a few outstanding men and women of the race who are genuinely interested in substantive measures," he was encouraged by the response. Moton, Dr. R. R. Wright, president of Wilberforce University, Mordecai Johnson, president of Howard, Alain Locke, and other prominent Black dignitaries signaled their support. The bill, he concluded, "had a good chance to pass."[1]

If anything, Mitchell felt the need to tamp down the enthusiasm of those who wanted to petition Congress for its adoption. Don't apply pressure, he advised Maude Brown of Louisville: "Often these requests hurt rather than help. I am here on the scene and am sure I have enough influence to pass this legislation through at the proper time." While its fate might be different in the southern-dominated Senate, well-informed members of the House would view 5733 as the best piece of legislation "offered for the relief and welfare of the Negroes during the last quarter century." Even McCormick's *Chicago Tribune* agreed that the bill was "the most far reaching and constructive piece of legislation in the interests of the Negro for the past quarter of a century."[2]

An editorial published in late February by the *Defender* showed just how much Mitchell's enemies disagreed. Why had Mitchell, who had maintained that he had "no inclination to represent Black citizens beyond the confines of his own congressional district," introduced this bad piece of legislation? There were no commissions to defend the rights of Poles, Italians, Germans, or Jews. 5733 would make Black Americans a "ward of the government instead of a citizen group. Today, the Indians are the only people who live under a commission."[3]

A. N. Fields continued the assault in the same paper two weeks later. The author of 5733 was "a political abortion, clearly unfit" to be a congressman. Blacks were opposed to peonage, either mental or physical. They could not exist "as a political subdivision distinct from the body politic." Rather than wasting his time making up new laws, Mitchell should "apply some of his pent up energy" to seeing that existing ones were fully enforced.[4]

The *Guardian* was more severe. Mitchell's proposal was "the most vicious bill ever presented to the Congress in the interest of the Negro. . . . The government looks after the blind, the deaf and dumb, the insane, the tubercular, and the criminal. . . . To this category Mitchell would add the Negro." It would require "a firing squad to line up at sunrise every respecting Negro . . . and have them shot."[5]

The NAACP also opposed the bill. Would Congress take Mitchell's seriously? White wondered. He thought it was "a thoroughly bad piece of legislation" that dumps Black Americans into a "Jim Crow bureau" instead of having their problems "considered at first hand by the departments before which they should come."[6]

Elizabeth Ross Haynes, who agreed with much of what Mitchell had said in his Bethel speech, found his commission proposal inconsistent with his claim to represent only the First Congressional District. We are not wards of the nation, she wrote, but seek to be "an integral part of the body politic." Such a commission would be "a little Africanized grab bag of the selfish few." In a similar vein, David Jenkins, a Black contractor from Terre Haute, Indiana, wondered why Mitchell didn't stick as promised to representing his district. "I prefer," he wrote, "to have my privileges and activities governed by the same laws that regulate the lives of all other Americans . . . I think this is the feeling of most intelligent Negroes."[7]

Mitchell had a simple answer to these objections: "If you were in Washington and knew how little the heads of bureaus know about colored people, you would do the same thing I did—advocate an industrial commission." Other groups had their own organizations looking after their interests. If Black Americans had such guardians, they weren't very effective. The insult of Jim Crow laws, murder at the end of a lyncher's rope, and the agony of the mob's torch proved that.[8]

While waiting for hearings on his proposal for an Industrial Commission, Mitchell also laid the groundwork for increasing Black influence in Congress during these early months by his refusal to deal with the problems of those who were not his constituents. Hundreds of letters poured into his office from Black citizens in all parts of the country seeking his assistance. His response to Elliott Robins of Midway, Florida, was typical of answers that went to individuals who did not live in the First Congressional District: "Because of a Congressional courtesy which does not permit a Representative to take the initiative in the affairs of another's constituents, I am obliged to suggest that you take this matter up with the Congressman who represents the district in which you live."[9]

Some of his resistance to being cast in the role De Priest had adopted was practical. "Imagine," he later wrote to Edwards, "the confusion that would be caused if a Congressman from one state attempted to interfere with matters in another state." But there was more to his thinking. "I have found," Mitchell argued, "it matters not from what section of the country a Congressman comes, he likes to look after the interests of his constituents and is much averse to have any other Congressman meddle."[10]

This was particularly true in the South: "I contend that the sooner our people in the South learn to use the Congressmen who actually represent them . . . the sooner we will make some headway in strengthening ourselves with the lawmaking body. It would be a sad day indeed if we must depend on one man to represent us in a body of four hundred and thirty-five." Referencing the racial composition of his own district, he told an audience, "I don't see any more harm in a Negro representing a white man than a white man representing a Negro."[11]

Rather than bring their complaints to him, Mitchell consistently advised Black citizens to apply pressure on their own representatives. Such advice went to W. A. Bayfield, who wanted to form a Black Democratic club in Birmingham, and to many others. You are citizens, he assured them, and have the right—even the duty—to address the government for a redress of grievances. Do not take for granted that your representatives would not be interested in your concerns. They probably don't know what they are because you haven't told them: "They should be called upon to do their full duty toward their constituents."[12]

If raising issues with one's own congressman was one prong in the campaign to have the southern Black voters heard, the drive to register those legally entitled to cast ballots was a second. When William Kelso of Alexandria, Louisiana, first complained about Black applicants being rejected from the Civilian Conservation Corps, the letter provoked a typical response from Mitchell: "I wish our people could understand that Congressmen represent geographical districts and not racial groups." This followed the usual "I will do what you should have done, make your Congressman aware of the problem."[13]

But Kelso would not be put off. He wrote back that "there is not a Negro voter in this district." Therefore, its representative "is under no obligation to the Negro." As a matter of fact, "it is absolutely a disgrace" that Black voters weren't allowed to register in their congressman's hometown. This provoked a fourth letter in the exchange in which Mitchell suggested his general strategy for Black Americans who sought the right to vote as guaranteed by the Constitution. "Nothing is more important," he wrote, "than the exercise of the franchise." Kelso could render "no greater service" to the Black residents of his district than to initiate a movement to register all who were technically eligible to vote. At some point, Mitchell would be interested in coming to the region and speaking on the subject. "I hope," he ended, "that the people have not given up hope and will make some effort to qualify and vote."[14]

Mitchell believed that peaceful protest would eventually end voter suppression in the South. The barriers would fall if enough would-be voters committed themselves to local registration campaigns. Such repeated attempts would overwhelm existing bureaucratic structures over time. Passivity and acceptance of the status quo were not the answers to injustice, but neither was violence. Frustrating the bureaucracy in the performance of its functions was.

He elaborated on the theme in a 1936 exchange with W. L. Horne, a dentist in Weldon, North Carolina, who wrote to him about a young Black woman local officials had refused to register as a voter. According to Horne, she was a graduate of Hampton Institute, had earned an MA from Cornell, and was about to receive a PhD from the same university. The local registrar, whose "reading was poor, pronunciation more so," had read her the eligibility law and, when she could not repeat it verbatim, turned down her application.

Mitchell replied that registering to vote was not only "the privilege but the duty" of every Black voter "who measure[s] up to the requirements as laid down in the law of your state." The woman should find an able lawyer and bring suit. If she had trouble finding one, Mitchell knew a "gentleman" at nearby Livingston College who had been very successful in "forcing the registration of colored people in that locality. He can give you first class advice."[15]

Mitchell was himself free with advice on the growing demand that Congress do something to protect older Americans in their retirement years, particularly Black senior citizens. On this subject, he was dismissive of Huey Long's "Every Man a King" campaign. Anyone who saw the "Kingfish" as a "second savior" was dead wrong. "I have no brief for the Senator," Mitchell wrote, "and do not think that he is at all interested in the Race." Likewise, the Townsend Plan, which proposed that every American over the age of sixty receive $200 a month from the government, was "one of the greatest fakes that has ever been perpetrated upon the people." It was "no more than a fairy tale . . . absolutely unworkable and impossible." Instead, he supported the idea of "our great President" to provide support for retired Americans through social security legislation.[16]

Constituent letters on this subject bear witness to the divided nature of the First Congressional District. Writing in pencil on a faded piece of lined notebook paper, Ador Rodgers spoke to the desperation of many: "Sir: I am a 60 yer old Dependent woman stranded an in Pore Health and haven got fode or reament surfishent. Mr. Mitchel sir I am asking you please rember me in the old folks depenent pension as my dayes of working fore my sorporte is past an gone."

On the other hand, C. S. Boothby, the president of the Jahn & Ollier Engraving Company, thought he reflected the sentiments of responsible Americans. His protest, typed on an embossed piece of company stationery, attacked the proposed legislation: What "unworkable, unconstitutional and even silly laws and schemes will next be passed to harass the people who are carrying the load of this nation on their back?"[17]

His maiden speech to the House, on April 15, 1935, showed Mitchell to be more in sympathy with Rodgers than Boothby. Using Sylvester Harris as an example, he advocated for "this great piece of legislation." In the past government had come to the rescue of "the privileged rich"—the railroads, great industrial corporations, and insurance companies. Now industry was finally being asked to do its part to support those who had built the country.

But he also saw flaws in the proposed bill, particularly the provisions that excluded Black agricultural and domestic workers. He was new to Congress but hoped that those "who are versed in that sort of thing" would offer amendments to provide for "servants, farm workers, and casuals." They were those who needed help the most. The bill also left to the states broad discretion in how to implement its provisions. This discriminated against the residents of poor southern states such as Alabama and Mississippi, which might opt out of the plan. "Instead of helping the poor states that have no money," he argued, "you are trying to forget them." It was like telling sick people that they required a prescription, "but you cannot get the medicine you need until you can walk to the drug store." All states should bear the burden of the plan, whether they had their own pension plan or not.[18]

According to the *Chicago Tribune*, Mitchell "who has made a hit with his colleagues with his quiet ways," received congratulations for his speech from both northern and southern Democrats. This included Speaker Joe Byrns of Tennessee. Judge Armond Scott, whose nomination to the District of Columbia's Municipal Court Bench Mitchell had promoted, thought it "a masterpiece of logic and eloquence." It was also well received by the public. R. W. Morgan, who identified himself as a seventy-six-year-old Black retiree who had attended three national Republican conventions, was now living on a railroad pension of twenty dollars a month. He experienced a conversion when he read Mitchell's words: "When I see one of my own race championing a cause that is so close to my heart, I am indeed not a Republican any longer but a good Democrat and one who is willing to go to the limit for you."[19]

Despite his popular stand on Social Security, Mitchell seemed to go out of his way to alienate traditional Democratic bastions of support during these early days. When Daniel McLean of the Brotherhood of Railway Carmen lobbied him to promote a bill favorable to his union, Mitchell's latent hostility to organized labor surfaced. There are "three colored lodges in your district," McLean threatened, and they are being informed of your hostility "so they may take whatever action they may choose when the proper time comes."[20]

The draft of his response showed Mitchell unimpressed by the threat. He had always been a supporter of the working man, "not withstanding the fact organized labor has been one of the most oppressive agencies the Negro as had to contend with and is still so." The lodges you refer to, he told McLean, are not in my district, but even if they were, "I shall take no orders from you. I do not even care to continue to receive your correspondence. In so far as your threats go, I am not bothered about them."[21]

Just as striking was the upset he provoked when he charged Mordecai Johnson, the president of Howard University, with being a Communist. During a "Conference on the Economic Condition of the Negro" in June 1935, Johnson had "pointed to several features in the Soviet system as a solution to many of the problems found in the United States." Three days later, Mitchell appeared at Howard, expressing the hope that the university "was not inculcating such radical thinking as he heard it was doing." When Johnson responded that freedom of speech was more important than government funding, Mitchell introduced a resolution in Congress to investigate whether or not Communism was being "inculcated" at Howard.[22]

Close friends tried to persuade Mitchell to moderate his position. T. V. Smith, a professor at the University of Chicago and a former teacher of his, hoped that Mitchell would "pray twice" before continuing his attack "against our beloved Howard." But Mitchell was adamant. Johnson "has no regard for the truth. There is no doubt in my mind that he is a Communist." Mitchell was determined to protect Howard from "the most damnable influence that could be marshalled against any institution designed for character and citizenship building."[23]

Eventually, Harold L. Ickes, Roosevelt's secretary of the interior, investigated Mitchell's charges and found them unsubstantiated, but the damage had been done. The *Philadelphia Tribune* saw the incident as just another example of Mitchell's desire to curry favor with powerful southern Democrats. He has, the paper wrote, "the ability to carry his hat in his hand and lick the hands of his master like a cur dog." Howard's Chicago Alumni Association rebuked him, passing a unanimous resolution to "publicly condemn and denounce" Mitchell. It declared that "every act or utterance done and made [by him], has been inimical to the best interests of the Negro Citizens of America."[24]

When not in Washington during 1935, Mitchell was active on the speaker's circuit, becoming a popular spokesperson for the New Deal with southern audiences. He spoke to crowds in Raleigh and New Bern, North Carolina, and Nashville but also found time to address his favorite audience: Black college students. This included those at Morris Brown in Atlanta, Hampton Institute in Virginia, Lane College in Jackson, Tennessee, and Wilberforce University in Xenia, Ohio.

These speeches introduced him as a national voice calling on a new generation of Black leaders who had rethought their political affiliations. Republicans, he argued, "had used the Negro as a football, kicking him from place to place in the last twenty-five years." "The mistake," he observed, "lies in that we waited too long to learn that Lincoln is dead and with his death . . . died the best principles of the Republican party." Black hope for betterment now lay with the Democrats. Hoover had driven the United States into the mud; Roosevelt was getting the country back on the road. "We are not on the highway, but we are making our way to it."[25]

The *Afro-American* thought that Mitchell had "killed himself politically, socially and as an influential factor" with these attacks on Republicans, but others thought he had a point and had expressed it eloquently. J. F. Lane, the president of Lane College, wrote that Mitchell had "represented the present Democratic administration more ably than any one to whom I have listened in recent years. . . .Your party has a fine opportunity of showing that it is no longer Bourbon in interest and attitude." R. E. Clay reported to Speaker Byrns that Mitchell had spoken before three thousand people in Nashville and "made [a] wonderful impression." Clara Mann, later his third wife, thought his speech in New Bern "the greatest in the history of the city." Mary Ellen Vaughn raved that "you cannot thoroughly understand nor will you ever realize what your visit meant to Murfreesboro, to both white and black. Some of the White people said to me if you had spoken at the Courthouse there would not have been a standing place available."[26]

During these travels, Mitchell acted as a recruiter for potential Black leaders to what he saw as a more welcoming Democratic Party. When Alva B. Johnson wondered if he should help organize a Black Democratic club in his neighborhood, Mitchell's answer was frank: If Johnson undertook the task, he should expect "the stiffest sort of opposition from the old hide-bound Republican leaders who cannot understand modern politics nor modern methods." If he wasn't prepared to receive "all sorts of kicks, blows, and rebuffs," he shouldn't try it. But if he did accept the challenge, "there awaits you remarkable success."[27]

He also used his speeches to defend his anti-lynching legislation. At the Morris Brown Founders' Day celebration in Atlanta, he told his listeners that lynching would not be stopped by legislation but only by "Christian education." His "Southern friends" would provide "salvation," but northern whites lacked an understanding of the problem. That was why he had introduced "the only bill that is going to pass."[28]

W. A. Fountain, the president of Morris Brown, thought that speech "one of the finest . . . I have ever heard." But it drew this from the ANP: "The unthinking element of his audience was pleased with the address. The thinking element was very much disappointed and distressed." The *Atlanta Daily World* was also critical, prompting Mitchell to complain to Fountain that "we have so many people trying to mold thought and sentiment who are themselves incapable of doing serious thinking."[29]

Despite fierce opposition, Mitchell persisted in advocating for his anti-lynching bill. To a May audience he predicted that Costigan-Wagner, if it passed in the House, would be filibustered and die in the Senate. Besides, legislation was not the cure for lynching; that came "from molding the sentiment of influential people in the community." Still, the principle of a law was important. He was from Alabama and knew "what sacrifice the fight for principle entails, but I've decided to put my trust in God and go ahead."[30]

That faith was not rewarded in Illinois despite the fact that the *Defender*, in a rare moment of support, defended his bill as a "masterpiece of federal legislation," one that "will ultimately result in the stamping out of lynching." In mid-May, Mitchell was "flayed as very few public men have ever been" by the president of the Illinois State Conference of the NAACP at a Springfield gathering where the audience appeared "somewhat amazed and greatly chagrined" by his opposition to Costigan-Wagner.[31]

Mitchell's bill received a more favorable reception in the South where the *Anniston* (AL) *Star* praised Mitchell for "recognizing that he can help his race only in proportion as he works with and not against the dominant race on this continent." The *Star* went on to claim that there was not another civilized country in the world where a large minority had as small a voice as in the United States and that it would be good to have one or two Black representatives "of the Mitchell type" in every state legislature.[32]

His speeches also brought Mitchell to the attention of Senator Hugo Black of Alabama, who complimented Mitchell on being so different from De Priest and those Blacks who "had gone over this land holding aloft the ancient torch of prejudice, passion, and hate, thereby contributing no benefit to the people of their race." Mitchell thanked Black for his praise: "I shall feel greatly heartened because of this and expect to work harder in the future than I have in the past to make this land not only safe and prosperous but a happy one as well for all American citizens."[33]

Over the following months, the battle between Mitchell and the NAACP degenerated into name-calling. Mitchell, who claimed to have been the only member of the organization in Alabama for many years and to have sent copies of the *Crisis* to white friends, now charged that the NAACP was "fighting this bill for all it is worth, not because it is a bad bill, but because it is not their bill." White's organization responded that Mitchell's "ravings" were just another example of his obsession with "currying favor with the reactionary and vicious elements of the South." If Costigan-Wagner failed, Mitchell would be responsible. "Willful lynching" senators, such as Huey Long of Louisiana, "Cotton Ed" Smith of South Carolina, and Walter George of Georgia, were saying "if Mitchell is satisfied with a milder bill, why enact Costigan-Wagner or any bill?"[34]

As this controversy simmered, Mitchell returned to the Industrial Commission legislation. Sumners had honored his promise of an "early hearing," scheduling it for June 18, 1935, and asking Mitchell to select the witnesses he wanted to appear. As that date approached, Mitchell told T. V. Smith that the "chances are two-to-one that we will be able to pass my bill." As evidence, he claimed to have addressed audiences in twelve states and received letters or telegrams "from thousands in thirty states," including fifteen governors, 99 percent of which supported his proposal.[35]

When the Judiciary Committee assembled, Sumners paid Mitchell the compliment of stepping aside and asking him to interview those he had selected to testify. This was, Chicago Democrats boasted later, "the first time in the history of Congress that a colored Congressman has conducted hearings on legislation introduced by him."[36]

Those he invited to appear spoke to Mitchell's purpose. While the commission would address all Black concerns, he intended for it to concentrate its efforts on the condition of those living below the Mason-Dixon line. This included the agricultural and household workers excluded from participation in the Social Security program.

Moton went first, telling the committee that those living in the South were "pretty near the bottom" of the national economic ladder. New York bankers did not think of spending money south of Baltimore and Washington. 5733 would force them to concentrate on the nine million Black Americans who were being ignored. T. V. Smith termed the standing of Black workers "the shame of American democracy." Perry Howard also emphasized the benefit of the bill to the South but warned that it was opposed by "radicals" for whom there "was no place in this country." Joseph E. Mitchell, editor of the *St. Louis Argus*, could not imagine any piece of legislation "that would be more beneficial generally to my group." Emmet O'Neal, a Democratic congressman from Kentucky, praised "one of the first attempts to get at a problem which is very fundamental in our country." He had many Black constituents who "have worked on a farm all of their lives and who are lost in the city." They would be helped by the commission. Alain Locke saw the bill as a combination of "constructive statesmanship and practical justice" since the crux of Black problems was economic and industrial. 5733 created a body that was needed because existing groups "rarely initiate new or special remedial programs for the Negro." John Dingell, the Democrat from Detroit, thought it "absolutely mandatory" that Congress address the problem Mitchell had brought forward. "We cannot solve the problem merely by denying that it exists." Scipio Jones, an Arkansas attorney famous for defending Black victims of a 1919 race riot against murder charges, argued that the commission would take the time to present Black grievances to the government, something whites had never done. Kelly Miller presented himself as a competent witness because he "was born a barefoot colored boy in South Carolina." "Segregation is a fact," he testified, "and it will be a fact until we can remove it. God only knows when, but in the meantime let us pass this measure and do the best we can." John Kee, Mitchell's colleague from West Virginia, was the last witness. His district, he asserted, had twenty-eight thousand Black miners working under ground. No matter how many schools were built, they always end up back in the mines "because they are not given the same opportunity to rise above their origin and environment." The commission would help to change that.

At the conclusion of this testimony, Mitchell read into the record letters of support from P. B. Young, Mordecai Johnson, and Mary McLeod Bethune, "the indisputable leader of the Black Cabinet," an informal but influential group of leaders Roosevelt consulted on a range of issues. A personal friend of Mrs. Roosevelt, "Ma Bethune" expressed "genuine approval" for Mitchell's concept, terming it "vitally important." Among other letters was one from C. C. Spaulding, the president of the North Carolina Mutual Life Insurance Company and "the most powerful black businessman of his era." White southerners were suffering because of the Depression but received maximum benefits from the government. It was common knowledge that their Black counterparts "do not receive anything like equal consideration." His office knew that large numbers of them were "literally starving." If the commission was successful only in obtaining "sufficient food to sustain life, a most humane service would be rendered."[37]

Before closing, Mitchell noted that Charles H. Houston, special counsel for the NAACP, had asked to file a brief in opposition to the legislation. Unpublished because of its late arrival, it argued that the commission was merely "political pap for politicians to dangle in front of the public." All it would do was create "a few political jobs and mislead the Negro people into a false notion that Congress is actually concerned with their welfare."[38]

After the hearing, Moton congratulated Mitchell on the "masterful way" in which he had handled the inquiry. Sumners's willingness to let him preside was just another example of "your shunning of publicity and the effective way in which you move in and out of Congress."[39]

Hoping to capitalize on what he saw as his success, Mitchell appealed to Sumners to have 5733 reported out of the Judiciary Committee. There were more than twenty-five thousand Black residents on relief in his district alone, "the majority of whom will never be employed in Chicago." They had been charges of the government that had fed, housed, and clothed them for the last five years. This could not continue. "Some plan must be worked out by which these people can be returned to the farms and become producers as well as consumers." At the same time, Mitchell cautioned A. C. MacNeal, president of the Chicago branch of the NAACP, that MacNeal's association represented an "extremely short-sighted and most hypocritical" group. "I have no sympathy," he concluded, "with your organization in the foolish attitude it has taken in this matter."[40]

White had even less sympathy for Mitchell. Reading in an Arkansas newspaper that his adversary had congratulated "Cotton Ed" Smith on a speech the senator had given in opposition to Costigan-Wagner, the executive secretary settled on a strategy of scuttling the Negro Commission as his revenge.[41]

On July 17, the Chicago Branch of the NAACP passed a resolution denouncing the hearings, chaired by a congressman who did not represent the majority of Black Chicagoans, "at which citizens purporting to have knowledge of Negro affairs" had appeared. A commission that "curbs subversive propaganda will curb dissemination of knowledge and limit protest." Rather than pursue the creation of a body that would set Black Americans back seventy-five years, Mitchell should introduce legislation to punish southern states that had disfranchised Black citizens and should inquire into acts of discrimination in New Deal agencies.[42]

Denouncing Mitchell as a "political charlatan," William Pickens, field secretary for the NAACP, launched a press assault. The congressman represented neither white nor Black voters and had "messed himself up" since his election by many mistakes, the idea of an industrial commission being the most egregious. It was "the dumbest thing ever offered as a threat to our race." The idea that the race needed special guardians to protect them from Communists and Socialists was almost as offensive as the assertion that they "are lost in the city." The commission would only be a "buffer for those in government who want to avoid facing problems, a dumping ground for all protests": "Bureaucratic government is bad for white American citizens. For American Negroes it would be fair hell."[43]

The *Defender* agreed. Mitchell "happens to be a temporary occupant of a seat in Congress." In years to come, serious thinkers will view his bill as "an associate of the Dred Scott decision." He and his friends were "political lepers whose very contact poisons the streams of usefulness in our social, economic, and political process."[44]

Roy Wilkins, assistant secretary of the NAACP, told MacNeal on August 12 that there was not "the faintest chance" that the bill would be voted on during the present session of Congress. However, he warned, Mitchell would reintroduce it in the next session "so that the positions created can be filled and utilized as an argument in the 1936 campaign." To prevent that the NAACP should be ready to "work with liberal organizations on the dangerous nature of this bill and especially the clause on subversive propaganda."[45]

"The NAACP is doing all it can against the measure," Mitchell admitted to J. E. Mitchell on July 31. "They are even telling Congressmen that the Colored People of the United States do not want it." But his optimism had faded. Now he only hoped that the Judiciary Committee would report favorably on the bill. Even that news would be "very heartening and encouraging to the Negroes of the Country."[46]

The appeal fell on deaf ears. Two weeks later, Mitchell admitted that 5733 would die in committee, blaming the result on the opposition of the NAACP and the *Defender*. The *Argus* 's Mitchell added the ANP to the list of the guilty, charging that P. L. Prattis, its city editor, "had connived and consorted with political enemies of the Illinois representative to injure his good name" and deny him reelection in 1936 by telling "all manner of lies."[47]

In response, Prattis swore that the ANP had been "as fair as humanly possible" with Mitchell. But it was true, he admitted, that the ANP had never censored Pickens for his diatribe, as opponents of 5733 were "men and women of more than ordinary responsibility and integrity in their communities."[48]

Editor Mitchell forwarded both letters to Arthur Mitchell, swearing him to secrecy. The congressman assured his St. Louis friend that Pickens wasn't worth attention, that his "lies" would soon be yesterday's news and "will be the means of putting the finishing touch on him." Pickens, however, was proud of his role: "The little editorial on Mitchell's Negro Affairs bill has had a large circulation and a stirring influence."[49]

Despite the demise of 5733, Mitchell saw his first session as a success. "If I had not done anything else except change the minds of 100 or more men in Congress" about the abilities of Blacks to legislate, he wrote, "I should feel that my presence was richly rewarded." He told P. B. Young that "he had received a most sympathetic hearing" from his colleagues because of his ability to work behind the scenes, not attracting publicity. "I have made a host of friends, North and South," he boasted to Ad Wimbs, "in the House and Senate who will go the whole distance in helping pass any legislation which I propose."[50]

Official Washington seemed to agree. When Mitchell asked Speaker Byrns for a letter testifying as to "my work in the Congress" that he could use "not only to my personal advantage but for the advantage of the Democratic Party," he received a positive reply: "You have made a fine record and won the confidence and friendship of your colleagues."[51]

Other congressmen concurred with the Speaker. Jed Johnson of Oklahoma had "been very much impressed with his ability. He is sincere and conscientious and is getting along fine here. I must say he is a great improvement over De Priest." A similar note of approval came from Charles Faddis of Pennsylvania: "I have formed quite a high opinion of Mr. Mitchell [and] can assure you that he is held in high opinion by the members of the House. . . . The fact that he is such a contrast to his predecessor has marked him as a man deserving favorable consideration."[52]

But what Mitchell might have considered the highest praise came from Nat Patton (TX-7), the "ultra-conservative" member for East Texas. When fifty white schoolchildren visited him, he asked Mitchell to come and talk with them in the Speaker's office. The Illinoisan thought that "quite an honor." So did P. B. Young, who speculated that "it is a very good sign for better racial relationships and political understanding when Southern whites accord you such recognition as you have received at their hands."[53]

Buoyed by these endorsements, Mitchell wrote to Marvin McIntyre, Roosevelt's assistant secretary in charge of appointments, thanking the president for the "wonderful recognition and cooperation" he had been given by the White House and promising to "use all of my influence for the best interests of the Administration and our great program. Whatever you wish me to do during the vacation of Congress, you have only to command me."[54]

Command him the White House did, sending Mitchell to Alabama and Georgia as an advocate for a New Deal, a plan that guaranteed equality before the law and "justice in the distribution of wealth," a program directed by a president "who had restored confidence in democracy at a time when revolution threatened." Mitchell exulted in this role. Addressing a largely Black audience in Athens, Alabama, he listed all the New Deal legislation, including the creation of the Tennessee Valley Authority, that had benefitted them. "Haven't you been happier," he then asked, "since Mr. Roosevelt became President than at any time during the administration of Mr. Hoover?": "Every heart beat of the man is for the masses" and the New Deal "the salvation of the Negro." Therefore, he concluded, "the Democratic party may not want me, but I want the Democrats."[55]

A local newspaper thought that "a more masterly address or greater tribute to President Roosevelt has never been delivered in the South." Many listeners did as well. Emma Clements of Nelson, Georgia, had previously not "cared a whit" about politics; now she was "eaten up with zeal to work in the coming campaign . . . for the greatest president since Lincoln." How could she contribute? Mitchell responded that her attitude was "sensible and sane. The success of the colored people of the south depends much on that point of view." Clements should "get involved with the people of your neighborhood."[56]

In Macon, Georgia, Mitchell focused on Black Republicans, inveighing against the "false leaders of our own race . . . who magnify our troubles in our own minds," preventing the race from cultivating the friendship of those who want to help us. "Let us lay down this hate which has been holding us back," Mitchell said. "Let us realize that we are all God's children and work together to enjoy life's blessings."[57]

Critics were as outraged about these speeches as they had been about the proposal for an Industrial Commission. "Mitchell is impossible," the *Defender* raged. "One would expect such tommy rot coming from an ex-Confederate slave-holder," but for a Black congressman to say such things was "almost incredible." Newspapers, it added, "are institutions. Congressman Mitchell is an accident. Institutions are fixtures, accidents just happen, and those responsible for them never fail to perfect a remedy to prevent their recurrence."[58]

7

"Not a Republican Dared Move"

When the Second Session of the Seventy-Fourth Congress convened in January 1936, Mitchell continued to bask in the limelight of the favorable impression he had created among his colleagues during his first year. Writing for the ANP, Davis Lee described him as one of the "best mannered, deported, and respected" congressmen. During a debate on army appropriations, Lee saw "member after member come to his desk, shake his hand, and put his arm around Mr. Mitchell." He interviewed one Alabama representative who held all Black people in contempt before meeting the new congressman. Now, Mitchell "has convinced me that the Negro is human, intelligent, and entitled to the same respect accorded to other races." A South Carolina colleague concurred: "He has minded his own business and made friends. One thing he has done is to change the attitude of many southern gentlemen toward your people." A third from West Virginia added that Mitchell should be the model for "every ambitious Negro boy. He knows how to handle whites as well as blacks." In reaction to this praise, Lee quoted Mitchell as saying, "I don't give a snap what people think or say about me. I have nothing to say about myself. A man's work and deed will speak louder than his mouth."[1]

His technique, he explained to John J. LeFlore, the secretary of the Mobile, Alabama, branch of the NAACP, was to work quietly and behind the scenes because he was interested in accomplishing a goal rather than grandstanding for publicity. Nobody has paid much attention to the fights he himself had made against discrimination, Mitchell told LeFlore. Nevertheless, "much has actually been accomplished which would not have been accomplished had I gone about it with the beating of drums and the flying of kites."[2]

Mitchell credited McDuffie, who had just resigned from Congress to assume a federal judgeship, for much of what he had accomplished. Your advice, he told his mentor, had led to his making scores of friends, colleagues from Alabama, Texas, and Mississippi being as cordial as those from Massachusetts, New York, and Ohio. "I feel," he reflected, "that I am doing something in the way of bringing about a better understanding between the two [races]. No one knows better than you how thoroughly devoted I have been to that type of work for the past quarter of a century."[3]

George Huddleston, the Alabama congressman who represented the district where Mitchell's mother and brother lived, appreciated his efforts, writing that "your success in Washington has shown the country that a Negro can be a real Congressman. I have been particularly pleased by your avoidance of low agitation of race prejudice and of anything which might foment hatred and ill will among the races. I feel that your service and example has been of high value to our party and to our nation."[4]

Wondering how many of his Democratic colleagues shared this appreciation, Mitchell wrote to all 321 of them. Under the guise of proposing to write a book about "the first Negro Democrat in Congress," he asked them to evaluate his work to date.[5]

John Dingell of Michigan believed his service "has already accomplished more toward breaking down racial barriers and bigoted views than anything else I have ever witnessed in Congress." Thomas Ford of California congratulated him on his "enlightened stand" and the "great service" he had rendered to Black Americans. Byrns hoped that his record "will serve as an example to members of your race throughout the country, upon whom you have reflected great credit." Sam Rayburn thought he "had the respect of every member." John McCormack of Massachusetts saw that "the constructive service you have rendered, with broad vision and gentlemanly conduct, has aroused the admiration and the respect of everyone."[6]

That respect did not extend to the NAACP, which by now had witnessed what Mitchell had predicted: the failure of Costigan-Wagner in the Senate after a filibuster led by southern opposition. In response, Mitchell had reintroduced his anti-lynching legislation, a bill White's organization continued to find unacceptable. Rather, it launched a campaign to repackage Costigan-Wagner in a bill sponsored by Joseph Gavagan, the New York representative for Harlem.

The NAACP's publicity campaign in support of Gavagan's bill was graphic and, at times, seemed aimed at Mitchell. A photograph of a lynching victim appeared, bearing the caption "This could happen in Chicago." White also wrote to other Democratic members of Illinois's house delegation, lobbying them to abandon him. These efforts failed. When he was approached, Raymond McKeough, the representative for the neighboring Second District, told White that he was committed to Mitchell and that if the House were to adopt anti-lynching legislation, "Mr. Mitchell's contribution to that happy result will be greater than that of any other single member of the House." When Leonard Schuetz (IL-7) indicated that he also supported Mitchell because he "is the representative of your people," Schuetz received this rebuke: "We have never presumed that you serve only the foreign element which happens to have the same background element as you. You have deliberately avoided the issue presented to you. . . . [You] are totally incapable of understanding the English language."[7]

Knowing that Gavagan's bill would not be reported out of the Judiciary Committee since it faced Sumners's opposition, White settled on calling a caucus of congressional Democrats to force a discharge petition. Mitchell warned him that this procedure was "irregular" and potentially "embarrassing to me in getting through certain legislation which I regard as vitally important to the race." But when he met with White for an hour and a half, the secretary showed no inclination to cooperate with him. "I cannot permit him," Mitchell wrote, to "intimidate me and cause me to do something which is unwise and even dangerous." If he tries to put me in a "false light, I shall expose him from the floor of the House."[8]

White answered Mitchell directly. Writing in the "kindliest spirit," he reproached his adversary for taking the survey about his performance. "Why does a man have to ask other people to testify to his record? The record should speak for itself. If a man came to me and asked me to certify, in writing, that he is honest, I would promptly begin to doubt his honesty." Mitchell, White continued, was being naive to think that southerners would support him once he was no longer useful to them, and that many members thought he was acting as he did because he doubted reelection and wanted "a lucrative job either in Washington or Illinois." "You have been very valuable," White ended, "to those who are opposed to the Negro in giving them an excuse for not facing the Negro question squarely."[9]

He also issued a statement to Illinois voters charging that Mitchell had "not furnished any assistance" to anti-lynching activity and had seduced his Illinois colleagues into following him. Representatives from the "rotten boroughs of the deep South" commended him while "Negro hating southern Congressmen" called the Association, a point of pride, their worst enemy. If voters didn't write to their congressmen stating their opposition to Mitchell's anti-lynching legislation, White warned, that would mean that Mitchell "truly reflects the attitude of all of the Negroes in Illinois."[10]

MacNeal urged White to step up his assault. "The issue seems to be clearly drawn between you and Mitchell," the head of the NAACP's Chicago branch wrote, "and he may as well be exposed as public enemy number one among Negroes. To be delicate in the matter would be fatal. You may as well throw a gang of bricks and you may as well discard powder puffs and use tanks and ten ton trucks."[11]

Mitchell used a Cleveland speech to document the correspondence he and White had exchanged. He also suggested a conference between the two of them and any other congressmen the NAACP might wish to have attend. The passage of an anti-lynching bill was so important that it "should not be toyed with or handled in such a way as to make its ultimate passage impossible." He promised to work unceasingly for the passage of appropriate legislation, "but I do not promise to adopt the tactics of some other person who has made a miserable failure covering a period of practically fifteen years."[12]

The 1936 anti-lynching effort ended when White's call for a caucus failed to attract the required number of attendees. Mitchell then warned MacNeal that White should abandon his hostility to the advice being given by so many House members "who really want to see this legislation passed." Scores of them had called the caucus strategy "irregular and unhelpful," but White "would not listen to any of them. I know he did not listen to me."[13]

Instead of listening, White attacked, insisting that Mitchell had not heard the last from him. His archenemy was only in Washington because of Harry Baker's death and a New Deal landslide. He was offering aid and comfort to southerners. "One would think he was of the oldest, whitest stock. . . . The late Huey Long was a sphynx on the legislation compared to Mr. Mitchell."[14]

While absorbed with this issue, Mitchell found time to prepare for what would be perhaps the most famous speech of his entire career. Seeing his survey as proof that Democrats would view him as a responsible voice, he planned carefully. This included research at the Library of Congress and consultation with Representative William Bankhead, an Alabama congressman and the House member who would ascend to the Speakership upon the untimely death of Joe Byrns in June 1936.[15]

On April 22, 1936, Mitchell addressed the House for twenty minutes, delivering a dramatic call for what he termed the political emancipation of his race. More than two million Black Americans would be eligible to vote in 1936 and the Democrats expected to wage a vigorous campaign for their share of those ballots. When they voted, they would show the nation that they stood "politically emancipated" from a Republican Party that has "abused the Negroes more than it has abused this country." They would give Democrats and "the great President that I love so dearly the largest vote that any Negro group has ever given a President."

There was no truth, Mitchell argued, to the assertion that "Lincoln was elected . . . for the purpose of freeing the slaves." All one had to do was read the Republican platform of 1860 that referred to the "inviolate right of every state to order and control its institutions" to understand this. Listeners should also consider his 1861 inaugural address in which he said, "I have no purpose directly or indirectly, to interfere with the institution of slavery in the states where it exists." Mitchell's Lincoln was a politician, and a good one. But the Emancipation Proclamation was the result of the exigencies of war, not a desire to liberate the enslaved from bondage. Furthermore, the best of the

Republican Party had died with the assassinated president. In the seventy years since then, the "beautiful promises" of Republicans have "led us dumb and hopeless and voted us . . . then forgot us again until they needed our votes."

Turning to the Democratic side of the House, Mitchell declared that since the election of Roosevelt, his party had given his race "a larger degree of justice [since 1933] than we have had under the Republican party." Amid cheers and applause, he proclaimed, "You are our friends and I hail you as our friends today."[16]

Mitchell described the drama of the historic moment: a Black Alabamian was telling more than four hundred white colleagues that the Democrats who controlled southern state governments where every sort of outrage was perpetrated against Black Americans were better friends of his race than the party of Lincoln. "Not a Republican dared move during my speech," he told a friend. "The Democrats were leaning forward in their seats when they were not cheering." He claimed that thousands of letters and telegrams praising him for his speech had come to him from "people of all parts of the country."[17]

Among those who wrote, Moton waxed enthusiastic that "it could not have been done better. Just think of all the Democrats, north and south, standing to applaud a Negro. It was truly a great achievement." Kelly Miller thought Mitchell's remarks about Lincoln and the Emancipation Proclamation "unnecessary and unfortunate" but saluted "the Negro's Declaration of Independence." Woodson was "delighted to read what you said and the manner in which it was received." A colleague from Connecticut wished "it were possible to place a copy of your remarks in the hands of every citizen in the United States." A listener in the gallery told Mitchell that the reception his speech received was "the greatest ovation ever given to a man of color in the life of our race in this country."[18]

Even some usually negative elements in the Black press reported on the enthusiasm with which the speech had been received. An ANP reporter thought that Mitchell had taken "the present day milk and water Republicans and punched them in the solar plexus. He called them hypocrites, ingrates and sophists, if not rascals." The *Afro-American* was surprised by "a political attack coming from such an unexpected quarter" but saluted the speaker's "debunking of Abraham Lincoln as a superman." It also surveyed twelve members of Congress, most of whom responded favorably to Mitchell's declaration of independence. The *Pittsburgh Courier* noted that Democrats offered "a loud and lusty ovation. Republicans meanwhile sat amazed and silent." The *Atlanta Daily World* apparently kept time. Mitchell, it reported, "caused a 10-minute unanimous demonstration by Democrats as Republicans sat dumbfounded."[19]

North and South, the white press took note of a unique moment that saw Democrats from all parts of the country applauding a Black speaker. The *New*

York Herald Tribune informed readers that "a half-dozen times through the twenty-minute speech, Democrats applauded loudly." The *Washington Evening Star* thought that the sight of both northern and southern Democrats cheering him on was an "amazing spectacle. . . . It may be a fore runner of political changes of considerable importance." The *Anniston* (AL) *Star* described a scene where "a fiery House speech . . . brought cheers from Democrats."[20]

There were passionate detractors as well. Pickens denounced a "half-intelligent, half-black member of Congress who is trying to curry favor with arrogant grandsons of slave holders. . . . The crowning asininity of Mitchell's asinine political career is this gratuitous and fortunately futile and impotent attack on the memory of the great man." Perry Howard, Mitchell's pool-playing friend at the Mu-So-Lit and the Republican Committeeman from Mississippi who had sent Mitchell to Chicago in 1928, was outraged: "Thousands of us deny each and all these allegations of yours. The Democratic party is responsible for all the infamy, shame, degradation, ignorance, and obnoxious laws imposed on us." Oscar De Priest told the ANP that "Mr. Mitchell himself enjoys the right to stand and address so distinguished a body as our Congress through the philanthropy and justice of the Republican Party and the martyred life of the distinguished Lincoln."[21]

Perhaps the bitterest denunciation came from Eardlie John, assistant cooperation counsel of the City of New York. How, John wondered, could Mitchell call people "your friends" who force you to eat in the kitchens of Washington and Alabama, who compel you to ride in the train's baggage cars below the Mason-Dixon line, who make Jim Crowism legal? These are the same individuals who lynch and burn us after "the most brutal, vulgar, and harrowing torture" in order to make us "good niggers, who foist upon us a system of education designed to give us a perpetual inferiority complex and a white supremacy fixation, who deny us the right to vote and shackle us in a vicious and cruel vice of economic peonage."[22]

Rather than retreat, Mitchell broadened his attack to include northerners such as John who were "false friends" of the Black American. When Roswell A. Benedict from East Norwalk, Connecticut, wrote to him to complain about southern bigotry, Mitchell scolded him for his "utter ignorance" of history. Where, he wondered, did Benedict think "the large estates in Connecticut owned by Yankees of today" originated? It was in the fortunes of the ships' captains who brought the enslaved from Africa to the colonies. Did those "traffickers" and "promoters" of "human slavery" deserve to be admired?[23]

John Robsion of Kentucky responded for the Republicans. He began by critiquing Mitchell's "great desire for preferment and his zeal for his new-found political friends" that led to his attempt "to belittle, misrepresent, and assail the great services rendered by Abraham Lincoln." If his Illinois colleague chose to align himself with those whose ancestors did all they could to keep his parents in bondage, who dominated a Supreme Court that gave the country the Dred Scott decision, who tried to prevent the passage the Thirteenth, Fourteenth, and Fifteenth Amendments, who fought against right to be born a freeman and the right to vote, "that is a matter that addresses itself to his own conscience." But Mitchell had taken Lincoln out of context by quoting only a few sentences from the 1860 platform and inaugural address. Why not be fair and read from the 1856 Democratic platform that "stood unfalteringly for the continuation of Negro slavery?"

Mitchell, Robsion charged, was nothing but a "renegade Republican," and hence the real obstacle to progress. Northern and western Democrats came and went, but southern Democrats stayed forever. The chairmen of the twelve most powerful committees in the House all came from their ranks. The fact that Roosevelt would not confront them was why every anti-lynching bill had gone into a "long Rip Van Winkle sleep" despite the reality that a lynching had occurred every fifteen days since Roosevelt had been elected and 95 percent of the victims had been Black. Mitchell, Robsion declared, should go to Texas and try to vote in a primary or attend a Democratic convention, or to South Carolina, where he would be permitted to vote if he could document that he had voted for an ex-Confederate officer who had run for governor in 1876.

What Mitchell should tell the voters, Robsion concluded, was that "I would not be holding a high office and would not be here to address you . . . and my own father and mother [would have] continued to feel the sting of the lash and would have died in their chains but for Abraham Lincoln and the Republican party . . . that will live on to save our country and fight for the rights of the colored race."

Mitchell asked for the floor to respond to Robsion's "tirade." What he had just heard was "a typical Republican campaign speech" designed to continue the "political slavery" of Black Americans. But 1936 was not like the 1870s. "Vision and ambition" had taught Black Americans that they had been Republicans for too long. Hadn't the debt of gratitude been paid? Rather than linger in the past, Robsion's party should "tell the aspiring youth of this country [what it] proposes to do in 1936 and the years to follow." "Neither party wants us," Mitchell admitted. "It is a question of which party offers us a better opportunity to rise in this country and live as citizens should live." It was the Democrats and, Mitchell said, "I shall use all the power and all the influence I possess to drive this truth home."[24]

In the aftermath of the exchange, Mitchell boasted that he "completely tore [Robsion] up in my reply." His adversary "was afraid for the public to see his speech and my answer in the same binding." Moton also saw Mitchell as the victor in the verbal exchange. He was "much pleased by the splendid way you took care . . . of Mr. Robison [*sic*] He did not detract one iota from what you said." Support also came from the *Washington Tribune*, which editorialized that Mitchell "had conducted himself in such a manner that challenges comparison with anything that has been said upon the subject of the Negro in politics."[25]

Emory B. Smith, his Washington friend from the 1920s, reported that his wife, a teacher, had devoted her class to studying the exchange and that "the response of the children was most enthusiastic." Smith himself had read it to his law office, where it "was received with the highest praise." "On so many occasions," he went on, "you have demonstrated such a remarkable degree of courage, tact and intelligence that I am certain you have broken down the opposition of your severest critics. You have not merely talked about the New Negro, you have presented a demonstration" of him.[26]

A further measure of how far Mitchell had come in wooing southern whites came from Thomas Blanton, a Texas colleague who had raise a point of order during Robsion's speech by insisting that his colleague from Illinois be addressed courteously. He now wrote to Mitchell thanking him for "the splendid service you have rendered . . . so very different from that of De Priest who was always trying to stir up trouble and getting nowhere." He was so impressed that he had written to the Texas Centennial Commission recommending Mitchell as "a wonderful speaker . . . you won't be disappointed in him."[27]

Mitchell's April 22 speech and exchange with Robsion were well timed, as they brought him to the attention of Democratic Party officials on the eve of their 1936 convention. Just as anxious to attract Black voters in 1936 as Mitchell was, the party had undertaken a "determined drive to corral" Black voters, naming Black delegates from border states. It also intended to have Black women serve as guides and to have Black operatives circulate on the convention floor with lists showing the number of Black voters in each state and the "super importance" of their votes in New York, Ohio, Illinois, Indiana, and Missouri.[28]

However, the influence of southern Democrats in the convention forced a delicate negotiation as to Mitchell's role. Ignoring his request to attend to study conditions and "make contacts," the party did not choose Mitchell as either a delegate or an alternate. Both Tittinger and Illinois Senator James Hamilton Lewis protested this slight, but to no avail. Farley then suggested a compromise: Mitchell would second the nomination of Roosevelt as a guest of the convention. Senator Ellison ("Cotton Ed") Smith of South Carolina objected to this, threatening a procedural complaint from the floor. To avoid this, Illinois governor Henry Horner was asked to give the formal seconding speech and Mitchell, wearing the badge of an alternate delegate, was offered a "seconding occasion."[29]

On the day of Roosevelt's nomination, Smith walked out as a Black minister was offering the opening invocation. "By God, he's as black as melted midnight," Smith shouted. "This mongrel meeting ain't no place for a white man." Then, after Roosevelt's formal nomination, Mitchell tried to speak. But "Cotton Ed," who had returned to the floor, broke in again. Reprising his previous exit, the senator from South Carolina announced that he "had had enough. This is the beginning of social equality. I'm leaving the convention to stay gone. I'm through." It was only after the ensuing uproar had subsided that Mitchell began his address, an act that made him the first Black elected official to speak over a nationwide radio network.[30]

The Roosevelt administration, Mitchell reminded the delegates, had been elected in 1932 with the distinct understanding that "the forgotten man should be remembered" and that the government should protect the "helpless and the hungry." Republicans listened to "the rich and privileged," but Roosevelt had listened to Sylvester Harris, "unlettered, dressed in overalls," who had sold his last cow to call the president, who in turn had saved his farm. This simple act of humanity on Roosevelt's part showed why the upcoming election "was the greatest opportunity for Negroes in four decades." Frederick Douglass had said that the Republican Party was the ship and all else the sea. "The Republican Party may be the ship, but [it] is on fire and, like the Morro Castle, is burning to the water's edge. The safety of my people consists in taking a life belt and plunging into the sea." Roosevelt was the "greatest President who has lived." He had thrown himself between "the American people and starvation." Mitchell's race was thankful for this and would never bite the hand that fed them. Therefore, they would stand with Roosevelt as they had stood with Crispus Attucks in Boston, as they had stood with Jackson at New Orleans and Teddy Roosevelt as he charged up San Juan Hill, as they had faced the German cannons in the Argonne. "History shows that we have always stood by our friends. We are with you all the way."[31]

Immediately after the convention, Smith's protest drew more attention than Mitchell's speech, but most of that scrutiny was negative. For many southerners who Mitchell had cultivated, Smith's protest went too far. Jimmy Byrnes, "the most influential Southern member of Congress between John Calhoun and Lyndon Johnson," was running for reelection to the Senate from South Carolina. When asked why he had not joined Smith in leaving, Byrnes told the ANP that he intended to appeal to "the reason of voters, not their prejudice." The *Birmingham News* saw Smith's performance as a "narrow-minded, small-spirited, and all together ugly act." It hoped that the rest of the country would not take it as being representative of the South's attitude. The Selma (AL) *Times-Journal* thought that Mitchell had overcome Smith's tantrum to deliver "one of the best speeches of the Convention."[32]

Mitchell told the Associated Press that Smith was "ignorant and steeped in prejudice," and probably a Ku Klux Klanner. "The sooner we get rid of his type, the better." If he intended to walk out of every Democratic function with Black participants, "he should go into training for a walkathon as he will have much walking to do." C. H. Hamlin, a member of the History Department at Atlantic Christian College in Wilson, North Carolina, wrote to Smith of his "humiliation and disgust" at the senator's actions, sending a copy to Mitchell, who appreciated the "fair expression of the feeling of the progressive Southern citizen."[33]

8
"The Top Expert Statistician of the Democratic Party"

At the beginning of the 1936 campaign season, reprints of Mitchell's Athens speech on the virtues of the New Deal, his April 22 repudiation of Republicans, and his response to Robsion were popular pieces of the literature handed out to Black voters. In Chicago, the Kelly machine portrayed his Athens address as the "best statement of the principles and ideals of the New Deal ever uttered by anyone on this subject" and ordered one hundred thousand copies for the upcoming election.[1]

As November neared, many Democratic candidates sought these items as campaign literature. "Please send 15,000 copies of your addresses to [Michael] Kirwan, [OH-19]," the publicity director of the Democratic National Campaign committee wrote in October. "He has a large industrial and colored population [in Youngstown] and is confident that the distribution of these speeches will materially aid his election." Alfred Beiter (NY-41) felt the same way: "I do not know of any campaign document that would be more effective . . . than your splendid speeches." Similar requests became so frequent that a waiting list for copies of Mitchell's pronouncements had to be established.[2]

Mitchell's written endorsements of colleagues running for reelection in districts with large Black populations were also valuable. When John Tolan of California asked for one, Mitchell described him as "not only cordial and agreeable, but deeply interested in measures that work toward the welfare of our group." Oklahoman Percy Gassaway received similar support. Mitchell saw him "deeply interested in the underprivileged citizens of the country . . . one of the members of the Congress that I could always depend upon."[3]

The retelling of the Sylvester Harris story also fit into the Democratic script. The NAACP's *Crisis* presentation of "Roosevelt the Humanitarian" did not mention Mitchell by name but did feature Harris, speaking in a distinctive if demeaning dialect:

> The phone in the White House rang. One of President Roosevelt's secretaries picked up the phone and answered "Hello!"
>
> A far away voice came over the wire: "Dis is Sylvester, an' I wanna speak to the President.["]
>
> Mr. Roosevelt, who overheard the distressed voice, took the receiver and said, "This is the President."
>
> "Mr. Roosevelt, I is Sylvester and these white folks down is gwine take my farm. I hear, you wouldn't let them do it if I asked you."
>
> When the President saved Harris it was "only one instance of the humanitarian spirit which has permeated President Roosevelt's administration."[4]

While Democrats celebrated the Roosevelt's coming to Harris's aid, Republicans portrayed it as an example of the president's cynical manipulation of the poor and illiterate. Pickens characterized Mitchell's bringing Harris to Chicago as a "publicity stunt" that "supplied a good laugh for a good many snobbish white people of the South and North, but was the weakest and most contemptible reason in the world why colored voters of Chicago or any other place should change their votes . . . just because Marse Roosevelt and his office staff had a little fun with a simple-minded Negro of the Mississippi bottoms and of course had paid the Negro for the amusement which he afforded them."[5]

Democratic Party officials were not amused at their prospects after the convention. Difficult as it is to believe in light of the result, they foresaw a challenging campaign for Roosevelt, one that he might lose. Emil Hurja, the president's pollster, thought the result was "very much in doubt," believing that Roosevelt had little chance to carry New York or Illinois and only a slightly better one in Ohio, Indiana, and Minnesota. Ickes agreed, confiding to his diary as late as July 21, 1936, "I am quite serious in my belief that we are in bad shape and in grave danger."[6]

Some of the peril lay in assuming that Black voters would support Roosevelt. To some Democratic strategists, this seemed similar to asking Jews to vote for Hitler. Why would they support a president who deferred to powerful southern voices in Congress, "side-stepped" on anti-lynching legislation, and seemed unperturbed by disfranchisement in the South? Compounding the problem, Paul Ward wrote in the *Nation*, was the perception that only Black elites voted, and they voted Republican. "The rest do not vote," Ward asserted. "They are voted. The Negro has been notoriously venal, placing his vote at the disposal of whichever machine at the moment can pay the highest price." What, he asked, could be done to guard against a massive influx of Republican cash at the last moment to swing the election in their favor?[7]

Mitchell's growing reputation as a talented orator and a committed New Dealer convinced party elders that he might play an important part in answering this question. Before the 1936 political season had even begun, the chairman of Ohio's Committee to Reelect the President had written to a Pennsylvania colleague that once someone heard Mitchell speak, the listener would understand why "the Negro race has in [him] one of its most useful, influential, and outstanding leaders of his generation." Agreeing and impressed by his April 22 speech to the House and his debate with Robsion, Farley had already asked how much time Mitchell could give to the Democratic Speakers Bureau in the campaign.[8]

Party elders thought Mitchell might have an important role to play in expanding Black turnout in a quartet of states—Illinois, Indiana, Michigan, and Ohio—they saw as critical to Roosevelt's reelection. To carry them, disadvantaged Black residents of the large cities—Chicago, Indianapolis, Detroit, Cleveland, and Cincinnati—had to be registered and then vote for the president. Many of the transplants who had relocated to these large urban centers during the Great Migration were now unemployed, demoralized, and ready to change political affiliations. Arthur Mitchell spoke their language and knew how to appeal to them.[9]

Mitchell was just as interested in seeing these votes in the Democratic column as was Farley. A committed New Dealer, he saw the president's efforts for the poor as a lifeline for the urban dispossessed. Just as important, if that appeal could also be translated into the election of Democratic congressmen beholding to minority voters, it would create a body of legislators sympathetic to his ideas about an Industrial Commission and anti-lynching legislation. Such a group would threaten the conservative alliance of Republicans and archconservative southern Democrats that opposed the passage of federal bills addressing Black personal safety, voting rights, and economic opportunity, all obstacles to Black Americans returning south. Equally important, a massive Black turnout in Midwestern cities could sweep an under ticket of city officials into office. Casting a straight Democratic ballot had the potential to bring a host of Black sheriffs, judges, and aldermen into positions of authority, benefiting all members of the "race."

Beyond these shared interests, Mitchell brought advanced organizational and analytical skills to the table. As early as July 26, 1935, he had written to Hurja that "we must make a better showing among the Negroes" in 1936. Six weeks later, he informed the pollster that he had ordered and received maps for seventeen states where he thought "the campaign should be waged." He intended to highlight every county with more than one thousand Black voters and suggested the establishment of youth boards consisting of college men, educational leaders, and other professionals to lead the drive to register voters.[10]

He also wrote to the Democratic National Committee in February 1936 that it would be impossible for the party to carry Illinois, Ohio, Indiana, Michigan, and several other states without a significant Black vote. He would be happy to come to New York to see "Mr. Farley and those in charge for the purpose of discussing this matter." For such a meeting, he had compiled detailed lists of the counties to be targeted, the number of registered voters in those counties, and unemployment statistics. Such calculations fascinated Mitchell, as an *Afro-American* reporter later discovered after hearing Mitchell detail Democratic election prospects. Showing "a weakness for charting and tabulating, [Mitchell] rubbed his hands with satisfaction. Like a school boy who had just devised a new kite, he showed me in roughly diagrammed markings just how he had doped out charts that could tell him at a glance every Democratic nose that could be counted in the whole [mid]western area."[11]

Farley, Roosevelt's campaign manager, had never been a leader in efforts to attract Black voters into the Democratic party. Nevertheless, Mitchell's many skills impressed him so he "urgently requested" Mitchell to become the Director of the Western Section of a Negro Division of the National Campaign Committee. In that position, Mitchell would be responsible to see that Kentucky, Tennessee, Ohio, Indiana, Michigan, Illinois, Wisconsin, Iowa, Kansas, Missouri, Nebraska, Oklahoma, Colorado, and California wound up in the Democratic column.[12]

When making the appointment, Farley told the *Baltimore Sun,* that his new Director was "the top expert statistician of the Democratic Party." From his knowledge of voting patterns, Farley announced, Mitchell knew that Roosevelt had received between 55 and 60 percent of the Black vote in 1932, but could get 75 percent in 1936. In addition, Black residents held the balance of power in 158 congressional districts where they could vote. Key concentrations were in Illinois (213,000 potential Black voters), Ohio (180,000), Oklahoma (174,000), Michigan (108,000) and Indiana (63,000). Mitchell's assignment would be to register and then make sure that these swing voters actually cast ballots. To give this effort structure, Farley would appoint a director for each state. They, in turn, would appoint a supervisor to each county with more than one thousand Black residents. Mitchell would supervise the directors and supervisors in the thirteen states for which he was responsible.[13]

The appointment infuriated Walter White, who considered Farley "stupid" for thinking the NAACP would be pleased with naming of a "knave and a fool" to such an important position. It would be a "spineless surrender" to let Mitchell's assignment go unprotested, especially since the Chicago branch of the organization was set to oppose his reelection. Wouldn't the honorable procedure, he asked Wilkins, be an open letter to prominent Democrats expressing disapproval of the appointment? A less volatile Wilkins "strongly advised" against this. "Our action," he warned, "would be interpreted as chagrin over the defeat of the anti-lynching bill."[14]

Figure 8. Walter White, the executive secretary for the National Association for the Advancement of Colored People, who opposed Mitchell on many issues. Mitchell viewed him as the silliest person he had ever seen "holding a responsible position" and referred to the NAACP, which he called the "National Association for the Advancement of Certain Persons," as nothing but a "racket." CC0, National Portrait Gallery, Smithsonian Institution. Clara Sipprell, photographer.

In the early stages of the campaign, Farley placed a low priority on making his "top expert" feel welcome or important. As an inducement to take the position, he had promised Mitchell that, before election day, his director could address the "underprivileged of the nation including farmers" in a fifteen-minute radio broadcast. Mitchell enthused that "this will mean thousands of votes to us . . . as I understand farming." But the pledge was never honored.[15]

Likewise, Farley slighted Mitchell when the latter asked that his headquarters be located in the same Chicago hotel as the National Democratic Campaign Committee. This, the congressman argued, would "keep down the question of Jim Crowism and will aid materially in demonstrating the absolute fairness of our party toward my people." "The Chief" refused, and Mitchell settled for a second choice.[16]

Mitchell was equally unsuccessful on the subject of a budget. He asked for $106,825 to reach all men and "a special campaign to reach women and young voters"; Farley gave him $25,000. C. B. Powell, Mitchell's counterpart in charge of Black publicity, was candid that this allotment reflected growing party confidence that previous concerns about a potential loss had abated as election day neared: "From the looks of things, they [the DNC] believe they have the Negro vote and they are not particular about appropriating any more money for same."[17]

Despite these rebuffs, Mitchell made do. To stretch his dollars, he engaged in practices that would be considered illegal today. For the first five or six weeks of his directorship, he used his own Chicago law offices as headquarters and paid his secretary and stenographer from his "congressional allowance." He also met expenses out of his own pocket, telling F. B. Ransom, in charge of operations in Indiana, that he never wanted to report to Farley that workers had gone unpaid, as it would hurt staff morale. He also hounded "The Chief" over the scarcity of "literature, buttons, lithographs, and other paraphernalia."[18]

What Farley and Mitchell did agree on was the need to concentrate resources in Illinois, Indiana, Michigan, and Ohio. As the ANP explained, the Democrats had broken voters in these states from their "almost solid affiliation with the Republicans but still needed to make a most determined effort" to turn these potential voters into casters of Democratic ballots. These were the "swing" voters who would decide elections from the top to the bottom of the ticket because, in all four states, their numbers alone were "from four to six times the majority claimed by either party."[19]

Based upon the recommendations of national committeemen and Democratic state chairmen, Farley appointed the state directors. Mitchell, however, was expected to remove bad choices, a task he performed with speedy efficiency. On September 7, he identified the original Ohio director as "a little slow" and in need of an assistant. Five days later, the unfortunate individual had become a "misfit" and been replaced by the hardworking Percy Jones. He almost fired Charles F. Davis in Nebraska after "an absolute flop due to the lack of arrangements." Davis was fortunate. Mitchell only warned him that he would be held personally responsible if anything similar happened again. An old enemy, William T. Thompkins, named to head operations in Missouri, did not fare as well after he took it upon himself to extend his efforts into Kansas. Stay out of

Kansas, Mitchell wrote. "I'm speaking plain to you because I am sick and tired of your method of snooping and double-crossing." Thompkins wrote back that this was "the most surprising letter I have ever received in my political career."[20]

In addition to finding competent state directors and approving budgets, Mitchell's duties included keeping Farley informed about party prospects, overseeing the delivery of a coordinated message that stressed the importance of voting a straight Democratic ticket, scheduling speakers, and serving as a resource when unexpected problems arose. While most crisis management and daily decision-making were made over the telephone, Ransom's written reports from Indiana detail the types of daily disruptions with which Mitchell dealt, and just how acute was his eye for detail.

In one case, the Republican candidate for governor in Indiana, who was the state commander of the American Legion, accused his Democratic opponent of being a "slacker" who had not served during World War I. Together, Mitchell and Ransom found another legionnaire to refute this. In a second instance, the GOP again attacked the Democrat running for governor for having a home in the area where two lynchings had taken place, suggesting that the candidate had somehow been complicit in the act. Ransom recommended that Mitchell send Katherine Bailey, the ex-president of the Indiana NAACP, to refute this charge, asserting, "It will mean everything to the Democratic Party." At the bottom of the letter, Mitchell wrote "sending Mrs. Bailey." In a third case, statewide charity balls were being staged by Democrats to raise money for a crippled children's hospital in Warm Springs, Georgia. Republicans charged that no Black children could be patients there. The Democrats countered that a percentage of donations were being withheld to be sent to local institutions for Black victims of infantile paralysis.[21]

Mitchell told state directors that their first obligation was to tie the Roosevelt campaign as closely as possible to state and local tickets. There was to be no separation between them. A vote for Roosevelt must be a vote for the complete Democratic ticket, including local candidates. To insure such discipline in each state's campaign, he supplied countless lists of speakers, methods for enrolling Republican voters who wished to register as Democrats but whose addresses could not be verified, influential contacts in each small city of a given state, Black appointees of the Roosevelt administration, and methods for countering Republican propaganda. At least in theory, the jokes told and music played in Cleveland, Ohio, and Kalamazoo, Michigan, should be similar.[22]

With his team of directors in place, Mitchell organized methods of communication between state offices and his Chicago headquarters. Supervisors were not to write to him; they were to report to the director of each state, who would then inform him if the news seemed important enough to pass on. But potential complainers were to remember that "you owe your job strictly to the

Democratic Party. . . . I hope that you will not bite the hand that is feeding you." This policy was rigidly enforced. When Mary Dawson warned of rumors that Black citizens of Columbus had lost confidence in "their colored leaders," Mitchell replied that he had daily reports from the state director and that there was absolutely no truth to the reports she had received. "I cannot take time," he added, "to answer all the silly letters that come to me."[23]

To him, discipline also meant waging war against the image of Democratic organizers being "chiselers," operators who were out for personal gain. This usually manifested itself in attempts to pad expense accounts, receive money for unauthorized speeches, or engage in unauthorized travel. These practices were so widespread that his Kansas director warned him that "nearly every political crook in the country has invaded Kansas." But warfare against "chiseling" also meant erasing the public's perception that Democrats paid voters for their ballots.

Although he had engaged in such practices in 1934, it was important to Mitchell for the American public to see Black voters refusing to do this in 1936. Rather than being seen as taking bribes, the American public must see them as making a conscious decision to vote in their own best interests, for Roosevelt.[24]

Bitter exchanges with Ransom illustrate the passion with which Mitchell fought against chiseling. Informed by his Gary agent that Republicans had a budget of $10–20,000 to purchase nine thousand Black votes in the city and advised that Democrats should "meet fire with fire," the Indiana director asked Mitchell to match Republican "walking around" money. "You know the history of Indiana politics," Ransom cautioned. Mitchell was unmoved. He expected last minute "corrupt actions" by the opposition, but there would be no competitive money. The president and he were "waging a clean, constructive, and educational campaign."[25]

The denial enraged Ransom, who "resented the implications" contained in Mitchell's refusal. Republicans were going to pay between five and fifty dollars a vote at the polls and they were to do nothing? The state committee cared only for the state ticket. Particularly vulnerable were the small towns of Indiana, where 250–500 Black people lived. Most of these voters were domestics, registered as Republicans but who wanted to vote Democrat. What am I to do, he complained, when "I have only one organizer, and he hasn't been paid." Again, Mitchell held firm. It was time for Black Americans to "learn that instead of holding out their hands at all times expecting money . . . every well-meaning Negro should roll up his sleeves and fight for the principle involved."[26]

W. F. Reden didn't want money but expected a federal appointment if he was to work in South Dakota. He received a similar rebuke: "The common interests of all the people are far more vital than the holding of an office by a few people. I have much experience in this matter and know that those who get into the party and work without thinking a great deal about themselves usually get the rewards. I expect to do everything in my power to get all the recognition for the Negro that any other group has, but I am just as deeply interested in having the Negro do his part so that the claim can be made."[27]

Once the ground rules had been established, Mitchell turned his attention to constructing mechanisms that converted potential voters into registered ones who would cast ballots. As he had argued when advocating for southern registration drives, Mitchell stressed the need for local organizations to take the lead on this.

In Ohio, two organizers visited the twenty counties where most Black voters lived. In Columbus, three hundred new Democrats were registered and seven meetings arranged for them to hear a Roosevelt radio address. By September 24, there were clubs in forty-four counties with the goal of increasing the Democratic vote by 50 percent. A week later Jones saw the situation in Toledo looking better than it had in years, with "500 new or renewed voters" having been enrolled. In Cleveland, a poll of 1,500 Black likely voters showed Roosevelt winning by a five to one ratio. Cincinnati was "one of our most fertile fields." Youngstown had an organization that "three months ago, I thought was impossible to perfect." There were "no worries" in Akron, even though Republicans controlled the city administration.[28]

Ohio recruitment of potential Democratic voters also took place at Republican events where Olympic hero Jesse Owens appeared. One in Cincinnati saw Jones operatives prepare and distribute a pamphlet titled "What the New Deal has done for the Negro." The Ohio director reported success with a similar operation in Columbus. There the Young Men's Democratic Club handed out eight hundred "national books" to those who had come to hear Owens tell them why they should vote for Governor Alf Landon of Kansas, Roosevelt's Republican challenger. Very few were left in the hall or on the street at the end of his appearance. Given the excellence of the statewide structure, a confident Jones told Mitchell a month before the election that 1936 would be the "greatest year in the history of Negro politics in Ohio."[29]

Other state organizations resembled Ohio in attention to detail. Indiana had a "set-up" not just in the twelve largest counties but in every ward, township, district, and precinct where Black voters were found. Ransom also toured the state to coordinate strategy with county and district chairmen of the regular Democratic organization, who were "tickled to death" to work with their Black counterparts. The Indiana group also made life difficult for Owens. On one occasion, some mysterious force decorated four of the nine cars in his parade with Roosevelt signs as it drove under a banner reading "Mr. Roosevelt: Our Savior."[30]

In Michigan, clubs existed in twelve congressional districts covering thirty-six counties with 169,453 Black residents. By October 15, Mitchell had received a proposal for twenty-five statewide "meetings" to be held before the election, three large ones in Detroit. The list of events contained proposed speakers and noted details such as the availability of sound cars.[31]

In Illinois, weekly reports listed the location of public gatherings and the anticipated size of the audience. In Chicago, Abbott's *Defender* posed a problem because of its staunchly Republican stance. Conquering his scruples about chiseling, Mitchell overcame this by paying the editor of the small *Metropolitan News* $250 to "to carry our matter, [and] from time to time espouse us editorially." By doing this, he bragged to an Iowa friend, he had "been able to work a miracle," one that would change many of the 192,000 Black votes in Chicago by giving Democrats visibility. This "conversion" of the *Metro* brought praise from Sam Rayburn, chairman of the Democrats' national Speaker's Bureau. "It was a great piece of work you did and you deserved great credit." Robert Wood, the secretary of the DNC, thought it quite "a remarkable achievement," an example of the "great work you are doing with your division."[32]

In Iowa, the Negro Democratic League's membership rose to 240 in one month, and C. Vernon Smith of Davenport congratulated himself on "what a good job we have done to capture some of the old dyed-in-the-wool colored Republicans." In large measure, this success was due to the Speaker's Bureau having sent the "first member of our race ever to speak to a colored Democratic organization in the city."[33]

In Nebraska, success was measured by new voters in Omaha. There, Charles F. Davis, the state director, was able to pressure the city to establish a registration site "in the heart of the Negro District." As a result, on one day, 259 new Democrats enrolled, as opposed to 82 Republicans.[34]

As Democratic registration numbers multiplied, Mitchell's ability to provide talented speakers to address large gatherings gained in importance. Potential Roosevelt surrogates applied to the state directors, who then sent a list of approved names to Mitchell. He then assigned his choices to each state, sent out schedules, and told those selected how much they would be paid. He had, he judged, twenty or more outstanding Black orators available at any time, many of whom "compare favorably with any speakers in the United States of any group."[35]

Given the constraints on his budget, Mitchell was originally reluctant to send those selected west of the Mississippi or to gatherings where a crowd of fewer than one thousand was anticipated. Beyond these restrictions, he developed a form, similar to the one in use in his Washington office, to determine who should appear where. Among the many questions it asked were the inside and outside seating capacity of the proposed rally site, the number of loudspeakers available, the ability of the speaker to move a crowd, and the estimated urban-rural split in the audience and its racial composition. As with his personal appearances, it was important that the audience be a mixture of races.[36]

Mitchell himself was the speaker most in demand, particularly among House colleagues with large Black constituencies. Thomas Hennings (MO-11) implored Farley to persuade Mitchell to come to St. Louis. With one hundred thousand Black residents in his district, Henning was "particularly anxious" for him to speak as his "personality and achievements will be of tremendous effect here." Dow Harter of Ohio and Samuel Pettengill of Indiana were equally ardent in their pursuit. William G. Worthy, chairman of the Speakers Bureau for Illinois, was particularly worried about two downstate incumbents, Claude Parsons (IL-24) and Kent Keller (IL-25). He urged Mitchell to speak in the area because "you and only you can do a great deal of good in this vicinity where much help is needed." Byron Harlan, another Ohio colleague, was perhaps the most descriptive of the suitors. "I have to do something to influence the heavy colored vote here," he wrote. Give me a speaking date and "I will be just as happy as a kid with a stick of candy."[37]

Although honoring most of these requests, Mitchell found that he had to ration his appearances as so many colleagues asked him to speak. His guiding principle, he told Ransom, was "to speak only where you have to and let that be in [the Midwest] as far as possible." He explained this policy to Farley as scheduling appearances to which he could drive. This enabled him to spend morning hours at headquarters, drive to a location, and return home the same night.[38]

Being able to return home in the evening was not just a convenience. It enabled Mitchell to avoid the embarrassment he experienced in places such as Springfield, Illinois, and Dayton, Ohio. When he scheduled an overnight stay at "the home and resting place of Abraham Lincoln," his hosts first sent him to a small hotel where "Negroes stayed." He refused the accommodation, threatening to return to Chicago without speaking. At a second lodging, the bell boy tried to take him through the back door to register. He objected, and they entered through the lobby. When it came time for breakfast the next morning, the management told him that the meal would be sent to his room. When he refused this arrangement, he was told that Springfield was "a small town and purely southern in sentiment so far as the mixing of the races was concerned." He said he didn't care; he was taking breakfast in the dining room. The hotel gave way.

A similar situation presented itself when Mitchell visited Dayton to speak for Harlan. The latter arranged for his guest to stay at the Hotel Van Cleve, "one of the best in town." Unfortunately, the manager, blaming "narrow-minded guests," asked that the congressman take meals in his room. Harlan solved the problem by hosting a dinner in Mitchell's honor at his home.[39]

When he did speak, his addresses only reinforced Mitchell's reputation as a gifted orator. The *Akron Times-Press* reported that his campaign stop for Harter resulted in "the largest Negro rally ever held" in the city. A grateful Harlan described his coming to Dayton as an "earthquake" that awakened the Democratic organization. Mitchell himself thought his talk in East St. Louis in support of Parsons and Keller was "the largest Negro political meeting of any kind I have ever witnessed," estimating the crowd at twenty-five thousand.[40]

Mitchell's words succeeded not only in motivating Black voters to support the Democratic ticket; they also inspired many volunteers to join the campaign. James Le Vine described himself as "inspired and fired with new courage, new vision, and a new determination to go forward" after hearing him speak in Springfield. Inez Steele joined the Democratic campaign because she had always admired Black leadership that took care of the needs of her group without grandstanding: "You have done this. You have given action not words. God speed you on."[41]

But, as effective as these efforts were, it was Roosevelt's visit to Chicago in mid-October that gave Mitchell the opportunity to bring all of his state organizations together in a massive display of support for Roosevelt. When the president first proposed the visit in August, Mitchell had promised Farley that he would have "large representations from all the Western States to greet him." On October 8, Mitchell sent a circular letter to State Directors asking how many Black attendees would come to hear the president. He was, he reminded them, "most anxious that the Negroes of the Middle Western states show up in large numbers." He need not have worried. Ickes, himself a Chicagoan, thought the appearance came off as "the greatest political demonstration that the city had ever seen." Mitchell concurred, telling to a friend that the "demonstration" attained a level that "has never been witnessed in these parts before." He estimated the total crowd at five hundred thousand, a sizeable portion of it Black.[42]

With Democratic momentum gathering across his region, Mitchell peppered Farley with optimistic reports about the percentage of Black votes that Roosevelt would receive. As early as September 7, he estimated it at a range between 65 and 75 percent in the key states of Illinois, Indiana, Michigan, and Ohio, even raising the possibility that Democrats might win in Kansas, the Republican candidate's home state. He was just as confident in a report to Bankhead. On October 22, he told the Speaker that Roosevelt's election was "cinched," that the only question was the size of the victory. Seventy-five percent of the Black vote would go to the Democrats, with Roosevelt carrying Illinois, Ohio, Michigan, Indiana, Missouri, and "other states in which I am doing a great deal of work. The Republican campaign machinery is virtually demolished . . . the outlook is exceedingly bright."[43]

As the possibility of sweeping the states in the Western Division rose, so did Farley's appreciation for its director. At the outset of the campaign, "the

Chief" had downplayed Mitchell's role, warning him not to "in any way interfere or complicate our activities." By October 6, Mitchell was "doing a mighty fine job." Three weeks later, it was "quite evident" to the Chief that Mitchell's "work has been carried on in a most successful manner and will be manifest when the votes come in." Two days after that, a personal note allowed as how "you have certainly done a *real* [Farley's underlining] job, Arthur, and I am very grateful to you. Keep up the good work until the last minute." Just before the election, "The Chief" relaxed. "I am confident," he predicted, "that we will have a sweeping victory . . . [thank you] for the efforts you have put forth."[44]

For his part, Mitchell did as he was told and kept the pressure on. "Victory is won," he promised Farley on October 26. "Our job now is simply making the lines hold. I assure you we will do this. . . . We expect to drive up to the last minute." It was a message he hammered home to his directors. Speeches were fine, but getting the vote out through personal contact was what really mattered. "Let us not be too cocksure of victory and sit down before the count," he warned.[45]

Turner Catledge, the veteran political reporter for the *New York Times*, thought Farley's growing confidence in Mitchell well deserved. His October 26 newspaper column described visits he had made to Ohio, Illinois, Iowa, Michigan, and Indiana. In each state, Black voters "had done busted away" from their former political moorings out of gratitude for New Deal legislation. They were now saying, "I know that Mr. Lincoln ain't running this year." In some of these states, Black Democrats seemed better organized than white Democrats, even down to the level of the precinct worker. They were "the most honestly enthusiastic group of workers to be found in any of these states." Thanks to them, Catledge saw photographs of the president "in shops and windows in the black belt of every Midwest city of any size."[46]

Another on-the-ground-report from Emory B. Smith, a member of Mitchell's peripatetic speaker's bureau, testified to this exceptional enthusiasm. Writing to W. Forbes Morgan, the treasurer of the Democratic Campaign Committee on the same day as Catledge's story appeared, he described himself as "dumbfounded" by the tremendous reception the Democratic ticket was receiving from Black audiences in Illinois, Indiana, and Wisconsin. He had spoken to a crowd of ten thousand in Chicago the day before and "had never seen a more enthusiastic meeting of voters. There is no question in my mind but that substantial work is being done among the Negroes . . . especially in the West."[47]

When the votes were tabulated on November 3, 1936, the result was a massive personal victory for Roosevelt who carried forty-six states, losing only Maine and Vermont. Moreover, his coattails carried five additional Democrats into the Senate, reducing Republican representation in the upper chamber to seventeen. In the House of Representatives, Democrats gained an additional twelve seats, increased their already overwhelming majority to 334–89.

It was also a personal victory for Mitchell. Every incumbent for whom he made an appearance won. In Ohio, four additional Democrats were elected, decreasing the Republican contingent to only two members in a twenty-four-person delegation. In Gary, Indiana, a site where Mitchell frequently campaigned, the results were just as dramatic. In the largely Black Fifth Ward, Hoover had received 85 percent of the vote in 1932. In 1936, Roosevelt received 67 percent.[48]

Almost at once, observers realized that the “political sensation” of the election was the shift of the Black vote from the Republican to the Democratic column. One poll asserted that 75 percent of Black voters living above the Mason-Dixon line had supported Roosevelt. Earl Brown thought that the change was particularly noticeable in Ohio, Michigan, and Indiana where “nothing short of a revolution” had occurred. It was “as dramatic and sudden a change in political behavior as has ever occurred” in the United States, “perhaps the most dramatic shift in the history of American politics.”[49]

The states Mitchell was responsible for reflected this realignment, particularly in larger urban areas. There, Hurja’s post-election analysis found that Democrats enjoyed an “emphatic” increase in their vote in 143 of 157 cities with populations larger than 150,000. This was most obvious in the Black sections of Chicago, Cincinnati, Cleveland, Columbus and Detroit. Gunnar Myrdal’s research identified many of these Democratic gains in specific wards where more than 50 percent of the voters were Black.

Table 1. Gunnar Myrdal’s 1944 research identified many Democratic gains in specific wards where more than 50 percent of the voters were Black.

	1932	**1936**
Chicago (2)	25.4	47.9
Chicago (3)	20.7	50.1
Detroit (3)	46	71.4
Detroit (5)	50.2	75
Detroit (7)	53.9	79
Columbus (6)	27.9	47.7
Columbus (7)	23.2	46

Source: Gunnar Myrdal, with the assistance of Richard Steiner and Arnold Rose, *An American Dilemma: The Negro Problem and Modern Democracy* (New York: Harper and Row, 1962, ca. 1944), 496.

Additionally, in Cincinnati's Black Sixteenth Ward, the Democratic vote rose from 29 percent in 1932 to 65 percent in 1936. In Indianapolis, Black wards went Democratic 75 percent–25 percent. In St. Louis and Kansas City, Democrats carried thirty-nine of forty precincts.[50]

As Sean Savage has correctly noted, Mitchell's Colored Division was "not the dominant factor in this partisan realignment." Public works and relief programs, Roosevelt's personal charisma, his wife's activism, and the existence of a so-called Black Cabinet to advise the president were key elements in shifting public opinion. Beyond that, the reality was that economics trumped politics. New Deal policies had saved many from starvation. It was poor Black people who shifted dramatically to the Democrats; elites remained largely Republican. New Deal agencies, even if unfairly administered, still represented an advance for Black Americans over what had been. As one observer noted, "when you start from a position of zero, even if you move up to the point of two on a scale of twelve, it looks like a big improvement."[51]

Nevertheless, it is reasonable to suggest that Mitchell was an important "organizer of victory" by turning potential votes into actual ballots. Not only did most Black electors "know the story of Sylvester Harris," but its teller coordinated Democratic resources in a way that translated Roosevelt's message into actual ballots. He and his directors made sure that Black Democrats, an inchoate political group at the beginning of 1936, were identified, registered, attended speeches, kept in personal contact with local candidates, and appeared at proper locations on Election Day.[52]

Christopher Manning, writing in *William L. Dawson and the Limits of Black Electoral Leadership,* concludes that "Mitchell clearly did not have the skills to handle the demands of a national campaign" in 1936. Most contemporaries of Mitchell would have disagreed with this assessment. William H. Larrabee (IN-11th) spoke for many incumbent congressmen who had benefitted from Mitchell's efforts. "The work given our party in the colored precincts," he wrote, "speaks well for the splendid work that was accomplished by your bureau in this campaign."[53]

Farley also knew what Mitchell had accomplished. "The Chief" wrote to him with unusual emotion after the election: "Dear Arthur: I don't believe in long letters and this one is going to be short, but sincere. I want you to know that I appreciate, more than I will ever be able to tell you, the very generous assistance rendered by you. . . . I shall always remember your loyal cooperation. Jim."[54]

Yet, even at this moment of triumph, the man who had no problem employing his wife as "Keeper of Records" in Ohio or bribing a Chicago newspaper, seemed sanctimonious when he returned a thirty-dollar check to the Democratic National Committee. He was, he explained, "duty bound" to return the check because the worker to whom it was issued "was not at the closing of the campaign engaged in working for the general ticket but was rather working for me."[55]

This self-righteousness made enemies of many who had done much to assure his success. For example, Percy Jones, who had made Mitchell a hero in Ohio, had his final budget rejected with this note: "You know as well as I do that I have not authorized any of this. To me, it looks like an effort to chisel. Is this the way you do business? Please do not bother to send me any more of this type as it is a waste of time and I will not approve them." Some of this criticism even reached Roosevelt. After reading a letter of complaint from an Ohio speaker, Roosevelt sent it along to Farley. The writer "seems a good deal down on Congressman Mitchell," the president noted. "Perhaps you can get someone to look into it without bringing me in to it."[56]

Nevertheless, the director of the Western Division was riding high at the end of 1936. As Earl Brown noted after the election, "The pay-off in Politics is always on the winner, and Mitchell won. By virtue of his office, he is the foremost Negro politician in the country." Percy Jones, rising above the personal rebuff he had received, agreed. Mitchell was "the number one man in the nation in the political field."[57]

Mitchell was not modest about his accomplishments. He had played a role in effecting a transition "so profound that a majority of black voters never again supported a Republican presidential candidate." By doing so, he thought that he had acquired the respect and gratitude of House Democrats, emotions he intended to capitalize on when it came time for Congress to consider his prized piece of legislation, his anti-lynching bill. "I'm going back to Congress," he told the *Defender,* "to make history."[58]

9

"The Most Potent Man in Congress"

The Congress that met in 1937 did not, however, fulfill Mitchell's expectations because Roosevelt interpreted his sweeping 1936 victory as the country's unqualified endorsement of the New Deal. Fearing that a conservative, elderly Supreme Court might declare most of the statutes upon which it rested unconstitutional, the president seized the moment to move against what he thought to be an unpopular institution that had been repudiated by the voters. In a special message to Congress on February 5, 1937, he requested legislation that would permit him to appoint up to six additional Supreme Court justices, one for each judge who served beyond the age of seventy. With this authority, he explained in a fireside chat, he would select individuals "who will bring to the Courts a present-day sense of the Constitution, younger men who have had personal experience and contact with modern facts and circumstances under which average men have to live and work."[1]

Caught off guard, Mitchell at first offered qualified support for the proposal. The Court was "slow, sluggish, and in many respects irresponsible." It had to be brought "in touch with modern trends" if it was to protect the rights of the people. He did not believe that the number of Supreme Court justices should be increased but did think that "those who have passed the point of usefulness should be retired." His mind, however, was "open on the whole question."[2]

A month later, Mitchell had rallied enthusiastically to Roosevelt's cause despite the fact that Thomas D. Herd reflected the views of the vast majority of those who wrote to him that "the independence, courage, and isolation of the Supreme Court must not be impaired. It is the umpire of this nation and it enforces the rules. If the rules should be changed, the people can change them." Roosevelt's initiative, the congressman answered, aimed at more than the "carnivorous conservatism" of the 1937 Supreme Court. It also had the potential to seat judges more sympathetic to the New Deal and racial justice, transforming the judiciary into an agency for a modern presidency, by "deferring to the expertise of the newly enhanced administrative state." Roosevelt was "100% right and 100% plus in [fighting] against entrenched greed and power."[3]

Mitchell then evolved into an unsparing critic of those opposing the president. R. H. Fogler, a vice president at Montgomery Ward, provoked a wrathful response when he also invoked the Supreme Court's role in the system of checks and balances as a reason to maintain the status quo. What permitted Fogler, Mitchell wanted to know, to preach justice when he was part of a "commercial institution that doesn't even want members of my race as customers." The "damnable system" Folger represented had "robbed and deprived one-tenth of our population in their quest for economic freedom." "I am mighty glad to have your letter so I can express to you my deep feeling on this hypocrisy of which you must be a leading disciple," Mitchell wrote.[4]

He also spoke frankly to fellow Black Americans on the subject. The Supreme Court justices, he lectured W. W. K. Sparrow, were "nine antiquated old men whose minds are senile" and who represented an institution that "has struck down practically every measure passed by the Congress during the past seventy-five years which had for its purpose the lifting of burdens from the backs of Negroes." This was an opportunity not only to shift the composition of the court but also to move some elements of decision-making from an unelected, out-of-touch body to a "great humanitarian who sympathized the plight of the race. It seems to me that if we do not speak out now, we are muffing a good opportunity."[5]

The 1936 election presented Mitchell with what he saw as a good opportunity to advance two causes of significant appeal to "his race": civil service reform and the admission of Black Americans to the service academies. The Civil Service Commission had been established in 1883 to award government jobs on the basis of an impartial examination, not as a political reward. In reality, after 1900 it had developed into an agency practicing rank discrimination against both Black and female candidates. The Depression only aggravated this trend, as traditional lower-paying service positions, previously held by Black workers, were increasingly being awarded to unemployed white counterparts. By the late 1930s, six government agencies employed 29,046 individuals, but only 1,078 (3.7 percent) were Black. Of these, 870 were custodial positions.[6]

Mitchell railed against the commission as the "greatest curse we have connected with any department of government," one whose "hypocrisy and absolute unfairness" had to be ended. To accomplish this, he introduced a bill (HR 3691) that aimed at eliminating the three pillars supporting existing discriminatory policies. To him the most offensive rules were the requirement for photographs on a job application, the "rule of three" that gave appointment officials the authority to choose among the top three candidates after seeing these photographs but before making a hiring decision, and the ability of the hiring agency to change the gender designation of the individual to be appointed after an eligibility list had been produced.[7]

Kelly Miller, who claimed that his appointment to a civil service job in 1884 made him the oldest surviving Black appointee, saw the three rules as the "crux of the [discrimination] problem" because it granted "discretionary powers to petty appointing officials." Mitchell's bill, HR 3691, mandated the substitution of fingerprints for photographs. It also called for the hiring of the individual ranked first on the eligibility list and the elimination of a gender designation preference for any given position.[8]

Mitchell took pride in 3691, asserting to Barnett that, if it was enacted into law, "it will go a greater distance in solving our problems with the government than any bill that has been introduced in my lifetime." William E. Taylor, a professor of law at Howard, concurred, considering the bill "the most progressive piece of legislation introduced in the last fifty years." It would make the system fairer not only to Black applicants but to "white women not blessed with beauty or extreme youth . . . and [to] all types of American citizens who do not have influential friends able to pull strings for them."[9]

Traditional enemies also praised Mitchell's effort. The NAACP's *Crisis* saw 3691 as "a bill of tremendous importance to colored people . . . [that] deserves whole-hearted support from all groups interested in employment opportunities for the race." Even Roy Wilkins found reason to salute Mitchell in his *Watchtower* column. The congressman was "on sound ground and if he is successful will benefit thousands of Negro citizens." But, Wilkins added, "the boys of the press will give him more than his due if he will climb down off his horse and cease being a boiled, stuffed shirt."[10] Mitchell's bill died in committee, but all three reforms were eventually adopted after he had left Congress.

Another crusade Mitchell undertook in early 1937 was to see a Black graduate of the US Naval Academy. Since the end of Reconstruction, only two had, none in the twentieth century. Much of the responsibility for this lay in the fact that the navy's hierarchy was dominated by white men who "embraced the mores of the southern racial caste system." Believing that there was no place in the service for a Black officer, they had created an atmosphere where "a Black American at the Naval Academy had one chance in a million of surviving the first year."[11]

Given the racially mixed nature of his district, appointments to both service academies had posed problems for Mitchell from the beginning. The only member of Congress willing to make minority appointments, De Priest had nominated Black candidates to both service academies regardless of where they lived. Among these was Benjamin O. Davis Jr., who went on to become the army's first Black general. He graduated from West Point in 1936 despite receiving the "silent treatment" for four years.[12]

Mitchell began with a different policy, arguing that "white boys have just as much right to be named from [his] district as any other group." He admitted to having been tempted to make his first appointment a white man but

Figure 9. Mitchell with James L. Johnson, his appointment to the Naval Academy (1937). His "resignation" outraged Mitchell, who thought he had been "railroaded" out of the academy. Chicago History Museum, ICHi-026234; Wide World Photos, photographer.

was dissuaded by "the members of the organization in Chicago" who thought it imperative that his initial selection be of a "member of my own race . . . to meet the argument that I am neglecting the interests of the Negroes wholly in my official appointments."[13]

To relieve some of the pressure on him to follow De Priest's policy, Mitchell sought to persuade other members of Congress with large Black constituencies to join him in naming minorities. He even went so far as to volunteer to speak to an Arkansas representative on behalf of Little Rock resident Otis Harris, who had sought a nomination from him. Mitchell hoped, he told Harris, that eventually "these men from the South will make some appointments of colored boys."[14]

These attempts having failed, Mitchell became convinced that he had to follow De Priest by naming Black men to the service academies even if they were not Chicago residents. Approaching a 1936 nomination to Annapolis with care, he consulted with Henry O. Atwood, the instructor of the Cadet Corps at Dunbar High School in Washington, a school seen as having one of the nation's best collegiate training program for Black students. Together, they chose James Lee Johnson to be the first Black midshipman to be enrolled at the Naval Academy since 1879. Then a student at the Case School of Applied Science in Ohio, Johnson had been a "brilliant" pupil at Dunbar, where he did so well that his friends nicknamed him "Socks," equating his mental capacities with those of the Greek philosopher Socrates.[15]

After passing both academic and physical entrance exams, Johnson enrolled on June 15, 1936, with Mitchell's personal pledge of support. "Remember," his sponsor promised, "that you have thousands pulling for you. I shall never be too busy to come to your rescue if it is necessary. I am profoundly interested in your success."[16]

The summer of 1936 passed reasonably well for Johnson, but trouble came when classes began in the fall. He roomed alone and therefore could not keep up with last-minute changes in appointments. This led to tardiness and other supposed violations of the academy's regulations, which resulted in a growing number of demerits. As a father of another midshipman described the situation to Mitchell, "the upperclassmen are apparently sitting up nights studying the rules for technicalities on which they can trip up the colored boy." In spite of this harassment, the ANP reported in October that Johnson "is doing fine and is being well treated. He is engaging in athletic activities and is a broad jumper and runner." His academic performance was satisfactory in all subjects except English.[17]

So it was a surprise when Superintendent D. F. Sellers wrote to the Johnson's father on January 27, 1937, that his son had accumulated 181 demerits, a number that threatened his status. Johnson Sr. forwarded the letter to Mitchell, who complained to both Sellers and Roosevelt. In his letter to Sellers, Mitchell charged that Johnson was being held to a much higher standard than a white boy would be, a situation that was "true in this country in whatever line we find ourselves in." Johnson's jeopardy, he told Roosevelt, was that "rare occasion" when he felt he had to appeal directly to the president. There was no doubt in his mind that upperclassmen had recorded demerits in an attempt to force Johnson out: "Something should be done to guarantee him a fair and square deal."[18]

While Roosevelt did not answer, Sellers did the next day, assuring Mitchell that "no summary action will be taken or is contemplated." The superintendent also came to Mitchell's office to vouch for the fact that Johnson was being treated fairly, although he conceded that no one could combat "ingrained prejudice against associating with the negro race." Mitchell and Atwood went to Annapolis two days later, interviewed Johnson, and received a promise from authorities that the Naval Academy was bending over backward to be evenhanded. Feeling better, Mitchell informed James M. Mead (NY-42) that "Johnson is doing well and is well thought of by the faculty."[19]

Unfortunately, it was at this point that Johnson's vision suddenly deteriorated. It had been 20/20 on admission; when he took an eye exam on February

8, he failed.[20] The Naval Academy's Academic Board met on February 10 and unanimously recommended Johnson's dismissal. It justified this advice on 1) his grade in English; 2) his demerits; 3) his failing eyesight; and 4) the general observation that "he was not considered officer material." Handed a draft letter of resignation the next day and asked to sign it, Johnson protested that he wanted to talk to Mitchell. He was told that the letter was a mere formality that could be reversed if he signed, while his refusal to sign to would create ill will. He signed. On February 12, Claude Swanson, the secretary of the navy and a Virginian "with a litany of 'darky' jokes" in his repertoire, accepted Johnson's withdrawal.[21]

When Mitchell heard of the resignation, he fired off telegrams of protest to both Sellers and Roosevelt. The president then called Mitchell to the White House for a February 16 conference during which with the congressman apparently convinced Roosevelt that an injustice had occurred. Upon leaving, Mitchell told the United Press that he was sure the president would do the right thing. "If he has any race prejudice of any kind," Roosevelt's guest observed, "I am unable to detect it." However, Mitchell added, Johnson had only been enrolled at Annapolis because "the Navy knew I was fairly well regarded by President Roosevelt."[22]

Roosevelt did follow up, telling Swanson that dismissing Johnson was not in the navy's best interest, that he should be carried provisionally for the rest of the year, and asking his secretary of the navy to review the case. But Mitchell was suspicious of this recommendation. While praising Roosevelt publicly, he sensed that there was little he could do. "I am making a fight on [Johnson's] behalf," he told a confidante, "but I am afraid I will not be able to accomplish much."[23]

He was correct. Swanson reconvened the Academic Board, but it unanimously endorsed the decision to "accept" Johnson's resignation. Roosevelt refused to override that finding. Mitchell described the entire process to an Ohio colleague as "a Star Chamber investigation which meant white washing the culprits." "I have in my possession," he added, "facts which establish beyond all question . . . that Johnson was railroaded out of the Academy through the deliberate efforts of high class midshipmen and officials of the Academy."[24]

In the aftermath of the affair, Johnson's father expressed gratitude to Mitchell "for all you did. I doubt if any Colored boy would have stood what has been heaped upon James." Later, both Sock's father and mother blamed Roosevelt for the outcome. "We know you would have taken further steps," they wrote to Mitchell, "had it not been you were so confident of the President's investigation."[25]

Refusing to give up, Mitchell gathered evidence to substantiate his "railroading" charge with typical tenacity and eye for detail. A rumor informed him that one of the midshipmen who had led the efforts to remove Johnson had been motivated by hatred for all Black people because his father had been murdered by one. Pursuing this, Mitchell asked Charles H. Houston at the NAACP if the organization could supply him with "info" as he intended to demand a congressional investigation into the incident. He also had Claude Holman, his secretary, investigate. That inquiry revealed that the father, a streetcar motorman, had in fact been shot and killed by a Black man during a 1933 holdup that had netted the criminal, who was now serving a life term in prison, two dollars.[26]

This fight for Johnson brought Mitchell some of the rare hate letters he kept. One read: "You yellow nigger, you have a lot of gall trying to force a nigger into the Naval Academy. . . . You are just breedin trouble as fast as you can. The less you are seen and heard, the better." Another threatened: "If you niggers don't quit pushing yourselves where you have no business, your are going to make a lot of trouble for yourselves. You know there is no place in the Navy for Nigger officers and you would do well to pipe down on this line. Keep it up and see what happens."

The Black press, however, celebrated his effort. The *Defender* editorialized that "this manly procedure adds justifiable laurels to his position as Congressman." William N. Jones, writing in his Day-by-Day column for the *Afro-American*, thought that Mitchell's "slashing onslaught against the social royalty at Annapolis" might make him "the most potent man in Congress."[27]

For his part, Mitchell felt that while he had lost a battle, he would win the war. He told John P. Davis, the secretary of the National Negro Congress, that he would "immediately appoint two other Colored students to the Academy. . . . I am not at all worried about the outcome." A similar message went to the American Society for Race Tolerance, with Mitchell adding, "anything you do to help my appointees in the way of fighting the cruel discrimination at the school would be highly appreciated." "The fight for Negro rights at the Academy," he reported to Emmet Scott, "has just begun." Preparing for battle, he wrote to Swanson, requesting copies of the college transcripts for the Annapolis officials involved in Johnson's dismissal, as well as their graduation dates, birthplaces, and assignments held as officers prior to their appointments at the Naval Academy. But to be successful in changing navy policy he would need the help of Black Americans, who should write to their representatives demanding justice. Our weakness, he told James Wetlock, lay in the "indifference of Negro voters in calling upon the Congressmen for whom they voted to do something in the way of wiping out these inequalities. . . . Until they are willing and ready to do this there can be no changes brought about."[28]

In the next round of their attack on what the *New York Amsterdam News* characterized as the Navy's "poisonous attitude toward Blacks," Atwood and

Mitchell selected George Trivers as Johnson's replacement. Another Dunbar graduate, he was enrolled at a local teacher's college. As the breadwinner for his family, Trivers was at first reluctant to abandon his career choice but eventually applied, passed all the entrance exams, and enrolled at Annapolis on June 10, 1937. Again, things did not go well. Like Johnson, Trivers was forced to board alone. Within two days, he had accumulated thirteen demerits for not having the shade in his room rolled up to the proper height and the discovery of dirt in the overflow hole to his sink. When upperclassmen told him to "come here, nigger," he had to respond "aye, aye, sir." He was kicked while marching in rank. Someone spat on his plate in the mess hall.[29]

After two weeks, the commandant, Forde Anderson Todd, called Trivers in for a conference. He told Mitchell's nominee that he should resign because "a successful life for a man must necessarily primarily depend upon his having a congenial occupation. At this stage of amalgamation of [your] race into general society [you are] rendering a disservice to [your] people by forcing [yourself] on other young men who as yet [do] not have themselves under control, and thus [you are] stirring up antagonism in [your] work and play." Trivers talked with his mother about this "advice," and she said she needed him at home. Although Mitchell had warned him "to communicate with me should the least thing appear wrong or against him," Trivers did not follow his sponsor's advice and resigned on July 3, after only seventeen days at Annapolis. Todd described the resignation as a "miracle." He reported to Sellers that Trivers "appeared in my office and to my utter amazement said he had talked over the matter with his mother and that they both thought he should resign, and he had his resignation in his hand. . . . As it stands we are very fortunate in being rid of Trivers."[30]

Mitchell, who had gone to Annapolis to investigate the circumstances surrounding the resignation, was furious, but more with Trivers than with the naval authorities. The congressman sent out a press release that described Trivers as not the "fighting type. . . . I am impressed rather strongly that he does not wish any position that requires strenuous effort, that he is like many young men I have known—he wishes to move along the line of least resistance." I would never have appointed him, he told P. B. Young, "had I not been led to believe that he had in him more ambition, courage, and real fight than he has shown."[31]

By and large, Black newspapers agreed with Mitchell. To the *East Tennessee News*, Trivers was a "lounge lizard . . . a typical example of the spineless, thoughtless young men of the Negro racial group who are to be found in far too great numbers in every section of our land." The *Afro-American* thought his resignation without consulting the congressman "inexcusable." He "was not made of the stuff to meet the challenge of this hotbed of color prejudice.

What any young man of color who goes to the Naval Academy [must know] to begin with is that the moment he enters the place, so far as he is concerned, THE WAR IS ALREADY ON." The *Defender* was crueler in its judgment. Its editorial, "Mama's Boy Returns Home," characterized Trivers's complaints as being against "the customary school pranks that even the most timid of country girls in some unknown boarding school would endure without a whimper. . . . Congressman Mitchell should be greatly relieved now that mama's boy has gone home where he may cuddle under the protective arms of an indulgent mother."[32]

In the aftermath of a second failure, Mitchell reflected to Eustace Gray, the managing editor of the *Philadelphia Tribune,* that the unfair treatment of Black individuals "might be more pronounced at the Academy than at other places, but we find it in all our institutions. . . . We should fight [against this] with good judgment, common sense, courage and uncompromising determination. I see no other way by which we are to overcome." But he was undaunted. Trivers had not shown "the type of courage that I think should have been shown by one placed in his position, [but] I will find the man and the man will do the job."[33]

But he never did. Six months after Trivers's resignation, when Charles H. Houston of the NAACP asked what his strategy was for calling attention to the "color bar" against Black midshipmen at Annapolis, Mitchell bristled. The navy might be more prejudiced than any other department in government, he responded, but unless Black candidates at least applied for appointments, what could he do? He had had to recruit both Johnson and Trivers. He had gone further than anybody else in attacking the problem. But, he said, "I have not had the cooperation and help of the organizations of the colored race that pretend they are interested in breaking down prejudice. This refers as much to your organization as to any other. If you have a man who is competent and who wishes to be appointed to the Naval Academy you have only to give me his name and to put him in touch with me and I will make the appointment." He followed up with the suggestion that the *Crisis* should publish his letter, as "this should drive men to make application if they are interested." Most, he warned Houston, "will not submit to the rigid discipline at these [Annapolis and West Point] institutions."[34]

Mitchell enjoyed greater success at the United States Military Academy with his appointment of James D. Fowler, another Dunbar graduate, who arrived at West Point a year after Johnson had begun at Annapolis. His reception was similar to that afforded Johnson and Trivers: demerits for appearance, no roommate, being excluded from dances and local convenience stores, being kept up at night to provoke drowsiness in class, and the silent treatment. "Those of us who were his classmates," a fellow cadet remembered, "suffered the usual indignities . . . but even we could distinguish between our treatment and that reserved for 'Mister Fowler.'"[35]

However, Fowler succeeded where Johnson and Trivers had failed. The *Afro-American* followed his freshman year in detail. He was "doing fine" academically and had been "vociferously applauded by thousands" of fans at the Army-Harvard football game. Three weeks later, he sat through a downpour at the Army-Navy game, "while hundreds of white cadets sought shelter."[36] Between the two reports, Fowler found time to write to Mitchell, boasting that "through you I have been able to prove to myself and to others that the Negro is one hundred percent man." At the same time, he complained that "it would take too long to list the obstacles that I have had to face . . . surmounting seemingly impassable barriers daily [with] very, very little opportunities to study." By the following July, Fowler grumbled to his parents that "Cong. Mitchell will have to do something about my demerits. I can't do anything about it. I'm skinned [given a demerit] if I take a deep breath."[37]

Mitchell offered little sympathy in response. Fowler shouldn't make excuses, he lectured. His mother was visiting too much and he was spending too much time writing to her. He should be left alone to "devote [himself] exclusively to [his] duties." Mitchell continued: "If you do this, I know you can make good. If you don't do it, of course you will flunk. Those who flunk have only themselves to blame. There is no excuse you could offer me that I would accept in lieu of success." In another exhortation he told Fowler to "lay aside much of the foolishness in which you are now engaging . . . the damn fool things you are saying which show how silly and light you are thinking. I want you to cut this thing out and be a real man."[38]

While holding his nominee to a high standard, Mitchell also sought to remove the "obstacles" Fowler faced. He protested to Brigadier General Jay L. Benedict, the superintendent at West Point, in a letter he copied to Roosevelt. "There has been," he asserted, "a most determined effort on the part of some of the cadets to make it impossible for Fowler to remain at the Academy because of the fact that he is colored." "I know young Fowler well," he added. "It is difficult to find a more outstanding and deserving young man regardless of race or color." Then the mailed fist emerged: "I have talked about this with the President and know that it is his desire that absolute justice be done in this case."[39]

Benedict dismissed the protest. Fowler had not been harassed. On the contrary, there was "considerable feeling in the Corps that [he] is not being held to the same high standards as are other cadets. He is presuming upon his being the only colored cadet . . . and does not endeavor to maintain the high standards of dress and conduct required of his classmates." But this time Roosevelt supported Mitchell. He sent a memo to his military advisor, Edwin "Pa" Wilson, that read, "I want the colored boy, James Fowler Jr., to graduate."[40]

Fowler did graduate in 1942, receiving a greater ovation than that offered to the cadets who finished both first and last in the class. By then, Mitchell seemed reconciled to the realities at West Point, if not at Annapolis. Conditions there were no worse than "discriminations against colored boys at other northern schools." The service academies' purpose was to train "officers who will be called upon to bear unusual burdens," and the regimentation certainly did this. Those "looking for a good easy berth and an opportunity to escape hard work of course failed."[41]

10

"The Greatest Statesman His Race Has Produced in a Century"

THE ANTI-LYNCHING DEBATE reopened in January 1937. Chagrined by the Senate filibuster that had doomed Costigan-Wagner in 1935 and the failed caucus strategy of 1936, White and the NAACP changed tactics. In 1937, they planned to start with a House bill. Fearing that Sumners would bottle up any proposed legislation in the Judiciary Committee, they also urged support for a discharge petition. Through this method any anti-lynching bill would avoid the Judiciary Committee and come to the House floor for an immediate vote as soon as 218 members signed the request for this to happen.[1]

Of the forty-one bills submitted for approval, the NAACP chose to reintroduce the Gavagan version. This enraged Mitchell, who considered Gavagan "a demagogue of the worst type, a man who meant nothing good for [Blacks]." He was "a politician," and a northern one at that, someone who did not understand the lynching phenomenon. Besides, his bill was "unconstitutional and doomed." Rather than support this "farce," Mitchell chose to reintroduce his own. His objective was to get a law, any law, into the statute books. Once there, it could be strengthened over time.[2]

Gavagan's bill was placed on the House docket on January 5; Mitchell's three days later. Although both made lynching a crime, the differences between the two were significant. Mitchell's dealt only with "victims seized from official custody"; Gavagan's "with all instances of mob violence." Mitchell's had officials found guilty of conspiring with a mob sentenced to from two to ten years in prison; Gavagan's from five to twenty-five. Mitchell's was silent on when federal intervention should occur; Gavagan's stipulated that it should begin after thirty days if local or state authorities had failed to act. Mitchell's imposed a fine of between two and five thousand dollars on the county where a death occurred; Gavagan's held both the county of abduction and death, if different, liable. Gavagan's also "exempted from creditors' claims damages assessed against the county on behalf of the victim's survivors."[3]

Clearly, the Gavagan bill treated lynchers and their accomplices more severely than did Mitchell's, but Mitchell believed that his was superior because it had a chance to become law; Gavagan's did not. It offered supporters the moral high ground but would only provoke another Senate filibuster and, even if adopted by the Senate, be declared unconstitutional by the Supreme Court. Its sponsors knew that. Their aim was not to pass important legislation but rather to create an "issue" that would raise support, and money, for the NAACP. "There are many people," Mitchell charged, "talking about this legislation simply to be talkers. That is, instead of working in an effective manner, they are using it as propaganda to promote themselves rather than bring about the actual passage of a bill." He warned Wilkins that the NAACP's tactics were also wrong. No bill forced to floor by a discharge petition had ever passed in the House of Representatives.[4]

Conversely, Mitchell saw a path forward for his bill, written as it was to take advantage of existing circumstances. Given his careful cultivation of a relationship with Sumners, the Judiciary Committee might report it favorably to the whole House. In the Senate, "Southern forces were themselves predicting passage without lengthy obstruction" of some type of anti-lynching legislation. Surely a bill authored by a Black southerner, less threatening in its provisions, would be more favorably received in the Upper Chamber than one coming from a Tammany Hall "hack." Hugo Black, then still a senator and Mitchell's fellow Alabamian, had gone out of his way to praise Mitchell when the latter arrived in Congress. Now, Black hinted that he could vote for an anti-lynching bill. Reinforcing this optimism, a March 1937 poll conducted by the American Institute of Public Opinion showed 70 percent of the country in favor of an anti-lynching bill. In the South, the percentage of support was 65 percent.[5]

Should his bill fail, Mitchell promised to fall in line behind Gavagan. "I expect," he told Pickens, the NAACP official who had done so much to torpedo his Industrial Commission, "to vote for whatever anti-lynching bill we are able to get before the House." He thought his was the better bill, but "authorship of the bill means little to me as compared with the importance of the legislation itself." Pickens answered with a handwritten note showing how the relationship had evolved: "Believe me, personally very grateful for the brave fight you are making along many lines." The *Pittsburgh Courier* noted that if concerned Black leaders worked together, the House might pass "meritorious legislation . . . that means so much to colored people."[6]

Agreement, however, was not to be the order of the day. Battle lines had been drawn between White and Mitchell, forcing congressmen to choose sides. Many supported Mitchell. Arthur Aleshire (OH-7), a newly elected beneficiary of Mitchell's Ohio efforts, was one. He informed White that he "had been working along with Mr. Mitchell and feel he is getting somewhere. . . . I have every reason to believe that Chairman Sumners will cooperate with Mr. Mitchell and afford hearings so that action can be taken."[7]

White's discharge petition rapidly accumulated 170 signatures in March, but Mitchell refused to sign, advising his colleagues to follow his lead. At this point, Sumners agreed to hold a hearing, the announced purpose of which would be to consider all anti-lynching legislation. The chairman made clear that he was opposed to, and would vote against, any anti-lynching bill. But, Sumners told White, if one had to come from his committee to the House floor, he did not believe that the NAACP would have "the nerve to oppose passage of a bill introduced by the one Negro member of Congress."[8]

On March 8, Mitchell wrote to his House colleagues announcing the hearing while predicting that some anti-lynching legislation would be reported out of the Judiciary Committee. "It is my candid opinion," he added, "that the bill which I have before the Committee is the best of the group." Writing to Barnett, he called Sumners's willingness to hold a hearing a "signal victory," a thought he expanded upon in a letter to the editor of the *Quarterly Review*. Sumners's action was recognition of his (Mitchell's) "unreserved efforts" to make a "favorable impression" on his fellow congressmen. He was franker still in a note to a friend at this moment of apparent triumph. If his position in support of anti-lynching "has not convinced my critics, then they can go to h . . . as it is quite apparent they are either too ignorant to be informed or they are too vicious to concede the fact."[9]

The NAACP thought itself neither ignorant nor vicious. Wilkins warned Mitchell that the organization was "deeply suspicious" of Sumners's sudden concession of a hearing. It was only a delaying tactic, designed to prevent the discharge petition from gaining the needed 218 signatures. Why hadn't Mitchell signed? The effect of Mitchell's letter, he predicted to MacNeal, "will be to confuse friendly Congressmen and to give doubtful Congressmen an excuse for not signing the Gavagan petition." Wilkins added that Sumners was bragging that "he has anti-lynching campaigners in his pocket and can delay a hearing as long as necessary."[10]

The Black press was divided. As was so often the case, southern papers tended to agree with the editor of the *St. Louis Argus* that Mitchell had "won a great victory in getting this legislation before the Judiciary Committee. [Sumners's] action is an expression of high respect for you and your opinion." But the *Afro-American* supported the NAACP, terming the call for a hearing "a trick," while the *Defender* warned that Mitchell had "assumed the dubious role of 'front man' for congressmen who are known to be unalterably opposed to any anti-lynching bill."[11]

Mitchell refused to believe that he had been tricked. "I have talked with Sumners at length about my bill," he assured Lewis L. Boyer (IL-15). "While we do not agree on some details, he is as much opposed to lynching as I am and is in favor of working out any kind of program which will wipe out the crime. He is anxious to have the best thinkers of the country come before the Committee and give testimony."[12]

As the NAACP "bombarded" members of Congress with demands that they support discharge, Mitchell remained confident. "I cannot understand what more can be desired," he wrote. "My bill will be reported favorably and will pass the House in this session. There is no reason to sign the Gavagan petition. It is only 'political propaganda for public consumption.'" He would, however, sign the petition "if it becomes apparent that that is the only way a bill can be passed."[13]

He had reason to be hopeful. Many of his supporters were fiercely loyal. Brooks Fletcher (OH-8), another beneficiary of Mitchell's 1936 efforts, objected to the NAACP's efforts to oppose Mitchell. Why was he bothering his friend? he demanded of White. "He is one of the most brilliant and useful members of Congress. Everyone has confidence in him and everyone knows he is working in the best interests of the colored people."[14]

Ever more confident, Mitchell sent another letter to his House colleagues in which he announced the hearing for the last day of the month. At this hearing, all anti-lynching bills would be considered. He was "most anxious that representative citizens in reasonably large numbers appear before this committee for the purpose of giving testimony relative to the crime of lynching and its cures."[15]

He sent invitations to testify to many of the southern supporters who had appeared at the Industrial Commission hearing. These included Ransom, Young, J. E. Mitchell, and C. C. Spaulding. Interestingly, he included for the first time a white, southern newspaper editor, Virginius Dabney of the *Richmond Times-Dispatch*. Mitchell confided to Dabney, "I am in close contact with the Judiciary Committee. Since my entry into Congress I have sought to make friends for this legislation. I have made them. Mr. Sumners is not in any way fighting the passage of this bill." This was a reassurance that he also extended to F. D. Patterson, now the president of Tuskegee: "I have just had a conference with [Sumners] and can assure you that the hearing is going to be on the broadest plane. It is very important that . . . distinguished people of the South appear and state fully their views."[16]

As a favor, Mitchell asked Patterson to persuade Dr. Monroe Work, the head of the Department of Records and Research at Tuskegee whose *Negro Yearbook* was considered the most accurate summary of lynchings then available, to attend. Patterson, who saw himself more as a college president than a race leader, did as requested. But Work refused, writing that "inasmuch as Tuskegee Institute has been content throughout the years to merely report statistics on lynchings, his appearance at the hearing would jeopardize the influence of his work." Work's refusal outraged Mitchell. Terming him a weak and foolish coward, he told Patterson the statistician "belongs to that type of Negro who talks much at the big gate but [is] unwilling to go and speak where a word is needed and might do his people some good. I am thoroughly disgusted with his conduct."[17]

Mitchell was careful to include potential opponents, particularly the NAACP, among those invited to testify. He told Wilkins that he was sure one of the anti-lynching bills would "pass the House this session of Congress. I hope at least one member [of the NAACP] can appear and give testimony."[18]

Walter White tried to block the hearing. "Action is imperative," he warned Illinois NAACP chapters in Chicago, East St. Louis, and Springfield, "even before you lay this letter down." Sumners, the "notorious arch-enemy of anti-lynching legislation, had resorted to the desperate and unprecedented maneuver" of a hearing. White implored that they should see to it that each Illinois congressmen who has not signed the discharge petition is "showered with telegrams." At the same time, they should arrange for as many church meetings as possible opposing the hearings and send telegram encouraging resistance "to any political clubs that you are in contact with."[19]

The hearing was held on March 31, 1937, running from 10 a.m. until 5 p.m. Two accounts of it exist in the Mitchell papers. One, perhaps written by Holman, is titled "Judiciary Committee of House of Representatives holds hearing on anti-lynching legislation." The other, "The Truth about the Anti-Lynching Bill," was composed by Perry Howard, the Black Republican committeeman from Mississippi, who assisted Mitchell in running the meeting.

In the Holman rendition, Sumners opened the session by invited Mitchell to conduct the hearing, a "glowing tribute" as it marked "the first time that a Congressman not a member of a committee has been called to conduct hearings for the committee." Howard confessed that he held "no brief for Democrats" but conceded that Sumners had made a good choice. He thought that Mitchell's "presentation of the case . . . was one of the finest that I have witnessed by any lawyer of any group."

The testimony focused on the evils of lynching, not the merits of a particular bill. Mitchell spoke first, supporting federal legislation. He was followed by eighteen witnesses including Congressmen Pettengill, Koppleman, and Ford. White spoke for the NAACP. The *Afro-American* had him stealing the show, his testimony pointing out that some unnamed bill (Mitchell's) "would produce situations wherein officers could hold off until the mobs got in their deadly work."

Howard's notes paint a different picture. They described the executive secretary as rambling on at length about why he had left Georgia as a young man and finally being asked to sit down. Charles H. Houston replaced him and summarized the organization's views on the constitutionality of anti-lynching legislation.[20]

The day after the hearing, the Judiciary Committee forwarded Mitchell's bill to the entire House with a favorable recommendation after approving it by a vote of eight to seven. Until recently the only piece of anti-lynching legislation ever so recommended, the report concluded: "The Committee on the Judiciary, to whom was referred House Resolution 2251 . . . after consideration, report the same favorably to the House . . . with the recommendation that, as amended, the bill do pass."

According to the *Afro-American*, this approval was as the result of "unparalleled trickery" on the part of southern congressmen. Twice, the newspaper reported, Gavagan had offered to substitute Mitchell's name for his as the author of his [Gavagan's] legislation, but Mitchell had refused the change, "following the instructions of Southern Congressmen, particularly Chairman Sumners." The committee voted thirty times, it asserted, all ballots resulting in support of a recommendation for adoption of the Gavagan bill. "Whereupon, some members of the committee, thinking the issue had been settled, left the meeting." When enough had departed, a move to reconsider resulted in the 8–7 vote.[21]

Writing for the majority, Emanuel Celler of New York focused on refuting the southern contention that lynching was essentially murder and that, since the federal government had no right to intervene in murder cases, it had no right to intervene in lynchings: "In murder one or more individuals take life, generally for some personal reason. In lynch, the mob sets itself up in the place of the State and acts in the place of the processes of law to mete out death as a punishment to a person accused of a crime. The mob sets itself up as judge, jury and executioner. In murder, the accused merely violates the law of the State. In lynching the mob arrogates to itself the powers of the State and the function of the Government. It is therefore not against the act of killing that the Federal Government should exercise its power but also the act of the mob in arrogating to itself the functions of the State and substituting its actions for the due process of law."

Denying the need for any anti-lynching legislation, Sumners wrote for the minority. A law was unnecessary because of the decline in the number of lynchings in recent years, a decrease "which cannot be approximated with reference to any other major crime." This drop "comes from constantly developing public sentiment to suppress lynching," which has been produced by "the greatest of all stimulants, the sense of exclusive responsibility." Taking this responsibility away from individuals and placing it in the hands of the federal government would not accomplish the bills' objective. On the contrary, it would diminish the stimulant working against lynching: public opinion.

Moreover, the bills under consideration "directly attack the basis of good accord and respectful cooperation between the States and the Federal Government, essential to efficient governmental cooperation."

An ecstatic Mitchell wired the *Defender* that the "Judiciary Committee has just made favorable report on my anti-lynching bill and [it] will probably pass next week." He then seized the moment to make a personal appeal to his fellow House Democrats in a letter showing emotion he seldom permitted himself to display. "I have tried to conduct myself," he wrote, "in such a way as to secure not only the respect but the cooperation of my fellow members. As a personal favor to me and as recognition to my group, I am asking that you pay no attention to adverse propaganda but that you wholeheartedly support me in my effort to pass this bill." A second letter to a supporter on the same day anticipated the fight that Mitchell knew lay ahead. The NAACP had "opposed me and my bill all the way through. They are whipped to a frazzle now and, the cowards that they are, they are skulking away with the hope, I think, to throw a monkey wrench in the works next week."[22]

He erred only in the use of the singular form of "monkey wrench." Walter White threw several. On April 1, he wrote to Roosevelt pleading with him to "use his influence" to defeat Mitchell's bill. His own letter to members of Congress came two days later. It denounced the "emasculated" Mitchell bill that had been reported out "wholly and solely" to defeat the Gavagan petition. Any effort, he warned, "to jam through an ineffective measure will be most displeasing" to forty million Americans who support effective legislation.[23]

Representative Sol Bloom of New York spoke for many recipients of these dueling letters when he passed White's on to Mitchell: "I received the enclosed letter from Mr. Walter White and do not quite understand what this is all about. Please advise me and return this letter to me." Harlan was also confused. He had read the two bills and would "admit it [the controversy] is all very much a mystery to me. However, I assure you that it will take the most cogent arguments to persuade me to vote in favor of any anti-lynching sponsored by anyone but you. If you do not have the interests of the Negro population at heart, I would be at a loss to know where to find that interest."[24]

Sensing Mitchell's strength, White airmailed a special delivery letter to MacNeal in which he damned "the perfidy and treachery which we are up against." A drunk southern congressman had boasted to him that Mitchell's bill "didn't have much in it to begin with and we have cut all of that out." Mitchell needed to be inundated by telegrams from his Illinois colleagues "demanding that he repudiate the emasculated and worthless bill bearing his name." Telegrams should also be sent to the Democratic whip, majority leader, and Farley, warning that proponents of effective legislation "will bitterly resent the trickery" that is being engaged in.[25]

MacNeal complied, if grudgingly. He would follow national orders, he replied, but marshalling effective opposition to Mitchell would be very expensive. There was a feeling in the chapter that "our funds should directly benefit Chicago citizens." Helping White would be "at a decided financial sacrifice and is done frequently in the face of objections on the part of local people."

Nevertheless, MacNeal wrote to Mitchell asking him to publicly support the discharge petition and to abandon his usual language "of benign accord with *some* type of language to combat the national disgrace of mob violence. We would like to have your frank and unequivocal statement as to whether or not you will act as suggested above [to support Gavagan] and we would appreciate a reply that is not vague and general."[26]

As requested, MacNeal also swamped the Illinois congressional delegation with messages of opposition to Mitchell's bill. Frank Fries spoke for Mitchell's Illinois colleagues, all but one of whom supported their fellow Illinoisan, when he wrote back, "I cannot understand why you are opposing Congressman Mitchell as I am confident he is doing everything he can to assist the colored people. . . . He is held in high regard by his colleagues in Congress."[27]

Mitchell's final words on lynching came in a CBS radio broadcast aired at 6:40 p.m. on April 5, two days before the scheduled vote on his bill. Lynching, he told his listeners, is "a great national evil that has brought disgrace to what we call American civilization and justice." Governors and women's organizations in southern states have declared against a crime that the president has termed "a vile form of collective murder." He then explained the distinction between murder and lynching that Celler had made. In considering the various bill before Congress, his was the most likely to become law, "but I expect to vote for whatever anti-lynching bill we are able to get before the House. . . . Authorship of the bill means little to me compared with the importance of the legislation itself."[28]

As usual, Mitchell had meticulously counted votes. He thought that his bill would pass but knew that few Republicans would support him after his attack on Republicans for inaction on civil rights. To many, such as Bert Lord, the issue was personal. Lord's father, the New York representative wrote in response to Mitchell's April 2 appeal, was killed in the Civil War: "It did not come with very good grace when last year you condemned Lincoln and the Republican party who freed the Negro race. To my mind, the remarks you made were unbecoming one of your race."

Likewise, only a few southern Democrats would vote "yes." Allard Gasque (SC-6) was one of the few of them who even responded to Mitchell's personal appeal. "I have been proud of your actions and demeanor [and] we are glad to be with you on everything we think is right," he wrote, but on this he was wrong. Mitchell's bill "would be disastrous in my state." It was not fair to blame an officer who had been "overpowered by a mob" when trying to prevent a lynching.[29]

Despite this opposition, Mitchell thought he could get the majority of votes he needed for to pass his bill. There were eighty-eight Republicans in the House and 347 Democrats, counting Minnesota farm laborers and Wisconsin progressives among the Democrats. It was an historic majority, one where the dominant party held 80 percent of the seats and one which he had played some part in creating. One hundred of those Democrats came from states that had seceded during the Civil War and twenty-six from the border states of Missouri, Kentucky, and Maryland. At worst, that totaled 214 potential "noes," but some members of the potential opposition might be absent, some might abstain, and some even vote in favor of 2251 in deference to the way Mitchell had conducted himself in the House.

But, did not he—soft-spoken, reasonable, and promoting the first step in a process to advance the cause of racial justice that the vast majority saw as necessary—enjoy wide support among northern and western Democrats, many of whom were in his personal debt for his 1936 efforts? Had not his poll of his peers shown that? A majority supporting him was a distinct possibility. Further, if the House adopted his bill by regular procedure not a discharge petition, it had a chance to escape a Senate filibuster and then be declared constitutional by the Supreme Court because of the manner in which it had been written.

Walter White had reason to be worried, and he knew it. He saw many years of effort to obtain an "honest anti-lynch bill at risk due to the egomania, treachery, and trickery" of Arthur Mitchell. So he had Wilkins telegraph MacNeal the day before the vote: "Necessary wire Chicago Congressmen immediately and any others in group you know urging them to vote down Mitchell bill." MacNeal again complied, repeating his complaint about the expense he encountered from sending "messengers in cars and jitney cabs" all over the city.[30]

According to an official NAACP press release, the evening of April 6 White arranged for Congress to be flooded by a wave of telegrams from the "most influential" representatives of the Black press denouncing Mitchell. The *Courier*, *Afro-American*, *Amsterdam News*, *Opportunity*, and the *Crisis* all sent wires to that effect. The *Defender* would have, but Abbott could not be contacted. The NAACP also sent messages to 282 congressmen urging them to repudiate the "weak Mitchell bill."[31]

The House session of April 7, 1937, opened with "obstructive tactics," and "great confusion" characterizing the beginning. To the *Chicago Tribune*, "scenes of some disorder" unfolded as "Speaker William B. Bankhead frequently called upon the sergeants-at-arms in a futile attempt to preserve decorum." To be sure the opposition coalition was in place, Republicans insisted on a time-consuming roll call to establish that a quorum was present. Then Hamilton Fish, later characterized by Mitchell as a "notoriety seeking, insincere politician," insisted that the record of the previous day be read in full, adding that Mitchell "hasn't the support of a single prominent colored newspaper in America."[32]

Once these preliminaries had been dealt with, the watershed moment in Arthur Mitchell's career as a member of Congress arrived. As a master of detail, he must have appreciated its procedural character. The motion on the floor was not whether the legislation should be adopted, but only whether it should be debated as a first step toward becoming law. One hundred and twenty-two members voted that it should; 257 that it should not. An enraged Mitchell stormed off the floor. When J. Burwood Daly of Pennsylvania tried to intercept him to explain his vote with the majority, Mitchell's response was "you can go to hell." A shocked Daly stepped aside, mumbling "I thought you were a gentleman."[33]

Reflecting on the vote, Mitchell judged that Republicans were the real political winners in his defeat. It was "their method of seeking revenge" for his "blistering attack" of 1936 that had "cost them two million votes." The Democrats who joined them had not yet "learned to beware of Greeks bearing gifts." They had handed Republicans a perfect issue for 1938. The GOP could now go to Black voters and "take credit for wanting a much stronger bill." The voters that he had worked so hard to move from the Republican to the Democratic column might well swing back the other way. The reversal could be so severe that Republicans might organize the House in 1939. Gavagan's bill was unconstitutional, although "cunningly contrived" to win the support of northern and border-state Democrats. Nevertheless, "a poorly drawn bill is better than no bill at all." He would work "wholeheartedly and unreservedly" for its passage.[34]

The next day, he apologized to Daly for his outburst. He had been "somewhat peeved" at several Democrats "who had given me their solemn promise" of support and then voted to defeat his bill. These turncoats included James M. Mead and Alfred Beiter, two Buffalo Democrats, against whom Mitchell immediately plotted revenge. Two days after his defeat, he wrote to the editor of the *Buffalo Star* requesting "as large a list as you can of the colored voters and political leaders in the districts of Congressmen Mead and Beiter."[35]

Although he now supported discharge, Mitchell was certain that Gavagan's bill would never become law. To Kansas representative John M. Houston, he bemoaned the defeat of his bill: "While it was less drastic [than Gavagan's bill] it would have served to check the crime of lynching and, after all, that is all that can be desired or expected. It would have been far better than having no law at all, and I am afraid that that is going to happen."[36]

He was also explicit about who was responsible for his defeat. Promised support had been "overcome by spurious propaganda by an obnoxious association numerically small" but that "makes more noise than nearly fifteen million

Negroes who do not belong to it." The NAACP had engaged in "all manner of false, vicious, and unwarranted statements and releases" during a campaign characterized by the "idiotic maneuvering" by an individual who "had no sense of truth and appear[ed] to border on infantile insanity." Those who voted against him "have severely hurt the cause of anti-lynching rather than helped it."[37]

Some in Congress sympathized. Future Speaker John McCormack of Massachusetts, who had voted with Mitchell, was "very sorry that adverse action was taken." But what mattered more, and a lesson Mitchell took to heart, was the support he received from an unexpected source: the most liberal wing of the Democratic party, those he had viewed and denounced in his early days, as Communists or Communist sympathizers. One was Maury Maverick, a "shrewdly intelligent, exuberantly radical, and joyously explosive" congressman from Texas who led a group of thirty-five representatives "to plot strategy against conservative leadership" in Congress. Later termed "the most progressive representative in Congress who has ever come from the South," Maverick and his group had been some of Mitchell's most ardent allies. After being defeated for reelection in a 1938 primary, Maverick explained this support in a letter Mitchell cherished: "I am hoping I can get over to your people that your anti-lynching bill was the right one. Should you go too far, the Supreme Court will surely declare [legislation] unconstitutional. The main thing is to get over to the American people that lynching is a national disgrace and that the Federal Government is taking cognizance of it. Extreme measures in the matter of lynching bills will not pass in Congress nor be declared constitutional; nor if passed and accepted by the court will it be accepted by the people. It is not a southern question but a question that covers the whole United States of America. I salute you, not only as an honest Negro statesman, but as an honest American statesman, worthy of the respects of all people."[38]

Some members of the public also approved of Mitchell's attempt. George T. Kersey, appropriately an undertaker, summarized the mood of these loyalists. He sympathized with a man who had devoted such energy to a "meritorious measure" only to be deceived by "false promises at a crucial moment." Still, Mitchell should be proud of what he had achieved. To have received a favorable recommendation from the Judiciary Committee "was in itself a great victory for our cause and more than has been accomplished by anyone else."[39]

While Mitchell seethed, the NAACP and others celebrated. White termed the vote on April 7 "the complete routing of the unholy alliance" of Sumners and Mitchell. Future Supreme Court Justice Thurgood Marshall was pleased to see "an ineffective bill and merely an attempt to forestall a vote on an effective one" frustrated. Hours after Mitchell's defeat, the association sent out 176 telegrams thanking congressmen for their votes and 113 wires to members who had sided with Mitchell, inviting them to support the Gavagan discharge.[40]

Figure 10. Hatton W. Sumners, the powerful Texas chairman of the House Judiciary Committee, which recommended the adoption of Mitchell's anti-lynching legislation. After its defeat, he told colleagues that future historians might see Mitchell as "the greatest statesman his race has produced in a century." Library of Congress Prints and Photographs Division Washington, DC.

Most of the Black press also expressed relief. The *New York Amsterdam News* thought that opposition to Mitchell had been "well neigh unanimous" among Black Americans and his defeat "hailed with delight by all thinking citizens." The *Afro-American* regretted that "Mr. Mitchell, his good intentions notwithstanding, had been used." A week later, Dewey Jones, writing in his "Day by Day" column for the same newspaper, was less forgiving. "There is not a high school student in this country," he declared, who could not see what Sumners had been up to. Mitchell's "indefensible" fight had "dissipated every vestige that he is the type of sprig that will grow up into big timber."[41]

Six days after the rejection of Mitchell's bill, a lynching occurred at Duck Hill, Mississippi, where two Black men were tortured with blowtorches and then killed before five hundred spectators. Photographs of the "executions" received national attention. Sumners reacted to news of the event with outrage, telegramming Hugh White, the governor of Mississippi, that "these lynchings, both with regard to lynchers and officer involved, were as dastardly a crime as cowardice could devise and brutality execute. It is the sort of thing which makes it hard for us who are trying to protect the sovereignty of the states. It will be effectively seized upon as a demonstration of the [in]ability of states to govern. The State of Mississippi cannot escape this reflection upon its governmental capacity."[42]

The final debate on Gavagan's measure, discharged after securing the necessary signatures (including Mitchell's), took place on April 15. During it, Sumners, still simmering about Duck Hill, detoured from a speech defending states' rights to pay this tribute to the author of House Resolution 2251: "If Mitchell holds himself throughout the years as he is today, his head on his shoulders and his feet on the ground, he stands a chance to be recognized by the historian of the future as the greatest statesman his race has produced in a century."

This should have been a moment of triumph for Mitchell, a recognition of success for his cultivation of southern allies in Congress. One of their most powerful members had just declared him to be "the greatest statesman his race has produced in a century." What was not possible in the future?

Rather, it was an irate Mitchell who answered Sumners that "there is not any danger in this country . . . that so terrorizes the Negro and hinders him along all lines of development" as lynching. The Fourteenth Amendment had been adopted to protect newly emancipated slaves. Republicans had turned it into a device protecting corporations and their interests. Many Black Americans in northern cities would like to live in my "beloved Southland," but they feared for their lives and their property. "My voice represents the race that has suffered the most at the hands of the mob." That voice now says: "We have taken all that you have done to us. You have shortened our school terms and discriminated against us in a thousand other ways, but we have remained loyal. Then why not give us an equal opportunity along with you and let us develop our children the same as you do yours?" Why not encourage Black people "in their honest struggle to be citizens and to be useful citizens?"[43]

This answer drew praise from the same Dewey Jones who had found Mitchell "indefensible" a week before. Now the congressman from Illinois spoke to all southerners "who claim to be our friends as long as we stay in places they designate for us. It required courage to denounce the Dixie system of justice after a leading representative of that form of justice praised him, and yet that is what Mr. Mitchell did." Perry Howard thought his friend's response "the greatest made on anti-lynching." He called Mitchell's office to suggest that it be reprinted and "shipped all over the country."[44]

The afternoon of the Sumners-Mitchell exchange, the Gavagan bill was adopted by the House by a vote of 276 to 119, the only significant opposition coming from southern Democrats. When it arrived in the Senate, it endured a six-week filibuster, just as Mitchell had predicted it would. It was eventually withdrawn so that the Upper Body could pass on to other more pressing business.

The *Journal and Guide* was close to the mark in its analysis of Mitchell's failure. "When generals fall out over debatable points on the eve of an important battle," it observed, "the chances of an enemy victory are greatly enhanced." The *St. Louis Argus* was of the same mind. It didn't take the wisdom of Solomon to see that the anti-lynching bill sent to the Upper House "would be in much better shape to pass the Senate" if the NAACP and Mitchell had been working together.[45]

11

"N______s Ride in Second Class"

Although given to fits of anger, Arthur Wergs Mitchell was by habit an intentional man, one whose actions were calculated and seldom spontaneous. An objective observer is therefore permitted a degree of skepticism about his claim that, days after his humiliation in Congress, he just happened to find himself on a Rock Island train in rural Arkansas on his way to Hot Springs to enjoy a well-deserved vacation from his labors in Washington.

What cannot be doubted is that he was an angry and frustrated traveler. No good deed, he must have thought, goes unpunished in the House of Representatives. After spending two years attempting to make himself respectable and admired as a congressman, what had he to show for his efforts? He had been mocked by most of the Black press. His effort to create an Industrial Commission was going nowhere. His proposal for civil service reform was buried in committee. His attempt to integrate the Naval Academy had ended in failure. His effort to have the House pass anti-lynching legislation had failed to even be debated, replaced by a bill authored by a Tammany "hack," legislation that had no chance of passing into law. All the more galling, the loss had occurred in a House of Representatives with an historic Democratic majority, one which he had helped to create.[1]

And the future looked just as bleak. Republicans would never support him given his role in 1936. Most southern Democrats were also lost causes and this wasn't just "unrepentant bigots" such as "Cotton Ed" Smith. Mitchell now understood that "good southern" politicians would not be agents for change. Personal affection had its limits. The McDuffies and Sumners of the world might lament that "they labored in a conservative political structure, but they would not lift a finger to change that structure." Supporting such change through legislation "might imperil their political careers." The Speaker of the House, William Bankhead, was a prime example. Mitchell had voted for him in 1936 and thought of him as "one of the best friends I have in the world," "a great leader of men with a large humanitarian heart" who had been "absolutely fair to me in every way." Bankhead reciprocated, praising Mitchell's "fidelity, diligence, ability . . . [and] the high character of public service you have rendered." But a "best friend" was not a reliable ally when it came to casting a vote for antilynching legislation, the creation of an Industrial Commission, or civil service reform.[2]

Many Democratic representatives from outside the South had also failed him at a critical moment. He had asked them to pass a bill that had a chance to become law "as a personal favor to me and as recognition to my group." They had said no, supporting one that was bound to fail. White northerners did not understand the South and were just as prejudiced as southerners. But they enjoyed the support of Black elites who had fled their birthplace and now preached to the South from their safe havens in the North. Had he not warned, just before his defeat, about those who "will Jim Crow you to death if you allow them . . . the type of political leader who will sell you out to get a job for themselves. That type is [everywhere]. You must weed them out with a political house cleaning."[3]

Recent events proved that this "house cleaning" must include rejecting once and for all the "fossilized leadership we have too long catered to, too much afraid that we would displease somebody." It was time for Black newspapers to become reporters of actual events instead of propaganda sheets for the NAACP and the Republican party. Both were hypocritical organizations out to benefit themselves at Black expense. Black college students educated in the South who fled to the North were no more trustworthy. All they sought was admission to the world of white privilege. Neither could the pastors of traditionally Black churches be relied upon. White houses of worship might represent insincerity writ large, but Black ones were even more corrupt. Their ministers were illiterate "dog leaders" whose attitude was that "no one can say anything to them but God himself." He would never again appear before a group "whose purpose is simply that of raising money" for themselves. The fact was that "you can find more democracy and racial tolerance at a baseball game than you can in church."[4]

Since the legislative branch could not be relied upon to advocate for racial justice, he thought, perhaps the judicial could. But that change in approach necessitated a change in the stages upon which he would appear. The floor of the House must be replaced by the courtroom and the platform of the student unions at Black southern colleges. The accommodating Arthur Mitchell had accomplished very little. It was time for him to become an impassioned advocate for a new generation of Black southern leaders and an accomplished litigant.

If such was his thinking, Mitchell enjoyed such speculation from the comfort of a first-class Pullman chair, an accommodation he had purchased in Chicago because the humiliating conditions that Black travelers in the South suffered under had not changed since he had railed against them to Congress in 1919. Twenty years later, the Jim Crow cars were still "usually the first car behind the coal-fired locomotive that belched soot, fumes, and engine noise." Wooden, not made of steel, they were the death traps in the case of an accident. Often equipped with one filthy toilet, they lacked the heaters, water coolers, upholstered seats, and carpeting of first class. While Black passengers could not enter first class, white riders circulated freely in second to smoke, drink, and gamble. In short, Jim Crow railroad cars were still a daily, public humiliation for Black travelers.[5]

But there was another reason for his purchase of the Pullman ticket. When he paid the one cent surcharge for it, Mitchell created a contract with the Pullman company, one that technically did not exclude Black passengers from its coverage. Until now, the reality that few Black travelers could afford Pullman accommodations had made this distinction virtually moot, but it was important to Mitchell.[6]

While the Jim Crow cars might not have changed, Mitchell's understanding of how to fight them had. As a lawyer and congressman, he had come to appreciate the 1887 act creating the Interstate Commerce Commission. It found its justification in the Commerce Clause of the Constitution that gave power to Congress to "to regulate commerce among the several states." It also made it illegal for railroads to subject "any person to unreasonable or undue prejudice or disadvantage in any respect whatsoever" when traveling between states. Although aimed at discriminatory freight rates at the time it was written, the language "seemed broad enough to cover inequitable treatment of black passengers as well."[7]

He also knew of 1914 Supreme Court ruling in *McCabe v. Atchison, Topeka, & Santa Fe Railroad*, a suit brought by four Black Oklahomans who claimed that the state's separate car rule violated their Fourteenth Amendment rights to "equal protection." The Supreme Court had ruled against the plaintiffs on a technicality: they had never purchased tickets or attempted to board a train. But one justice had made a revealing comment. The railroad and State of Oklahoma had argued that "black demand for first class service was so limited that they would suffer enormous financial losses if they had to run separate Pullman cars for blacks." The justice in question found this argument to be "without merit. It made a constitutional right depend upon the number of persons discriminated against, whereas the essence of a constitutional right is that it is a personal one."[8] That justice was Charles Evans Hughes. He was now chief justice of the Supreme Court.

Even more importantly, the legal proceedings that followed suggest that, with the typical thoroughness, Mitchell had visited the congressional law library and read the supplementary note filed by John H. Ferguson, the judge whose ruling in 1896 had cast him as the defendant in the infamous Supreme Court case. From that he would have learned that Ferguson, born in Massachusetts and the son of a Baptist abolitionist, had sympathized with Homer Plessy, the litigant in the famous "separate but equal" case, but felt that it had been poorly argued. His separate cars were legal; many courts had said so. Plessy's successful argument would have been not that the cars were separate but that they were not equal. As no one had raised the issue, Ferguson felt that he had had no recourse but to rule that Plessy "was simply deprived of the liberty of doing as he pleased."[9]

Mitchell also knew the story of William Henry Harrison Hart, a Black man who had run an orphanage for Washington's Black children from 1897 to 1906 and died penniless in 1934. Motivated by respect for Hart, Mitchell had introduced legislation requiring the federal government to pay Hart's heirs $48,756 for services rendered. But what impressed Mitchell was that Hart had established the precedent of a citizen's right to sue the government over the "separate car" railroad laws. In 1904, Hart had been traveling from Washington to New York in a "white car." When the train passed into Maryland, the conductor ordered him into the "black car." He refused to go, was arrested, and fined five dollars by a local court. He appealed the penalty to a higher state court that found the arrest to have been an improper restriction on interstate commerce and awarded him one dollar in compensation. This symbolic act of defiance, the *Pittsburgh Courier* wrote, might have "laid the basis for the nationwide elimination of Jim Crow travel had his example been followed."[10]

Mitchell had also personally experienced the application of Jim Crow statutes and sensed their weakness in law. When, in 1935, he had tried to purchase a Pullman accommodation in Goldsboro, North Carolina, the ticket agent for the Southern Railway Company told him that none were available. Investigating and finding this untrue, he complained "most strenuously" as a member of Congress to the railroad. Having previously purchased Pullman accommodations in Birmingham, Atlanta, and Spartanburg, South Carolina, he had been "inclined to believe that it is the policy of the Railroad Company to deal with decent people regardless of color on the same plane," but this was obviously not the case. In response, Frank L. Jenkins had written that Mitchell had not properly identified himself as a member of Congress and that the railroad "could not very well afford to establish a precedent of this sort" for an ordinary Black passenger. In the future, if he showed identification, "every consideration will be shown."[11]

So it was a passenger well versed in his rights that conductor Elbert W. Jones approached as the Rock Island neared Forest City, Arkansas. Having ejected at least twelve Black riders from "his train" over a career of thirty-two years, Jones was no stranger to controversy himself,[12] but his encounter with

Mitchell was to ignite a four-year battle that ended before the Supreme Court in the case of *Mitchell v. United States*.

The words Jones used when confronting Mitchell later became the subject of contention. In his version, Jones had himself saying "there are vacancies in this car, but there are none you will be permitted to occupy on this train. You will have to ride in the second class coach and no other place or I'll stop this train and have you locked up." According to Mitchell, Jones's message was more succinct: "Niggers ride in second class," words the congressman found "vile, opprobrious, profane, vulgar and filthy." In any case, the threat was real. Mitchell protested that he had a first-class ticket, but to no avail. To avoid being arrested, he moved to second class, completing his journey to Hot Springs in a car he described as "poorly ventilated, filthy, filled with stench and odors emitting from the toilet, and other filth."[13]

At the end of his Arkansas vacation, Mitchell returned to Chicago on the Missouri Pacific, a railroad that sent an agent aboard to see to his comfort. As he later explained to the *New York Times*, he chose to leave Hot Springs in a "Jim Crow car of another railroad which was equal in accommodations to that furnished to white people."[14]

Once returned to Chicago, he sought out Richard E. Westbrooks, a local attorney and personal friend, who had practiced law there for twenty-five years, serving for some of that time as the honorary consul for the Republic of Liberia. Westbrooks had also been a founder of the Cook County Bar Association whose aim was to inform Black citizens "as to those judges who are unfair and discriminate in their decisions against Colored people." The two agreed that an injustice had occurred that required a legal remedy. Westbrooks agreed to take the case on without charging a fee.[15]

At 10:54 a.m. on May 10, 1937, Westbrooks filed a grievance with the Interstate Commerce Commission charging that the Rock Island had forced Mitchell into second class, "even though he had a first class ticket, solely because of his race." Therefore, this action violated the Nondiscrimination Clause of the Interstate Commerce Act. For good measure, Westbrooks and Mitchell added that the Rock Island, acting in compliance with the Arkansas separate car law, had denied Mitchell "the equal protection of the laws guaranteed by the Fourteenth Amendment."[16]

In filing this action, they recognized that it was unlikely to succeed at this level. The ICC typically accepted the "railroads' claim that they were providing Black passengers equal though separate accommodations." In addition, even if the commission found for a complainant, it was likely to rule that the body had no regulatory authority, giving the railroad an excuse to ignore the ruling. But the Westbrooks and Mitchell had a long-term strategy. They expected to lose before the ICC, but, as Westbrooks announced, their action was "merely the first strategic move in a well-laid plan to carry the Jim Crow car rule . . . to the Supreme Court." After his appearance before the ICC, he reported to Mitchell, "I believe it needless to say that the matter went over with a bang. . . . You are now being proclaimed as the 'THE GREATEST CONGRESSMAN OF ALL TIMES.'"[17]

In their planning, Mitchell and Westbrooks assumed that a two-car railroad and all similar legislation aimed at separating the races had become settled law when the Supreme Court ruled in *Plessy v. Ferguson.* Given the temper of the 1930s, appeals to the equal protection guarantees of the Fourteenth Amendment would fail in a contest with states' rights. But they saw, as Ferguson had, that *Plessy v. Ferguson* contained within itself a poison pill that could bring down Jim Crow railroad cars and eventually the structure of segregation. That pill was "equal," a common English word whose meaning was generally agreed upon. It didn't matter that he might be the only Black passenger in America who wanted a first-class Pullman accommodation on a given train. He was an American citizen engaged in interstate travel whose personal constitutional rights had been abridged.

Mitchell had chosen to attack an entire Jim Crow system at a weak point: availing himself of a service that almost no Black American could afford or railroad could offer if "separate but equal" meant what it said. He had contracted with a private company for interstate travel, paying a premium based on distance to travel in a first-class Pullman carriage. This contract entitled him to access to drawing rooms, lounges, the dining car, and bathrooms with running water, soap, and towels. The Rock Island and the State of Arkansas, acting through the conductor, had forced him out of the accommodation for which he had contracted and into a second-class car, which did not even approach being equal, simply because he was Black. As the Rock Island could not admit that this was the case, it would have to fall back on an economic rationalization: there was not enough demand from Black customers for first-class travel to justify offering equal accommodations. This argument violated his rights as guaranteed under the Interstate Commerce Act of 1887 and had been dismissed by Hughes in *McCabe* as "without merit."

Friends and some foes praised the challenge. Bethune, the informal leader of the "Black Cabinet," presciently wrote that "this experience happened to come to the right man at the right time. We shall all be interested in the courageous fight that you are giving to this matter and trust that the result will be of help to the entire race." A newly appreciative Pickens knew that "your friends must all applaud your attack. . . . Let us know what we can do to help you. More power to your arm." The complaint even drew a sympathetic response from abroad. Luis de Oteyza wrote from Havana that "when I think of the rudeness to you in that train, I felt again the shame I always feel in my travels in your country when I see signs in the waiting rooms of stations and railroad coaches reading 'Negroes not permitted.'"[18]

A few papers mocked Mitchell, the *Tribune* among them. Its editorial, "A New Dealer goes South," ridiculed "the Chicago New Dealer who made the adventurous experiment of trying out the New Deal in the New Deal South." But much of the Black press supported him. In the *Afro-American*, William Jones saluted Mitchell's "impulsive courage" that "may become one of the milestones in the change of racial status in this country." His actions had created "one of the best cases we have ever had to take to the Supreme Court and have a showdown." The *Defender* was also complimentary. "Whether he likes it or not," Dewey Jones declared, Mitchell "has become the Negroes' symbol of freedom. He is in a position to do and say for them what they cannot do and say for themselves. . . . Their Congressman has at last come to their rescue."[19]

Tacit support also came from the railroads who could not afford equal accommodation for nonexistent customers. As early as 1891, Louis Martinet, a Louisiana creole who led the legal opposition to the Jim Crow cars law that ended in *Plessy v. Ferguson*, had perceived that "the roads are not in favor of the separate car law . . . owing to the expense entailed, but they fear to array themselves against it" because of the anticipated wrath of white public opinion. Now, the *Pittsburgh Courier* saw that Mitchell had attacked Jim Crowism in a manner that brought him the same powerful industrial ally: "the railroads themselves are against Jim Crow. . . . Extra cars and separate waiting rooms cost additional money and the railroad companies are anxious to make all the money they can."[20]

Mitchell himself took a broad, moralistic view of his action in a form letter he sent to supporters: "I know the good people of the United States are not at all in sympathy with the grave injustice visited throughout the Country in almost every avenue of life. It is difficult for me to understand how we can constantly boast of our Christianity and civilization and at the same time deal so harshly and unjustly with such a large portion of our citizenry. I believe [a] sufficient number of our citizens will eventually rise up and condemn this sort of thing so that a very much larger degree of justice will be enjoyed by my people."[21] He then set about managing his case against the Rock Island with the same strategy that had motivated previous crusades: to pursue an attainable goal with a limited focus, such that the effects of a minor success could have profound rippling consequences on society as a whole. To do this he pursued a two-level approach. On the one hand, he complained about the Rock Island because its facilities were not equal. The treatment he had received on his return via the Missouri Pacific proved this. "I am not aiming at all railroads," he claimed, "merely those who operate dirty, filthy equipment my people are forced to ride in." But he had a broader aim in mind as well. He soon introduced legislation in Congress making it "unlawful to segregate any persons traveling as interstate passengers on any carrier, . . . in railroad stations, waiting rooms, lunch rooms, restaurants, [or] dining cars." He was optimistic about the future of the first, small-bore goal. The second, however meritorious, was an exercise in public relations for the present. What he did believe was the achievement of the first goal must eventually lead to success for the second.[22]

Concentrating on proving the inequality of accommodations, Mitchell asked Scipio Jones to find a photographer to memorialize the scene of him riding in second class. The picture cost twenty dollars and ran in *Life* magazine's May 24, 1937, issue. He also asked his Arkansas friend to secure affidavits from local residents as to "the actual conditions of the Rock Island railroad prior to April 23, 1937." Jones was less successful with this request. "Most of the people I have approached," he reported, "are a little timid." He advised they might have better luck with people "who reside outside of Arkansas."[23]

When *Life* ran the picture, Mitchell approved of the photo but objected to the caption, which claimed that he was not crusading for the elimination of Jim Crowism "but merely for the equal accommodations stipulated in most of state laws." This was incorrect, he disingenuously complained. "A person of the dullest conception and understanding" would understand that his words should not be taken literally, that his ultimate target was Jim Crow. In response, Van Meter assured Mitchell that *Life* would "watch for the earliest possible opportunity to set these matters right."[24]

Mitchell did nothing to resolve this confusion, perhaps intentionally. On the one hand, he told the *New York Amsterdam News* that his aim was simply to force southern railroads to furnish "equipment for people of my race equal to that furnished for any other race." More candidly, he explained to Carl Murphy, the publisher of the *Afro-American*, that his suit was narrowly focused so it could be successful. *Life* 's statement that he was not fighting Jim Crowism outright was "absolutely false. I am fighting Jim Crowism, have always done so, and shall always do so. I am opposed to racial segregation in every form. It does not mean anything except oppression for the weaker race."[25]

This small-bore approach exposed Mitchell to ridicule as a self-serving individual interested only in his personal comfort. But Mitchell held that Black Americans had accomplished little since the Civil War with appeals to broad principles of equality. One could argue endlessly about the meaning of the Thirteenth, Fourteenth, and Fifteenth Amendments, but appeals to higher principles had fallen short. Action, not words, were required. When informed that the Elks had adopted a resolution opposing Jim Crow railroad cars in support of his ICC complaint, Mitchell responded, "We have been passing resolutions for more than half a century. It means decidedly more to go forward and do something."[26]

That something was to advance the proposition that the Rock Island had violated the Nondiscrimination Clause in the Interstate Commerce Act because of the provable differences between first- and second-class accommodations on the Rock Island. This charge permitted Mitchell to deny that he was "fighting for the social equality of my people in the South" when in fact he was, but by a circuitous route that denied the Rock Island the defense of *Plessy v. Ferguson*.[27]

To make the underlying threat explicit, he suggested to the Christian Methodist Episcopal Church a boycott of the Rock Island as "the only way to stop this inhuman treatment of our people. . . . It strikes me that leading Negroes have pussy-footed on this question long enough." He also thought "a little publicity stunt" in Chicago might help. Why not, he asked Westbrooks, host a dinner party for fifty "outstanding men and women—judges, newspaper men, lawyers, and minister" to highlight what had happened to him?[28]

Southern politicians, Mitchell's erstwhile allies, were appalled, not by what had happened to him but by his complaint about his mistreatment. Senator Pat Harrison of Mississippi warned that Mitchell had introduced a bill taking away states' rights to enact Jim Crow car laws and to segregate races in public places. Next legislation would make miscegenation legal, then the states would lose the right to say who could vote in their elections. After that, the federal government, "perhaps under the cover of bayonets," would "compel every state to permit Negroes to vote in white primaries of the South." "Beware, Beware," Harrison cautioned.[29]

But Mitchell relished his new cause and the positive response it provoked in the Black community. Shortly after the first filing with the ICC, Robert M. Ratcliffe, a young journalist for the *Daily World*, ran into him on an Atlanta street. Over ice cream the reporter asked the congressman if he thought his court case had a chance. "Young man," Mitchell answered, "I'm going to win that case." There was, Ratcliffe remembered, "determination and confidence written all over his face. He appeared to have what sports writers call 'bull dog tenacity.' If Brother Mitchell is what you might call tough, you must give him credit for being a fighter."[30]

Mitchell enjoyed being described as a fighter. Although he disparaged Black Americans for their celebration of Joe Louis's "fistic" accomplishments, he also attended several Louis bouts, leaving a graphic report of the one with James J. Braddock: "When Braddock took that final right, he crumpled and fell as if slugged with a club. . . . A stream of saliva spurted three feet from Braddock's mouth. When Braddock's managers lifted the fallen champ from the canvas, there remained a spot of blood as big as the brim of your hat."[31]

He was convinced that when the Rock Island took his final blow, it would crumble and fall "as if slugged with a club," and there on the mat would be Jim Crow segregation.

12

“The Negro Must Work Out His Destiny in the South”

COMPARED TO THE man who had gone back to Washington “to make history,” it was a chastened Arthur Mitchell who returned to the nation’s capital following the Congress’s refusal to debate his anti-lynching bill and his experience on the Rock Island. His congressional strategy had failed; it was time to change tactics. “All new thought,” Mitchell wrote when reflecting on this, “meets opposition from established thought. I do not quarrel with those opposed to progress. I rather pity them.” That applied not only to others but also to him, and he was moving on.[1]

He no longer envisaged the legislative branch of government providing remedies for the ubiquitous racism that plagued the country. But from where would new leadership emerge?

Black youths who had fled to the North to be educated were certainly not the answer. The last thing the South needed, in Mitchell’s view, was another generation of leaders whose only goal was to enjoy success in northern white society, not transform the South. There were many college graduates who had attained “honors from some of the best institutions in the country [that is the North], [but] do not know how to do the common things of life and are mostly helpless and pitiful.”[2]

To find his new leaders, Mitchell set out on a “good will” tour of the South in the fall of 1937. It lasted for six weeks, covering nine states: Virginia, North Carolina, South Carolina, Georgia, Alabama, Mississippi, Louisiana, Texas, and Oklahoma. Its purpose, he emphasized, was to have “heart to heart talks with leaders of both races.” During the trip, he met with several governors, toured more than seventy-five towns and cities and scores of colleges and high schools, and talked to churchmen of both races.[3]

North Carolina, “an outstanding example of what Negroes can do when they are organized and determined,” was the state that most impressed him. “When we stop petty bickering,” he told one audience, “stop fighting each other, and work for the common good of the race, the major part of our economic struggle will be solved." Black North Carolinians were getting what they deserved from state government because they were "organized and have less petty jealousies." Much of white North Carolina supported Mitchell's campaign. For example, a fulsome review for him came from the *Gastonia Daily Gazette* after Mitchell gave "a brilliant address on race relations" there. "Nothing," the paper editorialized, "but good can come from such speeches."[45]

He emerged from his tour convinced that "the Negro must work out his destiny in the South," with North Carolina as a model. What held the race back was the "bickering and dissension in our own ranks" that made it impossible to address problems "on a solid front." To achieve unity, Black leaders had to realize "who their friends are and work with them for the common good. I am talking about liberals both North and South."[6]

Northern friends included individuals such as Paul Douglas of the University of Chicago. "I do not believe there is a man in the whole country," Mitchell told the future senator, "who is better prepared to make a contribution to good government than you." A younger generation of ministers, such as Adam Clayton Powell Jr., also qualified. He earned Mitchell's praise for "the fight you are leading for a cleaner and more effective race leadership in the church." And there were millions of Perry Powers in the country. Describing himself as "half Irish and incurably Republican, but much more an American than partisan," Powers was disturbed by discrimination based on color. "Real superiority," he believed, "never expresses itself through assumptions, through . . . privileges not shared by others equally deserving through manner and conduct." "Would to God," Mitchell wrote back, "that we had our country filled with men [like you]."[7]

In the South, Mitchell saw "high class Southern white men with broad views and sympathetic feelings toward the Negro" as potential allies. They were "decidedly more interested in the welfare of the Negro than persons coming from other sections of the country."[8]

Educators were also potential recruits. Frank Graham, the president of the University of North Carolina, was "by all odds the South's most prominent educator and versatile public servant." Rethinking his former hostility, Mitchell also included Mordecai Johnson among possible mentors for his new generation of Black leaders.[9]

A new generation of southern journalists such as Grover C. Hall at the *Montgomery Advertiser* and Virginius Dabney of the *Richmond Times-Dispatch* also earned Mitchell's praise. "With your powerful pen," he told Hall, "you have wrought nobly in bringing about a better understanding between the races in the South. I rejoice that in you we have such a strong and courageous leader." He found Dabney's columns "high class and well-written."[10]

Unlike many of his generation, Mitchell placed surprising importance on the role women would play in building his new South. Many shared his belief that Eleanor Roosevelt was "the greatest white Democrat in America today" and that Mary McCloud Bethune should be held in high regard. But Mitchell went further, arguing that southern women, both white and Black, would be more sympathetic to his message than men. Seeing a biracial component to his new South, he would be a strong supporter of Black women seeking admission to white colleges and an early advocate for mixed marriages: "People should be left free to marry whomever they please. . . . I think [this] is the view of all informed, unbiased, and unprejudiced minds."[11]

Seeing education as the key to training a new generation of southern civil rights leaders, Mitchell placed special emphasis on Black schoolteachers, almost all of whom were women. "You are laying a foundation and building real citizenship," he told a conference of Alabama primary schoolteachers. "No persons in the United States are more sacred than the Negro school teachers in the Southland."[12]

Mitchell's focus on Black female teachers as opposed to white male politicians as agents for positive change reflected his newfound understanding that organic improvement would come from below, not above. "The strongest evidence," he wrote, "goes to prove that the mere passage of a law, or declaration of a court, would not solve the problem. While much can be done by the legislative body in Washington and the Supreme Court of the United States to bring about the practice of Negro rights, the major part of the work must be done by Negroes themselves in the communities and states where they live." Once he had thought the appointment of individuals to high government offices was the key to the race's advancement. Now he saw that it was more important "to make conditions better for a thousand in the lower brackets than it is to show special honor to some one or two in the higher bracket." That required an educational experience made relevant to Black children by teachers with whom they could identify.[13]

As an apostle for a changed South, Mitchell established new standards for his public appearances. When not addressing Black college students, he now insisted on speaking only to mixed race gatherings. Invitations should be extended to "both White and Colored . . . [so that] my appearance will serve to strengthen and make better the relationship between the races." "You would not put a bandage on your arm if the trouble was in your wrist," he complained after addressing an all-Black audience in Oklahoma City, "and that is precisely what we do when we meet alone to discuss America's problems." Further, it was not enough to invite just any white participants. They had to be prominent citizens and be placed in positions of high visibility on the dais. "Have some distinguished White people of your community seated on the platform," he instructed W. J. Trent, president of Livingstone College in Salisbury, North Carolina, before one speech, and be sure to include white women "who are in public life and whose work in the affairs of the nation and state play such an important part."[14]

What he said and how he said it were not to be open to negotiation. Hosts were not to limit his speaking time, and he would not "take suggestions about what I should say unless I ask for them. I resent this as strongly as I know how." Above all, care should be taken to insure that others did not dilute the value of his message whose purpose was to strengthen friendship between Black and white Americans and to "secure for the Negro a greater recognition of his rights as an American citizen. I hope there will be no other speaker who will in any way thwart the purpose of the meeting." Nor should music send a message other than that of national reconciliation. When Nannie Boyd wanted to begin one of his presentations with the singing of "Lift Every Voice and Sing," Mitchell answered that a rendition of the informal Black anthem would be fine later in the program, but he insisted "that you use the National Anthem of our country in deference to the Government which I represent" at the beginning.[15]

The message he constructed for adults would be unfailingly controversial. Progress would only come from recognition that Black Americans were often their own worst enemy, that, "if we have not gone forward it is because we have not chosen to pay the price." Those on perpetual welfare attracted his particular ire for the stereotype they created. When asked how he responded to the news that 69 percent of Black residents of St. Paul, Minnesota, were on welfare, Mitchell said that it showed "there must be too many good-for-nothing Negroes in St. Paul."[16]

Abandon "victimhood" as an explanation for all that was wrong or unfair, he advised. "I am tired of Negroes going through life with a chip on their shoulders. True enough, the ideal is far, far away. But I know of no other country where the opportunity" for a minority to better their condition is higher than in the United States. "I'm sick and tired of your talking about your constitutional rights and liberties," he told one Virginia crowd. "You ought to think about your constitutional duties and obligations."

Chief among the failings of Black Americans, Mitchell claimed, was their apathy, their unwillingness to attempt to register and vote no matter what the impediments. "I have never seen any people talk more about rights than we do. . . . The problems about which we complain will never be solved so long as the Negro has no say whatsoever in his form of government and those who hold office."[17]

Portraying yourselves as victims of racism cruelly reduced to lethargic indifference might meet a justifiable emotional need, he argued, but it did not lead to change. Those who complained were often "persons who wish to hide from the dominant race some of the conditions that do exist in our race that are discreditable. I certainly do not deny that these conditions exist. I think the remedy consists not in the denial of the truth but in working to change these conditions."[18]

Some of those conditions were outlined in a *Journal and Guide* editorial with which Mitchell agreed. "We Should Quit Singing the Blues" argued that Black Americans should "concentrate on some of the evils surrounding us and for which we are primarily responsible." These included "debt-burdened churches, an ill-educated clergy, ramshackle, dirty, and indifferent service in our stores, money wasted on 'bad liquor,' needless dances, and the numbers game." "Whites have not decreed," the editorial pointed out, "that colored citizens should be inefficient, lack discipline and solidarity, and disregard the laws of sanitation and hygiene."

An exchange of letters with W. H. Jackson, a Black man Mitchell met in Mt. Vernon, Illinois, during a campaign appearance, made the same point. Why, Mitchell asked him, was there so much racial segregation in southern Illinois? "I can see no reason why there should be the differences between the races that I found in this state which likes to pride itself as a state of liberality." Jackson responded that "most of our group that are living in this town do not live in a way to demand respect, and we can't just live like hogs and dogs and then expect the white man to bow himself down and pick us up. We must first do that ourselves and become dignified and straight forward citizens. . . . We will then be able to show the other race that we are no longer on a downward trend."[19]

Progress lay in striving to achieve equality using as a yardstick those standards by which a dominant white southern society measured success. We are treated better in the United States, he told Frederick A. Carter, "than any other place I have visited." Representing only one-tenth of the population, we could not expect to impose our will on a majority. "Our problems," he informed a North Carolina audience, "will be solved by our ability to encourage the white man to believe in us and work with us. We should foster a better estimation of ourselves in whites by solving our own problems."[20]

Working with southern society meant supporting the language, rituals, and institutions of the majority. He argued with Charles Thomas that it was ill-advised to demand to be called "Afro-American" rather than "Negro." C. C. Spaulding, who wanted to form "Negro Chapters" of his Brotherhood of Man organization because the races could not "fraternize harmoniously," was making a mistake. That was what white churches and fraternal organizations "do in reverse. There can really be no brotherhood worthy of the name until there is brotherly love and brotherly interest neither of which condones race discrimination." When a Black newspaper in Philadelphia urged him to join a protest against a "white rookie cop" who had killed an "innocent Negro," Mitchell refused to participate. "Negroes will get nothing and nowhere by always protesting about the White man doing [this] and the White man doing that. Instead, we should try to educate the White man to our problems through sane, sound, quiet reasoning." He was also opposed to the creation of congressional districts designed to elect Black representatives. That would "do only one thing, tend to create and spread class and racial hatred, the very thing I should like to see wiped out."[21]

Rather than engage in futile protest, the way forward was gradual reform through reconciliation. When B. H. Hardaway complained that his local school board was unsympathetic to Black needs, he was told that "it is the duty of the leaders of each community to try to cooperate with the leaders of the other race and work out their problems to the mutual satisfaction of both groups." When H. D. Dobson, a Black Atlanta merchant, found fault with white colleagues who demanded that he raise prices to avoid undercutting them, Mitchell urged caution. "Colored men who are just beginning a business," he warned, "should go to some trouble to get the cooperation of white businessmen. Because of [his] superior strength, it is not a good idea to incur his ill will."[22]

Figure 11. Mitchell addressing students at Howard University (1940). Mitchell's favorite speaking engagements were at southern Black colleges and universities, where he appealed to his audiences to remain in the South and lead a new generation of Civil Rights activists. Chicago History Museum, ICHi-026228; Scurlock Studios, photographer.

His idea was that local action supported by biracial community groups was the key to progress. When an admirer suggested that Mitchell should be appointed to the Supreme Court, he dismissed the idea as "silly." If you want to do something important to achieve a fairer judiciary, think "step by step." Begin by working with sympathetic white people to elect a county judge, then an appellate court judge, and so forth. The distance Black Americans have to travel is so great "that we cannot hope to make it in a single bound."[23]

That was also the message that Mitchell delivered over and over to Black college students, one that anticipated a brighter future for them than had existed for their parents or grandparents if they acted boldly and strategically. "I resent with all my soul and strength every racial discrimination practiced in this country," he told Howard students. "No such discrimination can exist within a genuine democracy. At the same time, I have sense enough to know that these things do not grow up over night. Nor can they be wiped out during one or two generations. I know we are making substantial progress . . . through patience, tolerance, struggle, prayer, and extreme effort. I plead for a continuance of the exercise of patience and the other virtues which we and our fathers have practiced."[24]

To lead, Mitchell preached, the rising generation had to be serious. "You are likely," he told Tuskegee students, "to put more emphasis upon the latest things in life rather than the lasting things of life." This included the veneration of athletic heroes rather than individuals who had improved conditions for the race. "I have been terribly disturbed because of the uproarious approval I have seen even in the so-called educated people of my race over the fistic victory of some man of small brain capacity when cold and indifferent" to the achievements of George Washington Carver. The successes of Joe Louis and Jesse Owens should be celebrated as more than athletic triumphs. They should be emulated because both "came up the rough way and triumphed. Soft treatment has never been known to develop one to a point where he can sustain hard knocks."[25]

The crux of his message became "If you [are to] succeed, you must do the work yourself. If you fail, you have only yourself to blame." The white man was not responsible for the shortcomings of the Black race. "Any Negro with fight and persistence could batter his way through all walls of opposition. . . . The main enemy of the Negro is the Negro himself, who is the most intolerant person with whom we have to contend."

To combat this, young people had to resist the instinct to seek success in what appeared to be the greener pastures of the North. Rather, they should "launch out in the deep of the sea and let your line down for the water in which you are now fishing is too shallow." Getting a degree represented only "one-tenth of what is expected of you." To be truly successful, he felt, young people must not seek to join northern white society but return to or remain in the South, where it is their duty to improve conditions.[26]

These were his notes for one college speech:

- Every man is in some sense a fisherman.
- What are you fishing for?
- Christ said "follow me and I will make you a fisher of men."
- Will you be content to catch the small fish which are always found near the bank and in the shallow water? Or will you seek to catch the large fish which abound in the deep water?
- You must have the courage to face danger.
- You will meet bitter criticism of so-called friends.
- Race prejudice: the very moment you leave these grounds. Character and worth will determine your reception.
- Go out into the South where the water is the deepest and where the largest fish abound.
- Which one of you will be the first rep. of Arkansas, Georgia, Alabama, Florida, etc. Which one of you will be the first Supt. of Education in some county?
- No colored woman has been elected to any law making body in the country. Are you afraid to launch out into the deep?
- How to regard those who are known to be against us. Absolutely refuse to recognize them as enemies. My experience in Washington.
- Only those who have achieved have also dared to launch out.
- To succeed you must hear, see, and do.[27]

He often offered this advice from Epictetus about facing prejudice. Circumstances reveal the person. When you run into difficulty, remember that God, "like the trainer of wrestlers, has matched you with a rough young man for what purpose? Why that you may become an Olympic Conqueror." But this is not accomplished without maximum effort. Avoid the temptations of a passive approach to life. Living is a serious business requiring confidence in self. "You must not be ashamed of your identity," he told students at Hampton Institute. "You must make no apology for the fact that you are colored. You had nothing to do with your color. . . . I want [you] to stand up and be proud."[28]

The younger generation must be the active party if conditions for Black Americans were to improve: "If you would succeed you will not wait around for chance or luck to aid you. [Do not] think that you must have a complete outfit of the finest tools before you can attempt to do anything. It is not fine tools and the best equipment or splendid opportunities, or influential friends, or access to money that makes great men. The greatness is in the individual or nowhere. The golden opportunity you are seeking is neither in your environment nor in luck. It is not in chance, nor in the help of others. It is yourself alone. You must forge your own key, unlock the door, and enter each for himself."[29]

"Crutches were intended for cripples," he told students, "and you're no cripple. Your best opportunity lies in yourself. Only a live fish can swim upstream. The force that will maintain you is coiled up inside you." The road to equality is a long and painful one, but "when a man puts away his childish complaints against the obstacles and frustrations of life . . . faith, hope and love come to abide in him and his success is assured."[30]

After an appearance in Minnesota, the *St. Paul Recorder* remarked one of these combative presentations: "He has chosen the unpopular way of telling his hearers what they ought to hear rather than what they like to hear. It takes courage to tell the Negro his faults. It's an unpopular and unpleasant task." "Wherever Mitchell goes," the paper continued, "he leaves in his wake heated discussions which last for weeks. It is good for the communities he visits." Calling him "the most positive voice of the Negro today," the *Dayton Forum* agreed. "The most overwhelming point in his favor is his brutal frankness," the paper opined. "Congressman Mitchell is the major prophet of the Negro race today. We had better hear him."[31]

13

"Betrayers of the Public Trust"

JUST BEFORE MITCHELL began his tour of the South, the White House offered him a dramatic opportunity to confirm his belief that the appointment of "high class Southern white men with broad views and sympathetic feelings toward the Negro" could improve Black prospects for full citizenship. Realizing that only "federally induced reform," not legislation passed by Congress could achieve this, Roosevelt made a dramatic move. Ten days after Mitchell sent his letter to Colonel McIntyre, Roosevelt nominated Senator Hugo Black of Alabama to replace retiring Supreme Court Justice Willis Van Devanter. While there is no evidence that Mitchell played any role in this decision, it is also true that if Roosevelt had wanted to select the single individual whose nomination would please Mitchell the most, the president could not have made a better choice.

Black's childhood paralleled Mitchell's in many ways. The future justice had begun life in a small village about thirty miles from the congressman's birthplace. Like Mitchell, Black came from an "impoverished, rural background." He also had "experience . . . among country sharecroppers." His father died when Black was young. His mother, like Mitchell's, was a deeply religious woman who valued education. Black was one of eight children; Mitchell one of six. After graduating from the University of Alabama Law School, Black returned to practice law in a community about the size of Panola. There he maintained a "meager practice" until a fire destroyed the town square and his office.

He then moved to Birmingham, where he came to the public's attention defending a Black inmate forced to work under the provisions of Alabama's "convict leasing" system after serving his sentence. Elected Jefferson County prosecutor, Black "dismissed thousands of cases involving alleged petty crimes by African Americans" while he "investigated and prosecuted cases of white police officers brutalizing and killing black suspects."[1]

Elected to the Senate in 1926 and reelected six years later, Black had proven himself one of the staunchest supporters of the New Deal. He introduced legislation that proposed a national minimum wage and a thirty-hour work week and was an advocate for the "court packing" proposal. Perhaps most importantly to Mitchell, he was the cosponsor of a bill to fund public education that Mitchell hoped to support if it could be amended to insure proper distribution to Black schools. Tarnishing these progressive credentials, Black had also been a southern loyalist on anti-lynching legislation, helping to lead the filibuster that defeated Costigan-Wagner.[2]

His nomination drew the contempt of the arch-conservative *Chicago Tribune,* which lampooned Black as "that celebrated liberal from Alabama, the New Deal's inquisitor general [and] self-anointed scourge of the 'power trusts.'" But it pleased Mitchell, who welcomed his nomination as an important step in turning the judiciary into a vehicle for reform. Realizing now that the legislative branch would not bring relief to Black southerners, he welcomed Black's selection as an important step in converting the judiciary into a vehicle for such corrective force. Might not a Supreme Court with Black as a member "disrupt southern politics by attempting to create a new legal order that challenged the localized structure of the American political system and emphasized a more inclusive democratic process?"[3]

The day after the announcement, the NAACP charged that Black had called African Americans "niggers" and that Black Americans could not expect a fair, unbiased, and impartial consideration from the nominee. His selection called for a "vigorous protest . . . at once." Mitchell thought differently, sending a congratulatory telegram to Black that affirmed the nominee as "truly progressive. I rejoice in your appointment." He was more forceful when speaking to the National Alliance of Postal Workers five days later: "There are those who say if a white man comes from the South he is essentially an enemy of the Negro. I know this is not true." Black's record as a prosecutor in Birmingham showed that he was "interested in justice for underprivileged people," that he had been a friend to Black southerners, and that he would make "a great justice."[4]

On August 16, the Senate's Judiciary Committee reported favorably on Black's nomination and he was confirmed by the Senate the next day by a vote of 63–16. On August 25, as a Supreme Court justice, Black wrote to Mitchell, thanking him for his support: "I am one of those who believe you have performed an excellent service as a member of the United States Congress. You have won the respect of your colleagues from every part of the United States and I believe that you can and will continue to render a great public service. I am happy that that service is being rendered by a native Alabamian."[5]

Shortly after his confirmation, a crisis developed with the discovery that the new justice had been a member of the Ku Klux Klan (KKK) during the 1920s. An unfazed Mitchell remained steadfast in his support. Anti–New Dealers and "reactionary Republicans" were using Black's membership in the Klan as a "political bludgeon." His fellow Alabamian, in Mitchell's judgment, was "a good man and a true liberal" who had, by joining the KKK, only made a mistake common at the time: "If you took every Senator who is a former member of the Klan out of Congress, you wouldn't have enough left to form a corporal's guard."

On the other hand, the revelation did disconcert Walter White, who later portrayed himself as believing that Black represented "an advance guard of the new South we dreamed of." He decided in the immediacy of the situation that he "had to speak for the membership and interests of the N.A.A.C.P." His telegram to Roosevelt minced no words: "This association urges most urgently . . . that you call upon [Black] to resign."[6]

Black eventually survived the uproar by going public with an explanation of his "mistake," but not before Mitchell's support for him reignited indignation for the congressman from enemies in the press. "As usual," the *Pittsburgh Courier* observed, "colored people are all out of step with Representative Mitchell." The *Defender* was more sarcastic in an editorial titled "Can Blind Men Lead." Mitchell "will have some explaining to do to Chicago voters at the next election on his "rejoicing" attitude over the appointment of Mr. Associate Klansman Black."[7]

After the fact, Mitchell took great pride explaining just that. He had, he boasted in 1941, been "three or four years ahead of the times" in knowing that his fellow Alabamian would be a voice for "the helpless and abandoned citizenry." Moreover, his support for Black bespoke the accuracy of turning away from viewing political leaders as agents of change, to empowering the judiciary, including "high class Southern white men with broad views and sympathetic feeling toward the Negro," with that responsibility. There was no inconsistency between Black casting racist votes in the Senate and becoming a leading advocate for the betterment of Black conditions as a Supreme Court justice. Politicians arrived at office through election, a process that forced individuals to honor the belief system of their constituents; Supreme Court justices, freed from those constraints, could allow their true convictions to emerge. Therefore, leading the Senate's 1935 filibuster to kill Costigan-Wagner in 1935, and becoming a leading proponent of Black rights on the Supreme Court, were not inconsistent. As a senator, Black had been forced to be a public racist; as a Supreme Court justice, he was free to be himself.[8]

The fate of Gavagan's anti-lynching legislation, adopted as a replacement for Mitchell's failed bill, only reinforced in Mitchell's mind the idea that redress of Black grievances would receive a more sympathetic hearing in a courtroom than in the halls of Congress.

Following the House's passage of the 1937 Gavagan bill via a discharge petition, the NAACP had returned to an emotionally charged campaign in support of the New Yorker's legislation. Typical publicity was a photograph of a Black lynching victim above a text that read "As the Cries, Prayers, and Wailing of the Victim gives way to the roaring flames, the cracking of guns, and the howl of the mob, and as the nearly lifeless form of the victim slumps into the consuming fire, the blood spreads out to Besmear the hands of every American citizen."[9]

Despite this effort, Mitchell's prediction that the Gavagan bill would be successfully filibustered in the Senate proved only too accurate. As that six-week talkathon took place, halting all other Senate business, his frustration boiled over in a Brooklyn speech. Debate on anti-lynching "has taken up more time than any other piece of legislation will during the rest of the session. Aren't we more interested," he asked, in "stopping lynching than in passing a particular bill? We have a group of leaders who say we must have a particular bill or no bill at all. I am tired of this paid leadership that will lead no further than the dollar will go."[10]

When the Senate abandoned attempts to break the filibuster and moved on to other concerns, the *Courier* blamed Mitchell for failing to denounce the Upper Chamber from the House floor. In an editorial titled "He Never Said a Mumbling Word," the paper quoted him as saying that it was not the filibustering senators who were damaging the anti-lynching cause. Rather, the fault lay with "filibustering Negroes who pretend to be our friends, but really are not." "So, once more," the paper concluded, "Congressman Mitchell lines up with the unreconstructed Rebels in Congress, completely out of step with the rest of the colored people in the United States." He "might as well have been in Kamchatka or Patagonia. For 47 days he sat supinely, afraid or reluctant to speak out, never saying a mumbling word."[11]

Discouraged by Congress's failure to adopt anti-lynching legislation, Mitchell was also less than enthusiastic about the Roosevelt administration's handling of the economic slowdown in 1937 and 1938 that retarded economic recovery. It was a problem caused by too early a retreat from relief programs. "It is now believed," he informed Lela Smith in July 1937, "that the depression is over and that the Federal Government must recede as rapidly as possible from relief projects." This meant retrenchment in the Works Progress Administration, a policy decision he had used "all the influence I had" to oppose. Restrictions are "the law of the land and undoubtedly will be enforced." Now more radical in his views, Mitchell disagreed with this assessment, seeing the change in policy a result of the newly developed southern opposition to Roosevelt's agenda. Black Americans had to be defended against the "irreconcilable Economic Royalists who have exploited the common people for the past fifty years. I am a member of a minority group that has been exploited to the nth degree. The time has come when the Constitution must have a liberal interpretation and must be enforced not only to protect capital but the laboring man as well."[12]

Despite sensing this wavering, Mitchell remained essentially loyal to Roosevelt and most New Deal initiatives. The president, Mitchell told B. S. Hendwork, was right 75 percent of the time. "He has accomplished more in the interests of the common people of the country than any President in my day." When J. D. Curtis complained about Roosevelt's policies, Mitchell answered that "this is not the first time I have seen the patient, after having received special hospitalization and treatment resulting in the saving of his life, later throw his crutches as the physician."[13]

In fact, crutches were hardly needed now. Banks were no longer closing, there were no soup lines, industrial activity was on the uptick. Highway construction, which Mitchell observed when driving from Chicago to Washington, was booming. Stock prices were up. "I hope," he concluded, "you will try to get some facts before you write to other people."[14]

George J. Farnsworth, the president of the Chicago Lumber Company, received a similar rebuff when he asserted that contraction rather than expansion of federal spending would solve the problem as it would have in 1932 if "the natural course of events" had been allowed to occur. Mitchell objected to both the message and the messenger: 1937–38 was not comparable to 1932 in any way. Then, President Hoover had been "doing nothing for the common people, his only concern being big corporations." Now "the President is working day and night to help those people who are without work and without means upon which to live." The country wouldn't be in this downturn if businesses such as Farnsworth's hadn't resorted to "practically every known device to embarrass the President and the Government in the honest efforts which were being put forth to rehabilitate businesses." Did Farnsworth realize that for every billion dollars the government had spent, the national income had increased between three and four billion? "All of the objections to the Administration's policies seemed to come from businesses that have enjoyed benefits from laissez-faire governments for the last century. . . . It is my firm belief . . . that all of our citizens along all lines will eventually become happy and permanently prosperous" if the president continued on his path.[15]

But loyalty to Roosevelt did not extend to those who had opposed his antilynching initiative. An undated Mitchell memo, probably written in early January 1938, declared that the most important issue to Black residents of Illinois, Michigan, Indiana, Missouri, Ohio, and Pennsylvania should be the demise of that legislation. "I propose," he threatened, "to expose every Democratic Congressman from these states who has a large Negro constituency in his district and who voted against this bill." They were "betrayers of [the voters'] trust" and "should be defeated when they come up for reelection." Mitchell expected to "leave no stone unturned in exposing that group which I regard as betrayers of their trust in so far as their Negro constituency is concerned." "I expect," he told Stephen Young, a former colleague from Ohio, "to do everything in my power to defeat every one of them, if exposing their lack of statesmanship and interest in their Negro constituency . . . will defeat them."[16]

Those who had voted not to debate his bill but now sought his help received curt dismissals. As early as March 1938, he told Democratic party officials in Ohio's Sixteenth Congressional District that it would be hypocritical for him to appear in support of the reelection of their candidate, William Thom. "Naturally, I do not feel any too friendly toward your Congressman." His vote had been a "blow below the belt." He was particularly embittered toward Louis Ludlow, a representative from Indiana, who had voted against him "solely because I am a colored man and he wanted Congress to consider an anti-lynching bill offered by a white man." He would not do anything for Ludlow "until he sees fit to straighten himself with me for the grave injustice he did me for which there is absolutely no worthwhile excuse."[17]

Conversely, Mitchell was fierce in his assistance of those who had supported him. They received lists of counties with a thousand or more Black voters along with a note stating that he was "deeply interested in your campaign and shall be glad to do anything I can to help you." A letter to Ambrose Kennedy (MD-4) and others offered personal endorsements to "the men who were outstanding in their sympathies toward legislation especially favorable to the Negro group." He spelled out his reasoning in deciding to support or ignore candidates to Fred Bierman (IA-4): "Had my bill been given the consideration to which it was entitled, and for which you worked hard, we would have on our statute books a Federal Anti-Lynching Bill."[18]

In the 1938 election to the House of Representatives, the Republicans gained eighty-one seats. Major elements contributing to this natural regrowth of a minority party in a two-party system included the so-called Second Recession of 1937–38 and the deep unpopularity of Roosevelt's "court packing scheme." But Arthur Mitchell's refusal to endorse House members who had disagreed with him dramatically diminished support in the Black community for many Democrats. Ludlow survived, but many others on Mitchell's targeted list did not. As the *New York Amsterdam News* reported at the end of the year, "last November . . . thousands of Negroes who voted for the Democrats in 1936, plumped for Republicans."[19]

Nowhere was this more evident than in Ohio. Going into the election, the Ohio House delegation Mitchell had helped to create consisted of twenty-two Democrats and two Republicans. After the 1938 election, there were nine Democrats and fifteen Republicans, a loss of thirteen seats in that state. Included in the debacle were defeats in both Cincinnati seats and in five of the seven districts where more than ten thousand Black voters were registered. A similar reversal occurred in other states Mitchell had been responsible for in 1936. The Wisconsin delegation lost eight Democratic seats, Indiana six, and Michigan three.

Even the Illinois delegation lost four Democratic seats. But it held the two downstate districts where Mitchell again personally appeared. Illinois Senator Scott Lucas thought it was "glorious victory in view of the trend in other states." Mitchell agreed. It was "a pleasure indeed to note the manner in which our state stood by the President's program" compared to what happened in Michigan, Ohio, and Indiana.[20]

"It has been apparent to me for some time," Mitchell wrote after the election, "that the Democratic party through its legislative efforts was running over many red signals. . . . I am sure the people think so."[21] But Mitchell had run over his own "red signals." In two years, "the foremost Negro politician in the country" had transformed himself into a pariah to the Democratic political establishment.

14

"Get Out of Congress as Early as Possible"

A STRONGER REPUBLICAN voice in Congress and its implied threat to relief measures so necessary to the poor clustered in northern cities led Kelly Miller and Mitchell to engage in correspondence about what could be done to help the "victims" of the Great Migration. Miller wrote first, summarizing what he saw as the future of Black Americans. In both the North and the South, race prejudice worked against them by restricting industrial opportunities above the Mason-Dixon line and civil and political rights below it. Nevertheless, if forced to choose, "a Negro family rooted and grounded in the agricultural life of Alabama has a much more promising prospect than if transferred to the sidewalks of New York. One shudders to predict the future of a Negro child brought up in a seven story flat of a Harlem tenement house." Cities, Miller argued, had absorbed as many Black residents as possible. The future in metropolitan centers was bleak as "it is unthinkable that [the race] should continue forever, or for long, to live on charity and relief." To him the farm represented not only their "best chance, but [their] only chance." The New Deal, through legislation such as the Bankhead–Jones Farm Tenant Act, a 1937 law that created a modest credit program to assist tenant farmers in purchasing land, represented at least promise of a better future as it showed Black Americans that the government was interested in them and willing to take "a first step towards self-proprietorship."[1]

Mitchell responded by drawing a parallel between the original settlers of New England and Black southerners who had fled the South during the Great Migration: "I am convinced that oppression, injustice, and the unsafety of life have always caused the oppressed to take refuge in some other part of the country, or some other country." Migration from the South had been the result of lynchings, disfranchisement, injustice in the courts, unequal education, and a "despicable sharecropper system." The South was gradually changing, but there was still much work to be done if the exodus was to stop. Throughout the

United States, there was too much stress on the idea that "this is a white man's country." Mitchell judged that Miller was correct in believing that the South "with its temperate seasons and agricultural possibilities offers the Negro his greatest possibilities." During his 1937 tour, the happiest people he had met were living in a resettlement project in Texas, aided by the government in securing farm land, comfortable houses to live in, and proper livestock, all under the supervision of "trained agriculturists. A special effort should be put forth to work out the problem of the Negro through this movement." If progress toward "protection and recognition" in the South were to continue, emigration would cease because rural electrification and an improved road system were bound to improve life for the poor. On the other hand, if advances toward civil and economic justice were not made, "the South will continue to lag behind all other sections of the country and justly so." Mitchell asserted that this effort must be led by a younger generation, both Black and white, arguing, "not only must the white man be fair and just to the Negro, the Negro must be thoughtful, patient, industrious and determined to make the largest possible contribution toward his own advancement regardless of the handicaps which he is called upon to face."[2]

Figure 12. Kelly Miller, a dean at Howard University, newspaper columnist, and Mitchell confidant. H. L. Mencken called him "the greatest black intellectual of his time." Mitchell said that "it was upon his shoulders that I leaned more heavily . . . than any other leader in the country." Schomburg Center for Research in Black Culture, New York Public Library Digital Collections.

When Mitchell went to see Roosevelt about a possible resettlement program, the president "appeared interested" in the idea. The congressman then issued a press release stating that he would introduce legislation for a "vast program to resettle destitute city-dwelling Negroes on the farm lands of the South." The program was not aimed at the "white collar" type of city dweller who "has made a place for himself in the city." Rather, it sought to better condition for the millions who were locked into desperate poverty where they lived. Although this would include whites "who went to the city in vain quest of employment and would like to return to the farm," the proposal was primarily aimed at the Black urban poor whose "economic and social plight is a reality [that] we might as well combat in a realistic and constructive fashion." It sought to "convert idle, unhappy city dwellers into happy productive farm dwellers."[3]

The Miller-Mitchell exchange attracted considerable attention. F. D. Buford, the president of the Agricultural and Technical College of North Carolina, thought the "Back to the Farm" concept "the most far-reaching effort that has been put forth concerning the rural Negro." F. B. Ransom, Mitchell's Indiana director in 1936, saw the Miller-Mitchell correspondence as putting the finger on "the real reason why the Negro is leaving the South in such large numbers." Even Roy Wilkins, often a bitter critic of Mitchell, conceded that "on this occasion, I feel you have stated the case as completely and as uncompromisingly as it could be stated."[4]

At the beginning of April 1939, Mitchell was given an opportunity to restate the case when Roosevelt asked the congressman to stand in for him as the speaker at Tuskegee's Founder's Day celebration. After receiving the request, Mitchell originally asked for a letter from the president to be read on the occasion "which might be interpreted as a message to the Negro and to the people of the South . . . of tremendous importance to the Democratic Party, and to the nation."[5]

Receiving none, he substituted a speech to the students on his vision of the future, combining an appeal for support of his resettlement program with the suggestion of a possible contribution his listeners could make to a rapidly mechanizing world. A renewed emphasis on southern agriculture, a proposal that he and the president had discussed "last week," would not only make it possible to remove many of the participants in the Great Migration from abject poverty but would also induce farmers to "not drift to our cities, as they are doing, where no jobs await them and where they are soon swallowed up and in most cases destroyed by the contaminating influences of city life." Booker T. Washington had recognized that the race must be producers as well as consumers. If he were alive in this age where the car has replaced the oxcart, he would take advantage of rural electrification to create a curriculum for resettled city residents that featured not only advanced farming techniques but also the repair of modern devices—radios, refrigerators, airplanes, automobiles and "hundreds of other mechanical devices." This training would "enable us to work and figure permanently in the development of these great mechanized forces which play a major part in education, democracy, and defense. Any program in this country which does not emphasize the dignity and importance of labor is unworthy of the name and will in the end prove worthless."

Discouragement, hardships, and handicaps, Mitchell told the students, "should drive you forward to do your best." Joe Louis, he argued, was a perfect example of this. He had been discriminated against in a manner that barred him from first-rate fitness facilities. As a result, he prepared in back alleys while his opponents trained in the best gyms. But those foes "went down because he [Louis] had learned in the world of hard knocks to overcome difficulties which these men had not been permitted to encounter" and that had given him "stamina and guts."[6]

In a letter to H. W. Faron, Mitchell expanded on his resettlement plan. The program, he explained, would be under "the expert supervision of trained agriculturists" from the Hampton and Tuskegee Institutes. Funding, he suggested to the *Afro-American*, would come from monies diverted from relief and housing projects in the North. Better these funds should be allocated to the purchase of "small farms back home where [the Negro] will be happy, where they will look to the future with hope, and where they will be an economic asset rather than a burden." Resettlement, he argued, would also "wipe out the despicable share cropping system" and provide economic security to "millions of Negroes on the farm who can find no employment elsewhere."[7]

The proposal drew immediate criticism as an attempt to force northern city dwellers to relocate to the South. In answer to this charge, the congressman complained that the press had yet again misrepresented his views: "Why can't you fellows ever get anything right?" There were thousands of city dwellers who, "through education and environment have become acclimated to city life." They would not be willing to trade "the bright lights of the city for Southern rural life." His proposal was not aimed at them but rather the millions who had not made the adjustment to a city. He knew that his plan would create "resentment among Negroes," but "the situation is a reality and there is no use sticking our heads in the sand."[8]

"Some resentment" proved an understatement. A few critics, such as Johnnie F. Moore of Matthews, Missouri, objected on logical grounds. Modern farming techniques, he wrote, made small farming impossible, so the plan wouldn't work. Far more shared Edward H. Burton's views, expressed in the *Defender* : "I cannot understand why on God's green earth any intelligent person should advocate any movement to return his people to virtual slavery." A

Black person, having breathed "the free air of the North," who wants to return to the South has "something wrong inside of his head."[9]

A fiery exchange of letters with Eugene Daniels summarized Mitchell's position. Look at what happened to you in Arkansas, Daniels reminded him. And you think we would be happy on a southern farm. Do you want us to return to a place "where they beat [and] burn us and where a Negro woman was hang by her heels and she was ripped open with a knife and a baby dropped out of her. So you seem to think we are surrounded with such conditions like these and when lynching of us is going on we will be happy?"

Mitchell wrote back that he usually didn't answer such letters, but that he would in this case because "I take your letter to be of a friendly nature." Most northern Black residents, he now argued, wouldn't return and "would be entirely worthless if they did." What he was interested in was only "helping the millions of those who must remain in the South to better their conditions." They "should have an opportunity to own the soil and should be able to rear their children in a wholesome environment." Future migrations to the North had to be prevented because "in Chicago today there are many thousand colored people who will never receive jobs in that city." How can they raise families? "The Negro race . . . must think seriously of the welfare of coming generations."[10]

Despite Mitchell's support, "Back to the Farm" never became a priority in Washington. When he asked Will Alexander of the Farm Security Administration about existing homestead projects, Mitchell learned that there were thirty-one throughout the South where 1,185 Negro families lived, but that such undertakings "constitute a relatively small part of our program." Undeterred, Mitchell appealed to Henry A. Wallace, Roosevelt's secretary of agriculture and soon-to-be vice president, arguing that: "Agriculture offers the Negro his largest opportunity in this country."[11]

Convinced of the value the program, by March 1940 Mitchell had visited twenty or more resettlement projects in the South and was impressed by what he had seen. In Alabama, thirty-four families had bought an average of fifty-eight acres, and the average net worth of the family had risen from $430 a year to $1,600. A year after his original proposal, he again wrote to Wallace: "I can see no hope for the Negro ultimately except through the extension of agricultural opportunity and development. The soil is not prejudiced and is as responsive to cultivation by the black hand as it is to that of the white hand."[12]

In conjunction with his resettlement plan, Mitchell undertook another southern study tour "to strengthen the bonds of friendship between the races and to secure for the Negro a greater recognition of his rights as an American citizen." This time he visited only North Carolina, the state he had found so attractive eighteen months before. It was, he thought, the most progressive southern state and the University of North Carolina "the most liberal university in the country." Moreover, the state had "done more for Negro education and has done more to build up a common understanding between the races than any other state."[13]

Nevertheless, borrowing Roosevelt's rhetoric, he warned an audience in Williston that his race was "the South's number one economic problem." One-third of the state's Black population was "ill-fed, ill-housed, and ill-clothed," a situation that was "threatening, disagreeable, distasteful, and harmful." But his people had to do their part in remedying the situation: "When we foster a better estimation of ourselves in the opinions of white men, [they] will in turn show us greater respect."[14]

Unfortunately, the Chicago political world chose this moment to show Mitchell fatal disrespect. As he knew was bound to happen, in January 1939 a majority of Black precinct captains in the Second Ward complained to Kelly that Tittinger paid them with "pats on the back . . . rather than jobs to earn bread." The good jobs in the district, they protested, went to white workers.[15]

Kelly investigated, going to Washington to seek Mitchell's advice. Although the congressman now considered Tittinger a political hack who "spends more time studying the race horses than he does looking after the interests of the Party," Mitchell defended his beleaguered patron as someone "who has done the finest work in the way of placing Negroes in office of any Committeeman anywhere." To rally support for his benefactor, he hosted a banquet, at his own expense, for precinct captains "who have worked so loyally" for the cause.[16]

It did no good. Kelly removed Tittinger as committeeman in November 1939, replacing him with William L. Dawson. Under the headline "Who's Who, What's What, and Who Gets the Coconuts," the *Daily News* announced the obvious: "Dawson is the man to see henceforth."[17]

Before Dawson's conversion, Mitchell had dismissed him as "one of the poorest excuses the Second Ward has ever had to put up with. I think I have rightly dubbed him 'Chicago's Ballyhoo Man Number One.' . . . He is not interested in the welfare of the people of the Second Ward. He is simply interested in William L. Dawson." Now, the loyal Mitchell who had lost interest in Congress reversed course. "In the language of the streets," he told Dawson, "you are going places. It is useless for me to say . . . that you can depend upon me to go down the line 100 percent with you." He reiterated this support to Farley: Dawson was working "heart and soul" for the Democratic party and was a "very able man." Mitchell "had never seen the Democratic spirit in the Second Ward so high."[18]

With the coconuts being distributed by Dawson, a Black politician with long-standing political alliances in Chicago, Mitchell knew that his days of usefulness to Kelley and Nash were numbered. In 1940, Roosevelt would send out a directive that no Democratic incumbents were to be opposed in primaries, but Mitchell and Dawson had already come to an agreement that the congressman would retire after his fourth term ended in 1943. As committeeman, Dawson ran Mitchell's successful 1940 campaign, taking care of his interests when the incumbent could not leave Washington. In this, his last campaign, Mitchell felt "absolutely safe in the hands of our Organization. I do not believe there is a better organization in the country." In one letter to Farley he even bragged that Dawson's becoming a Democrat was the result of the type of conversion he had effected on a national level in 1936 and in Chicago in 1938. These two elections had proved to a talented, Chicago-based Black politician that there was no future for him in the party of Lincoln.[19]

Committed to his idea of creating a new leadership group for the South and understanding his now limited effectiveness as a change agent in Congress, Dawson's rise did not upset him. It was time to move back to his "beloved Southland." "You once told me," he reminded a friend, that I should "get out of Congress as early as possible and give my time and ability in helping in the move to make the education of the Negro in the South [lead to change]. I am deeply inclined to a program of this kind."[20]

But where should he go? It couldn't be Alabama, where opposition to him had grown virulent after his filing against the Rock Island. This antipathy had gotten so bad that a college in Birmingham withdrew an invitation for him to speak in 1940 under pressure from the Alabama Council of Democratic Clubs with that organization circulating thousands of leaflets declaring that Mitchell's appearance would be an affront to the people of Alabama. "We call upon white men of the South," it read, "to see to it that our Southern ideas and traditions are respected. . . . We won't stand for another Reconstruction."[21]

North Carolina was an attractive option for relocation, but Mitchell settled on Virginia, largely because of the environment created there by "high class Southern white men," his proposed allies in building a more equal South. A political machine existed, run by Harry F. Byrd. But politics in Virginia were "reserved for those who can qualify as gentlemen. Rabble-rousing and Negro-baiting capacities, which in Georgia or Mississippi would be great political assets," were disqualifiers in the Old Dominion.[22]

The Byrd machine had eliminated many of the barriers to full citizenship for Black residents by the 1930s. Lynching had become a capital crime there in the 1920s and, in 1930, a US circuit court of appeals had ruled that its Democratic primary was "open to all citizens." By 1936, the ANP had reported that "Negroes rarely have trouble paying the poll taxes and registering in this state. Local courts and the State Supreme Court have outlawed in recent years all the subterfuge used to prevent Negroes from voting in the Democratic primaries and to bar them from registering." As a result, in 1936, more Black Virginians were registered to vote than during Reconstruction. The problem that remained was that disfranchisement was "self-imposed owing to Negro apathy and non payment of the poll tax."[23]

Attracted to the opportunities Virginia offered for him to contribute in a society more open to the political advancement of Black citizens, Mitchell applied for and was granted membership in the Langston Civic Club of America, an association honoring John Mercer Langston, the first dean of the Law School at Howard University, first president of what is now Virginia State University, and the first Black congressman elected to the House of Representatives from Virginia. The club's charter dedicated the group to the "reading and disseminating of information and books of value to and for the race."[24]

Langston had served as a trustee at St. Paul's Normal and Industrial School in Lawrenceville at the turn of the century, a position now occupied by Mitchell's friend, P. B. Young. It was probably at Young's invitation that the home-seeking congressman was asked to address St. Paul students. All Black schools in Brunswick County closed for the October 1939 occasion. At the event, "a massed group of students waved flags and cheered as the cavalcade . . . arrived on campus." They heard Mitchell tell local teachers that they "should take charge of the minds of their children and encourage them to appreciate the beauties of rural life." J. Alvin Russell the principal at St. Paul's, judged Mitchell's message to have been "sound." If Black Americans would listen, he said, "we will definitely make real progress."[25]

On December 4, 1939, less than three weeks after Tittinger's fall, Mitchell learned of a property available for purchase in Dinwiddie County about forty-five miles from the North Carolina border. Two weeks later, Mitchell bought it. The attraction might have been to make a contribution to rural education, but another thought lurked in his mind. Dinwiddie County was part of Virginia's Fourth Congressional District, extending south from Petersburg to the North Carolina border. Not only was it the smallest district in the state in the days before "one person, one vote," it was also one of the poorest. As such, might it be a launching pad for the election of the first Black politician from the Old Confederacy in decades? Across the back of the letter telling him of the availability of the property, Mitchell wrote "white 61,413, colored 79,943," what he thought voter registration in the district was, or could be.[26]

Within a month of putting down new roots, Mitchell had taken action to put his theory of local initiative to work on the educational front. Using a list supplied by the Jeanes Foundation, a charity that specialized in supplying educators for Black residents of rural communities, he wrote to all the Black teachers he could find in Dinwiddie County. "I am," he told them in his cover letter, "vitally interested in the educational work in your section and hope to do something in a substantial way to assist the teachers and the ministers in their efforts to build substantial citizenship among our group."[27]

His commitment to teachers began by providing them with materials to enhance the health of the students and mothers they served. Mitchell started by sending a series of pamphlets from the Children's Bureau of the Department of Labor to "more than a thousand colored school teachers in Virginia." Titles included "Infant Care," "Child Management," "Good Posture," "Guiding the Adolescent," "The Expectant Mother," "Well Nourished Children," and "A Better Chance for Every Child." Typical of the letters of thanks he received was one from Margaret Brooks, who found the pamphlets "so useful . . . in my work among rural children."[28]

In addition to expressions of gratitude, teacher letters back to Mitchell spoke to the many difficulties rural Black teachers faced in Virginia. For example, Maude Wyche, who described herself as living within three miles of Mitchell's home and being a registered voter, listed things she thought would improve education for Black children: consolidated schools, improved means of transportation, and modern equipment. Teacher salaries, she added, were among the lowest in Virginia. Nannie B. Speed taught Black children in a "tenant farm area," in a county where there was "supposedly compulsory education." But, when she reported to parents that their three small children were truant from school, the parents complained to their employer. They were told to "put the children in the cotton patch . . . or move." Maybe Mitchell could do something about this.[29]

Edith Brown, of Crewe, Virginia, had taken the initiative in seeing to the physical improvements in her building with the assistance of a "helpful few" who had raised fifty dollars to assist her in spreading the message of Black achievement. The money had been applied to physical improvements such as painting, wiring, and school supplies. Such self-help drew special praise from Mitchell for "doing the kind of work that colored school teachers must do if we are to lift our people to a higher plane of living and real usefulness." It also confirmed Mitchell's alarm that there were "no pictures of distinguished Negroes in these schools." Could Woodson, he had asked, send them portraits of Washington, Douglass, Dunbar, and Sojourner Truth?[30]

In keeping with his model, Mitchell also set out to attract the local white elites to his cause and to possibly support him as a candidate for Congress. In February 1940, he held a "wonderful meeting" at Chase City. At its conclusion, he wrote letters to the leaders of the white community who had attended. In one, he commended Frank C. Bedinger, an attorney, for his "early accomplishments and how you had fought off poverty and gone forward to achieve. There was a nearness [between us] which I do not always feel in meeting new people. We are closely allied in our problems and in our endeavors." He told Mayor C. E. Cohegen that he had "never enjoyed any meeting more. White and colored people in Mecklenburg County have pushed aside most of their bitterness and are working in a common cause to make our country the great place it should be." The people of your county have said "there is already too much hate, what we need is to learn to love."[31]

C. P. Green, the superintendent of education for the county, answered a similar letter. He was impressed by Mitchell because "white people are quick to realize the real qualities of leadership and character in the colored man as readily as he would recognize these qualities in a white man. . . . I am confident that we are all better citizens with a little better feeling towards one another because of your visit."[32]

When Young's *Journal and Guide* ran an article about the meeting, Mitchell found it "excellent" except for the fact that it did not mention the "prominent whites who attended," including Bedinger and Cohegen. "Do you not think," he asked Young, "that we should capitalize on these things if we are to build substantially, politically, and economically?"[33]

By 1941, many letters to Mitchell's Washington office were being answered by Ms. Ray because Mitchell was "away on his farm." That absence fed speculation that he was contemplating a run for Congress from Virginia. M. O. Bousfield, a director of the Julius Rosenwald Fund, an endowment established by a founder of Sears, Roebuck, and Company that supported the education of Black children in the rural South, "heard a rumor . . . that you are going to retire and seek residence in Virginia, and that you have some pretty definite plans for a program after you get there." Barnett heard similar conjucture. Mitchell did nothing to discourage this, prompting the ANP to wonder if he harbored "ambitions to be the first black elected from the South since Reconstruction." If he did, the service observed, there were many Black voters who would support him, if they bothered to register and pay the poll tax.[34]

15

"It Was My Privilege to See You in Action"

As Mitchell built his Virginia base, he continued to make periodic appearances in Washington when he thought the topic under consideration important. A final attempt in 1940 to pass anti-lynching legislation met this standard, although its prospects were dimmer than they had been in either 1937 or 1938 because, as Walter White admitted, "we face, frankly, the fact that there have been no considerable number of horrible lynchings to make public."[1]

Nevertheless, a rewritten Gavagan bill was now being shepherded through the House by Thurgood Marshall, who "worked more quietly than White" and enjoyed the support of Mitchell "with whom the Association [had previously] enjoyed an imperfect relationship." Mitchell was candid about this hostility: "The NAACP has not been able to control me in office and has conducted an avalanche of misrepresentations regarding my attitude on various questions."[2]

Mitchell, who had promised Gavagan "my cooperation to the utmost," delivered a passionate plea for the bill's passage in January 1940, his last formal presentation on a topic that had preoccupied him in his early days. He represented, he said, the disenfranchised, those now regularly and unjustly described as "rapists." What's more, Mitchell appealed to a history of enslaved Black southerners who during the Civil War protected the wives and daughters of Confederate men who fought to preserve and perpetuate slavery. Despite even this, his race now labored "under the most tremendous burden that has ever been placed on a group of people." Black southerners could not hold office, sit on juries, or vote: "They must leave their destinies in the hands of others who say they will take care of them."

He knew the South perhaps "as well as any Member of this House," and the bill asked for very little. It is a travesty, he asserted, to say that rape is the only cause of lynchings when eighty-one citizens had their lives snuffed out because they were accused of being impudent, perhaps failing to say "yes, sir" and "no, sir." For Mitchell, this bill was "more than just a measure to stop formal mobs. Its aim is to prevent any kind of group intimidation which prevented colored citizens from freeing themselves from oppressive racial discrimination by the exercise of the ballot."

Figure 13. Mitchell with Illinois congressman Raymond McKeough (left) and New York's Joseph Gavagan (right) in 1940. In that year, Mitchell supported Gavagan's anti-lynching legislation. In 1937, when they had dueling legislative proposals, Mitchell saw Gavagan as "a demagogue of the worst type" whose legislation was a "farce." Chicago History Museum, ICHi-026235; Acme Photo, photographer.

"This is our country," Mitchell thundered. "We have sweated for it like you have. By what authority do you tell me that we are not entitled to the full protection of the law?" Addressing southern House members, he charged that "my racial group has furnished the victims for [lynching]. You represent the group that has furnished the mob." Lynching, he added, had become a political bargaining chip. Republicans supported the Gavagan bill because they hoped to "buy back the Negro vote [in 1940]." On the other hand, southerners who spoke against the legislation "will expect to use that speech in their districts for reelection."

At this point, Hamilton Fish, the Republican congressman whose parliamentary tactics had contributed to Mitchell's 1937 loss, interrupted with a question: "Is the Negro vote for sale?" Mitchell snapped back that "every vote in the United States is for sale, not for money, but for rights and privileges. The day has come when you cannot fool the Negro like you used to. There are some of us who have the courage to tell the truth. We know who our friends are and we are going to stand by them."

Southerners, he finished, protest that "they love their mammy." We want this love to reach beyond that. "If you love us, give us the opportunity to be citizens like everybody else. You want to kiss us and hug us and claim us as your friends. We are not unmindful of all this hypocrisy. I want to see the Negro have an equal opportunity. We do not ask for any more; we will not be satisfied with any less."[3]

While friends supported him, much of the Black press reacted with hostility to the speech, particularly the exchange with Fish. Cliff McKay, writing in the *Atlanta Daily Mail*, complained that Mitchell, who had earned a "reputation of being a riddle as to just whom he represents" had just revealed why "he is held in such affectionate regard by fellow Congressmen of the South." His remark about Republicans trying to buy the Negro vote was just about the worst in a long series of "blunders" he had made. He should not be given any further chances "to perform such Galahad services for the white citizens of his native Chambers County." L. D. Powell, presiding elder of the AME Zion Church seconded McKay, accusing Mitchell of "playing into the hands of Southern Democrats," the very people who had denied him his constitutional rights on the Rock Island.[4]

Mitchell was unrepentant. "I certainly said what I knew to be true," he told Fred Moore. "There is entirely too much politics on both sides of the House when it comes to matters affecting the welfare of the Negro. Of course, no one expects those who play politics with such issues to come forward and make an open confession. Hence the noise on the Republican side with reference to my remarks." He was less diplomatic when answering Powell: "My presence and conduct in Congress has done more to soften and remove prejudice against the Negro race than anything that has happened since the passing of Booker T. Washington." It is "too bad our people have [your] type of leadership."[5]

On January 10, 1940, the last anti-lynching bill ever adopted by the House of Representatives passed by a vote of 252–131. This time, it did not meet with a filibuster in the Senate but rather with indifference. Consumed by neutrality legislation and other issues involving the war in Europe, the bill lingered for six months on the Senate's agenda but never came to the floor for a vote. Anti-lynching, as Robert Zangrando observed, "was an idea whose time had gone."[6]

What replaced it as a topic for domestic political consumption was the upcoming presidential election. Loyal to Roosevelt, Mitchell returned to the House floor on March 18, 1940, to speak on the topic of "The New Deal and the Negro." Designed to be used in the upcoming campaign, the speech was a long statistical review of how Black Americans had benefitted from government policies begun in 1933. The address aimed at refuting the charge, echoed by contemporary critics and later historians, that "Roosevelt, like all presidents since Reconstruction, had not meaningfully bestirred himself on behalf of blacks."[7]

In it he argued that the opposite was true: Black voters would not yield to Communism's allure precisely because of the improvement in their circumstances under Roosevelt. There followed in a detailed review of the seven agencies that had "touched the life of the Negro." They were the Works Progress Administration, Public Works Administration, Civilian Conservation Corps, Farm Credit Administration, Farm Security Administration, National Youth Administration, and United States Housing Authority.

"Every well-thinking Negro in the United States," he maintained, "if he is honest with himself, must admit that this administration has brought to the Negro his best opportunity and has created in him the strongest hope he has witnessed during his days of freedom. . . . A third term by Franklin Delano Roosevelt would mean continued progress for the Negro." There were still inequities, he admitted, "but the Negro has a greater opportunity in this country than he has anywhere else in the world. I am here because this is the greatest country in the world."[8]

Despite this loyalty to the New Deal, Mitchell's political influence had significantly declined from what it had been four years before. Not only was he unwelcome in Alabama, he was a scourge to much of the white South because of his Rock Island suit and his successful role in turning out the Black vote in 1936. Senator Josiah Bailey of North Carolina complained about "the catering of our party to the negro vote" in large northern cities, precisely the group that Mitchell had brought to the polls in 1936. A delegate from South Carolina to the upcoming convention painted with a broader brush: "Our national party is being led around by the negroism of the North. I am mortally afraid of the negro in our national party." In addition to alienating southerners, Mitchell's attack on "economic royalists" had offended businessmen including those in Chicago, where he was effectively a "lame duck." His 1938 refusal to campaign for Democrats who had voted against House Resolution 2251 had upset many northern members of his own party. Nor was he popular with many Black Americans because of his defense of Hugo Black. If that was not enough, he could also count among his enemies those he had accused of "chiseling" during the 1936 campaign.[9]

Undaunted, Mitchell campaigned to be named a delegate to the 1940 convention, this time successfully. Still the only Black member of Congress, party leaders asked him to second Roosevelt's nomination once the drama of whether or not the president would seek a third term had been resolved. But Mitchell was so out of favor, Ralph Matthews reported in the *Afro-American*, that his seconding speech was reviewed by a committee to guarantee that it "harmonized with party ideas and ideals."[10]

Delivered to "about as many spectators . . . as one might find in the Philadelphia ball park on a rainy Monday," Mitchell's address did not receive much attention. Radio stations in both New York and New Orleans took him off their nationwide broadcasts. Those in attendance heard Mitchell concentrate on two themes. The first was the loyalty of Black Americans to the United States as war loomed. Fifteen million citizens were "deeply conscious of the gravity of our present situation and . . . pledge to our country a continuation of that unbroken loyalty of spirit and action which has characterized our conduct . . . since 1619. We know no country besides America. There has not been and there will be no room for disloyalty in our hearts."

The second was a comparison of broken Republican promises to Black voters matched against the pledges kept by Roosevelt to "America's most forgotten" citizens. The president had not only appointed them to high positions, but the WPA and the CCC had saved the race from starvation. Funds had been approved for the construction of Black schools and colleges, thousands of children had been taught to read and write, the number of hospital beds available to Black patients had increased dramatically, slum clearance projects existed in nearly every large city, and thousands of rural Black homesteaders had been helped to purchase farms. There was no going back. 1936 had not been an anomaly. In 1940, Mitchell predicted, eight of every ten grateful Black voters would support Roosevelt.[11]

William R. Thom, the Ohio representative defeated in 1938 at least in part because Mitchell had refused to support him, praised his effort. "There were more inquiries about your speech and about your past life," he wrote, "than about any other person or incident in the whole convention. It is interesting that the inquiries were from non-members of your race. I feel safe in saying that no speech by a member of your race . . . has done so much for better understanding" between Black and White Americans. Mary MacLeod Bethune agreed, seeing the speech as vintage Mitchell: "My soul waxed warm as I listened to your silvery tones over the radio. . . . God give you more strength and more courage to meet the issues that are before us."[12]

But the *Defender* 's coverage quarreled with this positive interpretation. Its reporter quoted a Black Pennsylvania delegate who had wanted Mitchell to attack lynching, the poll tax, and discrimination in the armed forces: "A man is given the opportunity to voice the needs of his people and what does he do? He takes his hat off and bows and scrapes and offers thanks for being given only some of the things that are rightfully theirs and should have been given years ago."[13]

If there had been any possibility that Mitchell would be asked to reprise his 1936 role, he tried put it to rest with a letter to Farley, who was about to leave the administration after quarreling with Roosevelt about the president's seeking a third term. In it, Mitchell blamed the "disgruntles" from 1936 for his unpopularity within Democratic ranks. They were "particularly bitter toward me because I absolutely refused to allow certain people to ride on the payroll without rendering service to the Party." By doing that, "I committed an unpardonable sin when I protected the National Democratic Committee against exploitation." "I have," he concluded, "no person to suggest to manage the campaign, [but] I want it distinctly understood that I do not seek and will not take it. I am making my statement as strong as I know how." Mitchell need not have worried. He wasn't asked.[14]

Nevertheless, he played an important part in the 1940 campaign. His past speeches remained valuable, as Louis Ludlow, denied Mitchell's support in 1938 but nevertheless reelected, demonstrated when he asked for three thousand copies of "The New Deal and the Negro." So did his endorsements. Unlike in 1938, Mitchell now supported some of those who had opposed him, although it was obvious that the defeat of House Resolution 2251 still rankled. But, once again, it was Mitchell's reputation as a speaker that most appealed to Democratic Party officials who wanted to be sure that "candidates with substantial numbers of Negro constituents were getting a Negro Congressman who was also a renowned orator." As early as September 4, knowing of Mitchell's "ability as a public speaker and defender of Democratic principles," the Speaker's Bureau of the Democratic National Committee had asked about his availability outside his district. In particular, his reputation caught the attention of a freshman congressman from Texas who had been appointed to head the Democratic Congressional Campaign Committee. In mid-October, Edward J. Flynn, Farley's successor at the DNC, urged the party's best Black orator to see him "before you leave town" to coordinate campaign strategy with this rookie congressman.[15]

After hearing reports about Mitchell's appearances in Chattanooga, Louisville, and southern Illinois, Lyndon Johnson thanked him for the "splendid campaign" he was waging to keep the downstate Illinois districts in Democratic hands. As a token of gratitude, in agreement with Rayburn and Roosevelt, he had contacted some "good Democratic friends in Texas" and was sending the Illinoisan $400 to assist his own reelection campaign. Later, Johnson telegraphed Mitchell that he had more money available and wanted to be sure the First Congressional District remained in the incumbent's hands: "If very urgent, wire me absolute minimum and deadline. Give me estimate national ticket prospects and majority you expect your district."[16]

Mitchell answered that he believed his reelection was assured but that nothing should be taken for granted. Wendell Wilkie, Roosevelt's Republican opponent, had appeared in the First Congressional District three times because a "greater effort is being made by [the Republicans] to defeat me than to defeat any man in the House. They think that, if I can be defeated, they can again reclaim the Negro vote in the United States." If he could have $600, he could counter the Republicans who had bought the Baptist ministers by hiring "workers" who would provide him with a four-thousand-vote majority. He got the $600.[17]

It might have been Johnson, who valued Mitchell for "what you have done for the party and the various Congressmen you have helped," who asked him to make a last-minute appearance in Wichita, Kansas, where the incumbent Democrat, John M. Houston, "seems to be having trouble." The visit did not go well. In a repetition of the insults endured during 1936, the hotel where Mitchell was to stay refused to honor his reservation, and Houston's committee did not insist that their guest be accommodated. Because of this "most reprehensible" treatment, Mitchell not only refused to speak, but declined to refund the fifty-dollar travel allowance he had been given. This action drew praise from a local Black leader, Mrs. Carrie Robinson. Congratulations for not speaking because of your treatment at the hotel, she wrote: "All Democrats of Sedgwich County are proud of your stand." After the election, in which Houston was returned to Congress, Mitchell told Mrs. Robinson that some good could come from the incident. Houston had called him, asking to be absolved of blame but Mitchell had refused. He suggested that Robinson call a meeting of Black and white voters to which he would come and "place the blame where it rightly belongs. White men and women must understand that they owe their colored friends the debt of at least being fair to them when they are seeking the aid of our votes."[18]

An urgent telegram on November 4, the day before the election, revealed that Johnson had more than Kansas on his mind: "I have promised persons interested in your results and national picture to give complete report as soon as possible. Don't fail me. Good luck." When the numbers came in, Johnson was pleased with the national results. The Democrats gained seven seats in the House with Mitchell returned to Washington by slightly more than his usual margin. Nationally, Black voters cast ballots largely as they had in 1936, not as in 1938. Most importantly, the 1940 election solidified the perception of the Black vote as solidly Democratic.[19]

Johnson appreciated the role Mitchell had played in this outcome. "It was my privilege to see you in action, not only for yourself but for the party," he wrote. This was a sentiment shared by John McCormack, the future Speaker of the House: "The Democratic Party owes you a real debt of gratitude for your speeches." Mitchell was equally grateful for the future president's help. He was, he reported to Johnson, the only Democratic congressman in Cook County who had been reelected by a larger margin in 1940 than in 1938. He appreciated "not only the money you secured for me, but the personal interest you took in my reelection."[20]

Unfortunately, two Democratic colleagues who lost in 1940 were his friends from downstate Illinois, Claude Parsons and Kent Keller. Mitchell had been particularly proud of his efforts for them in 1936 and 1938, but now the seats returned to their traditional Republican orientation. After his loss, Parsons, previously the superintendent of rural schools and a newspaper editor in Illinois's second-least-populated county, wrote a touching note to the only Black member of the House, one that many could have written: "Your interest in me and mine is very deeply appreciated and I shall always remember with a great deal of warm personal feeling my service with you. I perhaps have been of some help to you especially when you first came here and you have been of a great deal of help to me and I hope our paths will continue to cross."[21]

16

"The Most Notable Decision Since Dred Scott"

By the time Roosevelt had been elected to a third term, Mitchell's case against the Rock Island had dragged on for more than three years, slowly coming to the attention of the Black public opinion. As early as March 10, 1938, the *Defender* promised to "give all the publicity" needed to the complaint, and this attention only increased as the suit worked its way through the legal systems.[1]

Two days later, the matter began its long trek to the Supreme Court when William A. Disque, an Interstate Commerce Commission examiner, held a hearing to adjudicate the case. During the proceeding, Jones, the conductor, admitted that the accommodations were not equal, that "it makes no difference whether a colored passenger pays a first-class fare or not, he cannot get first class accommodations." This left Westbrooks confident that the commission "has sufficient grounds for granting the relief prayed for in [our] complaint."[2]

To the contrary, Disque dismissed the protest on the grounds that the Rock Island could not afford to operate a separate car for such a small market. Mitchell professed himself to be "thoroughly at a loss to understand what course of reasoning" the examiner had followed,[3] but he and Westbrooks were not discouraged by the ruling. From the very first, their object had been to construct a case to be argued before the Supreme Court. There would be innumerable opportunities for both the commission and later lower courts to neutralize his "equal" argument by ruling in his favor. By losing, he could argue that he had sought redress at all appropriate levels and had been denied relief. Given his ultimate goal, Mitchell believed that he won by losing.

The legal partners then appealed to a quorum of eleven ICC examiners, who assembled on July 6 to hear Rock Island attorneys argue that Mitchell had not been denied a right and that Arkansas's two-car rule was a legitimate police action taken by a state. A railroad operating within a state had to comply with that state's laws. Mitchell and Westbrooks answered with this question:

Would a Black man possessing a first-class ticket purchased legally in one state be denied his constitutional rights to equal treatment when he enters a state where it would be illegal to purchase such a ticket?[4]

As with the Disque hearing, Mitchell seemed indifferent while waiting for the second commission ruling. "Whether I win or lose this preliminary skirmish," he told P. B. Young, "the case will be fought to the bitter end and I expect to take the case through to the Supreme Court if necessary. . . . In my estimation, this is the most far-reaching case of its kind that has been prosecuted before the Commission or in the Courts." Consequently, he was not disappointed by the commission decision reached before the 1938 election but announced only after it. A majority of the commissioners sustained Disque's ruling, but only by a vote of six to five. The Arkansas law, the majority declared, did not distinguish between inter- and intra-state passengers. Therefore, the Rock Island was "justified in assuming that the statute covered all passengers." Further, volume of traffic was a "legitimate consideration in determining whether certain services are warranted and whether a difference in treatment is justified." Incidental discrimination, of which this was an example, was "plainly not unjust or undue." The minority disagreed, although with varying degrees of intensity. The most outspoken declared that railroads that separated races "must serve equally well all passengers, whether white or colored, paying the same fare."[5]

Kelly Miller thought this ICC ruling established "something new in the theory and practice" of American law: the concept of "quantitative justice." It subordinated human rights to material interests. He also drew an invidious comparison: there was no difference between Germany depriving a Jewish man of his property because of his race and America denying Mitchell, "its foremost Negro citizen," his property rights "solely because he is a Negro."[6]

At the end of 1938, the *Afro-American,* so often a critic, awarded Mitchell a place on its yearly honor roll for exposing a "wholly un-American system . . . which makes a mockery of the United States Constitution and our claim to be a Democratic country." But Barnett wondered why Mitchell had lost as the facts "appeared indisputable." "Are you confident," he asked, that "all legal loopholes have been plugged?" Lawrence Sledge, one of the first Black lawyers in California and a leader of that state's NAACP, had great hope for the future if Mitchell could obtain the support of the attorney general in having the Arkansas law vacated "on the ground that it is an unwarranted interference with interstate commerce." The *Defender* agreed that the matter should be pursued at the level of the federal court. "The Mitchell case is as important to us as the passage of an anti-lynching bill," it editorialized. "It is important that the matter be settled once and for all if the Constitution, and our status under it, is not a farce."[7]

Given his strategy, it was not surprising that Mitchell welcomed this second "defeat." The 6–5 vote, he informed Castine Davis, was "far better than either of us [Mitchell or Westbrooks] anticipated." "I'm glad they refused us," Mitchell admitted to Westbrooks. "This gives us an opportunity to go direct to the [Supreme] Court. At the same time, the Court cannot say to us that we did not exhaust every remedy afforded by the ICC." The defeat also pleased one Talmas Jackson, but for a different reason. He agreed with the conductor who had "started to kick your rotten teeth out for arguing with him, just what he should have done you double-crossing scum. I'll be glad when you are dead."[8]

In the wake of this second defeat, Mitchell returned to his idea of a boycott of the Rock Island. When he learned that the National Negro Insurance Association was planning to utilize the line's services to transport delegates to its California convention, he wrote to C. L. Townes, the secretary of the association suggesting a boycott. If you knew the attitude of that railroad toward Black customers, you wouldn't use it, he argued. The Rock Island engaged in the "unfair treatment of the very group your companies serve." The letter had an immediate effect. The next day, Townes wrote to "All Members" that "any plans for the use of the Rock Island Railroad has been *absolutely* discontinued. The reason for this action is clearly set forth in the attached copy of a letter from Congressman Arthur W. Mitchell."[9]

As he promoted economic reprisals against the Rock Island, Mitchell continued to gather evidence of the railroad's most recent discriminatory practices. He learned that when Claude Barnett traveled on a Rock Island train between Houston and Dallas in 1938, the editor of the ANP thought it was "the lousiest arrangement I have ever seen on a railroad, a luxurious new streamliner [for Whites] with two seats in the baggage car to accommodate Negro passengers."[10]

His case nearing the Supreme Court, Mitchell continued to document instances of discrimination by other railroads as additional ammunition for his argument. When he traveled from Louisville to St. Louis in the fall of 1940, he was denied a first-class accommodation because a ticket seller told him that "the Louisville and Nashville did not sell first class accommodations to Negroes." Was this true? he asked J. B. Hill, the president of the company. The agent who refused him the ticket, Mitchell claimed, said it was Hill's personal policy. He would "like this information at once." Hill's answer was exactly what Mitchell hoped it would be. Hill denied that he was personally responsible but did admit that "the number of colored passengers desiring to make use of sleeping car accommodations on our line is so small that we would not be justified in offering extra cars."[11]

There was, however, something the changing legal structures of the country could do about the treatment Mitchell had received in Arkansas in 1937 or Hill admitted to in 1940. By 1941, the playing field for adjudicating Black grievances had been leveled dramatically.

A civil rights section of the Department of Justice had been created in 1939 as part of "a policy devoted to creating a new legal order designed to advance civil rights." It was headed by Frank Murphy, the former governor of Michigan who had risen to prominence during the strike at General Motors's Flint facility in 1937. As attorney general, Murphy, "a crusading spirit and a passionate moralist . . . completely changed the complexion of the Justice Department."[12]

In turn, the creation of this section influenced the behavior of the solicitor general of the United States, one of whose primary responsibilities was to appear for the government before the Supreme Court. In 1940, Francis Biddle, "an intimate of President Roosevelt's since their days at Groton" who was "at his best defending the rights of the little guy" now held the office. "Harvard-trained [and] a Philadelphia lawyer of historic ancestry, patrician bearing, and New Deal sentiments," Biddle found the denial of basic rights to Black Americans a "tragic mockery" of American ideals. At the same time, "like virtually every white American who considered themselves racially moderate in 1941 . . . Biddle was more than a petty racist himself." He believed, for example, that Black boys had a vocabulary limited to a few hundred words and once described Black babies as having the "glowing beauty of primitive children."[13]

Despite this, Biddle was an activist who defined the solicitor general's role as limited only by "the ethics of his own profession as framed in the ambience of his experience and judgment." He represented "the most powerful client in the world," the government of the United States. To him, that meant intervening before the Supreme Court "on behalf of an individual litigant to sustain his rights against racial discrimination."[14]

Even more important than the creation of the civil rights section or the presence of Biddle as the solicitor general was the change in the composition of the Supreme Court. Beginning with the elevation of Hugo Black to the bench, the process of replacing conservative justices with more progressive ones had gone forward. By 1940, Roosevelt's "Four Horsemen of the Apocalypse," bent on destroying the New Deal—Pierce Butler, James McReynolds, George Sutherland, and Willis Van Devanter—were gone, replaced by the less conservative Stanley Reed, Felix Frankfurter, William O. Douglas, and Frank Murphy. As a result, the court seemed ready to adopt "a policy devoted to creating a new legal order designed to advance civil rights."[15]

Of particular interest to Mitchell was the evolving court's 1938 ruling in the case of *Gaines v. Canada*. The suit involved the State of Missouri's claim that, because of limited demand, its offer to pay the out-of-state tuition for a Black student who wanted to attend law school amounted to "equal" treatment. By a

7–2 majority, the court, with Hughes writing for the majority, reaffirmed his 1914 sentiment. He ruled that "limited demand did not justify discrimination." Whether or not other Black students sought admission to law schools in Missouri was irrelevant. The right to equal treatment was possessed by the individual.[16]

Before appealing to this newly constituted Supreme Court, Mitchell sought redress in a district court, asking that it overturn the ICC ruling. A hearing was held on May 27, 1940, before a three-judge panel in Chicago. There, the ICC arguments were restated with the Rock Island attorneys, adding the further contention that the fact of Mitchell's proposed legislation to eliminate Jim Crowism being stalled in a House committee demonstrated just how complex the issue was. How could a railroad be expected to know what an infringement of constitutional rights was, they argued, when Congress could not?[17]

At the appeal, the appearance of an assistant attorney general of the United States for the defense angered Mitchell. "A black man coming into Court has two strikes against him," he objected. "I am ashamed for the great government which I represent, as I see an attorney general of the United States rise in this court to help fashion the chains of inequality and segregation around a fellow citizen, a member of a race which has been loyal to this country, which has performed its labor and shed its blood for its preservation."[18]

The appeal did not succeed. On June 27, the court dismissed Mitchell's argument in a brief decision. The ICC had not acted outside the law. Furthermore, because of the complexities of the case, the district court had no jurisdiction in the dispute.[19]

Having lost for a third time, Mitchell appealed to the Supreme Court, which agreed to hear the case on December 16, 1940. By this time, he estimated that litigation had cost him more than $7,000, expenses that he alone had borne. "No man of our race," he proudly declared, "has made any such sacrifice." In fact, he returned checks to willing donors, explaining that "outstanding Negroes who are in a position to wage incessant war against these unjust inequalities . . . should do so at their own expense rather than rely on any form of charity." At the same time, he admitted that he did not want help from the NAACP because he was unwilling to let the case "become a racket for the collection of money from the people." He saw his refusal of outside funding "as a departure from the custom heretofore built in such cases and think it is deserving of special attention."[20]

An exchange of letters in early 1941 with Fred R. Talbot testifies to Mitchell's feistiness as he prepared to appear before the Supreme Court. Talbot had written that an attempt to ban Jim Crow railroad cars was both unconstitutional and a waste of time. No self-respecting Black passenger wanted to mingle with white passengers and vice versa. Enclosing news clippings that reported on various crimes committed by Black individuals, Talbot concluded that the congressman would do more good trying to make "members of your race more law-abiding."[21]

An incensed Mitchell wrote back that Talbot was not smart enough to see what was involved. His case dealt simply with the enforcement of a contract that sought to establish that both races were entitled to the same kind of accommodations for the same amount of money. It had nothing to do with segregation or Jim Crowism. Moreover, given the same opportunity, a Black person would compete favorably with a white person in any area of life. Look at Joe Louis in the physical arena and countless examples in the intellectual. Character and ability were what mattered, not race. As to Talbot's assertion that Black people tended to be criminals, Mitchell pointed to John Wilkes Booth, Jesse James, Al Capone, and John Dillinger. Talbot represented, he was told, "a passing group who has nothing to add to the welfare of the country."[22]

On March 3, 1941, a legal bombshell landed that altered the trajectory of *Mitchell v. United States*. Biddle wrote that, after careful consideration, he could not support the decision of the district court and was filing a memorandum "for the United States, setting forth my views." He enclosed the note to be sent to the Supreme Court, the critical phrase in which read "so long as white passengers can secure first-class reservations on the day of travel and the colored passengers cannot, the latter are subjected to inequality and discrimination because of their race."[23]

Mitchell was elated, boasting to Ulysses S. Keys that it looked as if the case was "practically won." At least, he told his brother, "things are breaking my way." He was certain, in a letter to Julius J. Adams of the *New York Amsterdam News,* that he and Westbrooks would triumph: "I want the victory to be as complete as possible. I regard this as the most important case affecting the Jim Crow situation brought by any member of our race before the Supreme Court." He was so confident that he asked permission to appear before the Supreme Court in person. Since he was not licensed to argue before that body, it took the recommendation of Wesley Disney, a representative from Oklahoma, to give him this opportunity.[24]

Oral arguments in *Mitchell v. United States* were heard on March 13, 1941. Chief Justice Charles Evans Hughes, "a venerable, bearded figure of imperturbable dignity and the object of iconic popular veneration as the spirit of the laws incarnate," presided. Biddle painted the courtroom scene with a description that says much about racial attitudes in 1941 even among forceful proponents of Black rights: "It was an important case," he remembered, "and the court swarmed with Negroes—friendly, hopeful, respectful, wonderfully attired—one of them beaming and immense, in a short-tailed cutaway with the sleeves just below his elbows." Also in attendance was Barbara Goodall, who described herself as a "Negro orphan from Texas." When I saw you arguing before the Supreme Court, she confessed to Mitchell, "fighting for a right, recognition, and a chance for advancement for millions of Negroes, I could hardly keep back the tears."[25]

Figure 14. Mitchell with his coadjutor Richard E. Westbrooks (1941). They became two of the few Black attorneys to argue successfully before the Supreme Court when that body found unanimously in their favor in *Mitchell v. United States*. Westbrooks judged his partner to be "one of the most able and earnest men I have ever known." Chicago History Museum, ICHi-026227.

Westbrooks and Mitchell argued the case themselves. The justices' decision, they asserted, would be far-reaching and could do much to break down "the vicious wall of segregation" that had been built around Black Americans, denying them their citizenship rights in almost every walk of life. Mitchell personalized the argument: "Even when a member of our race reaches the highest position in the Government yet attained, he is still not entitled to more than second-class accommodations in a filthy coach." A Black American "paying a first class fare and traveling in interstate commerce" was entitled under the Constitution to the same services offered to white passengers. Further, *McCabe* and *Gaines* "had established that this right was not contingent on any volume of demand."

The Rock Island and ICC lawyers answered that demand for the services Mitchell had purchased was "virtually non-existent" and therefore unreasonable to expect. For example, it would be unreasonable for a Black passenger to expect a separate first-class dining facility on a train where there were no first-class Black patrons. As unimpressed as he had been twenty-seven years before when hearing *McCabe*, Hughes suggested that the solution might be to admit Black patrons into white dining cars. J. Stanley Payne, a lawyer for the ICC, countered that "the question would then be whether the railroad would have any other customers in the dining car" as there was "a sentiment for segregation in certain parts of the United States." At this point, Westbrooks reminded the court that the volume of traffic "has no bearing on the constitutional rights of citizens."

Biddle then took the side of the plaintiffs. The ICC and the lower court had erred in not taking into consideration "the Constitutional policy against racial discrimination" found in the Thirteenth, Fourteenth, and Fifteenth Amendments and should not permit "state power to reach into the field of interstate commerce in order to accomplish an end at variance with the basic policy of the Amendments." Both the Constitution and the Interstate Commerce Act made the guarantee of equal treatment one that was "personal to each passenger." Demand was not the issue. The majority of the commission had "considered that it was dealing with a question of 'colored traffic.' The Supreme Court, however, faced an issue of basic liberties and privileges of citizens." As he was leaving the court after making this argument, Biddle heard a spectator say "and now, I suppose, he's going over to have tea with the Japanese Ambassador."[26]

Later that day, Biddle wrote to Mitchell, "I thought you made an eloquent and able argument today." Mitchell responded that he was "deeply appreciative" of the solicitor general's intervention. "I firmly believe that if our great country is to have real democracy, we must improve our practice in our own home. How I wish this could be understood." He was candid in a letter to Grace M. Elliott on the same day: "I think this is the beginning of the end of the most cursed obstacle the Negro has had to face during his period of freedom in America. I have had lots of fun making this fight. . . . I have never made an investment that yielded me such large dividends."[27]

These oral arguments sounded the alarm bell for the southern judicial system about the threat posed by *Mitchell v. United States.* T. S. Lawson, the attorney general of Alabama, wrote to his colleagues that the case had become "of vital importance to all Southern states." He was seconded by Governor Frank Dixon, who warned that an adverse ruling would mean "the abolition of all Jim Crow laws, including those applicable to picture shows, trains, cafés, hotels, etc." He invited all governors to send their attorneys general to Montgomery to prepare a joint brief to be filed on their behalf.[28]

After this meeting, ten southern attorneys general filed an amicus brief in opposition to Biddle's memorandum on April 21. In it they argued that Congress, not the courts, was the proper forum for an appeal against segregation in transportation. Jim Crow railroad laws were "reasonable exercises of the states' police powers, designed to promote the general welfare and safety of the population."[29]

Writing in the *Alabama Journal,* Grover C. Hall saw little good coming from this initiative. At best, the governors and the attorneys general were "sticking their fingers in one hole in the dike." But it seemed inevitable that more and more holes would be punched in it. "One must ask," he mused, "will there be enough fingers?"[30]

Mitchell thought not, writing to W. G. Porter that he was "not a bit disturbed" by the meeting of the attorneys general. Their brief, he predicted, attacked the wrong target. They were arguing about the Constitution; he was arguing about a contract. But this case was the opening battle in a war to do away with white supremacy. The attorneys general "are simply whistling in the dark as you and all the people who follow this case will see when the final decision is handed down. I expect narrow-minded men to throw up their hands in holy horror. . . . However, there is one consoling thought: 'right will eventually win.'"[31]

Biddle's brief also captured the attention of the NAACP. To Roy Wilkins, now the editor of the *Crisis,* Mitchell continued to "act his part as the Greatest Mistake in Negro political history." Whatever the Supreme Court decided would not be because of anything he had done. The search for racial justice did not motivate Mitchell. What did was the fact that he had been forced to sit in a railway coach that was beneath his station in life. "He has intimated many times that if the coach had been clean . . . perhaps he would not have brought the suit."[32]

Two weeks later, the organization changed its mind, offering its support to Mitchell. William Hastie told him that "in these circumstances it has occurred to us that a brief . . . filed by the NAACP in support of your appeal might serve a useful purpose." Mitchell resented the overture. Why had the NAACP waited for more than a quarter of a century to express an interest in this type of case? There could have been "hundreds of thousands" of them every year, some involving officers of the association. Further, the NAACP's "attitude toward me and every official act I have done since being a member of Congress has been so false and unfair that I have no confidence whatever in the good faith of your offer."[33]

Wilkins reacted to this rejection by mistakenly claiming that this is "the first instance in which [Mitchell] is recorded as having done anything about jim-crow car travel with which he has been familiar all his life." Further, there had been a 1926 case in which the NAACP had intervened, but the association had "very weak ammunition in legal cases." Mitchell had "violently and abusively" rejected an offer of help. But what would you expect? When he was elected to office the first time, was he not endorsed editorially by the Black-hating Jackson, Mississippi *Daily News* ?

The Supreme Court's decision was announced on April 28, 1941. In a unanimous ruling read by Hughes, it declared that Mitchell's removal to second class was "manifestly a discrimination against him in the course of his interstate journey . . . based solely on the fact that he was a Negro. The comparative volume of traffic could not justify the denial of a fundamental right of equality of treatment, a right specifically safeguarded by the provisions of the Interstate Commerce Act." Because the suit did not challenge the legality of segregation, Hughes continued, the court had not considered the brief filed by the southern attorneys general. Both the Nondiscrimination Clause of Interstate Commerce Act and the Equal Protection Clause of the Fourteenth Amendment could be interpreted as permitting segregation, but "each guaranteed true equality of treatment to every individual."[34]

In a statement issued the next day, Walter White dismissed the decision as breaking no new ground. It merely provided for "substantial equality" in first-class transportation. "The time for real jubilation will come," he forecast, "when the courts unequivocally strike down all methods and modes of segregation." Other prominent Black Americans were more complimentary to Mitchell. Pickens, now a committed supporter, wrote that "you have won for all of us" by "your efforts in behalf of your race and . . . modern civilization." Bethune sent a telegram praising Mitchell's "signal victory . . . evidence of democracy as interpreted by the New Deal Supreme Court." William Henry Huff thought the judgment "a veritable blitzkrieg to the gigantic fortification of racial prejudice." C. C. Spaulding believed that "your achievements will go down in history." Raymond Pace Alexander, the Philadelphia civil rights leader, saw Mitchell's triumph as an "opening wedge and long step" toward the elimination of Jim Crow laws, one of the great victories ever won by a Black American in a court. Alexander added a long-term perspective: "When you have once struck a telling blow at a vicious and pernicious system, whether it be aimed at Negroes, Catholics, Jews, or what not, even if the blow is not quite a knockout blow, you are on the way to ultimate victory." But the letter that Mitchell may have appreciated the most came from W. E. Perkins, a school principal in New Orleans. "Millions," Perkins wrote, "had had the opportunity to do the same thing. None dared undertake it, either for want of courage, pride, wisdom, or means. But you did undertake it and won. That spells everything."[35]

The letter he may have appreciated the least came from William B. Simpson, a student at Lehigh University. Displaying unfortunate timing, Simpson wrote on the evening of the day the Supreme Court announced its decision. He thought Mitchell had been entirely wrong in pursuing the case. "You and your race would be happier in servitude than you are now. . . . The harder you work to make a place in the sun for your race, the more unhappiness you spread. . . . You Northern Negroes spend more time trying to prove that you are equal to anybody else than you spend on any other one thing. The southern Negro accepts his place as it is and therefore is much the happier man. I'm not trying to be insulting," Simpson concluded, but he wanted to know what Mitchell thought about a subject that was "very interesting to me."[36]

He found out a few days later. He was not a northern Negro, Mitchell wrote back. Simpson was wrong about that and "every assertion [he] ma[d]e." Mitchell continued: "I do not take your letter to be an insult, coming as it does from you. A person would have to have considerably more information and brain power than your letter discloses to be capable of offering me an insult. It is fortunate for the country that we do not have a great many of your type."[37]

Viewed from a broad perspective, Mitchell viewed the decision as nothing less than a "step in the destruction of Mr. Jim Crow himself, the first decisive step toward equal rights for Negroes in my lifetime." That, he added in an interview with the *Pittsburgh Courier*, meant the beginning of the end for "the vicious system of segregation which has enveloped Negroes in the South."[38]

In retrospect he saw Biddle's intervention as a key to the successful conclusion of his four-year battle. "I regard him as being one of the most outstanding lawyers in the United States," he told J. E. Mitchell, "not only well informed, but possessing plenty of courage." This was praise he repeated to Biddle later in 1941, when Roosevelt nominated his solicitor general to become attorney general: "With men of your caliber and courage in office, Democracy is bound to live." After he announced his retirement in 1942, Mitchell sent one final message to the man he felt had made victory possible: "I shall never be able to fully express my gratitude to you for your brave stand for justice."[39]

On the other hand, he had little respect for the attorneys general who had filed the brief supporting the Rock Island. After the Supreme Court's decision,

T. S. Lawson, Alabama's attorney general, issued a statement putting a brave face on the ruling. Mitchell, he announced, had won his case against the Rock Island, but "was defeated in his prime objective of invalidating the Jim Crow laws. . . . The present mode of segregation is unaffected by the opinion. It is travel as usual." Mitchell dismissed this judgment as just southerners "making noise, whistling in the dark." On the contrary, the decision represented "the greatest advance made in my lifetime to wipe out the old, traditional prejudices and mistreatment of the South."[40]

Press reactions were generally favorable to Mitchell, although some were quite restrained. The *Atlanta Daily World* saw the decision as limited to providing better seating, lighting, dining car service, and Pullman conveniences. "These will entail more preparations by railroad officials or a curtailment of Negro traffic in some sections." Charles P. Howard, writing in a column for the same paper, found Mitchell's refusal of NAACP help "insulting." "The NAACP," he predicted, "will keep up this fight when Arthur Mitchell is dead, buried, and forgotten."[41]

The *Afro-American* complimented Mitchell on his victory but complained that "the separation of races into Jim Crow cars was not addressed. . . . Somebody must be bold and manly enough to raise it. The Supreme Court decision is half a loaf. It is better than no bread." In June, it also published a poem by Langston Hughes titled "The Mitchell Case." Circulated by the ANP, the verse concluded:

> Mr. Mitchell, you did right well—
> But the rest of us ain't you
> Seems to me it would be simpler
> If the Government would declare
> They're tired of all this Jim Crow stuff
> And just give it the air
> Seems to me it's time to realize
> That in the U.S.A.
> To have Jim Crow's too Hitler-like
> In this modern age and day—
> Cause fine speeches sure sound hollow
> About Democracy
> When all over America
> They still Jim Crowing me.
> To earn a dollar sometimes
> Is hard enough to do—
> Let alone having to take that dollar
> To go and sue![42]

The NAACP reported the decision in the June 1941 issue of the *Crisis*, a copy of which Roy Wilkins sent Mitchell with the note "I thought this might interest you." The coverage was more favorable than had been Walter White's original reaction. Even if it affected only Black customers who had the funds to purchase a first-class ticket, the outcome was "an important milestone in the fight for just treatment of Negro travelers." Mitchell deserved "the thanks and congratulations which have been justly showered upon him" for carrying the fight on for four years. The *Defender* echoed this modest praise, conceding that "one thing you can say for Arthur Mitchell is that he is a fighter and can be counted upon to stay in the fight until the finish."[43]

Many Black newspapers were more enthusiastic. The *Pittsburgh Courier* praised Mitchell's strategy of not fighting Jim Crow on the grounds of mandated separation but rather on those of mandated equality: "This leaves the South without a leg to stand on. If Negroes persist in going to court and invoking the laws the Southern states themselves have passed, discrimination will be wiped out." Writing in a feature story about Mitchell's career on the eve of his retirement, the paper's William G. Dunn returned to this theme in extolling Mitchell's "greatest victory . . . the Dred Scott decision in reverse." "In 1857," he wrote, "the Supreme Court . . . decided that a slave was a slave in every state. In 1941 . . . it decided that a citizen is a citizen in every state."[44]

The *New York Amsterdam Star-News* agreed that the judgment was "the most notable decision since Dred Scott." It felt Mitchell had been exceptionally clever in making his case for equal accommodations and not "a direct assault on segregation." This had permitted Hughes to rule that the brief filed by the southern attorneys general was irrelevant. Moreover, Mitchell's victory was "brilliant" because "his thrust hit directly at the money belt of the railroads." Now, private industry and not the government might be forced to lead the way in eliminating segregation. "The case," the paper pointed out, "which some of the Congressman's critics considered one of minor importance, might turn out to be the fatal blow to complete [the] rout of Jim Crow cars all over the United States."[45]

William Pickens and Sgt. Floyd N. Alexander experienced an immediate effect from the Supreme Court decision less than two months after the ruling. Pickens wrote to Mitchell that he was traveling from Oklahoma City to Dallas in a Pullman sleeper "thanks to you and the Supreme Court." A month after that, Sgt. Floyd N. Alexander, on a trip from Maryland to Arizona, was denied Pullman accommodations in what the Judge Advocate's office declared "a clear violation of law as announced in the Mitchell case."[46]

But it was difficult to publicize news of the Supreme Court's ruling. J. E. Mitchell advised the congressman to ask Biddle to force the ICC to post the ruling in all railroad stations. If that wasn't possible, Mitchell should read the

Supreme Court's ruling into the *Congressional Record* and "circulate it among the people rather generally," but Roscoe Dunjee of the *Black Dispatch* wanted to target a particular group: "It will not hurt to have Southern crackers who read that document find out what the High Court has said on this subject."[47]

Mitchell thought that the importance of the ruling lay in the precedent it set. Dropping the pretense of seeking a narrow victory with an equality argument, he now pictured the Supreme Court's finding as "the furthest reaching decision of its kind ever rendered in behalf of the American Negro." "It makes me tired," he complained, to find people "trying to criticize this decision because it does not cover some fancy ground which they have in their own mind." Rather than complain about what the decision did not say, it was time for "other brave members of the race" to continue the battle he had begun, for those who agreed with him to wage "a never-ending fight" that had its precedent in *Mitchell v. United States*. "We have not fought enough for our rights," he told the ANP, but the way was now open "to force every railroad to grant proper service." "It is for others who are similarly treated," he advised Walter F. Anderson, to "make their fight in the courts, asking for damages and convincing the courts and the world that the decision reached in the Mitchell case must be adhered to." When Frank Adair followed his advice and filed a legal complaint about his treatment on a Louisville and Nashville train, Mitchell saluted his effort: "This is what I want to see men of your type do in a larger measure. Tell your friends: We can break much of this discrimination . . . by approaching the issue as you and I have done in our respective cases."[48]

Westbrooks thought Mitchell's argument would "be understood by the most humble members of the race," but Dunjee doubted that. In March 1942, he told Mitchell that he was swamped with letters requesting an interpretation of the decision "in the language of the crowd," an explanation he hoped Mitchell would supply. Six months later, George Hicks suggested that Mitchell contribute to a proposed newspaper column titled "Rights of Citizens as Guaranteed under the Law." Mitchell found the suggestion "necessary and worthwhile." "I am convinced," he admitted, "that not one-tenth of the benefits that should be derived from the Supreme Court decision . . . have been derived because people do not understand the decision and how their rights have changed."[49]

In September 1943, the Carl A. Hansberry Foundation published a pamphlet telling Black Americans how to take advantage of the Mitchell ruling. "You don't have to ride in a Jim Crow car," it advised its readers, "when you are travelling from one state to another." A railroad must furnish equal accommodations. Any conductor, trainman, or any other person who attempted to make them move from their seat or denied them the use of the dining car is guilty of a crime. The pamphlet advised that there were five steps to take when seeking guarantees emanating from the Mitchell decision: 1) read this pamphlet; 2) show it to a ticket seller or conductor; 3) call or wire the US attorney general; 4) appeal to the US marshall and district attorney for protection; or 5) call or wire the Hansberry Foundation.[50]

By 1944, Wilkins had to admit "countless instances . . . of Negroes in the southern hinterlands boarding trains and quoting this decision to conductors and others." The number of these instances encouraged the NAACP's Legal Defense Fund to take on more and more transportation cases, the rulings on which helped to develop the strategies successfully employed in *Brown v. School Board.* [51]

Over the next decade, thirty-two southern railroads decided "to risk occasional violations of southern law for reasons of cost and numbers" and developed "a kind of qualified desegregation in first class services." While second class remained segregated after World War II, profit-seeking railroads yielded to the inevitable and abandoned attempts to segregate first-class passengers, just as Mitchell had seen they would have to. From there, the path was open to the complete integration of interstate transportation: "By 1963," as Catherine Barnes writes, "the process launched by Arthur Mitchell in 1937 was finally complete."[52]

Although disappointed that its implications were never fully exploited, Mitchell always viewed "my case" and its resolution as his greatest contribution to the struggle for equal rights. He had a right to be proud. Joined by Westbrooks, the two alone had waged a four-year battle for a cause in which they believed, endured reversal after reversal, but stayed the course. Mitchell was particularly proud of the fact that he, refusing all contributions, had personally underwritten every penny of the expenses associated with the case. It was *Mitchell v. United States,* his shining moment, revenge for his 1937 humiliation. He and Westbrooks had walked into the Supreme Court, argued the case, and won. They had not only won but had been unanimously vindicated in their pursuit of justice. Countless plaintiffs could have made the "equal means equal" argument after 1896, but none had. Mitchell and Westbrooks had thrown the pebble of change into the American legal pond, confidant that the ripples from his "flawed but consequential legal challenge" would extend outward.[53]

One reached into the 1950s when Benjamin Mays, the minister who served as the "spiritual and intellectual mentor" to Martin Luther King Jr. and a designer of the Montgomery bus boycott, remembered Mitchell's "well laid legal strategy."[54] Another washed ashore with the passage of the Civil Rights Act of 1964 when Burke Marshall, head of the civil rights division of the Department of Justice, insisted that the groundbreaking legislation be based on the Commerce Clause of the Constitution and not the Fourteenth Amendment. Many members of Congress were disappointed to see such an important bill draw its "principal authority from a seemingly trivial clause of the constitution when it could be founded on the solid rock of the Fourteenth Amendment." But Marshall argued that he was committed to writing a bill that would be upheld by the Supreme Court, no matter in which section of the Constitution it was grounded. The Commerce Clause had sufficed for Mitchell; it would be good enough for Marshall.[55]

17

"What Is Democracy Anyway?"

PRIOR TO THE late 1930s, international affairs had merited little of Mitchell's attention. On the theoretical level, he hoped for the future that C. A. Ryan, the secretary-treasurer of the World Peace Organization, termed "democratic world government." When Ryan wrote suggesting that President Roosevelt hold a conference in Washington to establish such a structure, Mitchell responded favorably: "There is no question but that your suggestions in this matter are correct [and] should be adopted, but I don't think it possible to put it over at this time. . . . Airplanes, radios, and other agencies of communication and travel . . . will eventually help to bring it about."[1]

On a more practical level, he told Sam Goldfus, "I have always believed in peace, but I have never believed in peace at any price." Foreign countries marauding as bullies, such as Italy in Ethiopia or Japan in China, were threats. United States policy should be to "make no trouble, but protect our rights." The Spanish Civil War, for example, lay beyond the realm of American interests. In that case, "the only responsible thing to do is to attend to our business at home."[2]

But Mitchell was an early interventionist on one subject: Hitler's persecution of Jews. As early as December 1937, he told Abe Feinglass, the chairman of the Jewish People's Committee against Fascism and Anti-Semitism, "I have the deepest sympathy with the Jewish people in the great persecution they have sustained in various foreign countries. My people, who are sorely oppressed and discriminated against in almost every walk of life, are in the deepest sympathy with other racial groups suffering in the same manner."[3]

The Munich conference in September 1938 turned him into an even more strident supporter of Jews as victims of racial persecution at the hands of a Germany running roughshod over the European continent. Asserting that he spoke for Black Americans, he telegrammed Roosevelt that "we are greatly disturbed because of the intolerance of certain major groups toward the Jewish people residing in European countries and wish our voices heard in the interest of justice and fair play for all racial groups. We believe that the same spirit of intolerance which is working so tremendously against the safety and sacred rights of the Jewish people, if permitted to go unchallenged, will manifest itself sooner or later against all minority groups, perhaps in all parts of the world."[4]

This threat to the world order brought out the patriot in Mitchell. "I regard this as my home," he wrote in 1939. "This country has given me an unusual opportunity, greater, I think, than any other country would have given me. I would be an ingrate if I took any other position. I love it with all its faults and expect to die and be buried in it whenever the end comes."[5]

Such "patriotism" led him to a preoccupation with the internal threat posed by Nazi sympathizers. Unfortunately, this provoked a blanket condemnation of all those with German surnames. "I know several persons with names similar to yours," he told Paul Kammerling, the managing editor of Chicago's *Abendpost*, "who are engaged in an effort to disrupt the peaceful working of the American government and plant the damnable seed of fascism or Hitlerism in our institutions. [I will fight to the death to prevent] any attempt on the part of any foreign element to bring this country into the isms and troubles of Europe."[6]

As he later explained, Mitchell believed that "America needs a genuine housecleaning" and that these foreigners "who seek to undermind it should not only be exposed, but should be driven from our shores." To accomplish this, Mitchell pledged his "full support" to Martin Dies, a colleague from Texas, who had been named to head a Special Committee to Investigate Un-American Activities in 1938.[7]

However, it quickly became apparent to him that Dies, himself a member of the Ku Klux Klan, had little interest in examining the activities of the German-American Bund or the Communist Party USA. Rather, he seemed obsessed with ferreting out left-wing appointees in New Deal agencies. By February 1939, the committee had become an "absolute nuisance, completely out of sympathy with the Administration of which it should be a part." It was only a public voice for "bitter reactionaries who have sought and are still happy to destroy the New Deal and its great humanitarian program." Dies, Mitchell explained to Marvin B. Pool, "has made a genuine mess" of a worthwhile project and he would not vote for further appropriations if the Texan remained the chair of the committee. All Dies had done was to "make a joyful noise and go on ballyhooing rampages for the purpose of getting his name in the newspapers."[8]

Mitchell voted against appropriations for the Dies committee both in 1939, when he was one of only thirty-five representatives in opposition, and 1940, when he was one of twenty-five. He was proud of his vote, reflecting to John A. Lapp of the Chicago Civil Liberties Committee that he was "happy that I was one of the few who had the courage and backbone to do it." The *Chicago*

Tribune differed, denouncing him as a member of the "secret border patrol who carried the banner for the hammer and sickle." Mitchell's vote also provoked Hermann Weinberger to suggest that "you and the other twenty pinks should be kicked out of not only Illinois but the U.S.A. as well." To this Mitchell responded, "I wonder if Hitler is more tolerant than you. This is a free country where men can speak their opinions and vote their convictions without having to be kicked around by nitwits such as I think you are."[9]

While excoriating Dies for his failure to pursue Nazi sympathizers, Mitchell also viewed the threat of war with Germany as an opportunity to advance a pet project. Just after arriving in Congress, John White Galloway, an aspiring, young Black pilot, had written to him wondering what schools he could attend. Mitchell asked Claude Holman, his secretary, to research the question. After a "thorough investigation," Holman found that there were "no facilities at this time for training young colored men in aviation. [Therefore] we cannot assist you in your most laudable ambition."[10]

The problem still existed at the end of the decade, fueled by the War Department's view that potential Black candidates "lacked the requisite interest and aptitude for military aviation." But Roosevelt's conviction that war was coming and that air power would win it increased pressure for a change. When the president announced at a December 1938 press conference a plan to train twenty thousand civilian pilots, the project caught the eye of the *Argus*'s Mitchell, who wrote to his homonymous friend suggesting that Tuskegee be named a training site for Black airmen.[11]

Mitchell responded with alacrity. After securing the permission of Patterson, the president of Tuskegee, he took the idea to Carl Vinson, the chair of the House's Naval Affairs Committee, and Andrew May, Vinson's counterpart at Military Affairs. "They are both," he reported, "enthusiastic about giving the Negro his opportunity in this field. I know the thinking Negro public will hail with joy the announcement." He was, he told Carl Murphy, "highly elated" over the reaction in Congress to the proposal. "It seems to me that a new day is about to dawn for the Negro." I hope we "will keep a level head in this march upward."[12]

As a loyal supporter of the Roosevelt administration's foreign as well as domestic policies, Mitchell's views on American involvement in a European conflict evolved in step with theirs. By May 1939, he saw war there as inevitable but believed that "the strongest kind of preparation for war as the best way" to avoid it. By September, Cordell Hull, Roosevelt's secretary of state, was the greatest the country had had in his lifetime. Mitchell supported his advice that the United States should remain a nonbelligerent. No one wanted war, but circumstances indicated that the neutrality laws should be "properly amended" to deal with the realities of the situation. The following January, he was outraged by the Soviet Union's attack on Finland and wanted to support all those fighting Hitler but still opposed direct intervention.[13]

On May 1, 1940, Mitchell addressed Congress in a speech he titled "The loyalty of the Negro to America is pledged." In it, he denounced the National Negro Congress's resolution that, if war should break out between the United States and Russia, Black soldiers should refuse to fight. Communism, Mitchell warned, sought to divide the races, to use Black Americans' grievances as a tool to stir internal dissention. Further, John L. Lewis, the president of the United Mine Workers who had spoken in favor of the NNC resolution, was "the most dangerous leader in America today. . . . He wishes to be the American dictator." No matter what had to be endured, he reassured Congress, "the Negro will be found loyal to this Government. He is a lover of this country. It is his home. He knows no other. The Negro stands loyally by the American flag and will give his blood and his life to protect it against any foe. . . . We are Americans, all of us."[14]

Still, he was unwilling to completely abandon neutrality. A day after delivering his congressional address, he wrote Mrs. Stanley McCormick, a leading spokesperson for women's rights, that the "overwhelming feeling" of the American people was that this was not our fight. We had nothing to do with starting it, and we shouldn't become embroiled in European affairs. There was no excuse for sending millions of our boys to war, as we had twenty years ago only to "be left with the bag to hold." A month later, he was only willing to see the United States help the Allies repel German aggression "to the extent of our ability" or "later we shall have to shoulder the responsibility of putting [it] down ourselves."[15]

As war became more likely, Mitchell became more shrill. Correspondents with German surnames who disagreed with him were excoriated. E. A. Siebel was asked if he was German since he obviously was not a "real American." He told E. A. Eshleman that his name went a long way toward unmasking him: "You should be in Europe, where men of your mind belong." At best, the same fate awaited Edith Fischer, who also "had a German name. I know from the tone of your letter that you are a German sympathizer. I am wondering if you are a 'fifth columnist.'" If so, she belonged "either in jail or in a concentration camp."[16]

He was only slightly more restrained with Black Americans who expressed support for the position of the National Negro Congress. Julius Primus wanted to know what benefits those he spoke for had received for being loyal: "I rather die here than to die fighting for a country that don't recognize me as a citizen and don't give me any protection and respect. The Negro should not go to the next war." "It is silly," Mitchell answered, "to think of taking a stand which would mean annihilation rather than pursuing a course which promises a degree of relief in the end. It is very fortunate for the Negro race that your view represents the view of a very few."[17]

But when L. L. Lewis raised the issue of the discrimination Black soldiers faced in the armed forces, he struck a nerve with Mitchell. Enlisted Black soldiers, Lewis alleged, were "outrageously treated in the army," limited to being "grooms and horse holders." The navy was no better. The highest position to which a Black enrollee could aspire was "scullion or mess attendant." Why should Black Americans fight to defend such a country? To Lewis and the many others who wrote, Mitchell confessed to "grave concerns . . . as to the future of a country which practices that large a degree of hypocrisy known in practically every department of our government. They must surely know that a reckoning day is coming."[18]

Nevertheless, taking advantage of war to redress long-standing wrongs was unacceptable to Mitchell. When H. R. Arnette, the debate coach at the Agricultural and Technical College of North Carolina, sought materials from him to support the argument that "the American Negro should seize upon the present international crisis to gain full recognition and enjoyment of his Constitutional Rights," Mitchell told him he was wrong. Seizing on an international crisis to redress national wrongs was not the correct approach. It had failed in India and Ireland and would not be successful here. Rights could only be obtained by "the cultivation of good will and the resort to the courts."[19]

In the same vein, Mitchell asked Howard University's graduating Class of 1941 if the race should "go forward meeting all the demands of the emergency without regard to the injustices and discriminations and handicaps" that our government has placed upon Black Americans. The answer was unequivocally "yes." It was a painful fact that we must make "due allowance for years to pass over our heads while we fight for equality." Students would best serve the cause of equality by being "active leaders in your community," seizing every opportunity to deal responsibly with problems as they arose.[20]

One of those problems was the real meaning of democracy, as an exchange with W. A. Clifford of Eufala, Alabama, revealed. Is it wise, Clifford had asked, to agitate the race question at this moment? White southerners could never think of Black southerners as equals, so raising that prospect came with considerable risk. Given the uncertainty of the world situation, it might be unwise to push any people too far "towards something they cannot tolerate."[21]

By what manner of reasoning, Mitchell asked Clifford in response, can any sensible individual not see that Black men and women are American citizens and entitled to the full protection of the law. Indeed, they are entitled to full opportunity under the law. The sooner Clifford and those who think like him realize this, the sooner we will have real democracy. Judging people by their color brings those individuals down to the level "of Hitler and his cohorts." Some of the vast sums of money we are spending to protect the country from Hitler could better be spent here at home enlightening those who think that we can have one standard of justice and rights for both races. "What is democracy anyway?" Mitchell asked.[22]

By May 1941, Mitchell was "ready to vote for a declaration of war against Germany any day the recommendation comes from a proper source. . . . Hitler and his allies should be destroyed."[23] But preparations for war should not be endangered by racial protest, particularly by a mass demonstration. When A. Philip Randolph invited him to speak at the closing ceremonies of his proposed March on Washington as "an outstanding leader of the Negro people who has made a signal and constructive contribution to emancipate the Negro from civil and political bondage," Mitchell refused to appear. The very idea of gathering one hundred thousand protestors in the nation's capital at this moment made Randolph "the most dangerous Negro in America." He agreed with the president that "nothing will stir up racial hatred and slow up racial progress more than a march of that kind."[24]

Randolph eventually abandoned the march but wrested a concession from Roosevelt in the form of Executive Order 8802, the "first comprehensive federal act to ban discrimination both in federal hiring and in the government workplace," by creating a Committee on Fair Employment Practices to "receive and investigate complaints of discrimination in war industries and in government departments and industries."[25]

In an interview with the *Philadelphia Independent,* Mitchell rejected the claim that the threat of a "March on Washington" had led to the issuance of 8802. Roosevelt was "fair and unbiased" and did not fear marches. Rather, the congressman told a radio audience, the Executive Order was "only one of many provisions" in his Industrial Commission proposal that he had discussed with the president in 1935. Hopefully, the committee planned to deal with the defense contractors and unions who "would not use any Negro skilled worker, no matter what his ability or training," punishing those who advertised for "Caucasian race only" or announced "not at all interested in employing Negroes." Among the primary offenders he listed companies such as the Vultee Aircraft Corporation, the Baldwin Locomotive Company, Fairchild Aviation Corporation, and Glenn L. Martin Co. Among the unions that banned Blacks in their constitutions he named Airline Pilots Association and the brotherhoods of Railway Clerks, Car Men, conductors, locomotive engineers, switchmen, railway telegraphers, dispatchers, and yardmasters. "Could these conditions exist in a real democracy?" he asked. "I point to this defect in our present democracy as the weakest point in our fight for world democracy and our need to put our house in order."[26]

He returned to this point in an address to the Black veterans of World War I in November 1941, reading a letter from Sidney Hillman of the Office of Production Management, which declared that restricting Black workers

Figure 15. Mitchell with Black soldiers at the outbreak of World War II. Mitchell railed against the diminutive level of participation permitted to them. He was particularly concerned about the treatment they received at southern training facilities, warning that "unless something is done, I fear considerable bloodshed in the South." Chicago History Museum, ICHi-183203.

to unskilled jobs in the armed forces were "extremely wasteful of our human resources and prevented a total effort for national defense." To this Mitchell added, "They are more than wasteful. They are thoroughly undemocratic." The Black soldier, he told the veterans, had a duty to fight on two fronts in the upcoming conflict—to defeat Hitlerism and to wage "an uncompromising fight against all forms of race prejudice in our own country."[27]

Days before the attack on Pearl Harbor, he advised Black Americans to prove their loyalty to the United States by ignoring the "many leaders who are not particularly interested in the welfare of labor but who seek to use labor as for benefit of themselves. I regard such men as common racketeers." Lest there be any mistake as to whom Mitchell considered a "racketeer," he was explicit: it was John L. Lewis, the president of the United Mine Workers, whom he had previously denounced as a would-be dictator. Since then, Lewis had called upon his members to strike over an open as opposed to closed shop in a dispute with mine owners. Black workers, Mitchell now argued, could make no greater mistake that to allow Lewis "to influence and persuade them to follow him in his wild tirades."[28]

This denunciation brought a stinging rebuke from Willard S. Townsend, the international president of the United Transport Employees of America. Mitchell's attitude, Townsend wrote, might cast his race into the role of being strike breakers instead of supporting trade union practices: "Of all the blunders of your congressional career, this is the most asinine." It also provoked Morris Milgram, national secretary of the Worker's Defense League, to cancel an invitation for Mitchell to speak because he had "betrayed Labor's cause." But Mitchell was defiant. Labor had made serious blunders. If calling attention to them and asking his people to remain loyal to the United States "provokes your organization, then you stand forever provoked." The sooner we rid ourselves of the racketeer, Mitchell wrote, "the better for those of us who believe in good government and fair play for labor and for all racial groups."[29]

Immediately after the Japanese attack on Pearl Harbor and Roosevelt's "Day of Infamy" speech to Congress, the House prepared a formal declaration of war. Mitchell, "whom we all respect," was asked to speak by Carl Vinson, a Georgian and the powerful chairman of the Naval Affairs Committee, to second the declaration of war. "Beaming with pleasure," the congressman answered, "that will be easy for me. I've been a strong supporter of the president's foreign policies all along." Later, government leaders decided to act on the resolution without debate, but Mitchell read the remarks he had prepared into the *Congressional Record* anyway. In "The Pledge of Fifteen Million Negroes," he declared that Black Americans would give everything they had, including their lives, for success in the effort "to withstand Hitlerism." But he hoped that this contribution would cause the country to recognize "Negroes as full-fledged citizens." If they are good enough to die for their country, he observed, they "should be given the fullest opportunity to live for their country. We are loyal Americans and you can depend upon us."[30]

This included the "fullest opportunity" to become officers in the armed forces. Now willing to skirt legalisms to accomplish his goals, Mitchell renewed his campaign to have Black applicants admitted to Annapolis and West Point. Many of those he nominated were not residents of his district, a fact that he chose to ignore. His advice to Leland Jones was to use Mitchell's Chicago address to be "in technical compliance with the law." Moreover, the passionate opponent of the use of photographs on civil service applications added that Jones should "be sure to send a 'good photo' of yourself as the *Afro-American* and *Courier* wanted to publicize the nomination of a 'colored boy.'"[31]

Although willing to engage in these sleights of hand, Mitchell poured over applications to be sure his appointees met his standards. Lloyd J. Stark did not receive a naval appointment at least in part because of his letter. Mitchell's distinctive handwriting noted that he has spelled "anxious" as "anchious" and used "need" when "needed" was appropriate. Being less than honest was more disqualifying than having a poor grasp of grammar. When the congressman discovered that Toussaint Gadsden Jr. had lied about his eyesight, the applicant received this rebuke: "Let me suggest to you that above all else you must be fair and honest with persons whose aid you seek. This defect alone is enough to defeat you in any endeavor of life. You should overcome it or prepare for genuine failure."[32]

Mitchell never succeeded at the Naval Academy, but not for want of trying. In 1942, amid much fanfare that "one of his most cherished ambitions" was to see a Black midshipman, he made what he considered two outstanding appointments. One was rejected because he lacked the proper background in math and chemistry, the other because his "college certificate was not accepted."[33]

He had more success at West Point. Not only did Fowler graduate, but eleven Black cadets enrolled there between 1937 and 1945, most nominated by Mitchell, and eight graduated. The congressman hovered over these nominees as he had Fowler. When one objected to the demerits he had accumulated, Mitchell rushed to his defense demanding an investigation and threatening to go to Roosevelt if the situation was not remedied. The West Point superintendent responded that the plebe in question had been afforded "more consideration than the average cadet." There was "no basis for the belief that a considerable race prejudice exists now at the academy."[34]

He also rose in support of Black defense workers hired in the wake of Roosevelt's Executive Order 8802. In early 1942, some white residents of Detroit protested against the construction in their neighborhood of the Sojourner Truth House, a low-income residence being built to meet the needs of Black defense laborers. When its opening provoked demonstrations, Mitchell appealed to Roosevelt, alleging that city authorities "seek to take this project away from the group for which it was erected and by whom it is needed and needed badly." Concurrently, he wrote to Lester Granger, the executive secretary of the National Urban League, that "this is a common fight for rights and recognition of America's most loyal group. We can brook no compromise of rights now."[35]

He even reached out to Walter White, writing that he was "doing whatever I can in this matter and shall be glad to cooperate with you in every possible way to win the fight." His old adversary answered that he was organizing a protest, that it was "absolutely incredible to me that [officials] should continue to kick Negroes around and expect them to be enthusiastic for the war to preserve democracy." Mitchell endorsed the protest against this "nefarious robbery" without reservation: "The stronger the protest in the Detroit situation, the better."[36]

After a demonstration that saw forty Detroiters injured and 220 arrested, only three of whom were white, Black residents were permitted to move in. Mitchell thanked Roosevelt for his intervention, and White thanked Mitchell "for all you did in the Detroit housing matter. I'm glad the efforts we put forth had some effect."[37]

But Mitchell's primary concern during his waning days in Congress focused on the dangers faced by Black army trainees scattered across camps in his "beloved Southland." Even before Pearl Harbor, he had warned that the "treatment Negro soldiers are receiving in various parts of the South, if we are to believe the reports coming to us, is an awful thing." He also saw a future for the Black military after the war that would be filled with "difficulties and hardships, depression and unemployment such as we have never seen before."[38]

To improve the situation, he volunteered to form a morale committee to fight "subversive activities" designed to undermine Black loyalty to the country. Vinson thought the idea "a good one" and forwarded the offer to Frank Knox, who answered that "if it were practical, I should be very glad to avail ourselves of Congressman Mitchell's generous offer." But nothing came of it.[39]

A confrontation in Texas between the military police and Black soldiers confirmed Mitchell's fears. Black troops were relaxing at a bar in the Black section of Houston when a white policeman entered and delivered a lecture to "you nigger soldiers" on their shortcomings as representatives of the country. "I am not a nigger soldier," one answered. "We are American soldiers." "You are a nigger soldier if I say so," the policeman shot back, "and if you don't like it, I will kill you." An officer commanding the military police told an ANP reporter who had witnessed the confrontation and complained about it that "the army policy is to permit civil authorities and police to treat Negro soldiers as they see fit. They may talk to them in any way they wish."[40]

Motivated by a new sense of urgency the incident provoked, Mitchell told an ANP reporter that the single largest factor in the recent fall of Singapore had been Britain's refusal to recognize and use native soldiers. Yet the British handling of indigenous troops "is far better than the treatment which the American Negro soldier receives at the hands of a large portion of our civilian population and, I think, the war and navy departments themselves." In this spirit he wrote to Henry Stimson that "the morale of the Negro has been tremendously lowered by the treatment of the white population toward Negro soldiers" in several southern states. "I cannot emphasize too strongly," he added, the importance of the high command of the army taking a special interest in "what I am sure is a very grave situation." He also complained to Truman K. Gibson, who passed the warning on to William Hastie, an aide to Stimson charged with overseeing racial issues. Describing Mitchell as "a very cagey and smart individual" who "feels the war effort has been very unpopular with

Negroes," Hastie passed the letter on to Claude Barnett, adding that Mitchell had told him that "unless something is done, I fear considerable bloodshed in the South."[41]

Mitchell also alerted J. E. Mitchell at the *St. Louis Argus* of his fear. The editor observed that he didn't see how official Washington could "answer your letter and allow the conditions of which you speak to remain the same." The *Argus* intended to publish Mitchell's letter, and its editor suggested that the congressman read it into the *Congressional Quarterly* so that it could receive the publicity it deserved. But here Mitchell's patriotism overcame his sense of outrage. Stimson had told him that "suitable remedial action has been taken." "Let's wait and see," the congressman suggested.[42]

As had been the case since 1937, the navy remained a special target of Mitchell's wrath. Black sailors were "grossly discriminated against by [its] policies," he protested to Knox. Morale was very low and changes needed to be made. Knox brushed him off: "Policies were not discriminatory. They were designed to enable Negroes . . . to contribute substantially to the war effort." As had been the case with Johnson, an appeal to Roosevelt about naval policy did no good. "We must have the loyal support of all citizens," the president warned Mitchell. "I am informed by the Secretary of the Navy that the same basic training, including physical and vocational training, is accorded all recruits."[43]

To Mitchell, Roosevelt's support of Knox was misguided. It was yet another example of the United States' evolution to real democracy being thwarted by southerners clinging to the past. This group also included members who always opposed "giving a reasonable share of Democracy to the Negroes of the South because of the fear in their hearts." They were "low down" politicians who "use the Negro issue as a vote catcher." For half a century, they had stood opposed to all legislation designed to promote democracy: bills to prevent lynchings, relief for labor, the wage and hours bill, social security if it benefited Black Americans, and farm relief. It was a sad spectacle to observe their power because, to Mitchell's mind, there were so many good white people in the South who had never "bowed to Baal." Their number was increasing, but his race must fight with all its strength against false friends "who are constantly seeking to bind tighter around our ankles the chains of economic, industrial, and political slavery which they themselves have wrought and placed upon us." If a democracy was to live, its supporters had to understand that "the color of a man's skin has nothing to do with his citizenship rights." Where it does, "there is no real democracy." "Darker people throughout the world" want to remind the "arrogant white man" that "if a democracy is to live, it must shed the garment of hypocrisy. Let us strike with all our might," he urged, "for freedom and democracy in our own house."[44]

His last major speaking tour was to California in December 1942, where he became the first Black speaker to address the prestigious Commonwealth Club. There he predicted that the United States would win on the battlefields of World War II, but victory in the fight against racial and religious prejudice, which is what democracy is all about, was far less certain. We lost at the peace table twenty-five years ago, he told his audience, and could do so again. What kind of a world are we to have when the firing stops if discrimination in the armed forces is permitted to continue? "While we are adjusting the affairs of the world, we must not fail to adjust affairs in our own country, and in our hearts." His people were giving their lives to prevent Hitler from doing to the United States what millions of white people "have been doing to the Negro for more than 300 years."

"Several scores of men" would "rather see the Axis powers win this conflict than recognize the citizenship rights of Negro Americans." These same men "are loud and long in their acclaim for democratic rights of American citizens," but there had recently been a lynching in Mississippi, an act "just as repulsive as any crime which has been committed by the Nazis or the Japanese against our fighting soldiers." If we want to win at the peace table, "the color of people must no longer be a consideration. . . . That part of our Declaration of Independence which alleges that all men are created equal must be the basis of all our future plans if there is to be a lasting peace."[45]

Conclusion

"And So Goes on the Fight"

If revisionism, as Schlesinger argues, is "an essential process by which history through the discovery of new sources . . . enlarges its perspective and enriches its insights," then the Mitchell papers are a clarion call for us to rethink our appreciation of their compiler.

True, the Mitchell who emerges from them is exactly, in part, what his enemies charged him with being: a cog in Chicago's political machine who paid only nominal attention to his constituents, was unpopular with them, and won election and reelection only because the bosses considered him useful in securing patronage for the city.

But he was so much more. His primary goal was revolutionary in concept: to be the elected voice of disenfranchised southern Black voters in the political process from which they were excluded. It is against this standard that history should judge him.

Mitchell sought to establish nothing short of a new political elite to represent and to advocate for Black Americans. To do this, he saw his mission as replacing Black leaders who had done little to advance the cause of racial equality since the end of Reconstruction: the Republican party, the NAACP, and the northern Black press. But that could not take place so long as the siphoning of talented southerners to the North continued, a phenomenon that could only be halted by ensuring the physical safety of Black citizens, expanding their economic opportunities, securing Black access to national institutions and programs, and guaranteeing the right to vote. His responsibility, as he saw it, was to demonstrate to those for whom he advocated where their true interests lay, to promote legislation that advanced these goals, and to make a persuasive argument to a potential new Black leadership group that they should remain in his "beloved Southland."

Mitchell undertook this mission at a fraught moment when the Civil Rights Movement was, according to some, at its nadir, having gone underground, not to reemerge until 1954. But Henry Louis Gates Jr. challenges this characterization, arguing that "there is a constant thread between the end of Reconstruction and the reemergence of the civil rights movement of the 1950s."[1]

The Mitchell papers, which end abruptly with his retirement from Congress in 1943, bear witness to the existence of that constant thread and Mitchell's perception of himself as a chief weaver of it. That is certainly the suggestion contained in chapter titles he proposed for his never written autobiography: "Let the Record Speak," "Bills and Speeches in and out of Congress," "RR case—I won my case," Segregation—effect, cure," "What did I know?—The Truth," "Blazing the Way," And "My Plans Working Out."[2]

In retirement, Arthur Mitchell brooded over being misunderstood. In particular, he wanted posterity to understand the enormity of the challenges he faced and how those obstacles informed his strategy. His responsibility, he felt, was to create a sense of hope and clear the way to future progress. We "must sow today," he wrote in 1939, "cultivate tomorrow, and reap the harvest later in life." It was a message he expanded upon three years later: "The Negro in America is discriminated against in every department of our government and in almost every commercial enterprise. . . . It is absolutely futile to think that the conditions will be fully remedied [during our lifetime]. The cause of our mistreatment is too deep rooted and has taken too great a hold on the majority group for us to be able to overthrow it in a few years. I have done little more than make a visible dent. When you and I and thousands of others have exhausted our strength, the problem will still be here to be fought out by those who succeed us." It had been, he added, his responsibility to "leave a record which will inspire others to fight and sacrifice in order to change conditions and make our country a better place for all citizens."[3]

"Bend to the oar tho' the tide be against us" had been the motto of his first school and a cardinal principle for his career. He was "not of that type who would take the position that because I cannot travel a mile in one step that I will not start. I believe that all great moves are accomplished gradually, step by step." In this he was aided by his self-image as calm, reflective, and, above all, optimistic, a hopeful, forward-looking realist. "If there is one thing in my life for which I thank God above all," he reflected, "it is that I am a born optimist. I believe we are progressive beings and that while we might have set backs now and then, our general trend is upward."[4]

As it ended, he was convinced that his "presence in Congress has done more to soften and remove prejudice against the Negro race than anything . . . since the passing of Booker T. Washington." This was a sentiment with which Gordon Hancock, his ally in the "Back to the Farm" initiative, and many others agreed. After working with him, Hancock wrote, southern congressmen began to take Black participation in the legislative process more seriously. It was certainly the view of Hatton Sumners in the aftermath of Mitchell's defeat on anti-lynching legislation in 1937: "If Mitchell holds himself throughout the years as he is today, his head on his shoulders and his feet on the ground, he stands a chance to be recognized by the historian of the future as the greatest statesman his race has produced in a century."[5]

If overstated, Sumners's judgment focuses attention on Mitchell's congressional accomplishments and the building blocks he put in place for the future. His organizational skills contributed to the seismic shift in 1936 that moved much of the Black vote from the Republican to the Democratic column, a change that continues as a reality today. His proposal for an Industrial Commission hints at affirmative action well before it emerges as a mature political idea. Until recently, his anti-lynching legislation was the only anti-lynching legislation ever recommended to the full House of Representatives by its Judiciary Committee. All of his proposals to reform the civil service eventually became law. His campaign to integrate the service academies yielded important results, particularly at West Point.

Likewise, Mitchell saw with penetrating insight some of pitfalls that handicap race relations today. As early as 1935 he warned of the danger majority-minority districts could be in elections. He foresaw how the original formulation of Social Security would contribute to the growth of income inequality, as would the adoption of the GI Bill of Rights after World War II. Most obviously, he was unceasing in his warning that Chicago and other northern cities that witnessed population surges as a result of the Great Migration would not, in Martin Luther King Jr.'s words, turn out to be "the new Jerusalem."[6]

But equally as important were his accomplishments after he realized that the legislative process would fail to accomplish his goals. Chief among these was his advocacy for, and recruitment of, a southern vanguard to address the existing realities in the region. Mary Rambo, the Black woman living in New York who befriended Ellison's *Invisible Man,* could well have been Mitchell when she says, "It's you young folks that going to make changes. . . . You got to lead and you got to fight and move us all up a little higher. . . . It's the ones from the South that's got to do it, them that knows the fire and how it burns. Up here, too many forgits. They find a place for themselves and forgits the ones on the bottom."[7]

Mitchell would not have been surprised that when the Civil Rights Movement of the 1960s moved to the forefront of the national dialogue, its essential leadership was southern, not northern, as it had been in his day. His mission after abandoning the legislative process was to recruit just such a new generation of southern leaders, see to their education, and convince them to stay where they had been born, carrying on the fight based on the realities of the conditions they had experienced. "I succeeded here. You can and should as well" was his message.

It is interesting, if unknowable, to speculate as to whether or not the parents of Martin Luther King Jr., Ralph Abernathy, or many others ever heard Mitchell speak. We do know that the organizers of the Montgomery bus boycott were informed by his "well laid legal strategy" and the path it blazed leading to *Brown v. School Board*. We also know of the high regard in which Lyndon Johnson and Hugo Black, both southerners and key players in struggles of the 1960s, held Mitchell.[8]

Beyond all this, a 1963 *Ebony* interview with an eighty-year-old Mitchell sheds light on his view of his most important contribution to the fight for civil rights. In the exchange with the reporter, he declined to comment on the present Congress except to say that he disliked "extremists of any sort." He still could not "be bothered with small talk or cocktail parties," and he still was driving himself all over the South in his 1956 Buick. But in the trunk of his car he carried a record of *Mitchell v. United States* "to prove to many people that this is the leading case. . . . There are many Negro lawyers who do not know it is the leading case."[9]

By "leading case" he meant more than just the narrow legal judgment it had produced. To him it represented the triumph of his career-long drive to seek incremental improvement through the attention to detail that characterized his work. Appeals to lofty principles stirred the emotions; finding the weak line in a piece of legislation or the law achieved results.

At about the same time as the *Ebony* feature appeared, Mitchell replied to a survey titled "If I were young again." In it, he depicted himself as always working for "equal opportunity and equal treatment of Negro citizens," first as a school teacher, then as a lawyer, and finally as a member of Congress. Asked what he thought he had accomplished, he answered that he thought he had made a "worthwhile contribution" to the "perplexing race problem" and helped build "substantial American citizenship for minorities." If this inheritance was to be passed on and expanded upon by future generations, "the Negro youth must continue to fight for every right and opportunity all other citizens enjoy in this country. . . . He must never submit to race discrimination in any way. He must fight for every citizenship *guaranteed* by the American constitution." "The result of this fight," may mark "a new day in this country and perhaps in the world." But its successful conclusion depended upon the young, their energy and their sense of their own fate. "Give to the world," he advised, "the best you have and the world will give the best to you."[10]

His vision for the ultimate triumph of Black aspirations echoed the conclusion to his 1939 Founder's Day speech at Tuskegee. In it, he quoted from Carlyle that "the poorest day that passes over us is the conflux of two eternities. It is made up of currents that issue from the remotest past and flow onward to the remotest future." "Who knows," he added, "but this race of which you are members is being trained now through this world of hardship and drudgery and discrimination for the purpose of preserving civilization when the crucial moment comes?"[11]

It also found voice in a bit of doggerel he composed for his one of his final addresses to the House of Representatives:

> O, white man, why evade the issue?
> Your tin-god cycle's done
> You've held it down for centuries
> You've had a lot of fun
> Get ready for the Renaissance
> Your system's obsolete
> It's Providence you're up against
> And that you cannot beat
>
> You haven't settled anything
> In God's beholden sight
> For no question is ever settled
> Until it's settled right
>
> And so-goes-on-the fight.[12]

Notes

Prologue

1. Horace Bond Mann, *Negro Education in Alabama: A Study in Cotton and Steel* (New York: Atheneum, 1969), 175; *The WPA Guide to 1930's Alabama Compiled by Workers of the Writers Program of the Works Project Administration in the State of Alabama*; introduction by Harvey H. Jackson III (Tuscaloosa: University of Alabama Press, 2000), 4, 292, 296; Dennis S. Nordin interview with William E. Gilbert, Geiger, Alabama, April 12, 1971, Arthur W. Mitchell Sound Recordings, Chicago History Museum [hereafter CHM].

Introduction

1. Dennis S. Nordin, *The New Deal's Black Congressman: A Life of Arthur Wergs Mitchell* (Columbia: University of Missouri Press, 1997), x and 197; Earl Brown, "How the Negro Voted in the Presidential Election," vii, 2909–2913, 2912 in Arthur M. Schlesinger Jr., ed., and Fred L. Israel, assoc. ed., *History of American Presidential Elections, 1789–1984*, 14 vols. (Philadelphia: Chelsea House, 2002); Mia Bay, *Traveling Black: A Story of Race and Resistance* (Cambridge, MA: Belknap Press of Harvard University, 2021), citing Prattis to Wilkins, May 14, 1941, *ProQuest History Vault*, 001444-017-1491, 239; Melvin G. Holli, untitled review of Dennis S. Nordin's, *The New Deal's Black Congressman: A Life of Arthur Wergs Mitchell, Michigan Historical Review* 23 (1997): 220.

2. Nordin, *New Deal's Black Congressman*, vii–viii, 13–15; Melvin G. Holli, untitled review of Dennis S. Nordin's, *The New Deal's Black Congressman: A Life of Arthur Wergs Mitchell, Michigan Historical Review* 23, (1997): 220.

3. Nordin, *New Deal's Black Congressman*, vii.

4. Nordin, *New Deal's Black Congressman*, vii; J. W. Hubbard to Arthur W. Mitchell [hereafter understood], Arthur W. Mitchell Papers, 1898–1968, bulk 1934–1942 [hereafter understood], CHM, Research Center [hereafter understood] February 28, 1935, Box [hereafter understood] 6: file [hereafter understood] 4; Adams to, May 28, 1943, 66:3; Carver to, June 16, 1939, 45:10; Miller to, May 20, 1938, 38:11; Wright to, April 29, 1943, 60:3; Westbrooks to, October 4, 1938, 40:1.

5. Claude Barnett Papers [hereafter BP], Chicago History Museum, Research Center [hereafter understood], Claude Barnett [hereafter Barnett] to Frances Williams, November 15, 1934, Box [hereafter understood] 73: File [hereafter understood] 6 and undated memo, BP, 346:3, BP, 15: file for 4–February 13, 1935; Roy Wilkins, "Watchtower," *New York Amsterdam Star News*, March 29, 1941; BP, file for 5–November 22, 1934, 14:5; *Chicago Defender*, October 3, 1936; *Defender*, August 8, 1936; Edgar G. Brown, "Washington Scene," *Baltimore Afro-American*, December 26, 1942.

6. *St. Louis Argus*, January 17, 1936, 15:7; Arthur Mitchell [hereafter understood] to Leon Lewis, November 28, 1941, 63:6; to John Mitchell, March 7, 1941, 58:9; to Henry Huff, October 15, 1942, 67:6; to Dr. Hubert A. Davidson, December 10, 1941, 63:8.

7. To John H. Johnson, January 5, 1959, 71:9; *Afro-American*, July 20, 1946; "Ex-Solon Still Active 20 Years After Retirement," *Ebony* 18, no. 10 (August 1963), 41; William N. Jones, "Day by Day," *Afro-American*, February 27, 1927.

8. Mitchell's outlines are found on p. xx; Archie Motley, Chief Archivist, Chicago Historical Society, to, August 15, 1967, 71;10; interview with Lucious Edwards Jr., Petersburg, VA, March 15, 2022; email, Edwards to the author, April 5, 2022; James Janega, "Archie Motley, 67," *Chicago Tribune*, November 13, 2002.

9. Undated newspaper clipping, August 29, 1910, 1:1; Nordin, 14; Matthews, "Dries Dishes but He Is not Henpecked," *Afro-American*, February 29, 1939; to George Mitchell, February 18, 1952, 71:1.

10. *New York Amsterdam News*, November 27, 1937; to Dr. O. B. Williams, February 8, 1938, 36:7.

11. Morgan State Address, January 12, 1940, 43:9; Ben O'Brien, "Watching Washington," *Pomona Valley Weekly Tribune*, September 30, 1937, 33:2; Matthews, "Dries Dishes but He Is not Henpecked"; Malcolm B. Smith, *Pittsburgh Courier*, October 15, 1936; Lem Graves Jr., *Pittsburgh Courier*, July 20, 1949; to unknown, undated, 24:8; to Dr. J. W. Jones, March 14, 1935, 10:3; E. M. Hennessey, *Boston Globe*, January 6, 1935, 4:1.

12. Charles R. Branham, "The Transformation of Black Political Leadership in Chicago" (PhD diss., University of Chicago, 1981), 257.

13. Rodney Brock to, April 3, 1935; to Brock April 12, 1935, 8:9, "Expenses accounts, 1936," 22:4. Englestein to, July 1, 1940, 53:8; same to same, October 14, 1940, 55:4.

14. To James A. Farley, October 3, 1934, 2:4; to John C. Grimes, assistant treasurer, Democratic National Finance Committee, October 6, 1936, 22:6; to Bishop R. R. Wright, June 13, 1940; 53:3; *Norfolk Journal and Guide*, September 24, 1949, 70:2.

15. To C. Vernette Grimes, January 6, 1940, 49:1: Matthews, "Dries Dishes but He Is not Henpecked."

16. Nordin, *New Deal's Black Congressman*, 2; to William J. Edwards, October 8, 1913, BP, box 239; to Maude Scritchfield, August 20, 1943, 68:5.

17. For an appreciation of the danger for Blacks faced when driving in the South, see Bay, *Traveling Black*; Jill Watts, *The Black Cabinet: The Untold Story of African Americans and Politics during the Age of Roosevelt* (New York: Grove Press, 2020), 105; and Isabel Wilkerson, *The Warmth of Other Suns: The Epic Story of America's Great Migration* (New York: Random House, 2010), 219. To Carl Murphy, May 27, 1937, 31:2, and January 16, 1939, 42:1.

18. Arthur M. Schlesinger Jr., *A Life in the Twentieth Century: Innocent Beginnings, 1917–1950* (Boston: Houghton-Mifflin, 2000), 179.

19. Raymond Pace Alexander to, May 14, 1942, 66:2; C. S. Boothby to, May 12, 1939, 38:9. The Boothby-Mitchell exchanges are just one of many years-long verbal joustings that can be followed in the Mitchell papers.

20. To Ray Edmundson, January 18, 1939, 42:2; to Paul Williams, February 10, 1939, 42:8.

21. To Booker T. Washington Jr., October 6, 1937, 33:4; to Stafford B. Ash, February 10, 1937, 27:4.

22. To Broadhead, April 6, 1939, 43:10; Broadhead to April 10, 1939, 43:11.

23. To Van Duzen, March 11, 1940, 51:4; Van Duzen to, March 19, 1940, 51:6; to Van Duzen, March 25, 1940, 51:7; to Dunnigan, March 25, 1940, 51:7; to Van Duzen, n.d., 51:7.

24. To A. A. Quince, April 15, 1935, 9:1; to the Diamond Cab Company, April 24, 1935, 9:3; to M. C. John J. O'Connor, August 7, 1935, 13:2; to the Capitol City Engraving Co., December 19, 1935, 14:6; to Commissioner M. C. Hazen, March 31, 1938, 37:11; to the Grand Trunk Railroad, November 3, 1938, 40:7; to J. B. Hill, president, Louisville and Nashville Railroad, October 2, 1940, 13:11 [misfiled]; to the Postal Telegraph-Cable Company, January 17, 1941; to R. R. Tolson, n.d., 58:3.

25. To WRC Radio Station, March 15, 1937, 29:4.

26. Clinton to, September 8, 1935, 13:7; to Clinton, September 14, 1935, 13:8. There is no way to know whether or not Mitchell made the trip, but the Death Penalty Information Center does not record the execution of a "James Clinton" in Virginia between 1935 and 1940. See "Executions in the U.S. 1608–2002: The Espy File," Death Penalty Information Center (website), 2023.

27. To Lowell Mellett, ed., *Washington News*, February 19, 1936, 16:10. Mellett apologized, regretting "the ineptitude of the headline." Mellett to, February 20, 1936, *Washington News*.

28. To Carl Murphy, April 12, 1939, 44:1; to Mrs. Henry M. Robert Jr., president-general of the Daughters of the American Revolution, April 11, 1939, 44:1.; Meltsner to, March 15, 1941, 59:2; to Meltsner, March 18, 1941, 59:3.

29. Speech to Morgan State students, January 12, 1940, 49:3.

30. Pero Gaglo Dagbovie, *Carter G. Woodson in Washington, D.C.: The Father of Black History* (Charleston, SC: History Press, 2014), 98; to Woodson, February 3, 1940, 50:2; Woodson to February 5, 1940, 50:3.

31. *Atlanta Daily World*, October 13, 1935, *ProQuest* Historic Newspapers [hereafter PQHN]; to the Board of Regents, University of Michigan, August 11, 1938, 39:8.

32. "West, Irene," Martin Luther King Jr. Research and Education Institute (website), Stanford University; to West, April 10, 1942, 65:6; to same, September 23, 1942, 67:3; Luther Adams, "Chandler Owen (1889–1967)," Black Past (website), January 18, 2007; to Owen, November 27, 1941, 63:6; US Office of War Information, *Negroes and the War* (Washington, DC: Government Printing Office), Smithsonian Digital Volunteers: Transcription Center (website), Smithsonian Institute.

33. Owen to, July 20, 1937, 32:2; to Owen, August 23, 1937, 32:8; Owen to, August 30, 1937, 32:8, to Owen, August 31, 1937, 32:8; to Grace Allen Varney, April 6, 1942, 65:6.

34. Du Bois, "As the Crow Flies," *New York Amsterdam News*, November 11, 1939, PQHN; Wilkins, "Watchtower"; Maverick to, October 21, 1938, 40:5; Ruth and Aurelia Lindy to, February 20, 1938, 36:9.

35. *St. Paul Recorder*, October 7, 1938, 40:2; *Dayton Forum*, February 21, 1941, 58:6.

36. "From Plantation to Politics."

37. *Chicago Defender*, February 5, 1934, PQHN.

38. Adams to, May 8, 1942, 66:1; *Congressional Record*, Appendix for August 14, 1939,

76th Congress, 1st Session, vol. 84, no. 161, pp. 15,754–55; "If I Were Young Again," 72:6; Waldo Martin, "In Search of Booker T. Washington," in *Booker T. Washington and Black Progress: Up from Slavery 100 Years Later*, ed. W. Fitzhugh Brundage, (Gainesville: University of Florida Press, 2003), 38–55, 42; O'Brien, "Watching Washington; Malcolm B. Smith, *Pittsburgh Courier*, October 15, 1936, PQHN.

39. Prattis, *Pittsburgh Courier*, February 14, 1942, PQHN.

40. *Afro-American*, February 9, 1935, PQHN; *East Tennessee News*, February 14, 1935, 16:9. William N. Jones, "Day by Day," *Afro-American*, February 27, 1937, PQHN. Jones did add that his response to the phone slamming was to jump in a cab and be in a "chummy conversation" with Mitchell within minutes. "He's tight," Jones decided, "but not so tight."

41. To Clarence Muse, December 9, 1938, 41:1; to E. W. Taggard, November 23, 1934, 3:1.

42. Branham, "Transformation of Black Political Leadership in Chicago," 365, 368; "AFRO Interviews Eulalia Proctor," *Afro-American*, October 12, 1935, 13:12; to C. C. Wimbish, February 1, 1938, 36:6.

43. Christopher Manning, *William L. Dawson and the Limits of Black Electoral Leadership* (DeKalb: Northern Illinois University Press, 2009), 90; to Louis B. Anderson, January 10, 1938, 36:1.

44. *St. Louis Argus*, January 17, 1936, 15:7.

45. *Pittsburgh Courier*, October 15, 1936, PQHN; to LeFlore, February 15, 1936, 16:9.

46. BP, October 2, 1935, 349:5; to Claude Holman, October 1, 1935, 13:1; to Robert Vann, April 5, 1936, 19:1; to Charles L. Cuney, November 1, 1838, 40:7; *Afro-American*, February 2, 1935, PQHNN; to Mrs. Harriet Shedd Butcher, April 23, 1936, 18:7.

47. *Chicago Tribune*, January 11, 1938, PQHN.

48. Ralph Ellison, *Invisible Man* (New York: Modern Library, 1952), 255.

49. To William J. Nunn, July 3, 1943, to Arthur M. Weber, March 15, 1938, 37:6; to Antoinette Bowler, October 26, 1939; 47:9; [Oklahoma City] *Black Dispatch*, April 25, 1942, 65:9.

50. To P. B. Young, January 4, 1940, 49:1; to Dr. Robert W. Pallon, November 1, 1939, 48:1.

51. Undated item, 72:2. Boxes 72 and 73 of the Mitchell papers, largely noted for transcripts of his speeches, contain the items that cannot be dated. The only usable locator is the file number within the box where the item is located. In this case, it is Box 72, file 2.

52. Speech in Atlanta, February 14, 1939; *Daily Oklahoman*, October 9, 1939, 33:3.

53. Founder's Day speech at Tuskegee, April 2, 1939, 43:9; *Afro-American*, May 6, 1939, 44:9; January 10, 1940, 49:2.

54. The Insider, "The Nation's Capitol," *Amsterdam Star News*, February 7, 1942, PQHN; W. J. Edwards to, January 21, 1943, 63:8; Smith to, April 29, 1941, 60:3; P. L. Prattis, *Pittsburgh Courier*, February 14, 1942, PQHN.

55. Schlesinger Jr., *Life in the Twentieth Century*, 365–66, 449, 454.

56. Jill Lepore, *These Truths: A History of the United States* (New York: W. W. Norton, 2018), xix.

Chapter 1

1. Speech to Morgan State University students, January 12, 1940, 49:3; Nordin, *New Deal's Black Congressman*, 1–3; Perry R. Duis, "Arthur W. Mitchell: New Deal Negro in Congress" (Master's thesis, University of Chicago, 1966), 19–20; to Paul Crowder, July 21, 1938, 39:7; *Atlanta Daily World*, May 27, 1941, PQHN; to John J. Hagedorn, July 14, 1937, 31:9.

2. Morgan State speech; Nordin 4, Duis "Arthur W. Mitchell," 20; "The Principal's Story," *New York Age* reprint of a *Christian Science Monitor* article, April 2, 1912, 1:1. For a comparison of Mitchell's story to Washington's, see Booker T. Washington, *Up From Slavery* (Garden City, NY: Doubleday, 1963, ca. 1901), 33–38.

3. Blair L. M. Kelley, *Right to Ride: Street Boycotts and African American Citizenship in the Era of Plessy v. Ferguson* (Chapel Hill: University of North Carolina Press, 2010), 4; William Thornton, "More than 300 African-Americans Lynched in Alabama in 66 Years," *AL.com*, April 26, 2018; Equal Justice Initiative, *Lynching in America: Confronting the Legacy of Racial Terror*, 3rd ed., 2017, PDF; Rayford W. Logan, *The Betrayal of the Negro from Rutherford B. Hayes to Woodrow Wilson* (New York: DaCapo Press, 1997), 350.

4. On the restrictions adopted by the constitutional convention, see Michael Perman, *Struggle for Mastery: Disenfranchisement in the South*, 1898–1908 (Chapel Hill: University of North Carolina Press, 2001), 179; Douglas A. Blackmon, *Slavery by Another Name: The Re-enslavement of Black People in America from the Civil War to World War II* (New York: Anchor Books, 2009), 165; Albert B. Moore, *History of Alabama* (Tuscaloosa: Alabama Book Store, 1934), 653–54; and William H. Skaggs, *The Southern Oligarchy: An Appeal in Behalf of the Silent Masses of Our Country against the Despotic Rule of the Few* (New York: Devin-Adair, 1924), 136.

5. William Cohen, "Negro Involuntary Servitude in the South, 1865–1940: A Preliminary Analysis," *Journal of Southern History* 42 (February 1976): 48. On the convict leasing system, see Blackmon, *Slavery by Another Name*, 53–54, 66–69, 90, 171, 218, and 331.

6. Skaggs, *Southern Oligarchy*, 270; Ray Stannard Baker, *Following the Color Line: American Negro Citizenship in the Progressive Era* (New York: Harper and Row, 1964), 74, 76, 96, and 130.

7. *The Principal's Story*, 1:1; *If I were Young Again*, 72:6; "From Plantation to Politics," 1; *Congressional Record*, April 15, 1937, vol. 81, part 3, 3533.

8. Emmett J. Scott to, April 20, 1939, 44:4; to Frank P. Chisolm, May 14, 1937, 30:9; to C. H. Hamlin, February 3, 1938, 36:3; "Undated Items," 72:1; Morgan State speech; "From Plantation to Politics"; Carver to, May 27, 1939, 45:4 and to Carver, June 13, 1939, 45:9; to S. R. Redmond, July 30, 1941, 62:2.

9. Maureen S. Stocker, "Educational Theory of Booker T. Washington," New Foundations (website), last edited November 19, 2018.

10. Morgan State speech.

11. August Meier and Elliott M. Rudwick, *From Plantation to Ghetto: An Interpretive History of American Negroes* (New York: Hill and Wang, 1966), 179–81; Moore, *History of Alabama*, 657; Donald P. Stone, *Fallen Prince: William James Edwards, Black Education, and the Quest for Afro-American Nationality* (Snow Hill, AL: Snow Hill Press, 1990), 162;

Mike Wallace, *Greater Gotham: A History of New York City from 1898 to 1918* (New York: Oxford University Press, 2017), 837.

12. Nordin, *New Deal's Black Congressman*, 7; Robert G. Sherer, *Subordination or Liberation? The Development and Conflicting Theories of Black Education in Nineteenth Century Alabama* (Tuscaloosa: University of Alabama Press, 1977), 73–78; Glenn N. Sisk, "Negro Education in the Alabama Black Belt, 1875–1900," *Journal of Negro History* 22 (spring 1953), 135. The "Black Belt" references a crescent of counties from Virginia to Texas where the quality of the soil promoted the cultivation of cotton and where more than 50 percent of the inhabitants were Black.

13. Stone, *Fallen Prince*, 89, 94, 133, and 199.

14. Stone, *Fallen Prince*, 161–62, 192, 139, 134, and 144.

15. William J. Edwards, *Twenty-Five Years in the Black Belt* (Boston: Cornhill Company, 1918), xi–xii; to Edwards, May 21, 1912, BP, 239; Tuskegee Institute, *The Influence of Its Graduates in Founding of Off-Shoots of Tuskegee* (n.p., n.d.), 33–34.

16. Morgan State speech; To Edwards, June 20, 1903, BP, Box 239.

17. "State Board of Examiners license to teach," *Weekly Advertiser*, Alabama Department of Archives and History (Montgomery) [hereafter ADAH], May 19, 1904; *Greensboro Watchman*, ADAH, same date; Sisk, *Negro Education*, 133; Annie Gray Lomax to, December 4, 1934, 3:3.

18. *Greensboro Watchman*, November 30, 1939, M.P., microfilm; *Greensboro Record*, January 12, 1905, ADAH.

19. Allan J. Going, *Bourbon Democracy in Alabama*, 1874–1890 (Tuscaloosa: University of Alabama Press, 1951), 157; Baker, *Following the Color Line*, 84–85.

20. Moore, *History of Alabama*, 728, 737–39.

21. Blackmon, *Slavery by Another Name*, 105; William Warren Rogers et al., *Alabama: The History of a Deep South State* (Tuscaloosa: University of Alabama Press, 1994), 325; Baker, *Following the Color Line*, 247–48.

22. Baker, *Following the Color Line*, 247; Wilkerson, *Warmth of Other Suns*, 239, citing the *Jackson* (MS) *Weekly Clarion-Ledger*, July 30, 1903; William F. Holmes, "Vardaman, James Kimble," in John A. Garraty and Mark C. Carnes, gen. eds., *American National Biography* [hereafter ANB], 24 vols. (New York: Oxford University Press, 1999), 22:265–67.

23. Sherer, *Subordination or Liberation?*, 65–66; Stone, *Fallen Prince*, 131; Wilkerson, *Warmth of Other Suns*, 24; Blackmon, *Slavery by Another Name*, 356.

24. For lists of literature available, see Sisk, "Negro Education," 135; Mann, *Study in Cotton and Steel*, 256–59; Meier and Rudwick, *From Plantation to Ghetto*, 162–64; Rogers et al., *Alabama*, 325, 327; Henry Lewis Gates Jr., *Stony the Road: Reconstruction, White Supremacy, and the Rise of Jim Crow* (New York: Penguin Press, 2019), 91. For illustrations depicting African Americans as "either not human or fully human," see "Chains of Being: The Black Body and the White Mind," 109–23.

25. Blackmon, *Slavery by Another Name*, 304; Felix James, "The Tuskegee Institute Movable School, 1906–1923," *Agricultural History* 45 (July 1971): 205.

26. Claudio Saunt, *Unworthy Republic: The Dispossession of Native Americans and the Road to Indian Territory* (New York: W. W. Norton, 2020), 245–46, 311–12; WPA Guide, 296. Stewart E. Tolnay and E. M. Beck, *A Festival of Violence: An Analysis of Southern*

Lynchings, 1882–1930 (Urbana: University of Illinois Press, 1995), 45–46, 159; Equal Justice Initiative, *Lynching in America: Confronting the Legacy of Racial Terror*, County Data Supplement, updated February 2020, PDF; "White Mob lynched Negro on Suspicion. Afterward converted to cause of Negro education," unidentified newspaper article, 1:1.

27. It is unclear where Mitchell obtained his statistics, but a contract in his papers shows that he was an "enumerator" for the "colored people of Sumter County" in the 1910 federal census, 1:1; *Our Southern Home* [Livingston, AL], April 13, 1910, ADAH; undated note, 1:1.

28. *Sumter County Sun*, September 5, 1912, ADAH.

29. Arthur W. Mitchell, "The Struggle for Negro Self-Improvement," n.d., n.p., 1:1; John Rogers to, February 9, 1910, 1:1; "Resolution of the Salem African Methodist Zion Church, Fair Oaks, Alabama," *Sumter County Sun*, November 19, 1908, ADAH.

30. Rogers to, March 6, 1910, 1:1, Nordin, *New Deal's Black Congressman*, 9, citing Sumter County Court Records, Book 26, 153–54.

31. *Gainesville* [AL] *Times*, February 17, 1910, ADAH; Mitchell, *Struggle*, 1:1; [Arthur W. Mitchell], "Negro Americans, What Now?," n.d., n.p., 72:7.

32. *Struggle*, 1:1; unidentified clippings and notes, 1:1.

33. *Gainesville Times*, September 2, 1909, University of West Alabama, Julia Tutwiler Library [hereafter UWAL], Jud Arrington Collection, SF 2, D 2, folder 1, item 1; Allen W. Jones, "The Role of Tuskegee Institute in the Education of Black Farmers," *Journal of Negro History* 60 (1975), 259–60, 262–63; *Geiger Times*, February 16, August 5, and November 5, 1910, 1:1.

34. "Struggle," 1:1; Dennis S. Nordin interview with Fanoy Little, Panola, AL, April 13, 1971, Arthur W. Mitchell Sound Recordings, CHM. Little was eighty-nine at the time of the Nordin interview.

35. Bedford to, March 6, 1910, 1:1; Booker T. Washington, *Annual Report*, May 1, 1910, 1:1.

36. For details on pellagra, a disease common in rural America at the time, see Stephen J. Kunitz, "Hookworm and Pellagra: Exemplary Diseases in the New South," *Journal of Health and Social Behavior* 29, no. 2 (June 1988): 139–48, 145; to Edwards, August 17 and 29, 1910, BP, box 239. Nordin reports speculation among neighbors that Mitchell had locked his wife inside their house and "almost starved Eula Mae to death before having her committed to an insane asylum"; Nordin, *New Deal's Black Congressman*, 9–10.

37. *Springfield Republican*, n.d., 1:1; "Struggle," 1:1.

38. To Edwards, January 5, 1911, BP, box 239.

39. *Geiger Times*, November 1 and 9, 1911, 1:1; Nordin, Little interview. Nordin writes that "there are grounds for suspicion" that Mitchell set the fire himself, citing as evidence his "incineration of a barn on his Virginia estate some forty years later to collect on an insurance policy"; Nordin, *New Deal's Black Congressman*, 16.

40. *Geiger Times*, November 1 and 9, 1911, and July 25, 1912, 1:1; *Principal's Story*, 1:1.

41. *Waterbury Republican*, November 14, 1911, 1:1; Wallace, *Greater Gotham*, 837; ad promoting New York meeting, 1:1.

42. Edwin G. Burrows and Mike Wallace, *Gotham: A History of New York City to 1898* (New York: Oxford University Press, 1983), 811, 859; for a detailed account of the

incident, see Louis R. Harlan, *Booker T. Washington: The Wizard of Tuskegee, 1901–1915* (Oxford: Oxford University Press, 1983), 379–404.

43. To Washington, New York, December 15, 1911, in Louis R. Harlan and Raymond W. Smock, eds., *The Booker T. Washington Papers*, 14 vols. (Urbana: University of Illinois Press, 1981), 11: 417–18.

44. Louis R. Harlan, "The Secret Life of Booker T. Washington," in Raymond W. Smock, ed., *Booker T. Washington in Perspective: Essays of Louis R. Harlan* (Jackson: University Press of Mississippi, 1988), 118; Nordin, *New Deal's Black Congressman*, 17.

45. To Edwards, May 21 and 23, 1912, BP, box 239.

46. Nordin, *New Deal's Black Congressman*, 17–20, citing a Clara Mitchell interview and exchanges between Washington and W. C. Lloyd of the Postal-Telegraph Company, July 22, 24, and 27, August 3, 6, 25 and 27, and September 16, 1914, and an undated letter, Washington Papers, Library of Congress.

47. Nelle M. Jenkins, *The Heritage of Sumter County, Alabama* (Clanton, AL: Heritage Publishing Consultants, 2005), 242; "Geiger in the Heart of the Famous Black Belt of Alabama," UWAL, SF D3, folder 9; Jack Wheat, "What if They Built a Town and Nobody Came?," *Tuscaloosa* [AL] *Times*, July 29, 1984, UWAL.

48. Nordin interview with Gilbert, CHM; "Sumter County, Geiger," file SG 00626, UWAL; Wheat, "What If," UWAL.

49. Montgomery designed Mount Bayou to be a self-segregating community whose Black residents had only minimal contact with white people until full integration became a viable option. With the cooperation of "the best white people," he proposed to take "advantage of the disadvantages of segregation" by promoting independent Black economic development. Endorsed by Washington, the town prospered for two decades through the export of cotton, timber, and corn, growing to a population of eight thousand in 1911. The boll weevil and the Great Migration ended its success and its population declined. Mitchell was scheduled to be the town's graduation speaker at its fiftieth anniversary but declined at the last moment. See *Geiger Times*, July 25, 1912, ADAH; https://blackpast.org/aah/mount_bayou_1887; August Meier, "Booker T. Washington and the Town of Mount Bayou," *Phylon*, vol. XV, no 4 (1954), 396–97; 32:1.

50. *Geiger Times*, May 30 and June 12, 1912, 1:1; Lavender to, August 8, 1912, 1:1.

51. *Geiger Times*, July 11, 1912, 1:1.

52. *Geiger Times*, July 25, 1912, ADAH; *Montclair* (NJ) *Times* (?), August 10, 1912, 1:1.

53. *Boston Transcript*, December 11, 1912, 1:1 reprinted in the *Sumter County Sun*, December 19, 1912, ADAH.

54. Blackmon, *Slavery by Another Name*, 125; Stone, *Fallen Prince*, 157; Nordin interview with Gilbert; Dennis S. Nordin interview with John Pinson Jr., Geiger, AL, April 12, 1971, Arthur W. Mitchell Sound Recordings, CHM.

55. Gilbert and Pinson interviews.

56. Undated notes, 1:1.

57. Murphy to, January 13, 1939, 41:10; to Murphy, January 16, 1939, 42:1. Mitchell had offered a more dramatic version of the incident on the floor of the House in 1937: "I shall never forget how I stood with a Winchester rifle in my hand, how my wife stood with a pistol in her hand, waiting all night long for this mob to show up and snuff out our lives" (*Congressional Record*, 75th Congress, 1st Session, vol. 71, part 3, 3541).

58. To Edwards, June 7, 1912, February 3, 1913, October 8, 1913, and November 13, 1914, BP, box 239; *Geiger Times*, ADAH.

59. Duis, "Arthur W. Mitchell," 22; Nordin interview with Little and Pinson Jr., CHM.

60. *Choctaw Advocate*, February 24 and June 15, 1915, ADAH; Ann Harwell Gay, *Choctaw Names and Notes* (Meridian, MS: Brown Printing Company, 1993), 52–53.

61. Nordin, *New Deal's Black Congressman*, 24; Turner to, August 29, 1934, 2:3.

62. *Choctaw Advocate*, 4, January 5, 1916, and March 15, 1916, 1:2; "Resolution of Thanks for Opening of School Building of Armstrong to W. Butler Black Community," 1:2.

63. *Choctaw Advocate*, October 25, 1916, ADAH; Gay, *Choctaw Names*, 53; United States Congress, Committee on Interstate and Foreign Commerce, 66th Session, "Return of the Railroads to Private Ownership Hearings," 2029; Bay, *Traveling Black*, 108, 110, 117–18; Nordin, *New Deal's Black Congressman*, 26–27.

64. To Edwards, September 21, 1916, and February 20, 1917, BP, box 239; to the *Birmingham Ledger*, September 7, 1916, BP 346:5; to the *Meridian Dispatch*, reprinted in the *Choctaw Advocate*, September 27, 1916, 1:2.

65. *Choctaw Advocate*, May 30, 1917, 1:2.

66. At one point during his congressional career, the *Washington Merry-Go-Round* would rate McDuffie as one of the three most powerful figures in Congress; Robert S. Allen, *Washington Merry-Go-Round* (New York: Liveright, 1931), 244.

67. John McDuffie, *To Inquiring Friends, if Any: Autobiography of John McDuffie. Farmer, Lawyer, Legislator, Judge as Told to and Edited by Mary Margaret Flock* (Mobile, AL: Azalea City Printers, 1970), 91–92, 99–105, 112–13, 129.

68. *Birmingham News*, November 12, 1934, 2:9; to McDuffie, January 4, 1936, 15:3; to Loring B. Moore, November 4, 1948, 70:1.

69. Nordin, *New Deal's Black Congressman* 27; Jill Watts, *Black Cabinet*, 105; Wilkerson, *Warmth of Other Suns*, 219; Bay, *Traveling Black*, 125.

70. Nordin, *New Deal's Black Congressman*, 27, citing "Choctaw County Court Records, The Armstrong Agricultural and Industrial Institute vs. Arthur W. Mitchell, 1920–21."

71. R. R. Hunter to, February 26, 1941, 58:7; Gay, *Choctaw Names*, 53.

72. Lepore, *These Truths*, 4, 12.

73. Nordin, *New Deal's Black Congressman*, 24, 27.

74. Rogers et al., *Alabama*, 327; Stone, *Fallen Prince*, 171.

75. See Thomas Aiello, *The Grapevine of the South: The Scott Newspaper Syndicate in the Generation before the Civil Rights Movement* (Athens: University of Georgia Press, 2018); Lee to, August 17, 1936, 21:1.

76. To Lee, August 25, 1936, 21:2; Lee to, 30 August, August 30, 1936, 21:3.

77. To Lee, September 22, 1936, 22:5; to Lee, October 15, 1936, 23:1; Lee to, November 10, 1936, 24:3.

78. To Lomax, December 6, 1934, 3:4; to John Scott, February 22, 1936, 16:1; John Dolland, *Caste and Class in a Southern Town* (New Haven: Yale University Press, 1937), 65.

79. "The Hard Things," undated notes, 1:1.

80. Baker, *Following the Color Line*, 133.

81. *New York Age*, December 14, 1916, 1:2.

82. To Guy Harris, November 26, 1934, 3:1; Assertions of Mitchell's fondness for Alabama run throughout the Mitchell papers. For another example, see to Hobson Owen

Murfee, January 19, 1940, 49:5. To an unnamed newspaper, 1:1; Martin, "In Search of Booker T. Washington," 46.

83. Richard Wright, *Native Son* (New York: Harper Perennial Modern Classics, 2005, ca. 1940), 234; Charles Blow, *The Devil You Know: A Black Power Manifesto* (New York: Harper Perennial, 2021), 168.

Chapter 2

1. David Welkey, *Marching Across the Color Line: A. Philip Randolph and Civil Rights in the World War II Era* (New York: Oxford University Press, 2014), 56: Adam Hochschild, *American Midnight: The Great War, a Violent Peace, and Democracy's Forgotten Crisis* (New York and Boston: Mariner Books, 2022), 29–30.

2. E. Franklin Frazier, *Black Bourgeoisie: The Rise of a New Middle Class in the United States* (London: Collier-MacMillan, 1957), 164; Christopher Bracey, *Saviors or Sellouts: The Promise and Perils of Black Conservatism from Booker T. Washington to Condoleezza Rice* (Boston: Beacon Press, 2008), 31. For examples of the rules on "passing," see Audrey Elisa Kerr, *The Paper Bag Principle: Class Colorism and Race and the Case of Black Washington D.C.* (Knoxville: University of Tennessee Press, 2006).

3. Haynes Johnson, *Dusk at the Mountain: The Negro, the Nation, and the Capital: A Reporter's Problems and Progress* (New York: Doubleday, 1963), 29; David F. Krugler, *1919: the Year of Racial Violence; How African Americans Fought Back* (New York: Cambridge University Press, 2015), 96–97.

4. Bay, *Traveling Black*, 104–5; Kelley, *Right to Ride*, 7.

5. Return of the Railroads, 2026–29; Bay, *Traveling Black*, 105. Mitchell's testimony did not sway hearts or minds. In the general debate about the railroad bill, the Madden amendment failed by a vote of 142–12.

6. Real estate document, 1:3; to Mrs. L. W. Sanchez, May 25, 1937, 32:1; Hennessey interview, 4:1.

7. Nordin, *New Deal's Black Congressman*, 33.

8. *Atlanta Daily World*, November 18, 1934, PQHN; "Thirty-Five Years of Sigma," *The Crescent* [June 1949], 212; to Fred R. Banks, February 9, 1939, 42:7; to Thomas Reid, March 5, 1936, 17:4.

9. Watts, *Black Cabinet*, 96–97; Bracey, *Saviors or Sellouts*, 22–23; to Colonel [Marvin H.] McIntyre, June 27, 1935, FDRL, Official File [hereafter OF], 93; to Dr. F. D. Patterson, April 2, 1941, 59:8.

10. Meier and Rudwick, *From Plantation to Ghetto*, 296; Green, *Secret City*, 210; Daniel Donaghy, "Alain Locke" in *Encyclopedia of African American History, 1896 to the Present, from the Age of Segregation to the Twenty-First Century* [hereafter *EAAH*], 5 vols. (Oxford and New York: Oxford University Press, 2009), 3:199–201; to Locke, October 6, 1934, 2:4; Locke to, "Thursday" [November 8, 1934], 3:2.

11. Locke to, n.d., 48:9, same to November 4, 1936 [telegram] 23:9; same to October 27, 1938, 40:6; same to September 15, 1938, 39:11.

12. Carter G. Woodson, *The Mis-Education of the Negro* (Santa Barbara, CA: Book Tree, 2006), 157; to Woodson, May 5, 1939; Woodson, *Mis-Education of the Negro*, 160.

13. Woodson, *Mis-Education of the Negro*, 161; press release, *The Association for the Study of Negro Life and History*, July 22, 1934, 2:1.

14. To Woodson, April 24, 1935, 9:3; Woodson to, February 18, 1939, 42:11.

15. Slyvie Coulibaly, "Kelly Miller" in *EAAH* 3:325; Kelly Miller, "Address at Log Cabin Community Center, Sparta, Georgia, September 5, 1934," BP, box 14; *Afro-American*, January 20, 1940, PQHN; "The Passing of Dr. Kelly Mitchell," *Congressional Record*, January 18, 1940, 49:4.

16. Interview with Frank Marshall Davis, *Gary* [IN] *American*, November 16, 1934, 2:10; to Levitt, April 28, 1936; to A. C. Handle, May 11, 1938, 38:9.

17. Nordin, *New Deal's Black Congressman*, 10; Mitchell expense account, 1:4.

18. "Sixteenth and Twenty-Second Annual Preliminary Report of the Municipal Voter's League," *Municipal Voter's League*, n.p., n.d.; Chicago [Regenstein Library]; Lloyd Wendt and Herman Kogan, *Lords of the Levée* (Indianapolis: Bobbs-Merrill, 1943), 25, 351–52.

19. Adam Cohen and Elizabeth Taylor, *American Pharaoh: Mayor Richard J. Daley; His Battle for Chicago and the Nation* (Boston: Little, Brown, 2000), 29–30, 33, and 35.

20. St. Claire Drake and Horace R. Clayton, *Black Metropolis: A Study of Negro Life in a Northern City* (Chicago: University of Chicago Press, 1945), 348; Lisa G. Matterson, "Electoral Politics," in Stephen A. Reich, ed., *The Great Black Migration: A Historical Encyclopedia of the American Mosaic* (Santa Barbara, CA: Greenwood, 2014), 111. A small, statistically insignificant sliver of the Fourth Ward, completed the First Congressional District.

21. Christopher Robert Reed, *The Rise of Chicago's Black Metropolis* (Urbana: University of Illinois Press, 2011), 150; John M. Allswang, "The Negro Voter and the Democratic Consensus: A Case Study, 1918–1936," *Journal of the Illinois State Historical Society* 60, no. 2 (Summer 1967): 149.

22. Wikipedia contributors, "Pineapple Primary," Wikipedia, The Free Encyclopedia (website), accessed September 19, 2023; *Chicago Tribune*, April 8, 1928, PQHN.

23. Martin Kilson, "Political Change in the Negro Ghetto, 1900–1940," in *Key Issues in the Afro-American Experience*, ed. Nathan I. Huggins, Martin Kilson, and Daniel M. Fox (New York: Harcourt, Brace, Jovanovich, 1971), 183.

24. De Priest left no personal papers. For details on his career in Chicago politics, see Harold F. Gosnell, *Negro Politicians: The Rise of Negro Politics in Chicago* (Chicago: University of Chicago Press, 1967), 163–95, and Branham, "Transformation of Black Political Leadership in Chicago," 95–168, 240–57; *Twenty-Second Annual Report of the Municipal Voter's League* (n.p., n.d.), 5; George P. Robinson, "The Negro in Politics in Chicago," *Journal of Negro History* (April 1932): 225.

25. Manning, *William L. Dawson and the Limits of Black Electoral Leadership*, 83.

26. Karl A. Bosworth, *Black Belt County: Rural Government in the Cotton Country of Alabama* (Tuscaloosa: Bureau of Public Administration. University of Alabama, 1941), 10; Rogers et al., *Alabama*, 288.

27. Women's Civic Council of the Chicago Area, *A Partial Record of the Conduct of Elections in Chicago from December 1922 to [March 1938]* (Chicago[?]: n.p., 1938), I, 18, 35; II, 6–8, 21–22, 31. See also Cohen and Taylor, *American Pharoah*, 40–45, 129–30.

28. Reed, *Rise of Chicago's Black Metropolis*, 240n7.

29. *Pittsburgh Courier*, July 30, 1949, PQHN; Nancy J. Weiss, *Farewell to the Party*

of Lincoln: Black Politics in the Age of FDR (Princeton: Princeton University Press, 1983), 78; Duis, "Mitchell," 23.

30. *Afro-American*, June 6, 1936, PQHN; Mitchell to Hoover, March 30, 1929, cited in George F. Garcia, "Black dissatisfaction from the Republican Party . . . 1928–1932," *Annals of Iowa* 45 (Winter 1980), 465. For a discussion of lily-whiteism, see Donald J. Lisio, *Hoover, Blacks, and Lily-Whites: A Study of Southern Strategies* (Chapel Hill: University of North Carolina Press, 1985).

31. "From Plantation to Politics," 1; *Pittsburgh Courier*, November 14, 1942, PQHN.

Chapter 3

1. *Afro-American*, June 21, 1941, PQHN.

2. Rita Gordon, "The Change in the Political Alignment of Chicago's Negroes During the New Deal," *Journal of American History* 56, no. 3 (December 1969): 591–94; Weiss, *Farewell to the Party of Lincoln*, 84; Branham, "Transformation of Black Political Leadership in Chicago," 343–44.

3. See Alex Gottfried, *Boss Cermak: A Study in Political Leadership* (Seattle: University of Washington Press, 1962), 199–237.

4. To Rev. Powell, February 6, 1932, 1:7.

5. For items studied, see 1:7; *Pittsburgh Courier*, December 29, 1932, PQHN, Melvin Chisum to Barnett, December 29, 1932, BP, 346: file for 1930–35.

6. To Wayne Simpson, September 28, 1932, 1:7; W. H. Loving to, November 27, 1934, 3:2; Walter L. McDonald to, November 26, 1934, 3:2.

7. Cohen and Taylor, *Pharaoh*, 53; on the effectiveness of the Kelly-Nash machine, see Elmer Lynn Williams, *The Fix-It Boys: The Inside Story of the New Deal and the Kelly-Nash Machine* (Chicago: E. L. Williams, 1940); and Roger Biles, *Big City Boss in Depression and War* (DeKalb: Northern Illinois University Press, 1984).

8. McDuffie to, January 14, 1933, 1:8.

9. To Loesch, January 30, 1933, 1:8; Loesch to, January 31, 1933, 1:8.

10. To Miller, February 3, 1933, 1:8; to McDuffie, March 11, 1933, 1:9.

11. Branham, "Transformation of Black Political Leadership in Chicago," 300; Douglas Bukowski, *Big Bill Thompson, Chicago, and the Politics of Image* (Urbana: University of Illinois Press, 1998), 230.

12. To McDuffie, May 3, 1933, 1:9; Daniel Scroop, *Mr. Democrat: Jim Farley, the New Deal, and the Making of Modern American Politics* (Ann Arbor: University of Michigan Press, 2006), 106; McDuffie to Farley, copied to Mitchell, June 29, 1933, 1:9; same to same, September 13, 1933, 1:9.

13. To Kelly, April 15, 1933, 1:9.

14. To Tittinger, January 14, 1934, 1:11.

15. Duis, "Mitchell," 26; Mark H. Haller, "Policy Gambling, Entertainment, and the Emergence of Black Politics: Chicago from 1900 to 1940," *Journal of Social History* 24, no. 4 (Summer 1991): 728; Nordin, *New Deal's Black Congressman*, 50–51, citing 1970 and 1971 interviews with Tittinger.

16. *Chicago Tribune*, October 28, 1928, February 5 and May 9, 1934, PQHN; Wendt and Kogan, *Lords of the Levee*, 357–58; Dempsey J. Travis, *An Autobiography of Black Politics* (Chicago: Urban Research Press, 1987), 84.

17. *Chicago Defender*, March 2, 1935, PQHN; Duis, "Mitchell," 26; *Chicago Tribune*, May 9, 1934, PQHN.

18. Undated document, 1:8.

19. Undated postcard, 1:8; McDuffie to Kelly, March 6, 1934, 1:12; *Pittsburgh Courier*, March 31, 1934, PQHN; to Kelly, March 22, 1934, 1:12.

20. For official primary election results, see Chicago Public Library, Harold Washington Library Center, Municipal Reference Library, aperture cards 279–90.

21. McDuffie to, May 19, 1934, 2:1; Nordin, *New Deal's Black Congressman*, 54–55, citing Tittinger interviews. Mauvolvane Carpenter to Geary, May 11, 1934, 2:1; Precinct captains to Kelly, n.d., 3:9; Precinct captains to Nash, 3:8.

22. *Chicago Defender*, August 11, 1934, PQHN.

23. For De Priest's early travails in Washington, see BP, 349:3; Robinson, "Negro in Politics," 224; Gosnell, *Negro Politicians*, 184.

24. *Chicago Defender*, March 3 and 17, April 7, 1934, PQHN.

25. Gosnell, *Negro Politicians*, 163; Weiss, *Farewell to the Party of Lincoln*, 84.

Chapter 4

1. *Pittsburgh Courier*, October 6, 1934, PQHN.

2. Watts, *Black Cabinet*, 110–11, 157; Brown to, September 11 and 27, 1934, 2:3.

3. Sean Savage, *Roosevelt: The Party Leader*, 1932–1945 (Lexington: University Press of Kentucky, 1991), 95; Walter White, *A Man Called White* (New York: Viking Press, 1948), 169–70.

4. Scroop, *Mr. Democrat*, 122–23; Farley to September 18 and October 4, 1934, 2:3; 2:4; Roper to, October 27, 1934, 2:5.

5. McDuffie to Farley, September 2, 1934, 2:3. Here McDuffie ignored the fact that Mitchell had been a Republican as late as 1928. To Hurja, October 13 and 31, 2:4 and 2:5.

6. 2: passim; McDuffie to, September 21, 2:3; McDuffie to Farley, September 21, 1934, 2:3.

7. To Farley, October 3, 1934, 2:4; Chandler Owen to, October 17, 1934, 2:5; to B. F. Lindheimer, October 30, 1934, 2:5.

8. Weiss, *Farewell to the Party of Lincoln*, 34–35, 40.

9. Weiss, *Farewell to the Party of Lincoln*, 34–61; Watts, *Black Cabinet*, 62. For a detailed examination of Black complaints about the early days of the New Deal, see Clark Foreman, oral history interview, November 16, 1974, interview B-0003, Southern Oral History Program Collection (#4007), Documenting the American South, University of North Carolina–Chapel Hill; *Chicago Defender*, September 22, 1934, PQHN.

10. "Why De Priest Should Lose," dated "October 1934," by Chicago History Museum archivist, 2:4.

11. *Public Service Leader*, September 19, 1934, Regenstein Library, University of Chicago, microfilm JK 47.

12. Gene Delon Jones, "The Origins of the Alliance between the New Deal and the Chicago Machine," *Journal of the Illinois State Historical Society* 73, no. 3 (June 1974): 261, citing Howard F. Flanagan to Roosevelt, FDRL, OF 300, box 26.

13. Richard A. Keiser, *Subordination or Empowerment? African-American Lead-*

ership and the Struggle for Urban Political Power (New York: Oxford University Press, 1997), 30; Travis, *Autobiography*,121–22; Biles, *Big City Boss in Depression and War*, 92–93; Arnold R. Hirsh, "Chicago," in Richard Bernard, ed., *Snowbelt Cities: Metropolitan Politics in the Northeast and Midwest Since World War II* (Bloomington: Indiana University Press, 1990), 67.

14. To Kelly, October 18, 1934, 2:5; Kelly to, October 22, 1934, 2:5. Kelly addressing Mitchell as "Congressman" two weeks before the election is noteworthy.

15. Hennessey interview; to Louis B. Anderson, October 8, 1934, 2:4. "Hinky Dink" was a nickname supposedly given to the diminutive Kenna by Joseph Medill, the publisher of the *Chicago Tribune*, in the 1870s.

16. *Pittsburgh Courier*, October 6 and 7, 1934, PQHN.

17. *Herald and Examiner*, September 6, 1934, 2:3; Ralph Nelson Davis, "The Negro Newspaper in Chicago" (MA thesis, Regenstein Library, the University of Chicago, 1939), 163; *Chicago World*, 11 August, 2:2, and November 10, 1934, 2:8.

18. To Marie Kemp, October 12, 1934, 2:4.

19. "Why De Priest Should Lose," 2:4.

20. To Crewes, August 14, 1934, 2:2; *Chicago Defender*, August 22 and September 8 and 13, 1934, PQHN.

21. To Foster, November 1, 1934, 2:6.

22. To Locke, October 6, 1934, 2:4; to De Priest, 3, 15, and October 26, 1934, 2:4.

23. De Priest to, October 14, 1934, 2:4; *Chicago World*, October 20, 1934, 2:5; *Chicago Daily News*, October 20, 1934, 2:5; to De Priest, November 3, 1934, 2:6.

24. W. D. Allmons to, November 10, 1934; *Atlanta Constitution*, November 10, 1934, PQHN.

25. *Pittsburgh Courier*, November 17, 1934, PQHN. The story is dramatic but has recently been questioned. Watts writes that "Harris was far from a countrified rube; his farm was one of the most productive in the region" (Watts, *Black Cabinet*), 137.

26. *Columbus* [MS] *Commercial Dispatch*, October 28, 1934. The assistance of Ms. Bettye Brown and the Columbus-Lowndes Public Library in securing this article is gratefully acknowledged.

27. BP, 14: file for November 14, 1934; *Birmingham News*, November 12, 1934, 2:9.

28. Brochure found in 2:6; *Birmingham News*, November 12, 1934, 2:9.

29. *Chicago Tribune*, November 4, 1934, PQHN. Harris was still alive in 1957 when he was featured in Eleanor Roosevelt's "My Day" newspaper column. She reported that he then had a modern farm and lived in a house with many amenities, including "two TV sets." "I like to think of the story of Sylvester Harris," she wrote, "as being emblematic of a 'forgotten man' who went on to become a success with a little help from his government"; "My Day," February 3, 1957, Eleanor Roosevelt Papers Project, Columbian College of Arts and Sciences, George Washington University.

30. *Chicago Tribune*, November 4, 1934, PQHN.

31. *Chicago Defender*, October 20 and 27, 1934, PQHN.

32. BP, 14: file for November 5–22, 1934; Barnett to Morris Lewis [De Priest's secretary], November 8, 1934, BP: 346:3.

33. BP, 14: file for November 5–22, 1934; Branham, "Transformation of Black Political Leadership in Chicago," 300.

34. *Pittsburgh Courier*, November 3, 1934, PQHN; *New York Times*, November 4, 1934, PQHN; BP. 14: file for November 5–22, 1934.

35. Virgil W. Peterson, *Barbarians in Our Midst: A History of Chicago Crime and Politics* (Boston: Little Brown, 177); William H. Stuart, *Twenty Incredible Years* (Chicago: M. A. Donohue, 1935), 552–55.

36. BP, 14: file for November 5–22, 1934. For additional testimony as to the drama intendant on the outcome, see Edgar G. Brown to, November 8, 1934, 2:7; Alain Locke to, "Thursday,"2:11; G. R. Saxon to, November 9, 1934, 2:8; and Carter G. Woodson to, November 20, 1934, 2:11.

37. De Priest to, November 7, 1934 [telegram], 2:6; to De Priest, November 10, 1934, 2:8; *Pittsburgh Courier*, November 17, 1934, PQHN.

38. *Public Service Leader*, November 20, 1934; Municipal Reference Collection, aperture cards 01013–32.

39. *Chicago Tribune*, November 7, 1934, PQHN; Madden to, November 14, 1934, 2:10.

40. *Pittsburgh Courier*, November 24, 1934, PQHN.

41. Gosnell, *Negro Politicians*, 91; Barnett to William T. Carter [treasurer at Tuskegee Institute], November 8, 1934, BP, 346:2; Branham, "Transformation of Black Political Leadership in Chicago," 292.

42. To Roosevelt, March 4, 1935, FDRL, PPF, 22891.

43. Edgar G. Brown to, November 14, 1934, 2:10; Farley to, November 15, 1934, 2:10.

44. McDuffie to November 7, 1934, 2:6; to McDuffie, November 10, 1934, 2:8.

45. Travis, *Autobiography*, 125–26; to Geary, to Connelly, to Tittinger, to Kenna, November 24, 1934, 3:1.

46. Davis, *Gary* [IN] *American*, November 17, 1934, 2:10. Abbott's newspaper added a postscript to its reprint: if Mitchell means this, "his usefulness in Congress ends before it begins" (*Chicago Defender*, November 17, 1934, PQHN).

47. *Chicago Defender*, November 10 and 17, 1934, PQHN; Barnett to, November 8, 1934, 2:7.

Chapter 5

1. To E. W. Taggard. November 23, 1934; Hennessey interview.

2. "Specific Things for Which I Will work," misfiled in 64.3, Undated items, 1941.

3. *Chicago Defender*, November 17, 1934, PQHN; Dr. Richard W. Oliver to, November 16, 1934, 2:10.

4. *Birmingham News*, November 12, 1934, 2:10.

5. *Montgomery Advertiser*, November 9, 1934, 2:10. Hall also told Mitchell that "the state of Illinois is leading the country in how to be tolerant and magnanimous. It has a Jew for governor [Henry Horner], an Irishman for mayor [Kelly], and a Negro as representative of the first district," a remark that Mitchell passed on to Illinois's governor [to Horner, November 22, 1934, 2:11].

6. *Florence Tribune*, November 15, 1934, 2:10; *Nashville Banner*, November 16, 1934, 2:10; quoted in *The Crisis: Record of the Darker Races*, February 1935, 4.

7. "Plantation to Politics."

8. Carter to Barnett, December 6, 1934, BP, 346:2.

9. Wilson to Barnett, November 14, 1934, BP, 346:2.

10. Unknown to Wilson, November 16, 1934, BP, 346:2; BP, 14:5, file for November 14, 1934.

11. Barnett to Carter, November 27, 1934, BP, 346:2.

12. Wilson to Barnett, December 24, 1934, BP, 346:2.

13. To Harris, November 23, 1934, 3:1.

14. A reference to a civil rights case that received much attention during the 1930s. Nine Black teenagers were falsely accused of raping two white women on a train in Alabama. Originally sentenced to death, they escaped this fate at least in part the efforts of the International Labor Defense of the American Communist Party. The NAACP was not as vigorous in defending the accused.

15. Dewey R. Jones, *Chicago Defender*, December 1, 1934, PQHN.

16. Hennessey interview; questionnaire found in 12:6.

17. To J. W. Jones [telegram], November 27, 1934, 3:2: to Dr. William N. DeBerry, November 24, 1934; to A. J. Hammond, March 2, 1935, 6:5. *Afro-American*, May 18, 1835, 10:3; to Merritt, February 6, 1940, 50:4.

18. *Kansas City Star*, December 4, 1934, 3:3.

19. *Afro-American*, December 3, 15, and 22, 1934, PQHN.

20. Hennessey interview.

21. *Chicago Defender*, January 12, 1935, PQHN; Sabath to, January 9, 1935, 4:2.

22. To Britton, March 1, 1935, 6:5; to Tennon, March 1, 1935, 6:5.

23. "Jobs secured," March 3, 1937, 28:8; Caroline Davis to, March 17, 1940, 51:5. For additional lists of those employed see "Accomplishments by Congressman Mitchell—Patronage," 35:2 and "Post Office Letters-Xmas work," 41:5.

24. Barnett to P. B. Young, March 4, 1935, BP, 346:2; *Chicago Defender*, January 19 and April 13, 1935, PQHN; *Afro-American*, February 9 and April 20, 1935, PQHN.

25. *New York Herald Tribune*, January 28, 1935, PQHN; *New York Amsterdam News*, February 5, 1935, PQHN.

26. Westerfield to, January 29, 1935, 5:1; Jones to, February 2, 1935, 5:3; Keller to, April 6, 1935, 8:6.

27. *Chicago Defender*, February 23 and March 9, 1935, PQHN.

28. *Crisis*, February 1935, 6:4.

29. Bay, *Traveling Black*, 235; Weiss, *Farewell to the Party of Lincoln*, 97; Wolters, *Great Depression*, 276–77.

30. 72:1; 72:5.

31. To P. B. Young, May 21, 1938, 38:11. Many of Mitchell's contemporaries shared Mitchell's high regard for the *Journal and Guide*, considering it "one of the best edited, best written, well researched and organized papers of its day," see "Norfolk Journal and Guide," *PBS* (website), 2023. It should be noted that *ProQuest*'s Historic Black Newspapers [PQHN] does not include the *Journal and Guide* or any moderate southern voice. Its selection offers only geographic, not philosophical, variety.

32. BP, Box 15: file for February 18, 1935.

33. To C. Francis Stradford, February 7, 1935, 5:6; Woodson to, February 21, 1935, 6:1. Stradford was a cofounder of the Cook County Bar Association.

34. For the exact wording of the bill, see Hearing before the Committee on the Judiciary, House of Representatives, Seventy-Fourth Congress, First Session on H.R. 5733 to create an Industrial Commission on Negro Affairs [Washington: United States Printing Office, 1935] found in 11:5; Press Release, February 14, 1935, 5:8.

35. Weiss, *Farewell to the Party of Lincoln*, 108. See Wilkerson, *Warmth of Other Suns*, 59–62; Philip Dray, *At the Hands of Persons Unknown: the Lynchings of Black America* (New York: Random House, 2002), 344–51; *Chicago Defender*, January 5, 1935, PQHN, and BP, 14: file for 17–October 31, 1934, for summaries of the grisly event.

36. Robert L. Zangrando, *The NAACP Crusade against Lynching, 1909–1950* (Philadelphia: Temple University Press, 1980), 114–15.

37. *Afro-American*, October 19, 1935, PQHN; Ford to White, January 1, 1935, 73:6 (Nordin notes).

38. Beth Tomkins Bates, "A New Crowd Challenges the Agenda of the Old Crowd in the NAACP, 1933–34," *American Historical Review* 102 (April 1997): 357. See also Zangrando, *NAACP Crusade against Lynching*, 110, and Raymond Wolters, *Negroes and the Great Depression: The Problem of Economic Recovery* (Westport, CT: Greenwood Publishing, 1970), 337–40.

39. Zangrando, *NAACP Crusade against Lynching*, 113; Weiss, *Farewell to the Party of Lincoln*, citing Dyer to White, January 28, 1935, FDRL, Eleanor Roosevelt Papers, Box 1362.

40. To J. H. Petty, June 3, 1935, 11:1; *Washington Evening Star*, January 10, 1935, 4:2.

41. Lautier to White, February 2, 1935, 73:6 (Nordin notes).

42. Mitchell press release, 11:8.

Chapter 6

1. To P. B. Young, February 11 and 15, 1935, 5:7 and 5:9.

2. To Brown, March 11, 1935, 7:2; *Chicago Tribune*, April 29, 1935, PQHN.

3. "Mr. Mitchell in Congress," *Chicago Defender*, February 23, 1935, PQHN.

4. *Chicago Defender*, March 9, 1935, PQHN.

5. *Guardian*, March 9, 1935, 7:1. The city where the *Guardian* was published is unknown.

6. White to Louis Lautier, March 12, 1935, 73:6 (Nordin notes).

7. Elizabeth Ross Haynes to, February 3, 1935, 5:4; David Jenkins to, February 26, 1935, 6:4.

8. *Afro-American*, October 19, 1935, PQHN; Undated Items, 72:6.

9. To Robbins, March 2, 1935, 6:5.

10. To Edwards, June 12, 1939, 45:8; to George Leslie, January 18, 1937, 26:7.

11. To H. H. Dudley, March 28, 1935, 8:1; Undated Items, 72:6.

12. To Bayfield, September 2, 1935,13:7; to Betton, January 5, 1936, 26:3; to Bayfield, September 2, 1935, 13:7. As word of Mitchell's refusal to play De Priest's role as the national representative for his race spread, many denounced it as just another example of "Uncle Tom" Mitchell at work. However, William Jones, a columnist for the *Afro-American*, saw what others had missed, a centerpiece of the congressman's strategy to increase Black visibility in Congress. If he "refuses to accept the toga of race leadership," Jones wrote, "colored districts throughout the country will have to begin to look for Con-

gressmen who will. [Mitchell] might inaugurate a good-sized revolution in the Democratic Party"; William Jones, "Day By Day," *Afro-American*, January 26, 1935, PQHN.

13. Kelso to, June 28, 1935, 11:12; to Kelso, July 2, 1935, 12:1.

14. Kelso to, July 5, 1935, 12:2; to Kelso, July 9, 1935, 12:2. This was a point on which Mitchell differed dramatically from Washington. He was committed to "the critical importance of the ballot," a value that the founder of Tuskegee "had repudiated in the most public way possible" in his Atlanta compromise speech; Gates, *Stony the Road*, 248, 250.

15. Horne to, May 23, 1936, 19:6; to Horne, May 26, 1936, 19:6.

16. To Kelso, July 2, 1935, 12:1; to Nick Gentry, March 13, 1936, 17:6; to Sigmund Eck, April 17, 1935, 8:12.

17. Rodgers to, January 9, 1935, 4:2 (no attempt has been made to correct the spelling or grammar); Boothby to, May 17, 1935, 10:2.

18. For a full text of the speech, see *Afro-American*, April 20, 1935, PQHN; *New York Herald Tribune*, April 15, 1935, PQHN. This was a tenet Mitchell frequently returned to. In 1939, he told the House, "We do have poor counties and poor states, we do have rich people and poor people and if this Congress owes the old people of this Nation a duty to pension them, we ought to do it without regard to state lines"; *Congressional Record*, 76th Congress, 1st Session, June 9, 1939, 9733.

19. *Chicago Tribune*, April 29, 1935, PQHN; Scott to, April 19, 1935, 9:1; Morgan to, April 17, 1935, 8:12.

20. McLean to, May 18, 1935, 10:3.

21. To McLean, ("this answer not mailed"), May 21, 1935, 10:5.

22. *Pittsburgh Courier*, November 26, 1938, PQHN.

23. Smith to, June 9, 1935, 11:3; to Smith, June 17, 1935, 11:5.

24. Richard I. McKinney, *Mordecai: The Man and His Message. The Story of Mordecai Wyatt Johnson* (Washington, DC: Howard University Press, 1997), 86–91; *Philadelphia Tribune*, June 6, 1935, 11:1; Resolution, Executive Committee of the Chicago Chapter of the Howard Alumni Association, October 25, 1935, 14:1.

25. *Raleigh* [NC] *News and Observer*, February 18, 1935, 5:10; *Journal and Guide*, July 20, 1935, 12:8; *Afro-American*, March 23, 1935, PQHN.

26. *Afro-American*, March 25 and July 20, 1935, PQHN; Lane to, March 13, 1935, 7:2; Clay to Byrns (copy), April 8, 1935, 8:7; Mann to, May 11, 1935, 9:11; Vaughn to, March 13, 1935, 7:2.

27. Johnson to, March 2, 1935, 6:5; to Johnson, March 4, 1935, 6:6.

28. *Afro-American*, March 23, 1935, PQHN.

29. Fountain to, March 14, 1935, 7:3; BP, box 15, file for March 20, 1935; *Atlanta Daily World*, March 3, 1935, PQHN; to Fountain, March 21, 1935, 7:6.

30. *Afro-American*, May 4, 1935, PQHN.

31. *Chicago Defender*, February 2 and May 18, 1935, PQHN.

32. *Anniston* [AL] *Star*. May 9, 1935, 9:10.

33. *Pittsburgh Courier*, May 11, 1935, PQHN; to Black, April 30, 1935, 9:6.

34. BP, 349:5, October 2, 1935; to S. A. T. Watkins, July 29, 1935, 12:11; to Bishop S. L. Greene, August 6, 1935, 13:2; *Pittsburgh Courier*, September 14, 1935, PQHN; *Afro-American*, April 27, 1935, PQHN.

35. *Chicago Tribune*, April 29, 1935, PQHN; to Smith, June 1, 1935, 11:1; "Hearing

before the Committee on the Judiciary, House of Representatives, Seventy Fourth Congress, First Session on H.R. 5733 to create an Industrial Commission on Negro Affairs" (Washington, United States Printing Office, 1935), 1 in 11:5.

36. *Second Ward Square Dealer*, February 5, 1936, 16:6.

37. *Hearings*, 4–22, 11:5; Watts, *Black Cabinet*, 219, 180; Steven J. Niven, "Charles Clinton Spaulding," in *African-American National Biography* [hereafter *AANB*], ed. Henry Lewis Gates Jr. and Evelyn Brook Higginbotham, 8 vols. (Oxford: Oxford University Press, 2008), 7:341.

38. A copy is found in FDRL, OF 93: Colored Matters (Negroes), file 2, Memorandum of Charles H. Houston, June 21, 1935.

39. Moton to, June 21, 1935, 11:6.

40. To Sumners, July 15, 1935, 12:7; to MacNeal, June 27, 1935, 11:11.

41. Zangrando, *NAACP Campaign*, 142, citing Edward P. Costigan Papers, University of Colorado Library.

42. *Pro Quest History Vault. Papers of the NAACP, Part 12, Selected Branch Files, 1913–1939*. Series C, "The Midwest," folder 1427-004-0626 [hereafter *ProQuest, NAACP-Chicago*].

43. *New York Amsterdam News*, August 10, 1935, 13:2.

44. *Chicago Defender*, August 3, 1935, PQHN.

45. Wilkins to MacNeal, August 12, 1935, *ProQuest, NAACP-Chicago*.

46. To H. V. Gregory [and all members of the Judiciary Committee], July 31, 1935, 12:12.

47. To Scipio Jones, August 13, 1935, 13:3; J. E. Mitchell to, August 20, 1935; 13:5.

48. Prattis to J. E. Mitchell, August 21, 1935, 13:5.

49. J. E. Mitchell to, August 22, 1935, 13:5; to J. E. Mitchell, August 28, 1935, 13:6; Pickens to Barnett, August 22, 1935; BP, 376:7.

50. Undated item, 72:5; to Young, July 26, 1935, 12:10; to Wimbs, June 28, 1935, 11:12.

51. To Byrns, August 21, 1935, 13:5; Byrns to, August 30, 1935, 13;6.

52. Johnson to Henry Reed, July 17, 1935, 12:7; Faddis to Richard Workman, August 16, 1935, 13:4.

53. Robert A. Caro, *The Years of Lyndon Johnson: The Path to Power* (New York: Alfred A. Knopf, 1982), 270. To T. V. Smith, July 17, 1935, 12:7; Young to, August 3, 1935, 13:1.

54. To McIntyre, August 20, 1935, 13:4.

55. *New York Times*, August 11, 1935, PQHN.

56. *Athens* [AL] *Courier*, August 15, 1935, 13:3; Clements to, September 4, 1935, 15:6; to Clements, September 14, 1935, 15:7.

57. *Atlanta Daily World*, October 13, 1935, PQHN and 13:12.

58. *Chicago Defender*, September 28, 1935: 13:10. For similar sentiments see the *Pittsburgh Courier*, December 19, 1935, PQHN, and J. C. Jackson to the *Afro-American*, June 22, 1935, PQHN.

Chapter 7

1. Davis Lee, *ANP*, February 23, 1936, 17:1.

2. To LeFlore, February 15, 1936, 16:9.

3. To McDuffie, January 4, 1936, McDuffie Papers, 1775:249.

4. Huddleston to, January 24, 1936, 15:9.

5. To Democratic Members of the House of Representatives, January 28, 1936, 16:2.

6. A sampling from more than two hundred responses. See 16:2–17:9 for all the responses from Mitchell's colleagues.

7. *ProQuest*, NAACP, Chicago, 1427-004-0842; McKeough to White (copy), March 28, 1936, 17:11; Scheutz to A. C. MacNeal, January 20, 1936; and A. C. MacNeal to Scheutz, January 29, 1936, *ProQuest*, NAACP, Chicago, 1427-004-0841.

8. To J. E. Mitchell, March 25, 1936, 17:10.

9. White to, April 13, 1936, 73:7 (Nordin notes).

10. White Statement, *ProQuest*, NAACP, Chicago, 1427-005-0092.

11. MacNeal to White, May 8, 1936, *ProQuest*, NAACP, Chicago, 1427-005-0093.

12. Cleveland speech, BP, May 19, 1936, 349:5.

13. To MacNeal, May 25, 1936, 19:6.

14. *Crisis*, May 1936, 145.

15. See overdue notices for books on Lincoln borrowed from the Library of Congress, November 19, 1936, 24:5; *Afro-American*, April 25, 1936, PQHN.

16. Mitchell speech, April 22, 1936, *Congressional Record*, 80:6, 5886–88.

17. To James P. Darden, May 9, 1936, 19:2; to Major A. E. Patterson, April 25, 1936, 18:10.

18. Moton to, May 18, 1936, 19:4; *Washington Post*, May 5, 1936, PQHN; Woodson to, April 29, 1936, 18:10; Herman P. Koppelman to, April 30, 1936, 18:10; John P. King to, May 7, 1936, 19:2.

19. BP, *ANP* News Releases, April–July 1936, 19:2; *Afro-American*, May 2, 1936, PQHN; *Pittsburgh Courier*, April 30, 1936, PQHN; *Atlanta Daily World*, May 7, 1936, PQHN.

20. *New York Herald-Tribune*, April 23, 1936, PQHN; *Washington Evening Star*, April 25, 1936, 18:9; *Anniston* [AL] *Star*, June 1, 1936, 19:7.

21. BP, William Pickens, *ANP* News Releases, April–July 1936, 19:2; *Afro-American*, May 16, 1936, PQHN.

22. John to, April 24, 1936, 18:8.

23. Benedict to, July 15, 1936, 20:3; to Benedict, August 1, 1936, 20:6.

24. Robsion-Mitchell exchange, June 1, 1936, *Congressional Record*, 80:8, 8540–51.

25. To Percy D. Jones, June 4, 1936, 19:8; Moton to, June 10, 1936, 20:1, *Washington Tribune*, n.d., 19:8.

26. Smith to, June 4, 1936, 19:8.

27. *Afro-American*, June 7, 1936, PQHN; Blanton to, June 3, 1936, 19:7.

28. *New York Herald Tribune*, June 26, 1936, PQHN.

29. To Charles Michelson, June 16, 1936, 20:1; *Chicago Defender*, July 4, 1936, PQHN; *Pittsburgh Courier*, June 20, 1936, PQHN; *Afro-American*, July 4, 1936, PQHN.

30. Allan A. Michie Frank Rhylick, *Dixie Demagogues* (New York: Vanguard, 1939), 266, 281; BP, *ANP* News Releases, April–July 1936, 19:6; to Orrin Evans, March 20, 1940, 51:6.

31. Mitchell speech, 20:2. The *Morro Castle* reference is to a passenger liner sailing

between Havana and New York in 1934 that caught fire and was beached at Asbury Park, New Jersey, with a loss of 137 lives.

32. David Robertson, *Sly and Able: A Political Biography of James F. Byrnes* (New York: Norton, 1994), 126, quoting George Mowry; *Pittsburgh Courier*, July 15, 1936, PQHN; clipping enclosed in John Mitchell to, July 12, 1936, 20:4.

33. BP, *ANP* News Releases, April–July 1936, 19:5; Undated items—1936, 25:8; Hamlin to Senator Ellison D. Smith, June 26, 1936, 20:2; to Hamlin, June 30, 1936, 20:2.

Chapter 8

1. *Second Ward Square Dealer*, February 26, 1936, 17:1.

2. Charles S. Hayde to, October 7, 1936, 22:6; Beiter to, June 15, 1936, 20:1; E. W. Patterson to, October 5, 1936, 22:5.

3. Tolan to, July 27, 1936; to Tolan, August 3, 1936, 20:6; to L. L. Dolphin, June 5, 1936, 19:8.

4. "Roosevelt the Humanitarian," *Crisis*, October 1936, 298–99.

5. *Atlanta Daily World*, May 12, 1936, PQHN.

6. Marvin G. Holli, *The Wizard of Washington: Emil Hurja, Franklin Roosevelt, and the Birth of Public Opinion Politics* (New York: Palgrave, 2002), 67–68; Harold L. Ickes, The Secret Diaries of Harold L. Ickes, 3 vols. (New York: Simon & Schuster, 1953–1954), 1:643.

7. "Negroes: Jesse Owens Dashes to G.O.P. in Colored Vote Race," *Newsweek* 8:11 (September 12, 1936), 18; Weiss, *Farewell to the Party of Lincoln*, 209; Paul Ward, "Wooing the Negro Vote," *Nation* 143 (August 1, 1936), 119–20.

8. Brooks Fletcher to Fred High, March 27, 1936, 17:10; Farley to, June 8, 1936, 19:8.

9. Harvard Sitkoff, *A New Deal for Blacks: The Emergence of Civil Rights as a National Issue* (New York: Oxford University Press, 1978), 30–31; *New York Herald-Tribune*, January 26, 1936, PQHN.

10. To Hurja, July 26, 1935, 12:10, and September 17, 1935, 13:8.

11. To Democratic National Committee, February 28, 1936, 17:2. For samples of these lists, see 26:1–2 and 35:6; *Afro-American*, September 26, 1936, PQHN.

12. Scroop, *Mr. Democrat*, 121–22; to Nash, August 3, 1936, 20:6.

13. *Baltimore Sun*, July 30, 1936, 20:6; *New York Herald-Tribune*, July 30, 1936, PQHN.

14. White to Wilkins, August 4, 1936, and Wilkins to White, August 5, 1936, 73:7 (Nordin notes).

15. To Farley, October 6, 1939, 22:6.

16. To Farley, August 26, 1936, 21:2.

17. To Farley, August 7, 1936, 20:7; to George Crowley, September 21, 1936, 22:1; Powell to, September 29, 1936, 22:3.

18. To Farley, October 6, 1936, 22:6; to John G. Grimes, Assistant Treasurer, Democratic National Finance Committee, October 6, 1936, 22:6; to Ransom, September 21, 1936, 22:1; to Farley, September 22, 1936, 22:1.

19. BP, *ANP* News Releases, July–October 1936, 20:6.

20. To F. W. Littlejohn, August 15, 1936, 21:1; to Farley, September 7, 1936, 21:5, and September 12, 1936, 21:6; to Davis, October 10, 1936, 22:8; to Thompkins, August 18, 1936, 21:1; Thompkins to, September 4, 1936, 21:5.

21. Ransom to, September 22, 1936, 22:3; October 6, 1936, 22:6, and October 19, 1936, 23:3.

22. To George McDonald, September 21, 1936, 22:1. Mitchell's lists are exhaustive and invite further study. See boxes 25, 26, and 35:6.

23. To Percy Jones, September 29, 1936, 22:3; to Mrs. Marie Gregory, September 29, 1936, 22:3; Dawson to, October 6, 1936, 22:6, and October 13, 1936, 23:1; to Dawson, October 15, 1936, 23:2.

24. To E. E. Pruitt, October 5, 1936, 22:7; Davis Lee to, September 29, 1936, 22:3.

25. Andrew Means to Ransom, October 8, 1936, 22:6; Ransom to, October 19, 1936, 23:3; to Ransom, October 26, 1936, 23:6.

26. Ransom to, October 24, 1936, 23:6; to Ransom October 26, 1936, 23:6.

27. Reden to, October 1, 1936, 22:4; to Reden, October 3, 1936, 22:5.

28. Jones to, September 21, 1936, 22;1; Jones to Farley, September 24, 1936, FDRL, OF, 93:2; Jones to, October 1, 1936, 22:4.

29. Jones to, October 6, 1936, 22:6.

30. Ransom to, September 9, 1936, 21:7, and October 8, 1936, 22:7; Turner Catledge, "Democrats Count on Midwest Negroes," *New York Times*, October 26, 1936, PQHN.

31. Harold E. Bledsoe to, October 10, 1936, 22:8, and October 15, 1936, 23:1.

32. For the period October 27–31, see 23:7; Powell to, September 25, 1936, 22:2; to Lawrence Wood Robert, September 24, 1936, 22:2; to Utterback, September 24, 1936, 22:2; Rayburn to, October 1, 1936, 22:4; Wood to, September 28, 1936, 22:3.

33. Smith to, October 18, 1936, 23:3.

34. Davis to, October 13, 1936, 23:1.

35. To Ransom, September 12, 1936, 21:6; to Wm. G. Worthy, October 3, 1936, 22:5.

36. To Reden, September 12, 1936, 21:6; to Eugene V. Gavin, September 21, 1936, 22:1; 1936 audience survey, 23:1.

37. Henning to Farley, September 8, 1936, 21:5; Harter to, July 22, 1936, 20:5; Pettengill to, September 9, 1936, 21:7; Worthy to, September 29, 1936, 22:3; Harlan to, August 27, 1936, 21:3.

38. To Henning, September 14, 1936, 21:6; to Ransom, October 3, 1936, 22:5; to Farley, October 22, 1936, 23:5.

39. To Farley, September 14, 1936, 21:6, and memo to file, September 13, 1936, 21:6; Harlan to, October 8, 1936, 22:7.

40. *Akron Times-Herald*, October 9, 1936, 22:7; Harlan to, October 24, 1936, 23:6; to Farley, October 22, 1936, 23:5.

41. Le Vine to, September 15, 1936, 21:8; Steele to, October 12, 1936, 22:8.

42. To Farley, August 26, 1936, 21:2; to State Directors, October 8, 1936, 22:7; Ickes, *Secret Diaries*, 1:694; to Edgar G. Brown, October 15, 1936, 23:1.

43. To Farley, September 7, 1936, 21:5, September 12, 1936, 21:7, October 14, 1936, 23:1, and October 22, 1936, 23:5; to Bankhead, October 22, 1936, 23:5.

44. Farley to, August 20, 1936, 21:1, October 26, 1936, 23:6, October 28, 1936, 23:8, and November 1, 1936, 23:9.

45. To Farley, October 26, 1936, 23:6; to Henry Mease, October 26, 1936, 23:6.

46. Turner Catledge, "Democrats Count on Midwest Negroes," *New York Times*, October 26, 1936, PQHN.

47. Smith to Morgan, October 26, 1936, 23:6.

48. Martin Kilson, "Political Change in the Negro Ghetto, 1900–1940," in *Key Issues in the Afro American Experience*, ed. Nathan I. Huggins, Martin Kilson, and Daniel M. Fox, 2 vols. (New York: Harcourt, Brace, Jonvonavich, 1971), 2:190.

49. Patricia Sullivan, *Days of Hope: Race and Democracy in the New Deal Era* (Chapel Hill: University of North Carolina Press, 1996), 93, citing Frank R. Kent, "The Great Game of Politics," *Baltimore Sun*, November 12, 1936; Brown, "How the Negro Voted," in *American Presidential Elections*, ed. Schlesinger and Israel, 7:2911–12; Sitkoff, *New Deal for Blacks*, 95; Gordon, "Change in Political Alignment," 584; Kevin McMahon, *Reconsidering Roosevelt on Race: How the Presidency Paved the Road to Brown* (Chicago: University of Chicago Press, 2004), 59.

50. Holli, *Wizard of Washington*, 76; Weiss, *Farewell to the Party of Lincoln*, 206; Gunnar Myrdal with the assistance of Richard Steiner and Arnold Rose, *An American Dilemma. The Negro Problem and Modern Democracy* (New York: Harper and Row, 1962, ca. 1944), 496; William E. Leuchtenburg, "The Election of 1936," in *American Presidential Elections*, 7:2848. Sitkoff, *New Deal for Blacks*, 95–96.

51. Savage, *Roosevelt: The Party Leader*; Weiss, *Farewell to the Party of Lincoln*, 226 and 209–35 for a broader examination of the Black vote in 1936.

52. Weiss, *Farewell to the Party of Lincoln*, 228–29.

53. Manning, *William L. Dawson and the Limits of Black Electoral Leadership*, 75; Larrabee to, November 10, 1936, 24:3.

54. Farley, November 10, 1936, 24:3.

55. To Comptroller, DNCC, November 24, 1936, 26:4.

56. To Jones, November 13, 1934, 24;4; Roosevelt to Farley, FDRL, PPF 2289, n.d. but after January 15, 1937.

57. Brown, "How the Negro Voted," in *American Presidential Elections*, 7:2912; Jones to, July 26, 1937, 32:3.

58. McMahon, *Reconsidering Roosevelt*, 101; *Chicago Defender*, November 7, 1936, PQHN.

Chapter 9

1. Joseph Also, *The 168 Days* (New York: Capo Press, 1973), 48, 170; McMahon, *Reconsidering Roosevelt*, 70–71.

2. To Edith Bleili, February 11, 1937, 27:4; to Edward Schnakowski, February 17, 1937, 27:5.

3. Herd to, March 8, 1937, 29:1; McMahon, *Reconsidering Roosevelt*, 62; to Stephen Glut, March 8, 1937, 29:1.

4. To Folger, March 13, 1937, 29:4.

5. To Sparrow, April 1, 1937, 29:9; to Earl B. Dickerson, March 15, 1937, 29:4.

6. Margaret C. Rung, *Servants of the State: Managing the Federal Work Force, 1933–53* (Athens: University of Georgia Press, 2002), 73: Lawrence J. W. Hayes, *The Negro Federal Government Worker*, Howard University Studies in the Social Sciences, vol. 3, no. 1 (Washington, DC: Howard University, 1941), 106.

7. To Robert L. Johnson, President, National Civil Service Reform League, December 10, 1937, 34:6.

8. Miller to, January 19, 1937, 26:7; Rung, *Servants of the State*, 74; *Pittsburgh Courier*, December 25, 1937, 18. For details on how the "rule of three" and the use of photographs complemented each other, see Desmond King, *Separate and Unequal: Black Americans and the U.S. Federal Government* (Oxford: Clarendon Press, 1995), 51–59.

9. To Barnett, January 27, 1937, BP, 346:3; Taylor to, February 6, 1937, 27:3.

10. *Crisis* 44, no. 3 (March 1937), 81; Roy Wilkins, "Watchtower," *New York Amsterdam News*, July 17, 1937, PQHN. See also *Pittsburgh Courier*, February 13, 1937, PQHN and *Chicago Defender*, February 13, 1937, PQHN.

11. Robert J. Schneller Jr., *Breaking the Color Barrier: The U. S. Naval Academy's First Black Midshipman and the Struggle for Racial Equity* (New York: New York University Press, 2005), 50, 91, 133, and 268n2.

12. Schneller Jr., *Breaking the Color Barrier*, 65–71.

13. *Afro-American*, March 23, 1935, PQHN; to Mrs. Inez Gilbert Vicery, July 15, 1935, 12:7.

14. To George Sadowski, June 5, 1935, 19:8; to Otis Harris, May 20, 1935, 10:4.

15. Schneller Jr., *Breaking the Color Barrier*, 66, 79, and 83; Stephen Birmingham, *Certain People: America's Black Elite* (Boston: Little, Brown, 1977), 143–44; BP, *ANP* News Release, April–July 1936, 19:5.

16. To Johnson, July 28, 1936, 20:7.

17. Schneller Jr., *Breaking the Color Barrier*, 73–134; "An Annapolis Dad" to, February 27, 1937, 28:6; BP, *ANP* News Release, July–October 1936, 20:6; Johnson report card, 24:6.

18. Sellers to Johnson Sr., January 27, 1937, 26:9; To Sellers, January 29, 1937, 26:9; to Roosevelt, January 29, 1937, 26:9. Across this letter someone at the White House wrote "President wants an appointment with Mitchell."

19. Sellers to, January 30, 1937, 27:1; Schneller Jr., *Breaking the Color Barrier*, citing Sellers, Memorandum, 8 Feb. 1937, JMPJ, Midshipman Personal Jacket, James L. Jackson, Box 8, Special Collections and Archives, Nimitz Library; to Mead, February 11, 1937, 27:4.

20. Schneller Jr., *Breaking the Color Barrier*, 102.

21. James L. Johnson Jr., "The Circumstances of My Resignation," 27:4; Schneller Jr., *Breaking the Color Barrier*, 103–5.

22. To Sellers and to Roosevelt [telegrams], February 13, 1937, 27:5; *New York Herald-Tribune*, February 16, 1937, PQHN.

23. Schneller Jr., *Breaking the Color Barrier*, 104–5; to Inez Vickery, February 16, 1937, 27:7.

24. To Stephen M. Young, February 25, 1937, 28:4. See also Johnson Jr., "Significant Facts Regarding My Resignation," 32:5.

25. James L. Johnson Sr. to, February 13, 1937, 27:5; James and Gertrude Johnson to, undated but perhaps July 17, 1937, 32:1.

26. To Houston, March 8, 1937, 29:1; Holman to Roy Gavin, *Kansas City Call*, March 5, 1937, 28:9; Lucille Bluford, City Editor, *Kansas City Call*, to Holman, March 9, 1937, 29:2. Bluford added to her report that, if the son was involved in the Johnson affair, "that is material for a good news story."

27. Anonymous, February 17, 1937, 27:7; "A. Hint to the Wise" to, March 11, 1937,

29:3; *Chicago Defender*, March 6, 1937, PQHN; Jones, *Afro-American*, March 13, 1937, PQHN.

28. To Davis, February 17, 1937, 27:7; to the American Society for Race Tolerance, February 19, 1937, 28:1; to Scott, February 20, 1937, 28:2; to Swanson, July 19, 1937, 32:2. For data supplied see Swanson to, July 24, 1937, 32:3; to Wetlock, March 23, 1937, 29:6.

29. *New York Amsterdam News*, February 27, 1937, PQHN; Schneller Jr., *Breaking the Color Barrier*, 115–16.

30. Schneller Jr., *Breaking the Color Barrier*, 116, citing Todd to Sellers, July 19, 1937, General Correspondence Jan.–Oct. 1937 file, box 4, David F. Sellers papers, L[ibrary of] C[ongress] and Trivers interview by author, 1997; to P. B. Young, July 9, 1937, 31:9.

31. Mitchell press release, n.d., 31:8; to P. B. Young, July 9, 1939, 31:9.

32. *East Tennessee News*, August 5, 1937, 32:5; *Afro-American*, July 17, 1937, PQHN; *Chicago Defender*, July 31, 1937, PQHN.

33. To Gay, July 17, 1937, 32:1.

34. Houston to, March 12, 1938, 37:5; to Houston, March 14, 1938, 37:6, and March 21, 1938, 37:8.

35. Schneller Jr., *Breaking the Color Barrier*, 116, citing "James Daniel Fowler," *Assembly* 47 (July 1988): 188.

36. *Afro-American*, November 13, 1937, PQHN, and December 4, 1937, PQHN.

37. Fowler to, November 26, 1937, 34:3; Fowler to his parents, July 2, 1938, 39:5.

38. To Fowler, December 1, 1937, 34:4, and July 20, 1938, 39:7.

39. To Benedict, June 18, 1938, 39:3; to Roosevelt, June 23, 1938, 39:4.

40. Benedict to, June 18, 1938, 39:3; Schneller Jr., *Breaking the Color Barrier*, 124, citing Roosevelt to Watson, July 9, 1938, file "War Dept., U. S. Military Academy 1937–39," box 18, OF, 25c, FDRL.

41. Major General Francis B. Wilby, Superintendent, United States Military Academy to, June 4, 1942; to Thomas Campbell, September 13, 1940, 54:13.

Chapter 10

1. Zangrando, *NAACP Crusade against Lynching*, 139.

2. *Oklahoma Eagle*, October 16, 1937, 33:4; to William Worley, September 22, 1938, 39:11.

3. Zangrando, *NAACP Crusade against Lynching*, 142–43.

4. To George W. Crowley, March 5, 1937, 28:9, *Chicago Defender*, April 10, 1937, PQHN to Wilkins, March 11, 1937, 29:3. Mitchell was correct about the futility of discharge petitions. Between 1931 and 2003, 563 were circulated, forty-seven acquired the necessary signatures, only two promoted legislation that became law. Wikipedia contributors, "Discharge Petition," Wikipedia, The Free Encyclopedia (website), accessed September 19, 2023, citing Richard S. Beth, "The Discharge Rule in the House: Recent Use in Historical Context," Congressional Research Service, April 17, 2003.

5. Zangrando, *NAACP Crusade against Lynching*, 144, citing Walter White to Joel Spingarn, May 17, 1937, NAACP, Library of Congress, C-79; *Crisis*, March 1937, 81.

6. To Pickens, March 20, 1937, 29:6; Pickens to, March 22, 1937, 29:6; *Pittsburgh Courier*, February 13, 1937, PQHN.

7. Aleshire to White [copy], January 27, 1937, 26:10.

8. Samuel B. Pettengill (IN-3) to, March 22, 1937, 29:6; White, *Man Called White*, 172.

9. To House Colleagues, March 8, 1937, 29:1; to Barnett, March 9, 1937, BP, 349:3; to Editor, *Quarterly Review*, March 9, 1937, 29:2; to Roscoe C. Wright, March 8, 1937, 29:1.

10. Wilkins to, March 10, 1937, 29:2; Wilkins to MacNeal, March 11, 1937, 73:7 (Nordin copy) and *ProQuest*, NAACP, Chicago, 1427–005–0457.

11. J. E. Mitchell to, March 29, 1937, 29:8; *Afro-American*, March 20, 1937, PQHN; *Chicago Defender*, March 20, 1937, PQHN.

12. To Boyer, March 15, 1937, 29:4.

13. Pettengill to, March 22, 1937, 29:6; to Pettengill, March 29, 1937, 29:8.

14. Fletcher to White [copy], March 17, 1937, 29:7.

15. To House Colleagues, March 25, 1937, 29:7.

16. To Dabney, March 28, 1937, 29:7; to F. D. Patterson, March 26, 1937, 29:7.

17. Patterson to, March 30, 1937, 29:9; to Patterson, April 1, 1937, 29:9.

18. To Wilkins, March 26, 1937, 29:7. Others Mitchell invited to testify included editors Carl Murphy of the *Afro-American*, Robert Abbott of the *Chicago Defender*, Robert Vann of the *Pittsburgh Courier*, and Earl Dickerson. For a complete list of those invited and their responses, see 29:8 and 29:9.

19. White to Illinois State Conferences, March 26, 1937, *ProQuest*, Illinois State Conferences, 1936–37.

20. Holman (?), "Judiciary Committee of the House of Representatives holds hearing on anti-lynching legislation," 29:7; Howard, "The Truth about the Anti-Lynching Bill," 30:4. The Howard memorandum errs in dating the hearing on March 24.

21. *Afro-American*, April 17, 1937, PQHN.

22. To the *Chicago Defender* [telegram], April 1, 1937, 29:9; to House Members, April 2, 1937, 29:10; to A. M. Burroughs, April 2, 1937, 29:10.

23. White to Roosevelt, April 1, 1937, FDRL, PPF, 2289; White to Members of Congress April 3, 1937, 30:1.

24. Bloom to, April 5, 1937, 30:1; Harland to, April 5, 1937, 30:1.

25. White to MacNeal, April 3, 1937, *ProQuest*, 1427–005–0502 and 73:8 (Nordin copy).

26. MacNeal to White, April 3, 1937, *ProQuest*, 1427–005–0502; MacNeal to, April 5, 1937, 30:1.

27. Fries to MacNeal, April 7, 1937, *ProQuest*, 1427–005–0502.

28. CBS broadcast, "The Necessity of the Passage of a Federal Anti-Lynching Bill," April 5, 1937, 30:1.

29. Lord to, April 6, 1937, 30:1; Gasque to, April 6, 1937, 30:1.

30. White to MacNeal, April 5, 1937, Wilkins to MacNeal, April 6, 1937, McNeal to White, April 6, 1937, *ProQuest*, 1427–005–0502.

31. "Crushing Defeat," Press Service of the National Association for the Advancement of Colored People, April 7, 1937, *ProQuest*, 001423–008–0746. A copy of the release is found in FDRL, Eleanor Roosevelt, 100: Personal letters, 1937, WW-2. White was vague in his description of the final night's activities. All he said was "we marshalled our forces" (White, *A Man Called White*, 172).

32. *Chicago Tribune*, April 8, 1937, PQHN; to George Coleman Moore, May 9, 1938, 38:8; *New York Amsterdam News*, April 17, 1937, PQHN.

33. An amalgam of the accounts of the *Christian Science Monitor*, *New York Times*, *Washington Star*, and *Washington Post*, April 8, 1937, 30:2; *Columbus* [OH] *Advocate*, April 17, 1937, 30:4. John Robsion of Kentucky, Mitchell's opponent in 1936, voted in support of Mitchell. So did twelve of the thirteen Democrats in the Illinois delegation.

34. *Congressional Record*, April 7, 1937, 75th Congress, First Session, 30:2.

35. To Daly, April 9, 1937, 30:2; to A. J. Smitherman, April 9, 1937, 30:2.

36. To Houston, April 12, 1937, 30:3.

37. To Patrick Drewry [VA-At Large], April 9, 1937, 30:2; undated note, misfiled in 15:2.

38. McCormack to, April 12, 1937, 30:3; Schlesinger Jr., *Life in the Twentieth Century*, 277; Caro, *Years of Lyndon Johnson*, 545; Richard B. Henderson, *Maury Maverick: A Political Biography* (Austin: University of Texas Press, 1970), 75–79; *Crisis* 46:6 (June 1939), 181; Maverick to, December 21, 1938, 41:3.

39. Kersey to, April 8, 1937, 30:2.

40. White to MacNeal, April 10, 1937, *ProQuest*, 1427-005-0502; Marshall to Robert S. Hargrove, n.d., 73:8 (Nordin copy); Press Service of the NAACP, April 7, 1937, *ProQuest*, 0014-008-0746.

41. *New York Amsterdam News*, April 17, 1937, PQHN; *Afro-American*, April 10, 1937, PQHN; Dewey Jones, "Day-By-Day," *Afro-American*, April 17, 1937, PQHN.

42. Sumners to White, April 14, 1937, Wikipedia contributors, "Hatton W. Sumners," Wikipedia, The Free Encyclopedia (website), accessed September 19, 2023, citing Dallas Historical Society, HWS Collection, D 97–6. The author thanks the staff of the Dallas Historical Society for their unsuccessful attempt to locate any Mitchell-Sumners correspondence.

43. *Congressional Record*, April 15, 1937, 3533 and 30:4.

44. Dewey Jones, "Pointed Paragraphs," *Chicago Defender*, April 24, 1937, PQHN; Holman to, April 19, 1937, 30:5.

45. *Norfolk Journal and Guide*, April 10, 1937, 30:2; *St. Louis Argus*, July 30, 1937, 32:4.

Chapter 11

1. Caro, *Years of Lyndon Johnson*, 656 (ephemeral quote).

2. Anthony Badger, *New Deal/New South: An Anthony Badger Reader* (Fayetteville: University of Arkansas Press, 2007), 42; To Mrs. Marie Bankhead Owen, July 12, 1937, 31:9; Bankhead to, November 17, 1938, 40:10; Bankhead to, July 1, 1939, 46:3.

3. *New York Amsterdam News*, April 7, 1937, PQHN.

4. To Joseph Miller, June 12, 1938, 36:2; *East Tennessee News*, May 11, 1939, 45:1; to MacNeal Williams, July 16, 1937, 32:1; *St. Paul Recorder*, September 30, 1938, 40:1.

5. Wilkerson, *Warmth of Other Suns*, 192; Catherine A. Barnes, *Journey from Jim Crow: The Desegregation of Southern Transit* (New York: Columbia University Press, 1983), 15. For additional details on the differences in accommodations see the *Pittsburgh Courier*, May 14, 1938, PQHN.

6. Bay, *Traveling Black*, 89–90, 92–95, 233.

7. Barnes, *Journey from Jim Crow*, 6, 14.

8. Barnes, *Journey from Jim Crow*, i, 13.

9. Steve Luxenberg, *Separate: The Story of Plessy v. Ferguson and America's Journey from Slavery to Segregation* (New York: W. W. Norton and Company, 2019), 439.

10. Nancy T. Robinson, "William H. H. Hart," in Gates and Higginbotham (eds.), *AANB* 4:104; *Pittsburgh Courier*, May 22, 1937, 1.

11. To General Passenger Agent, Southern Railway Co., July 2, 1935, 12:1. Frank L. Jenkins to, July 17, 1935, 12:7.

12. See *Stenographer's Minutes before the Interstate Commerce Commission. Docket 27844. Arthur W. Mitchell vs. the Chicago, Rock Island and Pacific Railway Company*, 51–94, 37:3 and 37:4; *Chicago Defender*, March 12, 1938, PQHN.

13. *New York Amsterdam News*, May 13, 1937, PQHN; Stenographer's Minutes, 103–4.

14. *Afro-American*, May 22, 1937, PQHN; *New York Times*, December 4, 1940, PQHN.

15. J. Clay Smith, *Emancipation: The Making of the Black Lawyer* (Philadelphia: University of Pennsylvania Press, 1993), 385, 499.

16. Barnes, *Journey from Jim Crow*, 21.

17. Bay, *Traveling Black*, 70, 99–100; *Pittsburgh Courier*, May 22, 1937, PQHN; Westbrooks to, May 19, 1937, 31:1 The capitalizations are his.

18. Bethune to, May 17, 1937, 30:10; Pickens to, May 16, 1937, 30:10; de Oteyze to, December 30, 1937, 35:1.

19. *Chicago Tribune*, May 12, 1937, PQHN; *Afro-American*, May 22, 1937, PQHN; Dewey Jones, "Pointed Paragraphs," *Chicago Defender*, May 29, 1937, PQHN.

20. Luxenberg, *Separate*, 416, citing Martinet to Albion Tourgée, December 7 and 28, 1891, Tourgée Papers, Chataqua County Historical Society, Westfield, NY, documents 5837 and 5877; *Pittsburgh Courier*, May 22, 1937, PQHN.

21. To R. L. Gray [sample], May 12, 1937, 30:9.

22. *New York Times*, December 4, 1940, PQHN; *Chicago Defender*, January 15, 1938, PQHN.

23. Jones to, May 11, 1937, 30:8; to Jones, November 3, 1937, 33:7; Jones to, November 6, 1937, 33:7. Mitchell and Westbrooks had no trouble finding willing witnesses in Chicago.

24. To I. Van Meter, Editor's Assistant, *Life*, May 27, 1937, 31:2; Van Meter to, June 3, 1937, 31:3.

25. To *New York Amsterdam News*, May 15, 1937, PQHN; to Murphy, May 27, 1937. 31:2.

26. To T. C. Walker, May 26, 1937, 31:2.

27. Bay, *Traveling Black*, 236–37, citing D. W. Kellum, "Quiz Congressman Mitchell in Suit," *Chicago Defender*, March 12, 1938.

28. To Rev. C. E. Chapman, May 22, 1937, 31:1; to Westbrooks, July 21, 1937, 32:2.

29. *Chicago Tribune*, January 11, 1938, PQHN.

30. Robert M. Ratcliffe, 'Dixie Highlights,' *Atlanta Daily World*, May 4, 1941, PQHN.

31. *Afro-American*, July 10, 1937, PQHN.

Chapter 12

1. To G. L. O'Connor, January 14, 1938, 36:2.

2. To Governor Clyde Hoey of North Carolina, June 20, 1938, 39:4.

3. To Mayor of Roanoke, Alabama, September 7, 1937, 32:9, 35:1.

4. To Ernest Covington, October 23, 1937, 33:5; *Oklahoma Eagle*, October 16, 1937, 33:1; *Gastonia Daily Gazette*, September 17, 1937, 33:1.

5. *Gastonia Daily Gazette*, September 17, 1937, 33:1.

6. *Pittsburgh Courier*, November 28, 1942, PQHN; to C. Lavender, October 19, 1937, 33:4.

7. To Douglas, January 26, 1939, 42:3; to Powell Jr., January 15, 1941, 57:8. In 1944, Powell Jr. would win election to Gavagan's House seat; Powers to, May 7, 1942, 66:1; to Powers, June 10, 1942, 66:4.

8. To M. H. McIntyre, Assistant Secretary to the President, August 2, 1937, 32:5; FDRL, OF 93, x ref 1936–37, 82–83.

9. V. O. Key, *Southern Politics in State and Nation* (New York: Vintage, 1949), 206n1; B.P, *ANP* press release, October 2, 1935, 349:5; to Johnson, June 18, 1941, 349:5; Johnson to, n.d., 58:1.

10. To the Editor, *Montgomery Advertiser*, February 1, 1940, 50:1; to Dabney, October 14, 1944, 68:8.

11. *Waterbury Republican*, October 6, 1942, 67:3; for an example of Mitchell's advocacy for Black women to attend college, see to Harold C. Jacquith, President, Illinois College, October 3, 1936, 22:5 and Jaquith to, October 9, 1937, 22:7; to Arthur M. Weber, February 16, 1938, 36:8.

12. Undated item, 72:2.

13. To James A. Burns, January 5, 1939, 41:8; To Professor Charles M. Thomas, April 23, 1940, 52:6.

14. To E. B. Swope, March 7, 1941, 58:9; to Antoinette Bowler, October 26, 1939, 47:9; [Oklahoma City] *Black Dispatch*, April 25, 1942, 65:9. To Trent, April 11, 1939, 44:1; to George Longe, October 15, 1941, 62:11.

15. To Rev. Quentin Jackson, May 24, 1938, 38:11; to Trent, April 11, 1939, 44:1; to Boyd, February 14, 1940, 50:7.

16. Address to Howard University students, June 13, 1941, 60:5; *St. Paul Recorder*, October 7, 1938, 40:2.

17. *Atlanta Daily World*, May 27, 1941, PQHN; *Pittsburgh Courier*, November 28, 1942, PQHN; *Roanoke* [VA] *Times*, "Sound Advice to Negroes," February 6, 1940, 50:4; to Charles Williams, April 20, 1938, 38:3.

18. To Anna Goldsboro, October 5, 1938, 40:1.

19. To Jackson, October 29, 1940, 55:8; Jackson to, November 8, 1940, 55:10.

20. To Carter, July 1, 1940; 53:8; *Washington* [NC] *Star*, April 22, 1939, 44:5.

21. To Charles M. Thomas, April 22, 1938, 38:3; Spaulding to, May 25, 1937, 31:1; to Spaulding, May 27, 1937, 31:2; *Philadelphia Tribune*, "A. W. Mitchell Flays 'Cry Baby Negroes,'" August 10, 1941, 62:3; to Reverend William Hill, May 5, 1939, 44:9.

22. To Hardaway, May 2, 1939, 44:8; to Dobson, August 4, 1938, 39:8.

23. To Henry F. Huff, October 23, 1942, 67:5.

24. Address to Howard University students, June 13, 1941, 60:5.

25. Tuskegee Founder's Day Address, April 2, 1939, 43:9.

26. *Journal and Guide*, June 11, 1938, 39:2.

27. 67:11.

28. 72:1; 72:5; *Afro-American*, March 1, 1941, PQHN.

29. Howard University speech, June 13, 1941, 60:5.

30. 72:1, 6, and 10.

31. *St. Paul Recorder*, October 7, 1942, 40:2; *Dayton Forum*, February 21, 1941, 58:6.

Chapter 13

1. Henry J. Abraham, *Justices, Senators, and Presidents: A History of the U.S. Supreme Court Appointments from Washington to Clinton* (Lanham, MD: Rowman and Littlefield, 1999), 168; Steve Suitts, *Hugo Black of Alabama: How His Roots and Early Career Shaped the Great Champion of the Constitution* (Montgomery: New South Books, 2005), 168–82.

2. To Katye H. Steele, March 24, 1937, 29:7; Steve Suitts, "Hugo L. Black," Encyclopedia of Alabama (website), November 16, 2008, accessed September 19, 2023.

3. *Chicago Tribune*, June 27, 1936, PQHN; McMahon, *Reconsidering Roosevelt*, 17.

4. J. L. LeFlore to Roy Wilkins, August 13, 1937, 73:8 (Nordin copy); to Black [telegram], August 13, 1937, 32:6; Address to Postal Workers' Convention, August 18, 1937, 32:7.

5. Black to, August 25, 1937, 32:8.

6. *Afro-American*, October 9, 1937, PQHN; *Daily Oklahoman*, October 9, 1937, 33:3; White, *A Man Called White*, 177; McMahon, *Reconsidering Roosevelt*, 112, citing Howard Ball, *Hugo L. Black: Cold Steel Warrior* (New York: Oxford University Press, 1996), 100–101, 103; White to Roosevelt (telegram), October 16, 1937, 73:8 (Nordin copy).

7. *Pittsburgh Courier*, October 9, 1937, PQHN; *Chicago Defender*, same date, PQHN.

8. Mitchell made a similar argument when defending Roosevelt's 1941 nomination of "Jimmy" Byrnes to the Supreme Court. See to Roscoe Gilles, October 14, 1941, 62:10; to Roosevelt, May 17, 1941, 61:2; Byrnes to, May 20, 1941, 61:2.

9. Photo of May 22, 1937, *ProQuest*, 1427-005-0577.

10. *Afro-American*, February 26, 1938, PQHN.

11. *Pittsburgh Courier*, March 5, 1938, PQHN.

12. To Smith, July 21, 1937, 32:2; to Arlene E. Combs, July 24, 1937, 32:3; to I. H. W. Butsch, June 28, 1937, 31:7.

13. To Hendwork, December 6, 1937, 34:5; to Curtis, January 13, 1938, 36:2.

14. To Johnson, April 29, 1938, 38:6.

15. Farnsworth to, May 14, 1938, 38:9; to Farnsworth, May 17, 1938, 38:10.

16. Undated memo, 35:6; to Young, December 22, 1937, 34:8.

17. To Alfred L. Meacham, March 21, 1938, 37:8; to Dr. C. W. Reese, December 6, 1937, 34:5.

18. To David J. Lewis, June 21, 1938, 39:4; to Kennedy, October 11, 1938, 40:2; to Bierman, November 1, 1938, 40:7. For a complete list of 1938 candidate supported or opposed by Mitchell, see boxes 39 and 40, passim.

19. McMahon, *Reconsidering Roosevelt*, 101–2; *New York Amsterdam News*, December 31, 1938, PQHN.

20. McMahon, *Reconsidering Roosevelt*, 245, n. 7; Lucas to, November 19, 1938, 40:10; to Lucas, November 19, 1938, 40:10.

21. To Louis Rabaut, December 7, 1938, 41:1.

Chapter 14

1. Miller to, January 25, 1939, 42:3.

2. To Miller, February 7, 1939, 42:7. Mitchell proceeded to read the two letters into the *Congressional Record* of February 9, 1939, an act for which Miller thanked him: "You deserve credit for inaugurating a project which may result in great good for the race"; Miller to, February 13, 1939, 42:9.

3. Mitchell press release 12[?], April 1939, 44:1. The archival dating of the press release is probably incorrect. Mitchell refers to it in speeches on April 2 and April 5.

4. Buford to, March 30, 1939, 43:9; Ransom to, February 25, 1939, 43:1; Wilkins to, February 25, 1939, 43:1. For greater detail on the "Back to the Farm" movement, see Raymond Gavins, *The Perils and Prospects of Southern Black Leadership: Gordon Blaine Hancock, 1884–1970* (Durham, NC: Duke University Press, 1977).

5. To F. D. Patterson, February 7, 1939, 42:7; to H. M. Kannee, March 27, 1939, 43:8.

6. Founder's Day address, April 2, 1939, 43:9; and Arther W. Mitchell, extension of remarks on April 6, 1939, *Congressional Record*, 76th Cong., 1st sess., 1939, vol. 84, pt. 12 (Washington, DC: Government Printing Office, 1939), 1329–32. Mitchell wrote to Holman, "No speech which I have delivered since I have been a member of Congress has attracted such wide attention. Literally, thousands of letters have come to us"; to Holman, May 5, 1939, 44:9.

7. To Faron, April 1, 1939, 43:9; *Afro-American*, April 1, 1939, PQHN; to H. Frank Carroll, May 27, 1939, 45:4.

8. *New York Amsterdam Star-News*, April 15, 1939, PQHN.

9. Moore to, April 17, 1937, 44:3; Burton, "Views and Reviews," *Chicago Defender*, May 20, 1939, PQHN.

10. Daniels to, May 1, 1939, 44:8; to Daniels, May 2, 1939, 44:8.

11. Alexander to, April 8, 1939, 43:11; to Wallace, September 12, 1939, 47:1.

12. To "The Committee on the Library" [?], March 25, 1940; to Wallace, February 27, 1940, 50:11. For more on the Resettlement Administration see Watts, *Black Cabinet*, 234–36.

13. To President W. J. Trent, Livingstone College, April 11, 1939, 44:1; *New York Amsterdam News*, April 29, 1939, PQHN.

14. *Washington* [NC] *Morning Star*, April 22, 1939, 44:4.

15. *Chicago Defender*, January 24, 1939, PQHN; Biles, *Big City Boss in Depression and War*, 97–98.

16. To Thomas J. Price, May 27, 1939, 45:4; to Nash, June 27, 1938, 46:2; to Tittinger, June 27, 1938, 46:2; to Precinct Captains, September 8, 1939, 46:11.

17. *Chicago Daily News*, November 17, 1939, 48:4. Dawson had been defeated twice as a Republican candidate for Congress in 1924 and again by Mitchell in 1938. Following his second loss, he changed his party registration to Democrat.

18. To Francis S. Smith, December 21, 1938, 41:3; to Dawson, March 7, 1940, 51:3; to Farley, March 13, 1940, 51:4.

19. Biles, *Big City Boss in Depression and War*, 180, citing a Dawson-John Q. Wilson interview, September 24, 1958; Robert J. Blakely, *Earl B. Dickerson: A Voice for Freedom and Equality* (Evanston, IL: Northwestern University Press, 2006), 86, 89; William J.

Grimshaw, *Bitter Fruit: Black Politics and the Chicago Machine* (Chicago: University of Chicago Press, 1992), 78; to Joseph C. Coles, September 13, 1940, 54:13; to Corneal Davis, September 19, 1940, 55:1; to Farley, March 13, 1940, 51:4.

20. To P. B. Young, January 4, 1940, 49:1; to Dr. Robert W. Pallon, November 1, 1939, 48:1.

21. *Pittsburgh Courier*, May 4, 1940, citing the *Birmingham News*, April 21, 1940, PQHN.

22. Key, *Southern Politics in State and Nation*, 26.

23. George C. Rable, "The South and the Politics of Anti-Lynching Legislation," *Journal of Southern History* 51, no. 2 (May 1985), 207; Andrew Bunie, *The Negro in Virginia Politics, 1902–1965* (Charlottesville: University Press of Virginia, 1967), 119–20, 128; BP, October 21, 1936, 20:6; Virginia Writers' Project, *The Negro in Virginia* (New York: Arno Press and the *New York Times*, 1969), 246.

24. Charter, Langdon Civic Club of America, 47:9.

25. *Richmond Times-Dispatch*, December 31, 1939, 48:7; *New York Amsterdam News*, October 21, 1939, PQHN; *Afro-American*, October 28, 1939, PQHN; Russell to, December 21, 1939, 48:6.

26. N. D. Moore to, December 4, 1939, 48:4; to Russell, December 22, 1939, 48:6.

27. To Mary S. Bright, December 29, 1939, 48:8.

28. To Amanda White, January 26, 1940, 49:7; Brooks to, February 8, 1940, 50:3.

29. Wyche to, March 3, 1940, 55:1; Speed to, September 26, 1940, 55:2.

30. Brown to, January 12, 1941, 57:7; to Brown, January 14, 1941, 57:7; to Woodson, December 9, 1940, 56:6.

31. To Blackwell, February 20, 1940, 50:9; to Bedinger, February 20, 1940, 50:9; to Cohegan, February 20, 1940, 50:9.

32. Green to, February 22, 1940, 50:9.

33. To Young, February 22, 1940, 50:9.

34. Bousfield to, May 1, 1941, 60:6; Barnett to, May 23, 1942, 66:3; *New York Amsterdam Star News*, February 7, 1942, PQHN. Mitchell never did run for Congress from Virginia. He faced opposition from the Byrd machine, which controlled state politics down to the "level of dog catcher" and was not prepared to have a Black person in its Washington delegation. In addition, local Black political and social organizations resisted "an arrogant outsider from Chicago" (email from Lucious Edwards to the author, April 5, 2022).

Chapter 15

1. Zangrando, *NAACP Crusade against Lynching*, 163, citing White to Daisy Lampkin, November 30, 1939 (copy), box C-80, NAACP-LC.

2. Rawn James Jr., *Root and Branch: Charles Hamilton Houston, Thurgood Marshall, and the Struggle to End Segregation* (London: Bloomsbury Press, 2010), 155; to L. F. Coles, January 13, 1940, 49:3.

3. To Gavagan, November 26, 1939, 49:3; "An Appeal to the Nation for the Rights of the Negro," January 9, 1940, BP, 349:5; *Afro-American*, January 20, 1940, PQHN; *New York Amsterdam News*, January 13, 1940, PQHN.

4. Fred R. Moore to, January 16, 1940, 49:4; Woodson to, January 29, 1940, January 29, 1940, 49:9; Cliff MacKay, "The Globetrotter," *Atlanta Daily Mail*, January 14, 1940, PQHN; Powell to, January 19, 1940, 49:5.

5. To Moore, January 17, 1940, 49:4; to Powell, January 23, 1940, 49:6.

6. Zangrando, *NAACP Crusade against Lynching*, 165. Lynching, as public spectacle, largely disappeared from the national scene in the 1940s. Many would say it was replaced by "legal executions"; Tolnay and Beck, *Festival of Violence*, 233; Blow, *The Devil You Know*, 79, citing the work of Bryan Stevenson at the Equal Justice Initiative.

7. To Mrs. E. D. Prentice, September 19, 1940, 55:1; Kennedy, *Freedom from Fear*, 774; Badger, *New Deal, New South*, 34–42.

8. *Congressional Record*, March 18, 1940, 59:3.

9. Matthew W. Delmont, *Half American: The Epic Story of African Americans Fighting World War II at Home and Abroad* (New York: Viking, 2022), 41, citing Richard L. Dalfiume, "Military Segregation and the 1940 Election," *Phylon* 30, no. 1 (1969).

10. To Kelly, February 14, 1940, 50:7; Ralph Matthews, "Democrats Muzzle Rep. Mitchell," *Afro-American*, July 20, 1940, PQHN.

11. *New York Times*, July 17, 1940, PQHN; Emil J. Kochman to [telegram], July 16, 1940, 53:11; *Pittsburgh Courier*, July 27, 1940, PQHN; *Congressional Record*, July 16, 1940, 53:11.

12. Thom to, July 27, 1940, 54:3; Bethune to, July 22, 1940, 54:2.

13. John Lake, "Hat in Hand speech is criticized by Race Delegates," *Chicago Defender*, July 27, 1940, PQHN.

14. To Farley, July 23, 1940, 54:2.

15. Ludlow to, April 13, 1940, 51:10; to R. Goodwin Parrish, May 14, 1940, 52:10; to Parrish, May 23, 1940, 52:10. Caro, *Years of Lyndon Johnson*, 639–40; Jed Johnson to, September 9, 1940, 54:12; Flynn to, October 12, 1940, 55:5.

16. Johnson to, October 24, 1940, 55:7; to Laurence F. Arnold [IL-25], October 29, 1940, 55:8; Johnson to [telegram], October 29, 1940, 55:8.

17. To Johnson, October 29, 1940, 55:8; Caro, *Years of Lyndon Johnson*, 639–40.

18. Johnson to, November 1, 1940, 55:9; to Arnold, November 1, 1940, 55:9; Robinson to, November 2, 1940, 55:9; to Houston, November 3, 1940, 55:9; to Robinson, November 11, 1940, 55:10.

19. Johnson to [telegram], November 4, 1940, 55:9; Watts, *Black Cabinet*, 322.

20. Johnson to, November 15, 1940, 55:11; McCormack to, November 18, 1940, 55:12; to Johnson, December 3, 1940, 56:6.

21. Parsons to, December 3, 1940, 56:5.

Chapter 16

1. Westbrooks to, March 10, 1938, 37:5.

2. *Chicago Defender*, May 14, 1938, PQHN; Westbrooks to, April 21, 1938, 38:3.

3. Westbrooks to, May 6, 1938, 38:8.

4. Nordin, *New Deal's Black Congressman*, 262–63.

5. To Young, July 1, 1938, 39:5; *Chicago Defender*, December 10, 1938, PQHN; Nordin, *New Deal's Black Congressman*, 264; *Afro-American*, December 3, 1938, PQHN; Barnes, *Journey from Jim Crow*, 21.

6. Miller press release, November 30, 1938, 41:1.

7. *Afro-American*, January 14, 1939, PQHN; Barnett to, November 28, 1938, 40:11; Sledge to, November 29, 1938, 40:11; *Chicago Defender*, December 10, 1938, PQHN.

8. To Davis, December 9, 1938, 41:1; to Westbrooks, March 23, 1939, 43:7; Jackson to, April 14, 1939, 44:2.

9. To Townes, January 13, 1939, 41:10; Townes to All Members of the Negro Insurance Association, January 14, 1939, 42:1.

10. Gerald Horne, *The Rise and Fall of the Associated Negro Press: Claude Barnett's Pan-African News and the Jim Crow Paradox* (Urbana: University of Illinois Press, 2017), 27, citing Barnett to Randy Trice, December 22, 1938, Associated Negro Press Papers, reel 9, no. 215, Part III, Series A.

11. To Hill, October 2, 1940, 55:3; Hill to, October 7, 1940, 55:4. The Mitchell papers contain several dozen separate examples of him attempting to document railroad discrimination. In one, he claimed that a Pennsylvania Railroad conductor had refused to let him go to the lavatory until his ticket had been validated. The employee had been "abrupt and even insulting to me, not knowing that I was a member of Congress." The conduct of the brakeman on the same train had been even worse. When Mitchell complained about the heat in the car, he was told "Now listen, boy—there's nothing I can do"; to W. S. Franklin, Vice President, Pennsylvania Railroad, January 2, 1941, 57:5.

12. Francis Biddle, *In Brief Authority* (Garden City, NY: Doubleday and Co., 1962), 154; McMahon, *Reconsidering Roosevelt*, 105, 144–45.

13. *Philadelphia Ledger*, March 18, 1941, in Francis Biddle Papers, FDRL, container 13; Dominic J. Capeci Jr., "The Lynching of Cleo Wright: Federal Protection of Constitutional Rights during World War II," *Journal of American History* 72, no. 4 (March 1986): 871; Blackmon, *Slavery by Another Name*, 378.

14. Biddle, *In Brief Authority*, 94, 152–53.

15. McMahon, *Reconsidering Roosevelt*, 105.

16. Barnes, *Goodbye to Jim Crow*, 24–26.

17. Nordin, *New Deal's Black Congressman*, 266–67.

18. *ANP* news story, May 27, 1940, 53:1.

19. Nordin, *New Deal's Black Congressman*, 267. For the legal documents, see *In the District Court of the United States for the Northern District of Illinois . . . Arthur W. Mitchell vs. the United States of America. Findings of Fact and Conclusions of Law*, 53:7. When Mitchell moved the case from ICC jurisdiction to the federal courts, the defendant became the government itself.

20. To E. B. Hunter, March 1, 1941, 58:8; to Bishop R. R. Wright, June 13, 1940, 53:3; to Oliver Gray, December 10, 1940, 56:6; to Ulysses. S. Keys, March 11, 1941, 59:1.

21. Talbot to, January 2, 1941, 57:5.

22. To Talbot, January 14, 1941, 57:7.

23. Biddle to Westbrooks; Biddle to Mitchell, March 3, 1941, March 3, 1941, 58:8. The driving force behind the memorandum is disputed. Nordin attributes it to a "courageous decision" taken by Robert H. Jackson, the attorney general; Nordin, *New Deal's Black Congressman* 270 citing *Mitchell v. U.S., Memorandum for the United States.* McMahon attributes it to Biddle, who "had been decidedly more eager than Jackson to promote the work of the C[ivil] R[ights] S[ection]"; McMahon, *Reconsidering Roosevelt*, 161. Biddle thought the decision had been his; Biddle, *In Brief Authority*, 94. Jackson and Biddle must have conferred prior to its release. It is also difficult to believe that anyone would have issued the memorandum without Roosevelt's approval. In any case,

the memorandum created an unusual situation in American legal history: the country's lawyer, the solicitor general, had filed a brief in support of a plaintiff who was suing his client.

24. To Keys, March 11, 1941, 59:1; To John Mitchell, March 7, 1941, 58:9; to Adams, March 8, 1941, 58:9; to Westbrooks, March 11, 1941, 58:3; [Oklahoma City] *Black Dispatch*, March 11, 1941, 59:1.

25. Kennedy, *Freedom from Fear*, 333; Biddle, *In Brief Authority*, 162; Goodall to, July 9, 1941, 61:7. For additional reactions to Mitchell's appearance before the Supreme Court, see 59:2.

26. Associated Press news story, March 14, 1941, 59:2; *New York Times*, March 14, 1941, PQHN; Barnes, *Journey from Jim Crow*, 27–28; *New York Amsterdam Star-News*, March 15, 1937, PQHN; Biddle, *In Brief Authority*, 153.

27. Biddle to, March 13, 1941, 59:1; to Biddle, March 18, 1941, 59:3; to Elliott, March 18, 1941, 59:3.

28. Barnes, *Journey from Jim Crow*, 28; *Montgomery Advertiser* and *Alabama Journal*, March 13, 1941, 59:1.

29. Barnes, *Journey from Jim Crow*, 29–30.

30. *Alabama Journal*, March 15, 1941, 59:2.

31. To Porter, March 20, 1941, 59:4.

32. *New York Amsterdam News*, March 29, 1941, PQHN. J. E. Mitchell objected to this characterization of Mitchell's motives. The NAACP had a very weak record in fighting against Jim Crowism. Wilkins was "sitting back in his New York office criticizing the effort" while the Congressman was fighting for the rights of African Americans everywhere"; *St. Louis Argus*, April 4, 1941, 59:8.

33. Hastie to, April 16, 1941, 60:1; to Hastie, April 16, 1941, 60:1. Reprinted by the *ANP* and *Chicago Defender*, May 3, 1941, PQHN.

34. For the text, see 60:3; Biddle, *In Brief Authority*, 153; Barnes, *Journey from Jim Crow*, 29.

35. Pickens to, April 29, 1941, 60:3; Bethune to [telegram], April 29, 1941, 60:3 Huff to, April 29, 1941, 60:3; Spaulding to, June 10, 1941, 60:5; Alexander to, May 9, 1941, 60:8; Perkins to, December 2, 1941, 63:7. For additional congratulatory letters, see 60:3–60:8.

36. Simpson to, April 28, 1941, 60:3.

37. To Simpson, May 3, 1941, 60:3.

38. *New York Times*, April 29, 1941, PQNH; *Pittsburgh Courier*, April 3, 1941, PQHN.

39. To J. E. Mitchell, September 16, 1941, 62:7; to Biddle, draft of telegram, n.d., 62:6; to Biddle, June 10, 1942, 66:4.

40. *ANP* news story, May 4, 1941, 60:7.

41. *Atlanta Daily World*, May 2, 1941, PQHN; Howard, "The Lone Traveler," *Atlanta Daily World*, May 22, 1941, PQHN.

42. *Afro-American*, May 10, 1941, PQHN; Nordin, *New Deal's Black Congressman*, 276–77.

43. Wilkins to, June 9, 1941, 60:5. Across the note Mitchell scrawled, "I am not interested in anything your biased pen writes," *Crisis* 48, no. 6 (June 1941): 61:6; *Chicago Defender*, May 3, 1941, PQHN.

44. *Pittsburgh Courier*, August 16, 1941, 6, PQHN; Dunn, *Pittsburgh Courier*, November 21, 1942, PQHN.

45. *New York Amsterdam Star News*, February 7, 1942, and May 3, 1941, PQHN.

46. Pickens to, June 22, 1941, 61:5; Ulysses Grant Lee, *The Employment of Negro Troops* (Washington: Office of the Chief of Military History, 1966), 317; A. Russell Buchanan, *Black Americans in World War II* (Santa Barbara, CA: Clio Books, 1977), 77.

47. J. E. Mitchell to, August 19, 1941, 62:5; Mitchell followed this advice on September 18, 1941, titling the entry "My fight before the Interstate Commerce Commission and the Courts of the Country for equal accommodations for Negro passengers traveling interstate"; See *Congressional Record*, September 18, 1941, vol. 87, no. 168, pp. 4570–73 found in 62:8; Dunjee to, October 1, 1941, 62:9.

48. To Dunjee, March 13, 1942, 65:4; *Pittsburgh Courier*, December 6, 1941, PQHN; to Anderson January 20, 1942,64:5; to Adair, May 10, 1942.

49. Westbrooks to, October 14, 1941, 62:10; Dunjee to, March 10, 1942, 65:4; Hicks to, September 3, 1942, 67:2; to Hicks, October 1, 1942; 67:3.

50. *New York Amsterdam News*, September 11, 1943, PQHN.

51. Bay, *Traveling Black*, 240, citing Roy Wilkins, "The Negro Wants Full Equality," in Rayford W. Logan, ed., *What the Negro Wants* (Chapel Hill: University of North Carolina Press, 1944), 127.

52. Barnes, *Journey from Jim Crow*, 30, 32, 184; Klarman, *Jim Crow to Civil Rights*, 264–65.

53. Bay, *Traveling Black*, 104.

54. Benjamin E. Mays, *Born to Rebel: An Autobiography* (Athens: University of Georgia Press, 1971), 97. For a discussion of the legal links between *Mitchell v. United States* and *Brown v. School Board*, see Bay, *Traveling Black*, 247–65.

55. Bay, *Traveling Black*, 295, citing Robert Wallace, "Racial Trouble Shooter: An Intimate Report on Burke Marshall, Bobby Kennedy's Man in the Middle," *Life*, August 9, 1963, 78. For the historical interpretation of the importance of *Mitchell v. United States*, see Charles S. Johnson, *Patterns of Negro Separation* (New York: Harper and Brothers, 1943), 321, Loren Miller, *The Petitioners: The Story of the Supreme Court of the United States and the Negro* (New York: Pantheon, 1966), 366; Sitkoff, *New Deal for Blacks*, 236; Klarman, *Jim Crow to Civil Rights*, 281; William G. Ross, *The Chief Justiceship of Charles Evans Hughes, 1930–41* (Columbia: University of South Carolina Press, 2007, 216–17); and Paul Finkelman, "Supreme Court," in Paul Finkelman (ed.), E.E.A. H, 4: 417.

Chapter 17

1. To Ryan, May 27, 1937, 31:2.

2. To Goldfus, December 16, 1937, 34:7; to Joseph H. Levy, May 12, 1938, 38:9.

3. To Feinglass, October 23, 1937, 33:6.

4. To Roosevelt (telegram), October 12, 1938, 40:3.

5. To Dr. T. H. Allen, May 4, 1939, 44:9.

6. To Kammerling, March 23, 1939, 43:7.

7. To Ira Latimer, October 13, 1939, 40:3; to Dies, June 24, 1938, 39:4.

8. To Earl B. Dickerson, February 4, 1939, 42:5; to H. Jacobs, February 27, 1939, 43:1; to Pool, January 12, 1939, 41:10.

9. To Lapp, February 8, 1941, 58:4; *Chicago Tribune*, January 27, 1940, PQHN; Weinberger to, January 24, 1940, 49:7; to Weinberger, January 26, 1940, 49:7.

10. Galloway to, April 21, 1935, 9:2; Holman to Galloway, April 24, 1935, 9:3.

11. Delmont, *Half American*, 25–26; Robert J. Jakeman, *The Divided Sky: Establishing Segregated Flight Training at Tuskegee, Alabama, 1934–1942* (Tuscaloosa: University of Alabama Press, 1992), 87, 89–90; J. E. Mitchell to, January 5, 1939, 41:8.

12. Patterson to, January 13, 1939, 41:10; to Ira Bryant, Editor, *Nashville Defender*, January 19, 1939, 42:2; to Murphy, January 22, 1939, 42:2. For the evolution of the idea to the reality of the Tuskegee Airmen, see Jakeman, *Divided Skies*, passim. The account does not mention Mitchell.

13. *Washington* [NC] *Morning Star*, April 21, 1939, 44:4; to Lillian Pringle, June 28, 1939, 46:3; to Karl Edwin Seyforth, September 21, 1939, 47:3; to F. E. Jones, January 26, 1940, 49:7.

14. "The loyalty of the Negro to America Is Pledged," May 1, 1940, 52:8. Pickens, who had evolved from being a fierce opponent of Mitchell to being a strong supporter, thought the attack on the "foolish" resolution of the National Negro Congress was "entirely justified" and "one of the best things you have done in Congress"; Pickens to, May 9, 1940, 52:9.

15. To Mrs. Stanley McCormick, May 2, 1940, 52:8; to A. D. White, June 7, 1940, 53:2.

16. Siebel to, December 7, 1940, 56:6; to Siebel, December 11, 1940, 56:6; Eshleman to March 16, 1941; to Eshleman, March 18, 1941, 59:3; Fischer to, September 22, 1941, 62:8; to Fischer, September 27, 1941, 62:9.

17. Primus to, June 19, 1940, 53:5; to Primus, July 1, 1940, 53:8.

18. L. L. Lewis to, August 20, 1940, 54:7; to Charles B. Smith, January 14, 1941, 57:7.

19. Arnette to, December 10, 1940, 56:6; to Arnette, December 11, 1940, 56:6.

20. Address to Howard University students, June 13, 1941, 60:5.

21. Clifford to, March 14, 1941, 59:2.

22. To Clifford, March 18, 1941, 59:3.

23. To Richard Koppe, May 17, 1941, 61:2.

24. *New York Amsterdam News*, March 28, 1941, PQHN; Memo, June 4, 1941, FDRL, PPF 1248.

25. Watts, *Black Cabinet*, 342; Merl Elwyn Reed, *Seed Time for the Modern Civil Rights Movement: The President's Committee on Fair Employment Practices, 1941–46* (Baton Rouge: Louisiana State University Press, 1991), 15. For the March on Washington, see also Herbert Garfinkle, *When Negroes March: The March on Washington Movement and the Organizational Politics of FEPC* (Glencoe, IL: Free Press, 1959); Watts, *Black Cabinet*, 328–32; and Delmont, *Half American*, 55–59.

26. *Philadelphia Independent*, August 10, 1941, 62:3; Radio address, *Congressional Record*, July 24, 1941, 62:1, "Extension of Remarks," 63:6. Years later, despite the shortcomings of the order, especially the lack of enforcement powers for the FEPC (Watts, *Black Cabinet*, 342–47; Delmont, *Half American*, 60, 63, 135–37), Mitchell insisted that his Industrial Commission legislation was the bill "from which F.E.P.C. sprang." It had been "widely endorsed, but we could never get it out of committee"; to Brooks Hays, February 15, 1950, 70:6.

27. Address to the Negro Veterans of World War I, American Legion, Durham, NC, November 11, 1941, 63:3.

28. Melvyn Dubofsky and Warren Van Tine, *John L. Lewis: A Biography* (New York: Quadrangle/*New York Times* Book Co., 1977), 400–404; *Washington Evening Star*, November 20, 1941, 65:3; "Extension of Remarks," *Congressional Record*, November 28, 1941, 63:6.

29. Townsend to, November 21, 1941, 63:5; Milgram to, November 27, 1941, 63:6; to Milgram, November 27, 1941, 63:6.

30. Drew Pearson and Robert S. Allen, *Washington Merry-Go-Round*, December 18, 1941, 64:1; 63:8.

31. To Jones, May 13 and 20, 1942, 66:3.

32. Stark to, April 12, 1942, 65:7; to Gadsden Jr., January 29, 1942, 64:7. For additional applications and Mitchell's reaction to them, see boxes 65 and 66.

33. *Washington Afro-American*, May 30, 1942, 66:3; Leonard Draper, Bureau of Naval Personnel to, July 15, 1942, 66:9, and July 16, 1942, 66:10.

34. Schneller Jr., *Breaking the Color Barrier*, 162–63; to Major Gen. Francis B. Wilby, Superintendent, May 27, 1942, 66:3; Wilby to, June 4, 1942, 66:4.

35. To Roosevelt, January 10, 1942, 64:4; to Granger, January 17, 1942, 64:5.

36. To White, January 17, 1942, 64:5; White to, January 20, 1942, 64:5; to White, January 21, 1942, 64:6.

37. FDRL, PPF, 2289; to Roosevelt, February 6, 1942, 64:8; White to, February 14, 1942, 64:9; Delmont, *Half American*, 98–99. Unfortunately, the incident represented only an opening skirmish in the long struggle over the housing in Detroit (see FDRL, PPF, 2289), an issue that contributed to the far more violent race riot of June 1943; Alfred L. McClung and Norman D. Humphrey, *Race Riot* (New York: Dryden Press, 1943), 26, 28, 81; Watts, *Black Cabinet*, 361–65.

38. To Marguerite Johnson, August 25, 1941, 62:6; to Anna Alston, November 4, 1941, 63:2.

39. To Vinson, January 22, 1942, 64:6; Vinson to, February 4, 1942, 64:8; Knox to Vinson, February 3, 1942, 64:7.

40. Truman K. Gibson with Steve Huntley, *Knocking Down Barriers: My Fight for Black America* (Evanston, IL: Northwestern University Press, 2005), 96.

41. *Black Dispatch*, February 28, 1942, 65:2; to Stimson, February 14, 1942, 64:9; Gibson to Barnett, February 27, 1942, BP, 346:4.

42. J. E. Mitchell to, February 27, 1942, 65:2; Stimson to, February 23, 1942, 65:1; to J. E. Mitchell, March 2, 1942, 65:2.

43. To Knox, July 22, 1942, 66:10; Knox to, July 29, 1942, 66:11; Roosevelt to, August 4, 1942, 67:1.

44. *Congressional Record*, October 13, 1942, 67:4. Mitchell's eloquence led Dr. Walter A. Battle to write, "Your speech in Congress . . . will live forever in the history of this land. If it is your farewell address to Congress, it makes, without a doubt, a happy climax to an enviable record. The whole nation is richer for your having been sent to Washington"; Battle to, November 3, 1942, 67:6.

45. *Congressional Record*, December 14, 1942, 67:9.

Conclusion

1. Gates, *Stony the Road*, 37.

2. The outlines are found in 57:3.

3. To Willy Craye, July 22, 1938, 39:7; to Charles Augustus, January 6, 1942, 64:4; to same, January 20, 1942, 64:5.

4. 72:2. The final boxes of the Mitchell papers are unsorted. They can only be cited by box and folder number.

5. To L. D. Powell, January 23, 1940, 49:6; *Afro-American*, October 14, 1944, PQHN.

6. Wilkerson, *Warmth of Other Suns*, 386, 398.

7. Ellison, *Invisible Man*, 255.

8. Benjamin E. Mays, *Born to Rebel: An Autobiography* (Athens: University of Georgia Press, 1971), 97. For a discussion of the legal links between *Mitchell v. United* States and *Brown v. School Board*, see Bay, *Traveling Black*, 247–65.

9. "Ex-Solon Still Active 20 years after Retirement," *Ebony* 18, no. 10 (August 1963): 40–46.

10. 72:6.

11. Founder's Day speech at Tuskegee, 43:9.

12. *Congressional Record*, October 13, 1942.

Bibliography

Chicago History Museum, Chicago Illinois

Arthur W. Mitchell Papers, 1898–1968, bulk 1934–1942, 30 linear feet, 3 oversize folders, 1 microfilm reel. Descriptive inventory compiled by Diane Asseln, August 24, 1995.

Arthur W. Mitchell Photograph Collection (1980.0144 PPL)

Arthur W. Mitchell Sound Recordings

Gilbert, William E. Interview with Dennis Nordin. Geiger, AL, April 13, 1971.

Little, Fanoy. Interview with Dennis Nordin. Panola, AL, April 12, 1971.

Pinson, John. Interview with Dennis Nordin. Geiger, AL, April 13, 1971.

Claude A. Barnett Papers, 1918–1967, bulk 1928–1963, 414 boxes, 180 linear feet.

Series 1, Associated Negro Press 1920–1964, subseries 1: New Releases

Boxes 14–35: ANP News Releases, August 1934–March 1943

Series 4. Colleges and Universities. Subseries 2. Topical files on Black colleges and universities

Box 239: Tuskegee (Ala.) Institute Correspondence, 1934–1941

Series 10. Politics and Law. Subseries 3: Black Participants in Government

Box 346: Illinois politics, government, and Race Relations

Box 349, folder 2: Dawson, Congressman William

Box 349, folder 3: De Priest, Congressman Oscar

Box 349, folder 5: Mitchell, Congressman Arthur

Series 11. Race Relations.

Box 377, folders 1–4 NAACP: Pickens, William, Correspondence, 1936–1954

Johnston Memorial Library, Virginia State University, Petersburg, VA

The Arthur W. Mitchell Papers 1968–15, Special Collections and Archives. Processed by Lucious Edwards Jr.

Chicago Public Library. Harold Washington Library Center. Municipal Reference Collection.

Aperture Cards 279–90: Democratic Primary, April 10, 1934

Aperture Cards 01013–01132: General Election, First Congressional District, November 6, 1934

CX, E38w, vault: Ward Map, City of Chicago, 1931

Chicago Public Library. Carter G. Woodson Regional Library. Vivian G. Harsh Research Collection of Afro-American History and Literature

Abbott-Sangstake Family Papers

Box 11, folders 1–11: Chicago Defender
Box 78, folder 64: Correspondence, Mitchell, Arthur W.
Box 110, folder 6: Subject Files, 1940 election

Negroes in Illinois Writers Project

Box 12, folder 15: Notes on Tuskegee Institute and Tuskegee System
Box 25, folder 9: Statistical Analyses and narrative accounts of businesses in Chicago's South Side Black community, 1859–1938
Box 38, file 1: The National Association for the Advancement of Colored People
Boxes 41–42: Chicago Newspapers

Special Collections Research Center at the University of Chicago Library

Charles E. Merriam Papers

Subseries 5 and 12: The Administration of Mayor Kelly

Robert Merriam Papers

Box 98: Reports on Democratic Ward Committeemen, 1936

Thomas Vernor Smith Papers

Box 6, File 6: Mitchell, Arthur, 1934–38

Hoole Special Collections Department, Libraries of the University of Alabama, Tuscaloosa, Alabama

Papers of John McDuffie

Alabama Department of Archives and History, Montgomery, Alabama

Alabama Writers Project Collection: "Folklore and Folkways"

Newspapers:

Choctaw Advocate (1915–1922)
Gainesville Times (1910–1911)
Geiger Times (1906–1918)
Greensboro Watchman (1903–1943)
Our Southern Home (1903–1923)
Sumter Enterprise (1907–1911)
Sumter Sun (1905–1913)

Julia Tutwiler Library, Alabama Room, University of West Alabama, Livingston, Alabama

Arrington Collection

SF2 D2: Alabama, Tennessee, and Northern Railroad
SF2 D3, folder 9: Geiger
SF2 D3, folder 13: Livingston
SF2 D3, folder 18: Panola

Materials Concerning Sumter County

SF8 D1, folder 1: Newspaper Clippings, Rural Development
SF8 D1, folder 51: Arthur W. Mitchell, news clippings
SF8 D1, folder 54: John H. Pinson
SF8 D4: Maps

Franklin D. Roosevelt Library, Hyde Park, New York

Papers as Assistant Secretary of the Navy

Official file (OF)—files

25: War Department, containers 17–25: West Point
93: Colored Matters (Negroes), 1935–1943
253: Early, Stephen T.
259: McIntyre, Marvin H.
700: Palestine
1871: Democratic National Convention
1938: Brown, Edgar G.
2262: Democratic National Congressional Committee
2311: Peonage
2567: Johnson Jr., James L.
4245g: Committee on Fair Employment Practices

President's Personal File (PPF)—file

30: Colored Matters
270: Cummings, Homer S.
309: Farley, James A.
643: McDuffie, John
2099: Hurja, Emil E.
2289: Mitchell, Arthur W.
2670: Biddle, Francis
3166: Kelly, Edward J.

Papers of:

Francis Biddle

Steven Early, Diary of
Emil Hurja
Ross T. McIntire

Books, Theses, and Articles

Abbott, Edith. *The Tenements of Chicago.* Chicago: University of Chicago Press, 1936.

Abraham, Henry J. *Justices, Senators, and Presidents: A History of the U. S. Supreme Court Appointments from Washington to Clinton.* Lanham, MD: Rowman and Littlefield, 1999.

Abrams, Stacey. *Our Time Is Now.* New York: Henry Holt, 2020.

Aiello, Thomas. "Editing a Paper in Hell: Davis Lee and the Exigencies of Small time Black Journalism." *American Journalism* 33, no. 2 (Spring 2016): 144–68.

———. *The Grapevine of the South: The Scott Newspaper Syndicate in the Generation before the Civil Rights Movement.* Athens: University of Georgia Press, 2018.

Alabama. *The WPA Guide to 1930's Alabama, with an Introduction by Harvey H. Jackson.* Tuscaloosa: University of Alabama Press, 2000.

Alexander, Herbert B. "The Political Progress of the Northern Negro." *Negro History Bulletin* 4 (May 1941): 185–86.

Alexander, J. Trent. "The Great Migration in Comparative Perspective: Interpreting the Urban Origins of Southern Black Migrants to Depression-Era Pittsburgh." *Social Science History* (Fall 1968): 358–60.

Alexander, Raymond Pace. "The Upgrading of the Negro's Status by Supreme Court Decisions." *Journal of Negro History* 30, no. 2 (April 1945): 117–49.

Allen, Howard W., and Vincent A. Lacey, eds. *Illinois Elections, 1818–1990: Candidates and County Returns for President, Governor, Senate, and House of Representatives.* Carbondale: Southern Illinois Press, 1992.

Allen, Robert Sharon. *Washington Merry-Go-Round.* New York: Horace Liveright, 1931.

Allswang, John M. *Bosses, Machines, and Urban Voters.* Baltimore: Johns Hopkins University Press, 1986.

———. "The Negro Voter and the Democratic Consensus: A Case Study, 1918–1936." *Journal of the Illinois State Historical Society* 60, no. 2 (Summer 1967): 145–75.

Alsop, Joseph. *The 168 Days.* New York: Capo, 1973, ca. 1938.

Andersen, Kristi, *The Creation of a Democratic Majority.* Chicago: University of Chicago Press, 1979.

Anderson, Eric, and Alfred A. Moss, Jr. *Dangerous Donations: Northern Philanthropy and Southern Black Education, 1902–1930.* Columbia: University of Missouri Press, 1998.

Avery, Sheldon. *Up from Washington: William Pickens and the Negro Struggle for Equality.* Newark: University of Delaware Press, 1989.

Badger, Anthony J. *New Deal/New South: An Anthony J. Badger Reader.* Fayetteville: University of Arkansas Press, 2007.

Baker, Ray Stannard. *Following the Color Line: American Negro Citizenship in the Progressive Era.* New York: Harper and Row, 1964, ca. 1908.

Baldwin, Davarian L. *Chicago's New Negro Modernity, the Great Migration, and Black Urban Life.* Chapel Hill: University of North Carolina Press, 2007.

Ball, Howard. *Hugo L. Black: Cold Steel Warrior.* New York: Oxford University Press, 1996.

Bardolph, Richard. *The Negro Vanguard.* New York: Rinehart, 1959.

Barnes, Catherine A. *Journey from Jim Crow: The Desegregation of Southern Transit.* New York: Columbia University Press, 1983.

Barone, Michael. *Our Country: The Shaping of America from Roosevelt to Reagan.* New York: Free Press, 1990.

Bates, Beth Tomkins. "A New Crowd Challenges the Agenda of the Old Guard in the NAACP, 1933–41." *American Historical Review* 102, no. 2 (April 1997): 340–77.

Bay, Mia. *Traveling Black: A Story of Race and Resistance.* Cambridge, MA: Belknap Press of Harvard University Press, 2021.

Belles, A. Gilbert. "The Black Press in Illinois." *Journal of the Illinois State Historical Society* 68, no. 4 (September 1975): 344–52.

Best, Wallace D. "The Chicago Defender and the Realignment of Black Chicago." *Chicago History* 24, no. 3 (Fall 1995): 4–21.

Bethune, Mary McLeod. "My Secret Talks with FDR" in *The Negro in Depression and War: Prelude to Revolution,* ed. Bernard Sternsher, 53–65. Chicago: Quadrangle Books, 1969.

Biddle, Francis. *A Casual Past.* Garden City, NY: Doubleday, 1961.

———. *In Brief Authority.* Garden City, NY: Doubleday, 1962.

Biles, Roger W. *Big City Boss in Depression and War: Mayor Edward J. Kelly of Chicago.* DeKalb: Northern Illinois University Press, 1984.

Black, Hugo, Jr. *My Father, a Remembrance.* New York: Random House, 1975.

Blackmon, Douglas A. *Slavery by Another Name: The Re-enslavement of Black People in America from the Civil War to World War II.* New York: Anchor, 2009.

Blow, Charles. *The Devil You Know: A Black Power Manifesto.* New York: Harper Perennial, 2021.

Bond, Horace Mann. *Negro Education in Alabama: A Study in Cotton and Steel.* New York: Atheneum, 1969, ca. 1939.

Borucki, Wesley. "Robert Russa Moton." In *Encyclopedia of African American History, 1896 to the Present [EAAH],* 5 vols, ed. Paul, 3:390–91. New York: Oxford University Press, 2009.

Bosworth, Karl A. *Black Belt County: Rural Government in the Cotton Country of Alabama.* Tuscaloosa: Bureau of Public Administration, University of Alabama, 1941.

Bracey, Christopher. *Saviors or Sellouts: The Promise and Perils of Black Conservatism from Booker T. Washington to Condoleezza Rice.* Boston: Beacon Press, 2008.

Branham, Charles R. "The Transformation of Black Political Leadership in Chicago, 1864–1942." PhD diss., University of Chicago, 1981.

Brooks, Maxwell R. *The Negro Press Re-examined: Political Content of Leading Negro Newspapers.* Boston: Christopher, 1959.

Brown, Earl. "How the Negro Voted in the Presidential Election." In *Presidential Elections,* ed. Schlesinger, 7:2909–13.

Brown, James D. *The Education of Blacks in the South, 1860–1935*. Chapel Hill: University of North Carolina Press, 1988.

Brundage, W. Fitzhugh, ed. *Booker T. Washington and Black Progress: Up from Slavery 100 Years Later.* Gainesville: University Press of Florida, 2003.

———. "Reconsidering Booker T. Washington and *Up from Slavery*." In *Washington and Progress*, ed. Brundage, 1–18.

Bukowski, Douglas. *Big Bill Thompson, Chicago, and the Politics of Image*. Urbana: University of Illinois Press, 1998.

Bullard, Thomas Robert. "From Businessman to Congressman: The Career of Martin B. Madden." PhD diss., University of Chicago, 1973.

Bunche, Ralph. *The Political Status of the Negro in the Age of FDR*. Chicago: University of Chicago Press, 1973.

Bunie, Andrew. *The Negro in Virginia Politics, 1902–1965*. Charlottesville: University Press of Virginia, 1967.

———. *Robert L. Vann of the Pittsburgh Courier: Politics and Black Journalism*. Pittsburgh: University of Pittsburgh Press, 1974.

Burke, Bob. "Roscoe Dunjee." In *AANB*, ed. Gates and Higginbotham, 4:106–7.

Burroughs, Todd Stephen. "Associated Negro Press." In *EAAH*, ed. Finkelman, 1:98–99.

Burrows, Edwin G., and Mike Wallace. *Gotham: A History of New York City to 1898*. New York: Oxford University Press, 1999.

Calista, Donald J. "Booker T. Washington: Another Look." *Journal of Negro History* 49, no. 4 (October 1964): 240–55.

Capeci, Dominic J., Jr. "The Lynching of Cleo Wright. Federal Protection of Constitutional Rights during World War II." *Journal of American History* 72, no. 4 (March 1986): 85–87.

———. *Race Relations in Wartime Detroit: The Sojourner Truth Housing Controversy of 1942*. Philadelphia: Temple University Press, 1984.

Carney, Thomas E. "Carter G. Woodson." In *EAAH*, ed. Finkelman, 5:168–70.

Caro, Robert A. *The Years of Lyndon Johnson: The Path to Power*. New York: Alfred A. Knopf, 1982.

Carter, Dan T. *Scottsboro: A Tragedy of the American South*. Baton Rouge: Louisiana State University Press, 1969.

Catledge, Turner. *My Life and the Times*. New York: Harper and Row, 1971.

Chepsiuk, Ron. *Black Gangsters of Chicago*. Fort Lee, NJ: Barricade, 2007.

Chicago City Council. Municipal Voters League. *Twenty-second Annual Preliminary Report of the Municipal Voter's League*. Chicago: Hildmann, 1917.

Christopher, Maurine. *Black Americans in Congress*. New York: T. Y. Crowell, 1976.

Citizen's Committee on Public Information. *Out of the Red, into the Black: The Truth about Chicago's Municipal Government; A Frank Statement Reviewing the Years 1933 to 1938*. Chicago: n.p., 1938.

Clark, Jeanne Nienaber. *Roosevelt's Warrior: Harold L. Ickes and the New Deal*. Baltimore, MD: Johns Hopkins University Press, 1996.

Clay, William L. *Just Permanent Interests: Black Americans in Congress, 1870–1991*. New York: Amistad, 1992.

Clayton, Edward T. *The Negro Politician: His Success and Failure*. Chicago: Johnson, 1964.

Cohen, Adam, and Elizabeth Taylor. *American Pharaoh: Mayor Richard J. Daley: His Battle for Chicago and the Nation.* Boston: Little, Brown, 2000.

Cohen, William. *At Freedom's Edge: Black Mobility and the Southern White Quest for Racial Control.* Baton Rouge: Louisiana State University Press, 1991.

———. "Negro Involuntary Servitude in the South, 1865–1940: A Preliminary Analysis." *Journal of Southern History* 42, no. 1 (February 1976): 31–60.

Collins, Ernest M. "Cincinnati Negroes and Presidential Politics." In *Negroes in Depression,* ed. Sternsher, 258–63.

Coulibaly, Sylvie. "Kelly Miller." In *EAAH,* ed. Finkelman, 3:324–25.

The Crisis: A Record of the Darker Races. Vols. 41–50 (1934–1943).

Dagbovie, Pero Gaglo. *Carter G. Woodson in Washington, D.C.: The Father of Black History.* Charleston, SC: History Press, 2014.

Dalfiume, Richard M. *Desegregation of the United States Armed Forces: Fighting on Two Fronts, 1939–53.* Columbia: University of Missouri Press, 1969.

Davis, Ralph Nelson. "The Negro Newspaper in Chicago." Master's thesis, University of Chicago, 1939.

Delmont, Matthew W. *Half American: The Epic Story of African Americans Fighting World War II at Home and Abroad.* New York: Viking, 2022.

Democratic National Campaign Committee. "Roosevelt the Humanitarian." *Crisis* 43, no. 10 (October 1936): 298–99.

Diamond, Richard A., ed. *Congressional Quarterly's Guide to U.S. Elections.* Washington, DC: Congressional Quarterly, 1976.

Dollard, John. *Caste and Class in a Southern Town.* New Haven: Pub. For the Institute of Human Relations by Yale University Press, 1937.

Donaghy, Daniel. "Alain Locke." In *EAAH,* ed. *Finkelman,* 3:199–201.

Drake, St. Clair, and Horace R. Cayton. *Black Metropolis: A Study of Negro Life in a Northern City.* Chicago: University of Chicago Press, 1993, ca. 1945.

Dray, Philip. *At the Hands of Persons Unknown: The Lynching of Black America.* New York: Random House, 2002.

Dubovsky, Melvyn, and Warren Van Tine. *John L. Lewis: A Biography.* New York: Quadrangle/New York Times, 1977.

Duis, Perry R. "Arthur W. Mitchell, New Deal Negro in Congress." Master's thesis, University of Chicago, 1966.

Dyson, Walter. *Howard University, the Capstone of Negro Education: A History; 1867–1940.* Washington, DC: Graduate school, Howard University, 1941.

Edwards, William James. *Twenty-five Years in the Black Belt.* Boston: Cornhill, 1918.

Ellison, Ralph. *Invisible Man.* New York: Vintage International, 1995.

Epstein, Abraham. *The Negro Migrant in Pittsburgh.* New York: Arno, 1969.

Evans, Linda J. "Claude A. Barnett and the Associated Negro Press." *Chicago History* 12 (Spring 1983): 44–56.

"Ex-Solon Still Active 20 Years after Retirement." *Ebony* 18, no. 10 (August 1963): 40–46.

Farley, James A. *Behind the Ballots: The Personal History of a Politician.* Westport, CT: Greenwood, 1972.

———. *Jim Farley's Story: The Roosevelt Years.* New York: Whittlesey House, 1948.

Farrar, Hayward. *The Baltimore Afro-American, 1892–1950.* Westport, CT: Greenwood, 1998.

———. "Black Press." In *EAAH,* ed. Finkelman, 1:231–41.

Fine, Stanley. *Frank Murphy,* 3 vols. Ann Arbor: University of Michigan Press, 1975–1984.

Finkelman, Paul, ed. *Encyclopedia of African American History, 1896 to the Present [EAAH],* 5 vols. New York: Oxford University Press, 2009.

———. "Supreme Court." In *EAAH,* ed. Finkelman, 4:407–25.

Foner, Eric. *Reconstruction: America's Unfinished Revolution: 1863–1877,* revised edition. New York: Harper Perennial, 2014.

Foner, Jack D. *Black Bourgeoisie: The Rise of a New Middle Class in the United States.* London: Collier-Macmillan, 1957.

———. *Blacks and the Military in American History: A New Perspective.* Washington, DC: Praeger, 1974.

Freidel, Frank. *F.D.R. and the South.* Baton Rouge: Louisiana State University Press, 1965.

Fremon, David K. *Chicago Politics, Ward by Ward.* Bloomington: Indiana University Press, 1988.

[n.a.] "From Plantation to Politics." *Tuskegee Messenger* 10, no. 12 (December 1934): 1, 8.

Garcia, George F. "Black Dissatisfaction from the Republican Party . . ." *Annals of Iowa* 45 (Winter 1980): 462–77.

Garfinkle, Herbert. *When Negroes March: The March on Washington Movement and the Organizational Politics for FEPC.* Glencoe, IL: Free Press, 1959.

Garland, Phyl. "Journalism." In *Black Experience,* ed. Palmer, 3:1203–20.

Garraty, John A., and Mark C. Carnes, gen. eds. *American National Biography [ANB],* 24 vols. New York: Oxford University Press, 1999.

Gates, Henry Lewis, Jr. *The Black Church: This Is Our Story, This Is Our Song.* New York: Penguin, 2021.

———. *Stony the Road: Reconstruction, White Supremacy, and the Rise of Jim Crow.* New York: Penguin, 2019.

Gates, Henry Lewis, Jr., and Evelyn Brook Higginbotham, eds. *African-American National Biography [AANB],* 8 vols. Oxford: Oxford University Press, 2008.

Gavins, Raymond. *The Perils and Prospects of Southern Black Leadership: Gordon Blaine Hancock, 1884–1970.* Durham, NC: Duke University Press, 1977.

Gay, Ann Harwell. *Choctaw Names and Notes: Alabama's Choctaw County.* Meridian, MS: Brown, 1993.

Gibson, Truman K., with Steve Huntley. *Knocking Down Barriers: My Fight for Black America.* Evanston, IL: Northwestern University Press, 2005.

Goggin, Jacqueline. *Carter G. Woodson: A Life in Black History.* Baton Rouge: Louisiana State University Press, 1993.

Going, Allen J. *Bourbon Democracy in Alabama, 1874–1890.* Tuscaloosa: University of Alabama Press, 1951.

Gordon, Rita W. "The Change in the Political Alignment of Chicago's Negroes during the New Deal." *Journal of American History* 56, no. 3 (December 1969): 584–603.

Gosnell, Harold F. *Machine Politics: Chicago Model.* Chicago: University of Chicago Press, 1937.

———. *Negro Politicians: The Rise of Negro Politics in Chicago.* Chicago: University of Chicago Press, 1967, ca. 1935.

Gottfried, Alex. *Boss Cermak of Chicago: A Study in Political Leadership.* Seattle: University of Washington Press, 1962.

Green, Adam. *Selling the Race: Culture, Community, and Black Chicago.* Chicago: University of Chicago Press, 2007.

Green, Constance McLaughlin. *The Secret City; A History of Race Relations in the Nation's Capital.* Princeton, NJ: Princeton University Press, 1967.

———. *Washington: Capital City, 1879–1950,* 2 vols. Princeton, NJ: Princeton University Press, 1962–63.

Greene, Debra Foster. "Joseph E. Mitchell." In *AANB,* ed. Gates and Higginbotham, 5:632–33.

Gregory, Winifred, ed. *American Newspapers, 1821–1936: A Union List of Files Available in the United States and Canada.* New York: H. W. Wilson, 1937.

Grimshaw, William J. *Bitter Fruit: Black Politics and the Chicago Machine, 1931–1991.* Chicago: University of Chicago Press, 1992.

Grossman, James R. *Land of Hope: Chicago, Black Southerners and the Great Migration.* Chicago: University of Chicago Press, 1989.

Grossman, James R., and Anne Durkin Keating, Janice I. Rieff, eds. *The Encyclopedia of Chicago.* Chicago: University of Chicago Press, 2004.

Haller, Mark H. "Policy Gambling, Entertainment, and the Emergence of Black Politics: Chicago from 1900 to 1940." *Journal of Social History* 24, no. 4 (Summer 1991): 719–39.

Hamilton, Virginia van der Veer. *Hugo Black: The Alabama Years.* Baton Rouge: Louisiana State University Press, 1972.

———. "Hugo Black: The Road to the Court." *Southwestern University Law Review* 9, no. 4 (1977): 859–88.

Harlan, Louis R. *Booker T. Washington: The Making of a Black leader, 1856–1901.* New York: Oxford University Press, 1972.

———. *Booker T. Washington: The Wizard of Tuskegee, 1901–1915.* New York: Oxford University Press, 1983.

Hayes, Laurence J. W. *The Negro Federal Government Worker: A Study of His Classification Status in the District of Columbia, 1883–1938; Howard University Studies in the Social Sciences,* vol. 3, no. 1. Washington, DC: Howard University, 1941.

Hayes, William Edward. *Iron Road to Empire: The History of the Progress and Achievement of the Rock Island Lines.* New York: Simmons-Boardman, 1953.

Heard, Alexander. *The Costs of Democracy.* Chapel Hill: University of North Carolina Press, 1960.

Henderson, Richard B. *Maury Maverick: A Political Biography.* Austin: University of Texas Press, 1970.

Higgs, Robert. "The Boll Weevil, the Cotton Economy, and Black Migration, 1910–1930." *Agricultural History* 50, no. 2 (April 1976): 335–50.

"Historical notes" [Mitchell obituary]. *Journal of Negro History* 53, no. 3 (July 1968): 281–82.

Hochschild, Adam. *American Midnight: The Great War, a Violent Peace, and Democracy's Forgotten Crisis*. New York: Mariner, 2022.

Hogan, Lawrence D. *A Black National News Service: The Associated Negro Press and Claude Barnett, 1919–1945*. Rutherford, NJ: Fairleigh Dickinson University Press, 1984.

Holli, Melvin G. [Review of *The New Deal's Black Congressman*]. *Michigan Historical Review* 23, no. 2 (1997): 220–23.

———. *The Wizard of Washington. Emil Hurja, Franklin Roosevelt, and the Birth of Public Opinion Polling*. New York: Palgrave, 2002.

Holmes, William F. "Vardaman, James Kimble." In *ANB*, ed. Garraty and Carnes, 22:265–67.

Horne, Gerald. *The Rise and Fall of the Associated Negro Press: Claude Barnett's Pan-African News and the Jim Crow Paradox*. Urbana: University of Illinois Press, 2017.

House of Representatives. Office of History and Preservation, Office of the Clerk, US House of Representatives. *Black Americans in Congress, 1870–2007*. Washington: US Government Printing Office, 2008.

Houston, Charles H., and James L. Conyers Jr., ed. *Charles H. Houston: An Interdisciplinary Study of Civil Rights Leadership*. Lanham, MD: Lexington, 2012.

Huggins, Nathan I, Martin Kilson, and Daniel M. Fox, eds. *Key Issues in the Afro-American Experience*, 2 vols. New York: Harcourt, Brace, Jovanovich, 1971.

Ickes, Harold L. *America's House of Lords*. New York: Harcourt, Brace, and Company, 1939.

———. *The Secret Diary of Harold L. Ickes*, 3 vols. New York: Simon and Schuster, 1953–54.

Illinois, State of. *Blue Book of the State of Illinois*. Springfield: Office of the Secretary of State. various editions, 1909–1945.

———. *Emergency Relief Commission, Biennial Report, 1934–36*. Chicago: n.p., 1936.

Jakeman, Robert J. *The Divided Sky: Establishing Segregated Flight Training at Tuskegee, Alabama, 1934–1942*. Tuscaloosa: University of Alabama Press, 1992.

James, Felix. "The Tuskegee Institute Moveable School, 1906–1923." *Agricultural History* 45, no. 3 (July 1971): 201–9.

James, Rawn, Jr. *Root and Branch: Charles Hamilton Houston, Thurgood Marshall, and the Struggle to End Segregation*. New York: Bloomsbury Press, 2010.

Janega, James. "Archie Motley, 67." *Chicago Tribune*, November 13, 2002.

Janken, Kenneth Robert. *White: The Biography of Walter White, Mr. NAACP*. New York: New Press, 2001.

Johnson, Haynes. *Dusk at the Mountain: The Negro, the Nation, and the Capital—A Reporter's Problems and Progress*. New York: Doubleday, 1963.

Jones, Allen W. "The Role of Tuskegee Institute in the Education of Black Farmers." *Journal of Negro History* 60, no. 2 (April 1975): 252–67.

Jones, Glen Delon. "The Origins of the Alliance between the New Deal and the Chicago Machine." *Journal of the Illinois State Historical Society* 67, no. 3 (June 1974): 253–74.

Keiser, Richard A. *Subordination or Empowerment? African-American Leadership and the Struggle for Urban Political Power*. New York: Oxford University Press, 1997.

Kelley, Blair L. M. *Right to Ride: Streetcar Boycotts and African American Citizenship in the Era of Plessy v. Ferguson.* Chapel Hill: University of North Carolina Press, 2010.

Kennedy, David M. *Freedom from Fear. The American People in Depression and War.* New York: Oxford University Press, 1999.

Kerr, Audrey Elisa. *The Paper Bag Principle: Class, Colorism, and Rumor and the Case of Black Washington, D.C.* Knoxville: University of Tennessee Press, 2006.

Key, V. O. *Southern Politics in State and Nation.* New York: Vintage, 1949.

Kilson, Martin. "Political Change in the Negro Ghetto, 1900–1940." In *Key Issues*, ed. Huggins, Kilson, and Fox, 2:167–92.

Kirby, John B. *Black Americans in the Roosevelt Era: Liberalism and Race.* Knoxville: University of Tennessee Press, 1980.

Klarman, Michael J. *From Jim Crow to Civil Rights: The Supreme Court and the Struggle for Racial Equality.* New York: Oxford University Press, 2004.

Kneebone, John T. *Southern Liberal Journalists and the Issue of Race.* Chapel Hill: University of North Carolina Press, 1985.

Krugler, David F. *1919, the Year of Racial Violence: How African Americans Fought Back.* New York: Cambridge University Press, 2015.

Kunitz, Stephen J. "Hookworm and Pellagra. Exemplary Diseases in the New South." *Journal of Health and Social Behavior* 28, no. 2 (June 1988): 139–48.

Lee, Alfred McClung, and Norman D. Humphrey. *Race Riot, Detroit 1943.* New York: Octagon, 1968, ca. 1943.

Lee, Ulysses Grant. *The Employment of Negro Troops.* Washington: Office of the Chief of Military History, US Army, 1966.

Lepore, Jill. *These Truths: A History of the United States.* New York: W. W. Norton, 2018.

Leuchtenburg, William E. "Election of 1936" in Schlesinger and Israel, eds., *Presidential Elections* 7: 2809–2849.

Lewis, David Levering. *W.E.B. Du Bois: A Biography.* New York: MacMillan, 2009.

Lisio, Donald J. *Hoover, Blacks, and Lily-Whites: A Study of Southern Strategies.* Chapel Hill: University of North Carolina Press, 1985.

Locke, Alain. *The New Negro.* New York: Atheneum, 1969.

Logan, Rayford W.*The Betrayal of the Negro from Rutherford B. Hayes to Woodrow Wilson.* New York: Da Capo, 1997.

———. *Howard University: The First Hundred Years, 1867–1967.* New York: New York University Press, 1969.

Lucander, David. *Winning the War for Democracy: The March on Washington Movement, 1941–1946.* Urbana: University of Illinois Press, 2014.

Luxenberg, Steve. *Separate: The Story of Plessy v. Ferguson and America's Journey from Slavery to Segregation.* New York: W. W. Norton, 2019.

MacGregor, Morris J., and Bernard C. Nalty. *Blacks in the United States Armed Forces: Basic Documents*, 13 vols. Wilmington, DE: Scholarly Resources, 1977.

MacGregor, Morris J., Jr. *Integration of the Armed Forces, 1940–1965.* Washington: Center of Military History, US Army, 1981.

Mack, Connie. "Arthur W. Mitchell: Civil Rights Activist, Educator, Politician." In *Book Two,* ed. Jesse Smith, 477–78.

Mann, Kenneth Eugene. "Oscar Stanton DePriest: Persuasive Agent for the Black Masses." *Negro History Bulletin* 35 (October 1972): 134–37.

Manning, Christopher. *William L. Dawson and the Limits of Black Electoral Leadership.* DeKalb: Northern Illinois University Press, 2009.

Martin, Charles H. "Negro Leaders, the Republican Party and the Election of 1932." *Phylon* 32 (Spring 1971): 885–93.

Martin, Waldo. "In Search of Booker T. Washington." In *Washington and Progress,* ed. Brundage, 38–55.

Martis, Kenneth C. et al., eds. *The Historical Atlas of Political Parties in the United States Congress, 1789–1989.* New York: MacMillan, 1989.

———. *The Historical Atlas of United States Congressional Districts.* New York: Free Press, 1982.

Mason, Robert. *The Republican Party and American Politics from Hoover to Reagan.* Cambridge, UK: Cambridge University Press, 2012.

Matterson, Lisa G. "Electoral Politics" In *Great Black Migration,* ed. Reich, 275–79.

Mayberry, B. D. "The Tuskegee Movable Schools." *Agricultural History* 65, no. 2 (Spring 1991): 85–104.

Mays, Benjamin E. *Born to Rebel: An Autobiography.* Athens: University of Georgia Press, 1971.

McDuffie, John. *To Inquiring Friends, if Any; Autobiography of John McDuffie, Farmer, Lawyer, Legislator, Judge as Told to and Edited by Mary Margaret Flock.* Mobile, AL: Azalea City, 1970.

McGovern, James R. *Anatomy of a Lynching: The Killing of Claude Neal.* Baton Rouge: Louisiana State University Press, 1982.

McKee, James R. [Review of *The New Deal's Black Congressman*]. *Journal of Southern History* 67, no. 1: 204–05.

McKinney, Richard I. *Mordecai: The Man and His Message; The Story of Mordecai Wyatt Johnson.* Washington, DC: Howard University Press, 1997.

McMahon, Kevin J. *Reconsidering Roosevelt on Race: How the Presidency Paved the Road to Brown.* Chicago: University of Chicago Press, 2004.

McNeil, Genna Rae. *Groundwork: Charles Hamilton Houston and the Struggle for Civil Rights.* Philadelphia: University of Pennsylvania Press, 1983.

McWhirter, Cameron. *Red Summer: The Summer of 1919 and the Awakening of Black America.* New York: Henry Holt, 2011.

Meier, August. "Booker T. Washington and the Town of Mound Bayou." *Phylon* 15, no. 4 (4th Qtr., 1954): 396–401.

———. "Negro Class Structure and Ideology in the Age of Booker T. Washington." *Phylon* 23, no. 3 (3rd Qtr., 1962): 258–66.

Meier, August, and Elliott M. Rudwick. *From Plantation to Ghetto: An Interpretive History of American Negroes.* New York: Hill and Wang, 1966.

Michaeli, Ethan. *The Defender: How the Legendary Black Newspaper Changed America: From the Age of Pullman Porters to the Age of Obama.* Boston: Houghton, Mifflin, Harcourt, 2016.

Michelson, Charles. *The Ghost Talks.* New York: G. P. Putnam's Sons, 1944.

Michie, Allan A., and Frank Ryhlick. *Dixie Demagogues.* New York: Vanguard, 1939.

Milkis, Sidney M. *The President and the Parties: The Transformation of the America Political System since the New Deal.* New York: Oxford University Press, 1993.

Miller, Kristie. "Oscar Stanton DePriest." In *American National Biography,* ed. Garraty and Carnes, 6:461–63.

Miller, Loren. *The Petitioners: The Story of the Supreme Court of the United States and the Negro.* New York: Pantheon, 1966.

Moore, Albert B. *History of Alabama.* Tuscaloosa: Alabama Book Store, 1934.

Moore, Jacqueline M. *Booker T. Washington, W.E.B. Du Bois, and the Struggle for Racial Uplift.* Wilmington, DE: Scholarly Resources, 2003.

Myrdal, Gunnar, with the assistance of Richard Sterner and Arnold Rose. *An American Dilemma: The Negro Problem and Modern Democracy.* New York: Harper and Row, 1962, ca. 1944.

Nardulli, Peter F., ed. *Diversity, Conflict, and State Politics.* Urbana: University of Illinois Press, 1989.

"Negroes: Jesse Owens Dashes to G.O.P. in Colored Vote Race." *Newsweek* 8, no. 11 (September 12, 1936): 18–19.

Niven, Steven J. "Arthur Wergs Mitchell." In *AANB,* ed. Gates and Higginbotham, 5:623–24.

———. "Charles Clinton Spaulding." In *AANB,* ed. Gates and Higginbotham, 7:341–42.

Nordin, Dennis S. *The New Deal's Black Congressman: A Life of Arthur Wergs Mitchell.* Columbia: University of Missouri Press, 1997.

Norrell, Robert J. "Understanding the Wizard: Another Look at the Age of Booker T. Washington." In *Washington and Progress,* ed. Brundage, 58–80.

———. *Up from History: The Life of Booker T. Washington.* Cambridge, MA: Belknap Press of Harvard University, 2009.

Ogden, August Raymond. *The Dies Committee: A Study of the Special House Committee for the Investigation of Un-American Activities, 1938–1943.* Washington: Catholic University of America Press, 1943.

Ottley, Roi. *The Lonely Warrior: The Life and Times of Robert S. Abbott.* Chicago: Henry Regnery, 1955.

Painter, Nell Irvin. *Exodusters: Black Migration to Kansas after Reconstruction.* New York: Knopf, 1977.

Palmer, Colin A., ed. *Encyclopedia of African-American Culture and History: The Black Experience in the America.* 6 vols. Detroit: Thomson and Gale, 2006.

Palmore, Joseph R. "The Not so Strange Career of Interstate Jim Crow: Race, Transportation, and the Dormant Commerce Clause." *Virginia Law Review* 83 (1997): 1773–1817.

Patterson, James T. *Congressional Conservatism and the New Deal: The Growth of the Conservative Coalition in Congress, 1933–1939.* Lexington: University of Kentucky Press, 1967.

Perman, Michael. *Struggle for Mastery: Disfranchisement in the South, 1888–1908.* Chapel Hill: University of North Carolina Press, 2001.

Peterson, Virgil. *Barbarians in Our Midst: A History of Chicago Crime and Politics.* Boston: Little, Brown, 1952.

Phi Beta Sigma Fraternity. *The Crescent: 35th Anniversary Issue.* N.p.: n.p., Spring 1949.

Pride, Armistead S., and Clint C. Wilson. *A History of the Black Press.* Washington: Howard University Press, 1997.

Public Service Leader: Official Publication of the Regular Democratic Organization of Illinois. Chicago: n.p., 1934. University of Chicago Library, microfilm JK47.

Rable, George C. "The South and the Politics of Anti-Lynching Legislation, 1920–1940." *Journal of Southern History* 51, no. 2 (May 1985): 201–20.

Reardon, Karen. "Arthur Wergs Mitchell." In *Culture and History* 4, ed. Salzman, Smith, and West, 1831–32.

Reed, Christopher Robert. "Black Chicago Realignment during the Great Depression and New Deal." *Illinois Historical Journal* 78, no. 4 (Winter 1985): 242–56.

———. *The Chicago NAACP and the Rise of Black Professional Leadership, 1910–1966.* Bloomington: Indiana University Press, 1997.

———. *The Depression Comes to the South Side: Protest and Politics in the Black Metropolis, 1930–1933.* Bloomington: Indiana University Press, 2011.

———. *Knock at the Door of Opportunity: Black Migration to Chicago, 1900–1919.* Carbondale: Southern Illinois University Press, 2014.

———. *The Rise of Chicago's Black Metropolis, 1920–1929.* Urbana: University of Illinois Press, 2011.

Reed, Linda. *Simple Decency and Common Sense: The Southern Conference Movement, 1938–1963.* Bloomington: Indiana University Press, 1991.

Reed, Merl Elwyn. *Seedtime for the Modern Civil Rights Movement: The President's Committee on Fair Employment Practice, 1941–1946.* Baton Rouge: Louisiana State University Press, 1991.

Reich, Steven A., ed. *The Great Black Migration: A Historical Encyclopedia of the American Mosaic.* Santa Barbara, CA: Greenwood, 2014.

Robertson, David. *Sly and Able: A Political Biography of James F. Byrnes.* New York: Norton, 1994.

Robinson, George P., Jr. "The Negro in Politics in Chicago." *Journal of Negro History* 17, no. 2 (April 1932): 180–229.

Robinson, Nancy T. "William H. H. Hart." In *AANB* 4, ed. Gates and Higginbotham, 103–4.

Rogers, William Warren et al. *Alabama: the History of a Deep South State.* Tuscaloosa: University of Alabama Press, 1994.

Roper, John Herbert, Sr. *The Magnificent Mays: A Biography of Benjamin Elijah Mays.* Columbia: University of South Carolina Press, 2012.

Rosen, Elliott. *The Republican Party in the Age of Roosevelt: Sources of Anti-Government Conservatism in the United States.* Charlottesville: University of Virginia Press, 2014.

Ross, B. Joyce. *J. E. Spingarn and the Rise of the NAACP, 1911–1939.* New York: Atheneum, 1972.

———. "Mary McCleod Bethune and the National Youth Administration: A Case Study of Power Relationships in the Black Cabinet of Franklin D. Roosevelt." *Journal of Negro History* 60, no. 1 (January 1975): 1–28.

Ross, William G. *The Chief Justiceship of Charles Evans Hughes, 1930–1941.* Columbia: University of South Carolina Press, 2007.

Rung, Margaret C. *Servants of the State: Managing Diversity and Democracy in the Federal Work Force, 1933–1953*. Athens: University of Georgia Press, 2002.

Ryan, Yvonne. *Roy Wilkins: The Quiet Revolutionary and the NAACP*. Lexington: University Press of Kentucky, 2014.

Salzman, Jack, David Lionel Smith, and Cornel West, eds. 5 vols. *Encyclopedia of African American Culture and History*. New York: Macmillan Library Reference, 1996.

Saunt, Claudio. *Unworthy Republic: The Dispossession of Native Americans and the Road to Indian Territory*. New York: W. W. Norton, 2020.

Savage, Sean. *Roosevelt: The Party Leader, 1932–1945*. Lexington: University Press of Kentucky, 1991.

Schlesinger, Arthur M., Jr. *A Life in the Twentieth Century: Innocent Beginnings, 1917–1950*. Boston: Houghton-Mifflin, 2000.

Schlesinger, Arthur M., Jr., ed., and Fred L. Israel, associate ed. *History of American Presidential Elections, 1789–1984*, 14 vols. Philadelphia: Chelsea House Publishers, 2002.

Schneller, Robert J., Jr. *Breaking the Color Barrier: The U.S. Naval Academy's First Black Midshipman and the Struggle for Racial Equality*. New York: New York University Press, 2005.

Scroop, Daniel. *Mr. Democrat: Jim Farley, the New Deal and the Making of Modern American Politics*. Ann Arbor: University of Michigan Press, 2006.

Sherer, Robert G. *Subordination or Liberation?: The Development and Conflicting Theories of Black Education in Nineteenth Century Alabama*. Tuscaloosa: University of Alabama Press, 1977.

Simmons, Charles A. *The African American Press: A History of News Coverage during National Crises with Special Reference to Four Newspapers*. Jefferson, NC: McFarland, 1998.

Sisk, Glenn. "Negro Education in Alabama's Black Belt, 1875–1900." *Journal of Negro Education* 22 (Spring 1953): 126–33.

Sitkoff, Harvard. *A New Deal for Blacks: The Emergence of Civil Rights as a National Issue*. New York: Oxford University Press, 1978.

Skaggs, William H. *The Southern Oligarchy: An Appeal in Behalf of the Silent Masses of Our Country Against the Despotic Rule of the Few*. New York: Davis-Adair, 1924.

Smith, J. Clay. *Emancipation: The Making of the Black Lawyer, 1844–1944*. Philadelphia: University of Pennsylvania Press, 1993.

Smock, Raymond W., ed. *Booker T. Washington in Perspective: Essays of Louis R. Harlan*. Jackson: University Press of Mississippi: 1988.

Sosna, Morton. *In Search of the Silent South: Southern Liberals and the Race Issue*. New York: Columbia University Press, 1977.

Spingarn, Adena. *Uncle Tom: From Martyr to Traitor*. Stanford, CA: Stanford University Press, 2018.

Sternsher, Bernard, ed. *The Negro in Depression and War: Prelude to Revolution*. Chicago: Quadrangle Books, 1969.

Stone, Donald P. *Fallen Prince: William James Edwards, Black Education, and the Quest for Afro-American Nationality*. Snow Hill, AL: Snow Hill Press, 1990.

Stuart, William H. *The Twenty Incredible Years*. Chicago: M. A. Donohue, 1935.

Suggs, Henry Lewis. "Black Strategy and Ideology in the Segregation Era: P. B. Young and the *Norfolk Journal and Guide*." *Virginia Magazine of History and Biography* 91, no. 2 (April 1983): 161–96.

———. *P. B. Young, Newspaperman: Race, Politics, and Journalism in the New South, 1910–1962*. Charlottesville: University Press of Virginia, 1988.

Suitts, Steve. *Hugo Black of Alabama: How His Roots and Early Career Shaped the Great Champion of the Constitution*. Montgomery: New South Books, 2005.

Sullivan, Patricia. *Days of Hope: Race and Democracy in the New Deal Era*. Chapel Hill: University Press of North Carolina, 1996.

Sumners, Hatton W. *The Private Citizen and His Democracy*. Dallas: Southwestern Legal Center, 1959.

Sumter County, Alabama. *The Heritage of Sumter County, Alabama*. Clanton, AL: Heritage Publishing Consultants, 2005.

Takaki, Ronald. *Double Victory: A Multicultural History of America in World War II*. Boston: Little, Brown, 2000.

Thorton III, J. Mills. "Heflin, James Thomas." In *ANB* 10, ed. Garraty and Carnes, 496–97.

Tolnay, Stewart E., and E. M. Beck. *A Festival of Violence: An Analysis of Southern Lynchings, 1882–1930*. Urbana: University of Illinois Press, 1995.

Topping, Simon. "All Shadows Are Dark." In *Long Is the Way and Hard*, ed. Verney and Sartain, 3–15.

———. "Turning Their Pictures of Abraham Lincoln to the Wall: The Republican Party and Black America in the Election of 1936." *Irish Journal of American Studies* 8 (1999): 35–59.

Travis Dempsey J. *An Autobiography of Black Politics*. Chicago: Urban Research Press, 1987.

United States Supreme Court. Witt, Elder, ed. *Congressional Quarterly's Guide to the U.S. Supreme Court*, 2nd ed. Washington: Congressional Quarterly, 1990.

US Congress. House Committee on Appropriations. Committee on the Judiciary, House of Representatives, Seventy Fourth Congress, First Session. *Hearing before the Committee on the Judiciary . . . on H.R. 5733 to Create an Industrial Commission on Negro Affairs*. Washington: US Printing Office, 1935.

———. *District of Columbia Appropriations, 1902*. Washington: US Printing Office, 1902.

Van Riper, Paul. *History of the United States Civil Service*. Evanston, IL: Row, Peterson, 1958.

Verney, Kevern. *The Art of the Possible: Booker T. Washington and Black Leadership in the United States, 1881–1925*. New York: Routledge, 2001.

———. "To Hope till Hope Creates: The NAACP in Alabama, 1913–1945." In *Long Is the Way and Hard*, ed. Verney and Sartain, 105–20.

Verney, Kevern, and Lee Sartain, eds. *Long Is the Way and Hard: One Hundred Years of the NAACP*. Fayetteville: University of Arkansas Press, 2009.

Virginia Writer's Project. *The Negro in Virginia*. New York: Arno Press and the New York Times, 1969.

Wallace, Mike. *Greater Gotham: A History of New York City from 1898 to 1918*. New York: Oxford University Press, 2017.

Wallenstein, Peter. "P. B. Young." In *AANB*, ed. Gates and Higginbotham, 7:488–89.

Ward, Paul W. "Wooing the Negro Vote." *Nation*, August 1, 1936, 119–20.

Ware, Gilbert. *William Hastie: Grace under Pressure*. New York: Oxford University Press, 1984.

Washington, Booker T., Louis R. Harlan, and Raymond W. Smock, eds. *The Booker T. Washington Papers*, 14 vols. Urbana: University of Illinois Press, 1972–1988.

———. *Up from Slavery: An Autobiography*. Garden City, NY: Doubleday, 1963.

Waters, Enoch. *American Diary: A Personal History of the Black Press*. Chicago: Path Press, 1987.

Watts, Jill. *The Black Cabinet: The Untold Story of African Americans and Politics during the Age of Roosevelt*. New York: Grove Press, 2020.

Weir, Warren. *The Encyclopedia of African-American Military History*. Amherst, NY: Prometheus Books, 2004.

Weiss, Nancy J. *Farewell to the Party of Lincoln: Black Politics in the Age of FDR*. Princeton: Princeton University Press, 1983.

Welky, David. *Marching Across the Color Line: A. Philip Randolph and Civil Rights in the World War II Era*. New York: Oxford University Press, 2014.

Wendt, Lloyd, and Herman Kogan. *Lords of the Levee: The Story of Bathhouse John and Hinky Dink*. Indianapolis: Bobbs-Merrill Company, 1943.

West, Michael Rudolph. *The Education of Booker T. Washington: American Democracy and the Idea of Race Relations*. New York: Columbia University Press, 2006.

Wheat, Jack. "What if They Built a Town and Nobody Came?" *Tuscaloosa* AL *Times*, July 29, 1984, ID.

White, Walter. *A Man Called White: The Autobiography of Walter White*. New York: Viking Press, 1948.

Wilkerson, Isabel. *The Warmth of Other Suns: The Epic Story of America's Great Migration*. New York: Random House, 2010.

Wilkins, Roy. *Standing Fast: The Autobiography of Roy Wilkins*. New York: Viking Press, 1982.

Williams, Elmer Lynn. *The Fix-it Boys: The Inside Story of the New Deal and the Kelly-Nash Machine*. Chicago: E. L. Williams, 1940.

Wilson, James Q. *Negro Politics: The Search for Leadership*. Glencoe, IL: Free Press, 1960.

Wirth, Louis, and Eleanor Bernert, eds. *Local Community Fact Book of Chicago*. Chicago: University of Chicago Press, 1949.

Wolseley, Roland E. *The Black Press, U.S.A.* Ames: Iowa State University Press, 1971.

Wolters, Raymond. *Negroes and the Great Depression: The Problem of Economic Recovery*. Westport, CT: Greenwood, 1970.

Woman's Civic Council of the Chicago Area. *Dishonest Elections and Why We Have Them*. 2 vols. Chicago: n.p., 1938.

Woodson, Carter. *The Mis-Education of the Negro*. Santa Barbara, CA: Book Tree, 2006.

Wright, Richard. *Black Boy: A Record of Childhood and Youth*. New York: Harper and Row, 1964.

———. *Native Son*. New York: Harper Perennial Modern Classics, 2005.

———. *Uncle Tom's Children*. New York: Harper and Row, 1965.

Zangrando, Robert L. *The NAACP Crusade against Lynching, 1909–1950*. Philadelphia: Temple University Press, 1980.

Zangrando, Robert L., and Ronald L. Lewis. *Walter F. White: The NAACP's Ambassador for Racial Justice*. Morgantown: West Virginia University Press, 2019.

Zeigler, Robert H. *John L. Lewis: Labor Leader*. Boston: Twayne, 1988.

Online Resources

Carnegie-Myrdal Study of the Negro in American Research Memoranda Collection. Sc Micro F-13242. Schomburg Center for Research in Black Culture, Manuscripts, Archives and Rare Books Division, New York Public Library.

Equal Justice Initiative. *Lynching in America: Confronting the Legacy of Racial Terror*. 3rd ed. 2017. PDF.

"Executions in the U.S. 1608–2002: The Espy File." Death Penalty Information Center (website), 2023.

Foreman, Clark. Oral history interview, November 16, 1974. Interview B-0003. Southern Oral History Program Collection (#4007), Documenting the American South, University of North Carolina–Chapel Hill.

"Norfolk Journal and Guide." *PBS* (website), 2023.

"Population." Los Angeles Almanac (website), 2023.

Roosevelt, Eleanor. *My Day*. Eleanor Roosevelt Papers Project, Columbian College of Arts and Sciences, George Washington University.

Accessed at the Regenstein Library, University of Chicago

Congressional Record 79–89, 1935–1943

NAACP papers (11050072) Papers of the NAACP, Part 2 1919–1939, Correspondence of Selected NAACP Officials (11716110)

Papers of the NAACP, Part 12, Selected Branch Files, 1939, 1913–1939, Series C: The Midwest (11716167, folder 001427-001-0134, etc.)

ProQuest Historical Newspapers™

Atlanta Daily World, 1934–1943

[Baltimore] *Afro-American*, 1934–1949

Boston Globe, 1934–1943

Chicago Defender, 1918–1943

Chicago Tribune, 1918–1943

New Amsterdam News (and *Star-News*), 1934–1943

New York Times, 1934–1943

New York Tribune/Herald Tribune, 1934–1943

Pittsburgh Courier, 1934–1943

Washington Post, 1919–1943

Encyclopedia of Alabama (website)

h-1848 "Hugo L. Black," Steve Suitts

h-3889 "Geiger," James P. Kaetz

h-2972 "J. Thomas Heflin," Elbert L. Watson

h-3273 "John McDuffie," Brett J. Derbes

h-1353 "Arthur Wergs Mitchell," Dennis S. Nordin
h-3031 "Pineapple," Grant B. Hiatt
h-1593 "Southern Conference for Human Welfare," Rebecca Woodham

Index

The abbreviation "AWM" refers to Arthur W. Mitchell. Page numbers in italics refer to figures.